JOHN PENDLETON KENNEDY

SOUTHERN BIOGRAPHY

Andrew Burstein, Series Editor

JOHN PENDLETON KENNEDY

Early American Novelist
Whig Statesman & Ardent Nationalist

ANDREW R. BLACK

LOUISIANA STATE UNIVERSITY PRESS
BATON ROUGE

Published by Louisiana State University Press

Manufactured in the United States of America
First printing

Designer: Michelle A. Neustrom
Typeface: Adobe Caslon Pro
Printer and binder: Maple Press (Digital)

Library of Congress Cataloging-in-Publication Data

Names: Black, Andrew R., 1943–
Title: John Pendleton Kennedy : early American novelist, Whig statesman, and ardent nationalist / Andrew R. Black.
Description: Baton Rouge : Louisiana State University Press, 2016. | Includes bibliographical references and index.
Identifiers: LCCN 2015036498| ISBN 978-0-8071-6294-1 (cloth : alkaline paper) | ISBN 978-0-8071-6295-8 (PDF) | ISBN 978-0-8071-6296-5 (ePub) | ISBN 978-0-8071-6297-2 (MOBI)
Subjects: LCSH: Kennedy, John Pendleton, 1795–1870. | Statesmen—United States—Biography. | Legislators—United States—Biography. | United States. Congress. House—Biography. | Whig Party (U.S.) —Biography. | Nationalists—United States—Biography. | Legislators—Maryland—Biography. | Maryland. General Assembly—Speakers—Biography. | Novelists, American—19th century—Biography. | Politics and literature—United States—History—19th century.
Classification: LCC E415.9.K35 B55 2016 | DDC 328.73/092—dc23 LC record available at http://lccn.loc.gov/2015036498

The paper in this book meets the guidelines for permanence and durability of the Committee on Production Guidelines for Book Longevity of the Council on Library Resources. ♾

To Peggy

CONTENTS

PREFACE

People write books to answer questions. In this book, I try to answer three. First, what caused the American Whig Party to rise with such force in the 1840s, win two presidential elections, and then disappear completely a decade before the Civil War? Second, can the life and writing of John Pendleton Kennedy, our most prolific Whig and a resident of the antebellum borderland, help explain what went wrong with the Whig project? And finally, how can we, living in our present era, understand the issues of race and slavery as Kennedy and his cohorts saw them?

This book addresses the first two questions in its premise—that politics and literature were closely aligned for Kennedy and that his novels provide unique insights into Whig culture. Kennedy's best-known novel, *Swallow Barn,* is central to my analysis of this culture and of what made it shine so brightly for a time, then suddenly collapse. In approaching the third question, modern readers can find nineteenth-century views on race and slavery jarring. Earlier biographies of Kennedy dealt only marginally with these issues. However, Kennedy's evolving attitudes about race and slavery were as much an American story as they were his own. Though unsure and halting, they marked the country's first steps out of slavery on the long and as yet unfinished journey toward racial justice and equality. I try to describe those first steps candidly.

Several faculty members at Boston University were central to the conception and execution of this work. Most important were Nina Silber and Jon Roberts. Professor Silber generously shared her expertise on the antebellum South, its women, and its literature with me. Professor Roberts offered an invaluable understanding of the shifting intellectual ground on which Kennedy lived and wrote. Others such as John Matthews, Bruce Schulman, and Louis Ferleger helped improve my work in important ways.

For the transformation from manuscript to book, I am indebted to the people at Louisiana State University Press. I was lucky to have the help of Andrew

Burstein, editor of the Southern Biography Series. Professor Burstein is author of several books on the Early Republic and well versed in both its literature and politics. His tough questions and provocative suggestions sharpened the focus of my work. Rand Dotson, executive editor at LSU Press, helped shepherd this book through to publication. Julia Ridley Smith deserves special thanks for her bright and thorough copyediting. Having kept Kennedy's *Swallow Barn* in print over these many years, LSU Press was always my first choice of publisher for this biography.

Several institutions were of critical importance as I researched Kennedy's works. The American Antiquarian Society in Worchester, Massachusetts, the Peabody Institute in Baltimore, Maryland, and the Boston Athenaeum all deserve special mention for their extraordinary hospitality and helpfulness.

Biography writing is especially engaging. More than other forms of nonfiction, it draws an author in and transports him or her to another time and place. Fortunately, my wife Peggy understood this from the start. Without her patience and continuous support, I would not have attempted to investigate the life and writing of John Pendleton Kennedy.

JOHN PENDLETON KENNEDY

Introduction

> Where is Clarence?
> Where is the gentle Rivers, Vaughan, Gray?
> Where is the kind Hastings?[1]

Although U.S. congressmen often borrowed from Shakespeare to dramatize their speeches in the nineteenth century, few did it as effectively as John Pendleton Kennedy. As a freshman in the House of Representatives and the first member of the Whig Party elected from Baltimore, Kennedy was eager to take the floor against the rival Jacksonian Democrats. By the winter of 1839, the nation's economy had been mired in a grinding depression for nearly two years. Kennedy and his fellow Whigs blamed former president Andrew Jackson for causing the national crisis and his successor Martin Van Buren for allowing it to drag on.[2]

On this occasion, Kennedy selected his quotation from *Richard III,* Act IV, scene 4, wherein the distraught Queen Elizabeth cries out to the victims of the play's villainous monarch, all of whom he has murdered in his pursuit of unlimited power. Staying in the same dramatic register, Kennedy proceeded to remind his audience of the many cabinet members either dismissed or forced to resign during Jackson's turbulent eight-year presidency. "Where is Berrien, Branch, Ingham? Where is Duane, McLane, and other friends of the chief?" Kennedy asked, and promptly supplied his own answer: "Gone, Sir, immolated by the spirit which endured no free opinion." Kennedy's Whig colleagues were accustomed to vilifying Jackson as a "tyrant" and had actually passed a censure resolution against him to that effect in 1833. So they found the comparison between the ex-president and Shakespeare's nefarious despot most fitting.[3]

A *New York Times* correspondent who observed Kennedy on the House floor described him as a "striking personage." At forty-three, Kennedy was considered broadly handsome. He owed his athletic figure to his love of horsemanship, and he favored a somewhat elegant style of dress. Most who met Kennedy quickly fell under his charm, and one who knew him well described his wit and intelligence as "overflowing." The *Times* correspondent took special note of Kennedy's erudition and complimented his rhetoric for its "perfectness of its composition."[4]

Such praise came as no surprise to the newspaper's readers. By the time he took his seat in Congress in 1839, Kennedy was one of the most admired authors in America. His plantation novel *Swallow Barn* had been published in 1832 and was followed three years later by his Revolutionary War novel *Horse-Shoe Robinson.* Just as he entered Congress, Kennedy brought out an historical romance set in colonial Maryland, *Rob of The Bowl.* In quick succession, he had contributed three long novels to the thin shelf of indigenous literature. As his reputation as a novelist grew, Kennedy joined an elite literary circle that included such writers as Washington Irving and James Fenimore Cooper. Somewhat later, Kennedy would mentor the promising young talent from his native Baltimore, Edgar Allan Poe. Kennedy's novels would be reprinted numerous times during the nineteenth century and translated into multiple languages. On the hustings, his supporters would cheer him on as "Horse-Shoe," after the rugged hero of his popular second novel.[5]

Kennedy's most important novel, and the central focus of this biography, was *Swallow Barn.* With its disjointed structure and conflicting messages, this rambling description of plantation life in rural Virginia has both intrigued and puzzled those scholars who have studied it. Among literary critics and historians, there has been little agreement as to the novel's intent and significance. Several scholars have accused Kennedy of being a southern proslavery intellectual, while others have labeled him a northern-oriented industrialist. Some scholars have accepted *Swallow Barn* as an accurate depiction of the Old Dominion. Still others have considered the novel too distorted in its use of pastoralism and chivalric language to be taken literally. So, too, have scholars struggled to explain Kennedy's ambivalence toward race and slavery in *Swallow Barn.* Throughout the novel, Kennedy oscillated between degrading and humanizing descriptions of his black characters. Not surprisingly, his views on the institution of slavery and the planter class dependent on it were also inconsistent.[6]

By the time Kennedy sat down to write *Swallow Barn,* both his urban upbringing and political commitment made objectivity impossible. Although his mother came from western Virginia and he had spent boyhood summers there, he had long since become a Baltimorean and had lost much of his earlier nostalgia and sympathy for his mother's home place. More important, his deeply felt Whig principles—his ardent nationalism, his commitment to proactive government (especially federal support of internal improvements), and his faith in economic and social progress—all ran counter to the chronic localism and retrogressive political economy of the Old Dominion.[7]

Prior scholarship on *Swallow Barn* has suffered from a lack of attention to the historical context. The turbulent events of the early 1830s significantly influenced the tenor and contour of Kennedy's novel. The intensification of partisan invective that marked Jacksonian politics, the worsening of sectional tensions, and the 1831 Nat Turner slave rebellion shadow Kennedy's narrative. By 1830, the author felt betrayed and angered by President Jackson's sudden turn against internal improvements. The next year, the South Carolina–based nullification movement thoroughly soured Kennedy's perspective on politics across the South. During that summer, Nat Turner's uprising broke out in Virginia while Kennedy was vacationing there and finishing his novel. Such a catastrophe so close at hand destabilized the conclusion of *Swallow Barn* and contributed to the novel's seemingly haphazard structure and incongruous content.[8]

Previous studies of Kennedy have also failed to properly locate him in the antebellum borderland or to take into account how being a Marylander conditioned his writing and politics. Border Whigs such as Henry Clay, John Crittenden, and Kennedy belonged to neither the North nor the South and shared a sense of insecurity regarding future sectional relations. Living just inside the legal boundaries of southern slavocracy, Border Whigs were especially wary of the passions unleashed over the issue of slavery and the threat these passions posed to national unity. As Kennedy's friend John Latrobe put it, the antebellum borderland could either help forge "a united and homogenous people" or become "studded with fortresses." Much of Kennedy's ambivalence toward the institution of slavery in *Swallow Barn* stemmed from his need to mediate in his fiction and his politics between opposing sides of a dangerous, intractable conflict.[9]

Kennedy's political career was no less illustrious than his novelistic one. Following his early tutelage in the Maryland legislature, he represented his native Baltimore in the U.S. House of Representatives continuously, except for one year out of office, from 1838 until 1845. Given his reputation as an author and the soundness of his Whig principles, Kennedy quickly assumed the role of chief ideologue for his party. Both his "Whig Manifesto" and "Defense of the Whigs" helped codify the party's political thought and legitimize the new party in the eyes of the electorate. During the presidential election of 1840, Kennedy merged his political and literary interests to produce a scathing political satire entitled *Quodlibet,* wherein a combination of Jacksonian demagoguery and fraudulent banking practices lay waste to a fictional town.[10]

Just as his novelistic success gained him admission to an elite literary circle, Kennedy's time in government introduced him to a prominent cadre of Whig Party leaders. He established valuable friendships with John Quincy Adams, Henry Clay, Daniel Webster, Millard Fillmore, and many others. Entering the presidency, Fillmore appointed Kennedy as his secretary of the navy. In less than a year, Kennedy dispatched Commodore Matthew Perry to Japan and sent naval expeditions to the Arctic and Amazon regions. Once out of public office, Kennedy assumed the role of elder statesman in a deeply troubled Whig Party. Even though he marshaled his considerable personal skills and political connections to placate its dissonant factions, he could do little to slow the party's rapid disintegration after 1850. Following the disastrous defeat of its presidential candidate Winfield Scott in 1852, the Whig Party made a shambling exit from the national stage, never to return. Kennedy and other former Whigs scrambled to reorganize as a party of national unity and find a new political home for themselves.[11]

During the late 1840s and early 1850s, Kennedy also rededicated himself to his writing. In 1849, his biography of William Wirt was published to considerable critical acclaim. Although largely forgotten today, Wirt served as attorney general in the Monroe and John Quincy Adams administrations, was a renowned courtroom lawyer, and authored novels as well as a biography of Patrick Henry. Wirt was also an important mentor to the young Kennedy. In appreciation, Kennedy dedicated *Swallow Barn* to him.[12]

In 1851, the revised edition of *Swallow Barn* came to market. Kennedy had altered key portions of the novel to explain his behind-the-scenes support for the politically divisive Compromise of 1850 and its controversial Fugitive Slave Law. Kennedy also tried to clarify the reasons for the South's insistence on noninterference in its domestic affairs. He cautioned his readers that southern slaves were completely unprepared for immediate emancipation and warned of the dire consequences if such a course were taken. One of Kennedy's southern friends wrote that the revised edition of *Swallow Barn* was a much-needed "antidote" for abolitionist literature coming from the North. It is unclear whether Kennedy was aware that Harriet Beecher Stowe's *Uncle Tom's Cabin* had been running as a magazine series during the same year his revised edition appeared.[13]

The original edition of *Swallow Barn* in 1832 and the novel's revised edition in 1851 closely bracketed the lifespan of the Whig Party. The two editions of *Swallow Barn,* along with much of Kennedy's other writing, help to explain how a political party with enough momentum to challenge the Jacksonians in the 1830s could simply vanish two decades later. The answer must be sought in the underlying culture of the Whig Party and the conflicting impulses within it. For all their reforming energy and modernizing spirit, Whigs also had their conservative side. They believed that the American nation should move forward at a steady but slow pace. They eschewed sudden and precipitous changes that threatened a stable social order and a sound economy. When applied to small problems, these contradictory dispositions resulted in a balanced, modulated approach. But when facing large, complicated national issues, the tension between the Whig Party's reforming zeal and its ingrained conservatism produced a fatal indecisiveness that led to its early demise. Had they not had to deal with the problem of slavery, the Whigs might have muddled through.[14]

But the Whigs did have to deal with slavery. They were never able to reconcile the institution with their high moral standards and modernizing spirit. However much they tried, slavery's glaring inhumanity and anachronistic economic nature frustrated Whig efforts to incorporate it into even the most elastic conceptions of a diversified national economy and a well-ordered, hierarchical society. Kennedy similarly struggled to accommodate slavery in a fictional plantation setting, quaintly portrayed at a safe remove from most of his readers. Still, the tensions in *Swallow Barn* are palpable, attesting to slavery's grim and unsettling reality. In the end, both novel and party were undone by the failure to deal with the problem of slavery.

Because literature and politics were so closely aligned for Kennedy, his body of writing provides a unique window into the underlying culture of the Whigs well before they coalesced as a formal political party and chose a name. It took the leadership of Henry Clay and the codification of its principles by men like Kennedy to convert this cultural formation into a political party capable of winning elections. Using Kennedy's novels, satires, and essays as my sources, I show why Whigs became Whigs—what made them think differently from their rivals, the Jacksonian Democrats. No other Whig matched Kennedy's literary production. No other written legacy of the period sheds as much light on both the power and the frailty of Whig thought.[15]

My analysis begins with the "Swiss Traveller" essays, which Kennedy penned in the afterglow of the War of 1812, and the satirical *Red Book* series, coauthored with his friend Peter Hoffman Cruse. Then, I treat Kennedy's three novels in the order they were written. Like *Swallow Barn,* Kennedy's second and third novels were heavily freighted with his Whig principles. Though historical novels, both were as much about Kennedy's own time as the periods in which they were set. *Horse-Shoe Robinson* takes place in the Carolinas during the Revolution but was largely motivated by Kennedy's hatred of nullification. Consequently, it calls for a return to the redemptive values of the nation's founding. Set in colonial St. Mary's, Maryland, *Rob of The Bowl* recalls a well-ordered, deferential society free of political strife. In Kennedy's hands, early St. Mary's becomes a kind of Whig Utopia. Kennedy's political papers (before and after the Civil War) offer further evidence of the author's search for consonance. His pamphlet *The Border States* and a fictionalized epistolary collection, *Mr. Ambrose's Letters on the Rebellion,* are remarkable for their appraisals of southern secession and expectations for postbellum race relations in the South. These works have received little or no scholarly attention to date.[16]

The task of bringing the two Kennedys together—the literary and the political—is long overdue. Although several older biographies of Kennedy exist, none combine the study of his literary and political sides so as to illuminate the lineaments of Whig culture during its emergence. A holistic approach is necessary if we are to better appreciate the lively interaction between his novels and his politics and understand the meaning of his most enigmatic work: *Swallow Barn.*

Prior to this, literary critics have tended to speculate wildly about Kennedy's literary motives. In adopting the strategy I have described, we accomplish more, shedding new light on the life and death of the Whig Party. Its breakdown in the mid-1850s removed a vital adhesive, allowing the federal Union to be pulled apart. In that way, John Pendleton Kennedy's story is the portrait of a culturally confused America, a story that takes in the embattled mind, as well as the rhetorical performances, animating the contentious, fatefully sectionalized nation.[17]

CHAPTER I

The Early Years

Of Kennedy's earliest memories, the cold-water dunkings given to him by his mother stood out. After bathing her young son this way, she clothed him in the lightest possible garments, no matter what the season. This daily ordeal, he later learned, was intended "to save me against the prevailing effeminacy with which parents are apt to invade the strength of their children." By the time of his birth, on October 25, 1795, more tender forms of mothering prevailed in most of the country. However, Nancy Pendleton Kennedy was more traditionally southern in her child-rearing and in other ways. She would remain so all of her life.[1]

Kennedy had a happier recollection of his father. No more than four at the time, the boy watched from the third-floor window of his family's Baltimore townhouse as his father passed below in a funeral procession for the recently deceased ex-president George Washington. Mounted and wearing a light horseman's uniform, John Kennedy looked up and waved to his son.[2]

Kennedy's parents were an unlikely match. Nancy Clayton Pendleton traced her lineage back to seventeenth-century Tidewater Virginia. The Pendletons featured prominently in the Revolution and afterward increased their wealth and influence. Nancy's father and several other Pendletons had moved west to the Shenandoah Valley (to what became Berkley County, near present-day Martinsburg, West Virginia), where they attempted to replicate the plantation economy of their Tidewater counterparts. Although cultivating wheat required fewer slaves than tobacco did, the Shenandoah Pendletons hewed closely to the traditional patterns of plantation life and thrived in the relative isolation of their adopted habitat.

Kennedy's father hailed from humbler stock. Emigrating from Northern Ireland around 1784, probably at fourteen, he joined two much older brothers already successful as Philadelphia merchants. When he finished his apprenticeship, John Kennedy was dispatched to Baltimore with enough financing to start a copper-plating business selling to shipbuilders.[3]

Later, after helping President Washington quell the short-lived Whiskey Rebellion, Kennedy was returning home through the Martinsburg area, where Nancy Pendleton, the reigning local beauty, caught his eye. As a rising merchant and an impressive figure in uniform, John interested Nancy, too. Within weeks the two were married. The wedding was attended by Nancy's family and several other Pendletons living nearby.[4]

A year after moving to Baltimore with her husband, Nancy gave birth to John Pendleton Kennedy. Over the next half-decade or so, she had three more sons. As a consequence, young John had to fend for himself at a young age. He described himself as an "urban ruffian," shooting marbles with other children, drinking water from his hat, and playing pranks on unsuspecting adults. Good with his fists early on, he frequently engaged in boxing matches with other boys.[5]

As he began exploring his urban surroundings, the young Kennedy would have walked the length of Market Street, the town's main thoroughfare, where his family lived. The street was shaded in warmer weather with spreading locust trees, and cattle still mixed easily with pedestrians. As a sign of the town's growing prosperity, the disordered rows of low, hipped-roofed, wooden houses were giving way to more elegant homes, Greek revival townhouses with their Doric porticos and fine classical lines. In time, he probably roamed some of the town's seven hills, not yet leveled by order of the town council. He would have crossed the rushing streams that turned mill wheels not far from the town center, and in the town center, Kennedy would have observed the massive courthouse, complete with stocks, pillory, and whipping post before its steps. A few blocks away, he would have walked past St. Paul's Church, erected by Baltimore's large Catholic community.

However, none of this would have captivated a young boy's curiosity as much as the harbor. Kennedy would have watched ships arrive, seen exotic cargoes being unloaded, and listened to the strange interplay of foreign tongues. Around the harbor, especially near Fell's Point, huge shipbuilding yards, massive warehouses, and crowded piers vied for waterfront access. Not only were wheat exports leaving Baltimore for hungry, war-torn Europe, but a brisk re-export trade was being carried on with the rich sugar islands of the Caribbean. Although Napoleon attempted to stifle this commerce, Baltimore's fast clipper ships and evasive captains were establishing their own rules of the sea and becoming the stuff of local legend.[6]

In addition to these sights and sounds, Kennedy could not have missed the spirited political rallies for which Baltimore was becoming famous. In the opinion of many outsiders, the town's politics were the most rambunctious in the nation. Because Maryland had been the first state to abolish all property requirements for white male voters, and because it had become a Federalist redoubt against the ascendant Jeffersonian Democrats, politics in Baltimore achieved an intensity rare for the time. Massive political demonstrations and partisan parades became regular features of the town's life. Kennedy would have grown accustomed to them as a young boy.[7]

For a month or more every summer, Nancy returned to western Virginia and took her children with her. Kennedy remembered these visits as carefree and languorous. Most days he went barefoot, and there was even less parental control than in Baltimore. Slave children seemed to be everywhere and celebrated his arrival each summer with great fanfare. They taught him how to hunt and where to fish. Later in life, Kennedy would refer to them as "Nature's nearest cousins," but, as a child, he regarded them simply as playmates. "Whatever distinctions society may have created between master and slave," he recalled, "childhood abolished all."[8]

In this remote corner of Virginia, economic circumstances sharply divided white society. On the one hand, the poorer class, often of German or Irish descent, worked small farms, performed odd jobs, or hunted for a living. The plantation class, on the other hand, held the best land, benefitted substantially from slave labor, and controlled local politics. Kennedy's favorite relative in the area, "Uncle Phil," reigned over the Pendleton clan and set the political tone among his family and their neighbors, who rarely traveled far. Even after her marriage and move to Baltimore, Kennedy's mother routinely traveled back to her rural home place because of her "rooted love" for it. Rich or poor, these people behaved "like islanders," Kennedy remembered; they were deeply provincial and resistant to change. Many of these colorful characters would find their way into his first novel, *Swallow Barn.*[9]

Although he kept in touch with his Virginia relatives and never lost his love of the area's natural beauty, Kennedy increasingly committed himself to the dynamic life of Baltimore. As it made the leap from modest town to thriving port city, Baltimore's rapid and diverse economic development fostered a rich commercial and intellectual culture that was far more interesting than the staid patterns of rural life. With twenty-six thousand inhabitants at the century mark, Baltimore had doubled in the last decade and would do so again in the next. Because its livelihood was based on foreign trade and its location was congenial to both North and South, Baltimore was surprisingly cosmopolitan. It attracted Yankee peddlers, Virginia planters, Scotch merchants, French refugees from Santo Domingo, plus numerous Irish, German, and Dutch. A fifth of the town's inhabitants were black.[10]

Although Baltimore shared a number of salient features with the South, it was not, as one historian has mistakenly characterized it, simply an urban expression of that region. Rather, Baltimore was the most important town in the early nineteenth-century borderland. While its cotton mills and cigar factories connected it to the South, Baltimore was never economically dependent on the South. Although several thousand slaves lived in Baltimore at the turn of the century, they would soon be outnumbered by the burgeoning free black population. Still, race and slavery would preoccupy white residents of Baltimore during the antebellum period. As a Maryland legislator and spokesman for his state, Kennedy would find himself caught up in these issues.[11]

Perhaps because he was becoming too familiar with the streets of Baltimore, Kennedy's parents sent him to school at an early age. He first attended "Mrs. Coffee's school" and then, after two years, entered the "boarding academy of Mr. and Mrs. Priestly." At these institutions, he encountered two especially strong women who tamed his ruffian tendencies and earned his enduring respect. Although Mrs. Coffee was renowned for her creativity in classroom punishment, Kennedy admired her intelligence and great skill at archery. Mrs. Priestly, a powerfully built woman from the West, was rumored to have swum across the Ohio with a child on her back to escape marauding Indians. Kennedy credited her with teaching him his letters as well as deportment and good manners.

At the Priestly Academy, classical languages dominated the curriculum. "We measured off Virgil by the yard," Kennedy remembered. The bright spot was the old classicist William Sinclair. Nearsighted and a poor disciplinarian, Sinclair was so obsessed with ancient authors that he had only the faintest notion that there had been an American Revolution. Kennedy acknowledged the influence of his early teachers on him as "most significant in forming of the character [and] grinding the perceptions of childhood." Years later, in the pages of *Swallow Barn,* Sinclair would reappear as Parson Chubb and the Priestlys as Mr. and Mrs. Crab.[12]

As he learned from his teachers and immersed himself in Baltimore's vibrant culture, Kennedy was making friends with more educated children, meeting influential adult mentors, and falling in love with books. In doing so, he was partaking in a new rendition of American life, one taking shape in the nation's coastal towns and markedly different from that of its traditional inland communities. The young Kennedy joined a special subset of the post-Revolutionary generation that was growing up less dependent on family and village life, or what one sociologist has called the "chimney corner," and more under the sway of urban life, with its rich and varied texture.[13]

This was especially true in more populated areas and among better-off families. The interaction between individual development and the surrounding society became increasingly complex and dynamic for a select number of Kennedy's generation. Certain of his cohorts became more reliant on improved schools, proliferating clubs and associations, and the greater availability of printed material for their personal development. The increasing vitality of public life also broadened the perspective of this rising segment of the nation's youth. For the fortunate few, the path to adulthood lengthened and included a few years of college and some professional training. As members of this group extricated themselves from what had been the traditional matrix of kin and communal relationships, they became more autonomous and individualistic in their approach to life.[14]

The emergence of this more individualistic and autonomous mindset had important implications for how Americans would deal with economic, political, and moral issues during the early to mid-nineteenth century. Faced with rapidly changing economic and social conditions and their sometimes disruptive consequences, most members of the post-Revolutionary generation would fall back on traditional solutions to address the nation's problems. Others would seek more innovative, progressive options, ones better suited for coping with these often unsettling transformations. Although the boundaries between these mindsets were somewhat soft at first, they would become more fixed in response to the unfolding events and ensuing crises of the new century.[15]

These crises were not long in coming and would test Kennedy personally. His father's business failed because of some "unlucky speculation," probably beginning around 1804, and was exacerbated by international trade disruptions and a severe economic depression in Baltimore. Ironically, the same European conflicts that helped drive the insatiable demand for American foodstuffs during the first years of the new century also created chronic instability for American shippers in the form of maritime warfare. John Kennedy's copper-plating business depended upon the health of the shipbuilding industry that, in turn, was linked to the free flow of goods, mostly inland agricultural products, out of Baltimore. Even though the swift Baltimore clippers, with their sleek hulls and extra topsails, frequently evaded interdiction and confiscation on the high seas, they could do little about erratic and hapless American trade legislation meant to remedy these disruptions.[16]

The Embargo Act of 1807, signed into law by President Thomas Jefferson, virtually closed down the American export trade and had a devastating impact on Baltimore. The town's exports plummeted from $14 million in 1807 to $2 million the following year. The Non-Intercourse Act of 1809 attempted to reopen trade with nations other than England and France but did little to restore pre-embargo shipping levels. After war with England was declared in 1812, exports out of Baltimore dropped below $200,000 per year and stayed there for the duration of the conflict.[17]

Baltimore's economic collapse, which ranked among the worst in the nation, wiped out many of the town's wealthiest families, forcing them to sell their Georgian mansions, complete with Hepplewhite furniture, at distressed prices. Even though his brothers covered much of his indebtedness, John Kennedy gave up his Market Street townhouse and moved his family to a poorer neighborhood on the outskirts of town known as "Shrub Hill." The young Kennedy abandoned his plans to attend Princeton, the appropriate college for his class and region. Instead, he enrolled in the newly founded and less expensive Baltimore College.[18]

Biographers of John Pendleton Kennedy have ignored how his father's business failure hung darkly over the young Kennedy's account of these years and deeply affected him. He blamed his father unequivocally for the family's diminished circumstances. While he remembered his father as carefree, honest, and having many friends, Kennedy also accused him of being "careless and liberal in money matters" to the detriment of his family's well-being. More damningly, Kennedy wrote that his father "never possessed much talent and his cultivation was less still." Possibly recalling a happier time, he concluded that his father should have been a cavalry officer.[19]

It was significant that Kennedy's mother kept the family afloat financially during the Shrub Hill years. Although he never accepted her traditional thinking and provinciality, the young Kennedy still saw his mother as more intelligent and decisive than his father. These attributes gave her "a degree of command in her family," Kennedy remembered. Along with the strong women from his early school years, Nancy influenced the perceptions of womanhood that he would later articulate in his essays and novels. The character of Mildred Lindsay in his second novel, *Horse-Shoe Robinson,* is the strongest echo of these impressions.

His father's business failure was formative for the young Kennedy in other important ways. He made up his mind to be different from his father and actively sought role models suited to that objective. One was Judge Jebalin Hollingsworth, with whom Kennedy became acquainted shortly after the family's move to Shrub Hill. Taking a keen interest in the young man, Hollingsworth lent him books and encouraged him to further his scholarship. Welcomed into the old man's library, Kennedy listened as he walked around quoting Terence and Plautus in Latin. "What an influence such a man makes on a young student—such as I was!" Kennedy recalled.[20]

In this and other ways, Kennedy's response to his family's reduced status was individualistic and forward looking. Rather than try to defend his past privileges and regret his lost place in the traditional order of things, he accepted his new circumstances and established his own set of internal goals. "It was perhaps a fortunate circumstance for me," he later wrote, "that during my boyhood my father fell from affluence into poverty." His father's misfortune caused the young Kennedy to redouble his determination to succeed in some new and promising career. As an autonomous, self-directed personality, he never resisted change but embraced it as an opportunity.

"It was after our removal to the country that I gave myself so assiduously to study," Kennedy recalled. At Shrub Hill, he shared a small, cold garret with his younger brother, Andrew, and studied at a desk fashioned out of an old wooden box. Above this desk, Kennedy constructed an elaborate set of pigeonholes, where he organized his notes and compositions by subject and discipline. He embarked on a wide-ranging and intensive program of self-education, meant to go beyond what Baltimore College, which he had entered in 1808, could offer him. "I worked hard during those years, to accomplish myself in a whole circle of science and learning," he later recalled. "I studied Greek for a whole winter, by rising before daylight—read Locke, Hume, Robertson—all the Essayists and poets, and many of the metaphysicians,—studied Burke, Taylor, Barnum—worked at chemistry, geometry, and higher mathematics—although I never loved them—made copious notes on all subjects which came within my study—sketched, painted (very badly) read French, Spanish and *began* German—copied large portions of Pope's translation of Homer, and wrote critical notes upon it, as I went along—in short I thoroughly overworked myself."

Thoroughly exhausted and frustrated, Kennedy complained that his project of self-education suffered from a "want of structure." Although mentors such as Judge Hollingsworth could inspire and occasionally advise him, they could not provide the delicate balance between broad reach and particular focus that such a comprehensive and intense program required. One of his problems was the "overloading [of] my mind with a multiplicity of studies," such that concentration on any particular subject was difficult. He compared his studies to a "kaleidoscope," where impressions of the moment faded quickly and patterns sank into confusion. Another problem was a "tendency toward more imaginative speculation [and] castle-building" during flights of free fantasy. While recognizing the need for increased mental rigor, Kennedy also sought an overall construct upon which to organize his program of self-improvement.[21]

Fortunately, Kennedy and his ambitious cohorts could draw on a rich vein of didactic literature for support. Much of this work consisted of the eighteenth-century Scottish moral, or "common sense," philosophers. Among their various projects, these philosophers had identified what they deemed the attributes responsible for the success of cultivated individuals and civilized societies. The most influential of these philosophers for Americans of Kennedy's generation—writers such as Francis Hutchinson, William Reid, and William Robertson—had determined that the progress of nations depended more on social forces than on laws. The critical social forces were sound education, high moral standards, and cultivated manners. The Scottish moral philosophers stressed the malleability of personal character and encouraged self-improvement for the benefit of individuals and society alike.[22]

Closely related to the views of the Scottish moral philosophers were the middle-class essayists associated with the British magazine, the *Spectator*, founded in 1711 by Joseph Addison and Richard Steele. These writers and others in their circle promoted a culture of politeness and good taste. They differentiated themselves in politics from the Tory Party and in aesthetics from the

British upper class. They were bourgeois proto-Victorians who set the tone for the rising commercial class in British society and influenced everything from gentlemanly deportment to fictional prose to landscape design.[23]

Addison set the tone of what was later referred to as the neoclassical, or Queen Anne, prose style, which was widely imitated in England and the United States because of its seemingly effortless clarity, polish, and decorum. Such writing was highly urbane and relied heavily on cleverness and wit to accomplish its overall aesthetic effect. It used tolerant irony and gentle satire to smooth out the rough edges of daily life and presented its readers with an amusing but harmonious view of the world. While such writing could occasionally be didactic, it was rarely impassioned or emotionally extreme. Like their emerging bourgeois audience, these authors and essayists emphasized moderation and good sense above all else, striving whenever possible for the golden mean.[24]

Other writers contributed to this broad cultural movement. For their conceptions of human nature and its relationship to government, David Hume and John Locke were highly influential. Later, Edmund Burke reiterated that "Manners are of more importance than laws" and distinguished between orderly social change and what he considered the excesses of the French Revolution. Laurence Sterne and Jonathan Swift infused the neoclassical style with new wit and originality. Swift, somewhat of an outsider as a Tory sympathizer and native of Ireland, introduced a sharper satire than that of his contemporaries.[25]

Kennedy refers by name to many of the Scottish moral philosophers and polite-style British writers, whose works he probably borrowed from Judge Hollingsworth or other individuals wealthy enough to own books. Using Hollingsworth's privileges at the Baltimore Library, Kennedy would have perused periodicals such as the *Edinburgh Review,* where he would have read Dugald Stewart, popular on both sides of the Atlantic, who articulated a system of bourgeois ethics based on the work of these writers.[26]

Young students like Kennedy regarded these works less as a formal philosophy and more as a practical ethical system, the most valuable component of which was the concept of "faculty psychology." Developing one's various mental "faculties" and bringing them into perfect harmony would ensure the kind of intelligence, judgment, and equipoise idealized by Addison, Stewart, and others. This broad concept of self-improvement encompassed an individual's education, moral behavior, personal habits, deportment, and manners.

If pursued to its potential limits, this system contained the power of a secular religion.

It is important to note that Kennedy did *not* receive his inspiration for character building from the pulpit. While evangelicalism often combined with Scottish philosophy to sway members of the rising generation in the North, this did not happen with Kennedy. Although he had been baptized in Baltimore's First Presbyterian Church and attended Baltimore College while Presbyterian Samuel Knox was its president, Kennedy does not appear to have spent much time in church. In fact, while attempting to study the Scriptures as part of his broad program of self-education, he admitted to having a "deviant spirit" and was given to an excess of speculation about the nature of God and the hereafter.[27]

Though lacking a strong component of religiosity, Kennedy's campaign for self-improvement was zealous. He was motivated by the didactic literature he read and the mentor-exemplar figures he met. These influences, he later recalled, helped him develop a "tender conscience" and a "humble estimate of my moral qualities." Acknowledging his personal deficiencies, he embarked on a systematic program of character modification. His small failings were easy to correct. For example, after winning three dollars at loo, a popular card game at the time, from a student even poorer than himself, Kennedy resolved never to play cards again. His chronic fear of the dark was more serious. He attributed this fear to an overactive imagination and, taking an autonomous approach to his problem, never shared it with anyone. After weeks of waking at midnight and walking the woods until dawn, his hair standing on end from imagining figures in the darkness, Kennedy mastered his fear. "I felt conscious I was achieving a valuable triumph over a defect in my early character," he remembered.[28]

While Kennedy tended to look up to older and more accomplished individuals as role models, he often measured himself more directly against his peers. Having a strong desire for camaraderie with like-minded individuals, he joined various clubs and associations. He took careful note of the successes and failures of his fellow students and club members, lauding those who shared his own high personal standards and scorning those who "sank into dissipation." He saw his successful classmates as a "select citizenry," one in which he was proud to be included. This select, competitive group constituted a microcosm of the well-adjusted society the Scottish moral philosophers advocated. It was one in which each individual was inculcated with the high moral standards of the whole group and practiced properly sanctioned behavior. As a result of this ethically conscious socialization process, Kennedy's moral improvement program shifted subtly from having a purely individual to a more collective focus. In short, he began moralizing.[29]

Even as a student, Kennedy recognized that not every member of society was prepared to accept the moral strictures demanded by the Scottish moral philosophers. Bent so unwaveringly on his own self-improvement—and convinced that such a program was critical for the betterment of society—Kennedy looked upon any person who did not share his views with unmitigated disdain. In a reminiscence originally set down during his school days, Kennedy recalled the strange story of "Cud."[30]

Carruthers Swan, nicknamed "Cud" by his classmates, appears to have attended the Priestly Academy, Baltimore College, or both for a period of several years. His tuition paid by a rich uncle, the boy seems to have had little interest in education. He appears to have been the embodiment of slovenly, undisciplined youth. Kennedy described Cud as having an "awkward posture, boney arms" and being "coarsely dressed." But it was Cud's chronic truancy and disregard for school regulations that bothered Kennedy most: "Mischief, of every denomination, and trouble were his daily companions." He engaged Cud in more than a dozen school-yard fistfights and, according to Kennedy's telling of it, "whipped" him every time. While other students and the old classicist William Sinclair credited this spindly, scrappy boy with having "spunk," Kennedy was not so generous: "He performed no task—he obeyed no rule, but despised all profitable industry and whatever bore the resemblance of order and usefulness."

Finally, Cud's uncle became fed up and stopped paying the boy's tuition. Cud left school and shipped out as a cabin boy to Liverpool. Evidently, his behavior aboard ship was even worse than it had been in the classroom. Rumor had it that Cud killed a fellow sailor in a fight, and his dereliction of duty and general irresponsibility seem to have been associated with a disaster at sea. "It had often been predicted this little imp of iniquity would come to an untimely end," Kennedy wrote, "and although the catastrophe was not brought about by the folly and wickedness which marked his career, yet it had singular coincidence both in its hour and the speed of its approach with common predicament. He was enough to bring bad luck upon a whole ship's company."

Though Cud may not have been directly responsible for the fate of his shipmates, Kennedy implies that the disharmony he introduced into the tight-knit society aboard ship and its vulnerable operations at sea was lethal. Kennedy believed that Cud carried a "devilish, subtle spirit that fed upon riot and disorder." Whatever the truth, Kennedy saw these events as a clear warning about rebellious outliers in an otherwise properly functioning social group, and his telling of Cud's story signals the emergence of a strong element of didacticism in his world view.[31]

For modern students, steeped in relativism, the surety of Kennedy's moral views seems both naïve and extreme. But during this period, an unquestioning assumption of universal truths defined didacticism in its various forms. While this tendency toward absolutism often was associated with the intense religiosity of the time, Kennedy's didacticism took a more secular form. It was so self-assured because it was *self-constructed* from the didactic literature he read and the mentor-exemplars he observed. That others in Kennedy's peer group shared his principles and beliefs only helped reinforce them.

The construction of these principles and beliefs was conditioned by the period in which Kennedy and his generation came of age; as autonomous and individualistic as they were, they were influenced by many of the same experiences. On the one hand, the social and economic instability of the period impelled them to search the uncertain horizon for new moral bearings. On the other hand, the very existence of the new nation—endowed with what they perceived as superior political and social systems—offered the framework for a new moral order. Because Kennedy's generation had not lived through the Revolution, they were free to render its legacy as they saw fit. This project to sanctify the founding generation, while freighting their work with fresh meaning, became paramount with the outbreak of a second war with England in 1812.[32]

President Madison declared war in June, and the American invasion of Canada was under way by the time Kennedy graduated from college in September. Because of his age and location, Kennedy could hardly have avoided being caught up in the war. By winter, he was training as a private in a local militia unit. Imbued with martial spirit, Kennedy was also brimming with moral prescriptions to improve the war effort. He began seeking a vehicle through which to communicate his views.[33]

At some point in 1813, he was encouraged by an older friend to write a series of essays entitled "The Swiss Traveller." Since the last essay mentions the burning of the nation's capital, Kennedy must have worked on them through the summer of 1814. "The Swiss Traveller" was published anonymously two years later in the *Portico,* a local literary publication with an ultra-nationalistic tone. Later in life, Kennedy would dismiss these essays as "jejune and very mediocre." The few literary critics who have examined them have agreed. Kennedy's youthful attempt to mimic the graceful prose of Addison is ponderous and redundant, and his enthusiastic rhetorical forays on the character of the founding fathers and his jingoistic exuberance are not the products of a mature writer.[34]

It is difficult to know to what extent Kennedy's over-heated nationalism in "The Swiss Traveler" drew upon his own sentiments, was dictated by the editors of the publication, or simply reflected what was expected of writers at the time. During the second war with England, such nationalistic prose became almost conventional and bent even the most independent authors to write in the overwhelming spirit of the moment. Even Washington Irving, a future friend of Kennedy and a writer of exceptional wit and originality, succumbed to the inflated, bromidic wartime style. In short, Kennedy was speaking as much for the young, brash society he was part of as he was for himself.[35]

Nonetheless, "The Swiss Traveller" is valuable for helping us understand how Kennedy projected his moral values onto American society in a time of war and how the war itself shaped those values. While "The Swiss Traveller" has been aptly described as a panegyric to America's founding generation, Kennedy's essays were also censorious of his own generation and called for a reinvigoration of the national ethos.[36]

Kennedy used the device of writing as a fictional foreign visitor, a "Mr. Sidney," to communicate these concerns. A passionate lover of freedom, Sidney has been exiled from his native Switzerland by French invaders. He has journeyed to the land of "the freest government upon earth," hoping to find the same moral climate that gave birth to the country during its struggle for freedom. Will he discover that America is "still the abode of heroes and patriots," or will he find "human excellence languishing and expiring"?[37]

Kennedy never really answers that question. Instead, he provides his readers with two laudatory portraits of the founding generation, one of George Washington, long gone by Sidney's arrival in 1812, and the other of a "Doctor Manly," a former Revolutionary soldier turned man-of-the-cloth, living in retirement somewhere in the upper South. Both men embody the self-perfection envisioned by the Scottish moral philosophers and so ardently sought after by Kennedy.[38]

"His greatest superiority," Kennedy says of Washington, "consisted of his consciousness of well-directed virtue." All of Washington's mental faculties are in perfect balance. His "sober mid-way" is impervious to uncontrolled passions and never causes him "want of discernment." Even his gestures and physical carriage communicate courage, disinterestedness, and magnanimity. Manly, living in perfect harmony with his rural setting and encircled by adoring grandchildren, is a similar study in perfection. Everything about his small farm bears the "marks of attentive improvement," his outbuildings being packed with their "fruitful stores" and the neatness of his garden plots and fences showing that "Nothing was neglected." Manly's character is "highly perfected under the guardian care of a scrupulous conscience." Like Washington, Manly's body signals his moral perfection. "No contracted or ignoble principle controls its movements," Kennedy observes. Like Washington, Manly's faculties are in perfect equilibrium. "His prepossessions were fixed; all within his breast was peace and good will. There was nothing which could come in jarring contact with the world he inhabited."[39]

Had he sensed these noble traits in his contemporaries, Kennedy would not have written "The Swiss Traveller." But the reality of America's second war with England was far from ideal. In July 1812, Kennedy must have witnessed the bloody riots in Baltimore which killed or severely wounded a dozen Federalists and destroyed their newspaper. One of the victims was the Revolutionary War hero "Light Horse" Harry Lee, who was so badly beaten that he became an invalid. Kennedy was probably incensed that American merchants had continued to supply the British in Canada and the Caribbean with foodstuffs well into 1813. Just as disturbing would have been the lack of cooperation by state militias in the overall conduct of the war and the desultory performance of American soldiers in the invasion of Canada. As a final humiliation, the British easily captured the nation's capital and set fire to the White House in August 1814.[40]

Through the voice of Sidney, Kennedy stresses the need to instill in the post-Revolutionary generation the kind of moral perfection that had elevated men such as Washington and Manly to their great tasks. "A radical evil increases with the degeneracy of the times," he warns, and "the smallest blemish may become a resting place for the fulcrum of a powerful lever in the hands of a strong man, a factious demagogue." Kennedy catalogues the many dangers facing the country: "despicable and unmanly private interests," "enervating and unrestrained luxury," "domestick faction," and "the lethargick indolence of peace." After thirty years of prosperity, Americans had become dull, slothful, and far too comfortable. It was time to "chasten and instruct."[41]

In assessing the country's moral tenor, "The Swiss Traveller" devotes considerable attention to women and their influence on society. Women had "fired Greece and saved Rome, civilized and subverted empires." While praising American women for their stalwart service in the Revolution and for their uniquely "undisguised and open" character, Kennedy still worries about their susceptibility to extravagance and luxury. "The ladies in all countries," he warns, "establish the criteria of luxury." Since men are inclined to gratify these feminine fancies, he reasons, women must be held responsible for resisting the debilitating effects of luxury on America's nascent and fragile ethos.[42]

The specific causes of the war are irrelevant, Kennedy argues. Wars are the "agents of the Almighty province," meant to purify and regenerate a people. During the war, he predicts, Americans will give up "productions of all other countries less favorable" and replace them with goods made at home. They will forget "opinions of foreign origins" and come to find "domestic virtue more admirable." Mothers will play a special role. It is they, Kennedy maintains, "who govern infancy and fix the character of the future men." Likewise, fathers will pass the nation's defining principles on to their sons with the same earnestness with which they inculcate religion. The future tar will triumph in battle, remembering that his father served on the *Constitution.* Behind this burst of chauvinism, Kennedy recognizes that creating a coherent public memory will be a vital component of America's national consciousness. "Nothing of war is left but remembrance," he concludes. Two decades later, Kennedy would help build this consciousness with his historical novels.[43]

Even allowing for its youthful exuberance and the time in which it was written, the intense nationalism of "The Swiss Traveller" is remarkable. Kennedy declares that the objective of his essays is "to promote a universal sentiment of patriotism." His own nationalism is unconditional, and he never mentions any loyalty except to the nation. "The surest road to national happiness," he declares, "is found in attachment to country." Though at times poorly composed and over-wrought, Kennedy's first published writing sets down sentiments that he would embrace for the rest of his life.[44]

There were reasons for Kennedy's intense nationalism. Despite his admiration for British letters, Kennedy shared the antipathy of many Americans for England by the time of the war. Hatred of the British was intense in Baltimore, due to its large number of French and Irish, and Kennedy's Scotch-Irish background may have heightened his own animosity. Moreover, Baltimore suffered disproportionately from the deprecations of the British navy on American merchant vessels. The impressments of American seamen, viewed as a purposeful postcolonial humiliation by the British, enraged the local citizenry. While it would discover new sources of prosperity after the war, Baltimore would never replicate the halcyon years of merchant shipping that preceded it. Kennedy partly blamed his father's business failure on British trade and maritime policies. His nearly fanatical pursuit of high tariff legislation in later years likely had its emotional roots in this period.[45]

Still, nothing fueled Kennedy's nationalism like going off to war, an experience he described as "the glory of my life, its vivid high point." Eighteen years old and just out of college, he was eager to join the prestigious militia unit in which his friends were training. The commanding officer of the United Volunteers was General William Winder, a prominent Baltimore lawyer completely lacking in military experience. Kennedy scorned those his own age who had not joined up. Resplendent in uniform, Kennedy strutted about the streets of Baltimore, basking in the gaze of its young ladies.

The week's training at Fort McHenry was still more exhilarating. Learning to maneuver in formation and practicing marksmanship with his Harpers Ferry musket were just the beginning. There were campfires, stories to tell, and the camaraderie of bivouac. These were the intoxicating conditions that drove men to perform great deeds. "True manliness and male companionship were more likely to be found on the camp grounds than in the drawing room," Kennedy observes in "The Swiss Traveller."

Things became more serious at the end of August 1814, when a large British fleet delivered over four thousand troops to the western shore of the upper Chesapeake Bay. These troops had the nation's poorly defended capital in their sights, and the role of blocking their advance fell on the Baltimore militia. In this moment of crisis, Kennedy's mother played the part of a Spartan matron. Handing her son his knapsack, she delivered a stern admonishment: "Do not let me hear, my boy, of your turning your back disgracefully upon the enemy." As his regiment marched out to meet the enemy at Bladensburg, Maryland, the young soldier was in high spirits. Expecting an easy victory followed by a ball in the nation's capital, he had slipped a pair of dancing pumps into his knapsack.[46]

The ensuing engagement was an embarrassing debacle. The combination of sweltering heat and senseless marching and countermarching by General Winder exhausted the Americans. Though causing little real damage, the British Congreve rockets terrified the green troops. Most of the militia fled the field so quickly that the battle was referred to in the nation's newspapers as the "Bladensburg races." Kennedy's regiment held firm under heavy fire, only collapsing before the British bayonet charge. Kennedy was contrite about the American performance: "We made a fine scramble of it." As he carried a wounded comrade from the field, Kennedy lost his musket in the melee. Having misplaced his boots the night before, he was wearing his dancing pumps.[47]

The defeat at Bladensburg opened the way for the British capture of Washington. Even though the burning of the capital added another humiliation for the Americans, the more strategic prize for the British was Baltimore. Fortunately, civic and military leadership had turned the city into a well-fortified camp. What is more, the British victory at North Point, only seven miles from Baltimore, proved a Pyrrhic one. Among the heavy British casualties was their ground commander, General Robert Ross. Kennedy participated in this battle too, but his record of it is fragmentary. In a letter to his Uncle Phil, Kennedy wrote that the Americans had come "to think more highly of the British regulars." In a "memorial" written a few years later, he noted that out of the seventy-eight volunteers from his company who fought at North Point, three were killed, ten wounded, and three taken prisoner. By this second engagement, American resistance had stiffened. Because of their heavy losses at North Point, the failure of their navy to reduce Fort McHenry across the Patapsco River from Baltimore, and the extensive fortifications thrown up around the city, the British decided against further activity in the Chesapeake. An anxious American public saw that the British were not invincible. Baltimore was saved.[48]

In "The Swiss Traveller," Kennedy declares that the only real legacy of war is "remembrance." This was true of the War of 1812. Little material gain was achieved by either side. The Treaty of Ghent returned all boundaries to their status quo ante bellum and left most other issues unresolved. None of this seemed to matter much to Americans, however, after their stunning victory over the British at New Orleans. On a single day in early January 1815, the myth of America's endowment as a divinely chosen and specially nurtured people seemed affirmed. How else could this miraculous victory against such superior forces be explained? Even the Battle for Baltimore, a military stalemate at best, produced the "Star-Spangled Banner," commemorating the young nation's indomitability against a more powerful, foreign power.[49]

In this and other ways, the War of 1812 was transformational for Americans. In the decade after the war, nationalism ran high. With the demise of the antiwar Federalists, the country became more politically unified, ushering in the so-called Era of Good Feelings. Furthermore, Americans began taking notice of their past and celebrating their native virtues. Physical monuments were constructed at places like Plymouth Rock and Bunker Hill. Written ones took the form of George Bancroft's magisterial history of the United States and James Fenimore Cooper's Hudson River Valley novels. Soon Kennedy would add his own indigenous tales to the nation's developing literature.[50]

After the war, the country began turning inward economically as well as culturally. American manufacturing gained a more solid foothold, and the supply of domestically produced goods rose sharply. Economic development shifted westward, reflecting a more robust interior commerce. President James Madison and the Fourteenth Congress supported road building, a central bank, a more protective tariff, and other measures to encourage economic self-sufficiency. If there was a lesson to be learned from the war, it was that America's political independence rested squarely on its economic independence.[51]

Although he had articulated it awkwardly in "The Swiss Traveller," John Pendleton Kennedy had anticipated many of these developments. In both his future literary production and his emerging political principles, he would devote himself to strengthening his once-vulnerable country. However inept his battlefield performance or naively rendered his patriotic sentiments, Kennedy's experiences in the defense of his country served as the crucible for his strong and enduring nationalism.

CHAPTER 2

Entering Public Life

It was July 1825, and the midday heat at Monticello was merciless. The front hall where Kennedy waited offered some relief, but he soon learned that Thomas Jefferson was ill again and not seeing visitors. Resigned, but still curious, Kennedy tried to peer through the glass-paneled doors separating the hall from Jefferson's apartment. There, in the dim space behind the waved glass, a tall, stooped figure moved slowly into view, paused, and then glided on. "He was in a costume long out of fashion—small clothes, a waistcoat with flaps," Kennedy noted, "and some remnants of embroidery." The silent specter did not return. "It was all I ever saw of the sage of Monticello," Kennedy remembered.[1]

There was, of course, the disappointment of not meeting Jefferson. But more than that, Kennedy may have experienced a disquieting sense of distance and incongruity between himself and the great man of Monticello, a generational separation accentuated by Jefferson's declining health and antique clothes. Kennedy may have felt that his half-sighting of Jefferson, so faint and fleeting, was more prophetic than anything the great man could have imparted to him. After all, what could Jefferson tell any member of America's rising generation about the challenges that lay ahead? Possibly, he might have repeated what he had written to a friend the year before—that one generation cannot "bind" another and that all laws and institutions are changeable according to the will of the people. The dead, Jefferson had written, have no control over the living. As he left Monticello, Kennedy probably understood this.[2]

Jefferson died the next year, and his vision of a purely rural, agrarian America should logically have died with him. After all, burgeoning urban centers—Baltimore among them—and proliferating textile mills in New England had created a very different nation. Still, the transition to a more diversified and integrated economy had not been an easy one. Even before the financial crisis of 1819 shook the country, many Americans were questioning the new economic order. President James Madison himself seemed to lose confidence, vetoing on constitutional grounds the 1817 Bonus Bill, which would have provided federal funds for road and canal construction. The "radical" Old Republicans applauded the Jeffersonian tone of his veto message. Arguing against the constitutionality of such federal programs, these radicals also claimed that such projects infringed on individual liberties and states' rights. Once the Panic of 1819 and the ensuing depression took their toll on the nation, the faith of many Americans in the economic nationalism of the postwar period evaporated.[3]

The Missouri Crisis of 1820 followed close behind this financial collapse. When certain northern members of Congress tried to make the exclusion of slavery a precondition for Missouri statehood, southern members rallied in an all-out defense of their peculiar institution. Even though a compromise was achieved, allowing admission of Missouri as a slave state but setting boundaries on the future expansion of slavery, the damage done to the Union was irreparable.[4]

In short, by the time of his visit to Monticello, Kennedy's dream of a prosperous and unified America was far less certain than it had been after the War of 1812. So, too, Kennedy was a lot less naïve and idealistic than he had been when writing "The Swiss Traveller" a decade before. As Jefferson and the Revolutionary generation continued to expire, Kennedy and those born after the founding era were coming of age and beginning to play a role in public life, deciding which noble creeds inherited from the founders should be defended, modified, or ignored. The role of Kennedy's generation, vis-à-vis what the founders had achieved, changed from laudation to interpretation.[5]

Tentatively at first but with increasing confidence, Kennedy entered public life. Between the end of his military enlistment and his Monticello visit, John Pendleton Kennedy embarked on a career in the law, pursued his literary ambitions, and engaged in politics for the first time. He was admitted to the Maryland bar in 1816, coauthored a series of social satires called the *Red Book* from 1819 to 1821, and served in his state's House of Delegates during the years 1820 to 1823.

Although there is no evidence that Kennedy used it himself, the word *career* entered America's vocabulary around this time and would have been familiar to him. Formerly used to describe a horse-racing track, the word now implied a break with traditional forms of work, a shift to more specialized occupations, and a degree of professional status as part of a more complex post-Revolutionary economy. During the first decade of the nineteenth century, Baltimore witnessed an explosion of career men. The number of teachers and clergymen increased dramatically, as did that of bookkeepers and insurance agents. During this time, the number of doctors nearly doubled and lawyers nearly tripled.[6]

Of course, lawyers were nothing new to America. Having usurped community leadership from the clergy during the colonial era, the power and prestige of lawyers had risen steadily ever since. They had dominated the independence movement as well as the writing of constitutions at the state and national levels. By the early 1830s, Alexis de Tocqueville described American lawyers as "the highest political class and the most cultivated portion of society." They had acquired an "aristocratic character" unlike the lawyers of any other country. William Wirt, a prominent Baltimore lawyer and mentor to the young Kennedy, agreed with this assessment. "Men of talent in this country have generally bred to the profession of law," Wirt observed, "and indeed throughout the United States, I have met few persons of exalted intellect, whose powers have been directed at any other pursuit."[7]

Baltimore boasted a large number of distinguished lawyers at the time Kennedy was choosing a career. In the years after the War of 1812, a legal aristocracy of sorts dominated the city's political life. Wirt stood at the top of this esteemed fraternity and would serve as attorney general under Presidents James Monroe and John Quincy Adams. Nearly equal in prestige was William Pinkney, ambassador to the Court of St. James, U.S. senator from Maryland, and attorney general under President Madison. Other luminaries in the field included Robert Goodloe Harper, also a U.S. senator from Maryland, and Roger Brook Taney, soon-to-be attorney general under President Andrew Jackson and eventually chief justice of the Supreme Court.[8]

Although he toyed with other career possibilities, Kennedy decided early on the law. College debating had taught him how to prepare his arguments, and Judge Hollingsworth had shown him how to make them more erudite by referring to the classics. Kennedy also chose the law because it offered status and security. Wirt had described the American bar as "the road to honor," and Kennedy took great pride in the distinguished jurists on his mother's side of the family. He craved the kind of respect men like Judge Philip Pendleton of South Carolina and Judge Edmund Pendleton of Virginia had commanded in their day. While he would later be regarded as a friend of industry, Kennedy never considered entering the rough-and-tumble arena of commerce. After witnessing his father's business failure, he was careful to insulate himself professionally from the perils of such endeavors.[9]

For an ambitious individual like Kennedy, especially one with a didactic strain and bias for social order, the law was a made-to-order career. The doctrine of judicial review, established early in the century by the U.S. Supreme Court, meant that the country's top lawyers served as the ultimate arbiters over the laws of the land. Any law emerging from the legislature was subject to review by the courts. For Kennedy, who had "read" John Locke but "studied" Edmund Burke, social order depended not on some theoretical contract between government and the people but on a well-run court system and the accretion of legal precedence it produced. Similarly, while the social forces identified by the Scottish moral philosophers contributed to an orderly society, such a society could not function without a robust legal tradition respected by its members. The establishment of that tradition fell to a select group of individuals with the training and intelligence to interpret the law for the general public. Kennedy intended to be one of them.[10]

In spite of its status and prestige, entering the ranks of the legal profession during the first decades of the nineteenth century was relatively simple. During this early, "pre-professional" phase of American legal history, colleges and universities produced only a few hundred graduates per year. Educated men were still a rarity, and any decent level of education usually qualified one for a career in the law. Although most apprentices were forced to struggle through Blackstone, Littleton, and Coke—and, in Kennedy's case, the drudgery of the *Maryland Reports*—actual admission to the bar was surprisingly easy. Many examiners for the bar believed that a candidate's knowledge of the classics and overall erudition were the most important criteria for joining the legal fellowship. When John Latrobe stood for the bar, a decade after Kennedy, his interview consisted mostly of questions regarding his command of Greek and Latin. The balance was spent discussing Edmund Spenser's *Faerie Queene*.[11]

Kennedy went about his legal training first under an uncle, another Edmund Pendleton, and later Judge Walter Dorsey. He went before the Maryland bar under the auspices of General William Winder, who, although inept as commander at the Battle of Bladensburg, was a well-connected Baltimore attorney. While little is known about his actual examination, Kennedy's assiduous attention to ancient languages, military service under Winder, and diploma from Baltimore College all favored his admission.[12]

Despite its lofty inducements, legal work proved boring and disappointing for Kennedy. Although Baltimore experienced a credit-driven, postwar boom from 1815 until the 1819 financial collapse, there was not enough legal work for young lawyers, especially those, like Kennedy, without wealthy and influential families to back them. Part of the problem stemmed from the low barriers to entry in the legal profession during this period. While they struggled to drum up business, Kennedy and several other fledgling attorneys were forced to share office space. Because most legal work was done in the courts during this time, clients rarely visited law offices. As a result, most of them were dismal places. They were cold, drab, and uncarpeted, their tables piled high with bundled briefs and correspondence. The prevailing atmosphere was heavy with the mustiness of old law books. It was far too easy for Kennedy and his young associates to put aside *Coke on Littleton,* Bacon's *Abridgments,* or Ferne's *Contingent Remainders* and turn instead to discussions of Addison, Sterne, and Swift.[13]

It was this environment that spawned the *Red Book,* a satirical collaboration between Kennedy and his office mate Peter Hoffman Cruse. Like Kennedy, Cruse was well versed in classical literature, loved the polite-style British essayists, and had already become an accomplished writer by his early twenties. Henry Latrobe, who often visited their office in his all-too-plentiful free time, described both Kennedy and Cruse as "addicted to literature rather than the law."[14]

Ironically, the same classical education and appreciation for literature that eased lawyers into their profession could tempt them from it. As a consequence, America's early history abounded in distracted or lapsed lawyers who became accomplished writers of fiction. Men such as Royall Tyler, John Trumbull, Hugh Henry Brackenridge, Charles Brockden Brown, and Washington Irving all left their marks in literature rather than jurisprudence. Even Kennedy's mentor, William Wirt, who reputedly lacked a profound legal mind but was unrivaled as a courtroom raconteur, found time to produce two novels, *Letters from a British Spy* and *The Old Bachelor,* as well as a highly fictionalized biography of Patrick Henry.[15]

A number of America's literary lawyers specialized in social and political satire. For example, Trumbull's *The Progress of Dulness* took aim at the religious fervor of the late eighteenth century and its New Light divines. Similarly, Tyler's *The Contrast* mocked the materialism of the post-Revolutionary period and its class pretensions. Somewhat later, Brackenridge's *Modern Chivalry* ridiculed the excesses of Jeffersonian democracy and its antiquated agrarian ideals.

Although they drew much of their literary inspiration from the polite-style British essayists, these literary lawyers could be hard and biting in their satirical attacks. What is more, because they were usually well educated and socially elite, they thought themselves qualified to censor social behavior and political conduct as they saw fit. In short, they saw themselves as eloquent and at times oracular stewards of the public good.[16]

Situation and motive may have been similar for Kennedy and Cruse, as they sat down to compose the *Red Book.* Granted, there was the sheer fun of the project for two young, bored lawyers. Both wished to exercise their literary abilities and hoped for a degree of local fame. These impulses mixed easily with the natural iconoclasm of youth. Yet, given the timing of the *Red Book,* which appeared six months after the Panic of 1819, sentiments of bewilderment, frustration, and even anger may also have influenced these young writers.

In the early nineteenth century, it was still customary for writers and authors to publish anonymously or use pseudonyms. This was the case not only for writers of newspaper and magazine articles but also for writers of literary forms not yet considered legitimate, such as novels. For the scathing satire Kennedy and Cruse had in mind, anonymity also offered the benefit of protection. What is remarkable about the *Red Book* is the extent to which its authors went to conceal themselves. Not even their publisher, Baltimore printer and bookseller Joseph Robinson, knew who they were. Using a system of secret mail drops, "J. Dilworth" and Robinson traded advice, corrected manuscripts, and brought out ten issues of the *Red Book* from October 1819 to March 1821. "It is in vain to seek its origins," the mysterious authors boasted in the first installment of the *Red Book.* "The authors are not to be known, though they mingle freely with their fellows; their situation protects them from scrutiny, even from suspicion." Kennedy and Cruse occasionally promised to appear in public but then failed to show up. Once they offered to set up two full-length wooden images of themselves and supply axes and broad swords so their outraged victims could hack the images apart. Of course, the authors never appeared.[17]

It was even unclear to their publisher and the public how many *Red Book* authors there were. There seemed to be at least three. One was Horace of Baltimore, who was "like the Roman Horace but altered to suit the times." This was Peter Hoffman Cruse, who wrote most of the mock-classical poetry. Then there were Sidrophel and Pentagruel. Sid, who was Swiss and probably Kennedy's creation, "wandered the mountains writing hexameters and killing rattlesnakes."

Pentagruel had a more Rabelaisian personality. He possessed a coarser sense of humor, was less preachy than Sid, and was probably a collaborative effort.[18]

The few modern critics who have examined the *Red Book* have dismissed it as too derivative and provincial to be taken seriously. There is no question that Kennedy and Cruse drew heavily on the style of Addison and Steele's *Spectator*. Nor is there any doubt that they borrowed recognizable themes and characters from Swift's *Gulliver's Travels*, Irving's *Salmagundi*, and Wirt's *The Old Bachelor*. Much of the satire directed at certain notables of Baltimore society has lost its relevance for modern readers, but the *Red Book* was an enormous local success during its brief life, quickly selling out every installment at Robinson's bookstore. Despite what they thought of it, the educated citizens of Baltimore and local literati could not get enough of these little red pamphlets. Furthermore, the *Red Book* earned the praise of two prominent Boston intellectuals, Edward Everett and Andrews Norton, neither of whom knew anything about Baltimore society but appreciated the strange little periodical for its wit and originality.[19]

Modern critics have ignored the historical context surrounding the publication of the *Red Book*. Even before the Panic of 1819 exposed the fragile finances of the city's business community, Baltimore society had been living in a kind of nostalgic dream state. After the war of 1812, the city's economy had shifted from relying on international shipping, the once lucrative trade with Europe and the West Indies, to emphasizing local manufacturing, mostly of consumer goods for growing inland markets. With this shift, former merchant shippers invested their wealth in local real estate and financial institutions, thereby transforming themselves into a rentier class. The wealthiest and most influential members of this class were known as the "Club" and controlled Baltimore's largest banks. A far less elite group of "new men," mostly former artisans from the city and millers from the adjacent countryside, led the rising manufacturing sector.

Even so, the old merchant shipping elite continued to set the tone of fashion and determined social status in the city. These families, with their elegant townhouses and country estates, hosted a full schedule of fancy cotillions, lavish costume balls, and sumptuous dinners that harkened back to the golden age of Baltimore. Social hierarchy was determined not by one's success as an enterprising manufacturer and the emoluments such success accorded but rather by one's acceptance into the select circle of the city's old merchant elite. Young, ambitious professionals such as Kennedy, Cruse, and their associates eagerly sought this kind of social advancement, attending balls, courting the eligible daughters of the city's elite families, and otherwise ingratiating themselves with members of this social stratum.[20]

The Panic of 1819 changed all this. In Baltimore, more than in any other city, the financial collapse and ensuing depression swept everything before it. The vulnerable City Bank went bankrupt, and other local banks struggled to stay afloat. Maryland banknotes fell to half their value. The Warren Manufacturing Company, worth over $200,000 before the panic, sold for $35,000 afterward. An estimated ten thousand workers lost their jobs, and a dozen soup kitchens opened to feed them. Rents in the city declined by 50 percent. Young professionals like Kennedy and Cruse saw many of their clients completely ruined.[21]

The financial collapse of 1819 was the worst in America's history up to that time, and the depression that followed lasted several years. There were many causes for the collapse. Among them was the overissuance of paper money by local banks in nearly every section of the country. The newly chartered Second Bank of the United States was clearly at fault for not reining in this practice until it was too late. This proliferation of paper money and a surfeit of credit, much of it from England, fueled a land-speculation frenzy and an overproduction of cotton in the South. The break in the cotton price during January 1819 set the groundwork for the collapse, and the general tightening of credit by the Second Bank, most local banks, and British exporters unleashed the full fury of the panic in May.[22]

Worse still for Baltimore, the city's elite families had participated in extensive bank fraud and other kinds of shady financial speculation. The investment firm of Smith and Buchanan, controlled by two of the city's prominent families and part of the powerful Club, had purchased stock in the Baltimore branch of the Second Bank with little or no collateral. This unsecured stock had been used to fund a series of questionable investments. (The cashier of the Second Bank, James McCulloch, who Kennedy had carried away from the fight at Bladensburg a few years before, played a significant role in this scheme.) Other elite families, such as the Joneses, Steretts, and Higginbothams, had played parts in the failure of the City Bank as well as the near collapse of the Union Bank of Maryland.[23]

The Panic of 1819 upended Baltimore's social conception of itself. The city's most elite families were morally disgraced and never recovered their reputations. The economic basis for the rentier class, with its stock jobbers, brokers, and shavers, was called into question. The trials of those accused of bank fraud dragged on for years. One delegate in the Maryland legislature went so far as to suggest that those found guilty should be hanged. Understandably, the fashionable style and social pretensions of the city's best families were publically condemned. Expensive cashmere shawls and Leghorn hats suddenly disappeared from the streets. More understated "cotton-cambric parties" took the place of cotillions and fancy balls. The city's most respected newspaper, *Niles' Register*, urged its readers to return to "the simplicity of our forefathers" and "exchange dissipation for temperance and vice for virtue."[24]

These attitudes are important in understanding what motivated the writing of the *Red Book* and accounted for its popularity. During a period of economic stress and public self-examination, the *Red Book* tapped into a strain of classical republican sentiment against luxury and fashion nearly as old as the country itself. These were the same corrupting influences that had been so glaringly exposed in "The Swiss Traveller." What is more, because neither Kennedy nor Cruse had as yet attained the emoluments of success in their own careers, they felt justified in criticizing the elite members of their community who had seemingly caused its moral breakdown.

In short, the *Red Book* was much more than a youthful literary romp. The unrelenting drive, razor-sharp edge, and sheer intensity of its satirical attack sprang directly from the circumstances in which it was written. As they observed the behavior of society around them, many readers of the *Red Book* seemed to accept its critical premise. "The world in our opinion needs correction," Kennedy and Cruse warn in their first installment. They declare it their purpose to "strike at the penetralia of society, and pluck from it the corruption that cowardly hands dare not touch." In the guise of Sidrophel, Pentagruel, and Horace of Baltimore, they walk the streets of the city, invade the haunts of its fashionables, and expose pretense, hypocrisy, and extravagance wherever they find it.

No one is spared. The older gentlemen of the city are subjected to withering attack. These superannuated elites have seen their "sparks of ambition too early and unhappily quenched" and now suffer from a "lurking consciousness of talents unemployed and an indolent infirmity of purpose." These old fellows hide "their flimsy pretensions under the solemnity of a pair of spectacles, or disguised them in the envelope of professional grandeur." Most idle away their days at exclusive clubs arguing over nothing or parading about the city with their "gold-handled canes" and "contemptuous dignity of carriage." The more ridiculous of them escort young women to the theater and "stooping to pick up a fan," can hear "their joints cracking under them."[25]

Foremost among these old gentlemen is the obnoxiously loud Mr. Boreas, who belongs to all the right clubs and "talks roaring and walks roaring," and the well-traveled coxcomb Mr. Oracle, an expert on nearly everything who mistakenly "believes himself to be one of the important units of creation." A more introverted member of this class, the wealthy but solemn Mr. Vanderbeef, "thinks money sanctifies dullness." While the actual models for these characters have been lost to memory, Kennedy and Cruse apparently sketched them from life and occasionally provoked the wrath of the targeted personages. Just after the first issue of the *Red Book* appeared, a rumor circulated that its mysterious (and presumably wealthy) authors had posted an immense sum to defend their publisher in the event of a libel suit.[26]

The wives of the city's elite class fare no better. Their fashion is "specious vulgarity," their salons "tawdry," and their learning "shallow." Their pretentious behavior and foolish extravagance are enough to drive their husbands away for long evenings of oysters, cards, and worse. Behind all their face paint and got-up resplendence, these doyennes of Baltimore society are ugly enough to "lead the apes of hell." So brutal was the *Red Book*'s treatment of the city's finest ladies that it was pointedly criticized by William Wirt.[27]

But worst of all are the social climbers, newcomers to the city's economic wealth and aspirants to the social status it might provide. The desperate rivalry among these arrivistes for social ascendency is satirized through the Hardoakes and the Apewells. "Solemn war was declared," Sidrophel (probably Kennedy) notes regarding this competition. "Their weapons were mansions, Sunday pews, marriages of their daughters, ballroom and parlor show." The Hardoakes were originally rural folks who "acknowledged no right to be idle" and, while always striving to appear sociable, "loved their animals better than their neighbors." The Apewells come from the city and have no real talents other than "the art of rising in life, like parasitical plants on some goodly tree." Nonetheless, they make remarkable progress in society. Somehow this family "twined and twisted and crept and expanded into importance." Their success is hard to explain except that they rely heavily on "their skill in French romances and French phrases."[28]

The society described in the *Red Book* was highly unstable. Following the

Panic of 1819, the old elite could expect little or no quarter from Kennedy and Cruse. Nor could those who would eventually replace them at the top of society. The Hardoakes are probably modeled after the former rural millers and Apewells after the former urban artisans; both groups had recently turned to manufacturing. Granted, the authors of the *Red Book* lacked the long-term perspective needed to make sense of these "multiple elites." Nonetheless, the authors questioned the credibility of the newly prosperous families because they adopted the pretensions and extravagances of the disgraced elite. What was required, the authors of *Red Book* implied, was a complete break from these discredited values and a return to a simpler way of life.[29]

In a nostalgic moment, old Mr. Bronze recalls a time when young men and women performed honest work and led simple, unembellished lives, before "the shopkeeper [was] transformed into a merchant or a director" and "the leger-worm first fluttered out a gilded, fashionable butterfly." Fashion, Mr. Bronze argues, is the true culprit. "The process by which nature makes a tulip out of dirt is not more mysterious than that by which I have known Fashion to produce hers; and I see by enchantment, sofas, side-boards and carpets, spring out of cheeses, bundles of tape and bohea-chests, like Cinderella's coach from the pompion."[30]

Somewhat later in the *Red Book,* Horace of Baltimore (Peter Hoffman Cruse) articulates the problem of fashion and blames it on young women in verse:

> To release you from Fashion's bewildering thrall,
> Who holds you unconscious how fast you are bound,
> In her magical circle still running the round;
> Like the wily magician whose mystical tones
> Turn'd maidens, the tale goes, to idiots and stone.[31]

The *Red Book* is even more didactic than "The Swiss Traveller" regarding the evils of fashion, at one point juxtaposing two fictional young ladies named "Good Sense" and "Fashion" in a meticulous side-by-side comparison. The *Red Book* examines their respective tastes in reading, social deportment, moral judgment, and eventual domestic success. Good Sense adheres to "tasteful simplicity of attire," reads "her Bible and sensible books," and always exhibits "modest behavior." Her rewards are a successful marriage, a devoted husband, and well-behaved children. Fashion, on the other hand, has a "high complexion and a showy figure." Always adorned in the milliner's latest offering, she parades her finery opposite the alehouse or, on Sundays, at church: "It was her chief pleasure to display there at the country church, to the dismay of the sober-suited matrons, and to the great edification of the boys in the church yard." Fashion changes her favorites "almost as often as her dresses" and ends up with spoiled brats for children and a husband who spends most nights at his club.[32]

Fashion was by no means Baltimore's only difficulty. There was the overarching problem of too much self-interest and competition for material success; boundless pursuit of personal gain had been one of the root causes of the city's financial collapse and lingering depression. The *Red Book* compares the mercurial soul of Baltimore to ancient Phoenicia and identifies Market Street as the "prize fighting ground to which everything patrician and plebian is referred for contest." Stationing themselves beside this bustling thoroughfare, Sidrophel and Pentagruel amuse themselves by guessing the occupations of the various combatants by the manner of their walk. "The lawyers walked in knots," Sid observes, "because, perhaps they deal in these articles, and are moreover of greater service to each other than to anyone else, and therefore fond of each other's company. The Doctors on the contrary, walked alone—I presume for the very opposite reason, as they are seldom known to admire or esteem each other."[33]

At such points, the *Red Book* takes on a lugubrious, almost cynical tone. With their careers going nowhere and the future growing dimmer, such a discouraged perspective seemed justified to the periodical's young authors. The tumult and confusion of Market Street was a far cry from Kennedy's Burkean ideal of a well-ordered and smoothly functioning society:

> The most cheerful looking man, was a bankrupt . . . the wisest looking man was a bank director . . . The most out-landish was a dandy . . . the most pompous, a lawyer . . . most dogmatick, a Parson . . . most learned in his own opinion, a doctor—the most dignified, a dancing master. The happiest of the whole group was the ash-man, lording over his decomposed essences of mortality—dust and ashes; careless and contented, whistling in the cloud that enveloped him as little affected by the din and clamour and vanity and folly of the scene around him, as the Mohawk chief in Drury-Lane.[34]

In spite of the human variety packed into these urban scenes, black people are conspicuously absent from Kennedy and Cruse's portrait of Baltimore. A fourth of the city's sixty thousand inhabitants were black in 1820; a third of these were held in bondage. Since most of the town's slaves either performed domestic work or were hired out as day labor, they were highly visible in the busy streets. While Baltimore was by no means in the grip of slavery, it was no stranger to it either.[35]

The most startling aspect of the "Journey to the Nether World" is its trenchant attack on southern slavery. Living in the borderland during a period of rising tension over slavery, it is surprising that Kennedy and Cruse chose to address this volatile topic at all. (In fact, the Missouri Crisis had been brewing for over a year when they broached the subject in the *Red Book.*) With good reason, the two satirists decided to attack slavery obliquely, using an allegorical tale with the unusual title, "Journey to the Nether World by Captain Symmes."

The source of their inspiration was as bizarre as the tale itself. In 1818, Clive Symmes, an ex-army officer living in St. Louis, published a theoretical paper postulating that the earth was hollow and consisted of concentric spheres, one within the other, which were habitable. Symmes claimed that these spheres could be entered through holes located in the vicinity of the North Pole. In the course of his lifelong obsession, Symmes would petition Congress twice during the mid-1820s for federal funding to locate and explore his polar holes. Controversial though they were, "Symmes' holes" fascinated the public. Henry Thoreau would even mention them in *Walden.*[36]

In 1820, a Philadelphia man, writing under the pseudonym of Captain Adam Seaborn, published a novel called *Symzonia: A Voyage of Discovery.* The novel describes Seaborn's trip to a land beneath Antarctica, the recent discovery of which was creating a great public stir. This sub-Antarctic land, called "Symzonia," is blessed with a morally perfect and superbly governed Utopian society. Seaborn and his crew are struck by the extraordinary whiteness of these Utopians. Not only are they dressed entirely in white, but their complexions are so white that the visitors, though Caucasians themselves, feel like "the sootiest of Africans" standing next to them. In spite of its fantastic premise, the novel sold poorly. A local reviewer found it "dull and uninteresting."[37]

It is unlikely that Kennedy and Cruse read *Symzonia* before publishing their own subterranean, antipodal tale. Their "Journey to the Nether World" appeared in the first week of March 1820, either coincident with or before the Seaborn novel reached the market. Furthermore, the fictional realm they describe, also located beneath Antarctica, is very different from that in *Symzonia.* The citizens of Vandalia, as the two authors call their strange country, especially the elite class living in the capital of Folliana, are far from moral exemplars and lead luxurious, sumptuous lives. At one point in the story, Captain Symmes asks his local guide who owns the resplendent townhouses along what appears to be the best street in Folliana. The guide answers that they belong to the "Tawney-Traders."

"Tawnies," Captain Symmes inquires, "what are they? " "They are a variety, it is believed, of our race," his guide explains, "but who have noses three inches long and, thin lips, and are altogether so ugly, that our priests, philosophers and Tawney-Traders hold them to be little better than apes, and under the particular displeasure of the gods." The guide goes on to explain that, despite the loathsome opinion of them, Tawnies are important to Vandalian society. Not only do Tawnies serve as docile laborers during their brief lives, but their remains are of great value after they expire. The most prized possessions of Vandalian ladies are their dressing-boxes (elegant feminine grooming kits), which, to qualify as truly prestigious items, can only be constructed from human bones. Since capital punishment in Vandalia is inadequate to supply such material, Tawney bones are now used exclusively.[38]

Recoiling in fear and horror, Symmes confesses that his own nose is rather long and that his lips are on the thin side. He asks his guide whether the Vandalians actually slaughter the Tawnies for their bones. Insulted, his guide quickly clarifies the situation: "God forbid, Sir!—that were contrary to the law: they are only put to hard labor, and their mortality is rapid enough to prevent so inhuman a procedure as you mention." Not only is the use of Tawney bones fully accepted by Vandalians, but Tawney-Traders are absolutely unassailable at the top of Vandalian society. The nobility of this ruling class, it is pointed out, is determined by "the degree of uselessness and worthlessness" of its members. Their extreme indolence is admired and aspired to by the "Lollers" and "Lickspittles," who are positioned below the Tawney-Traders in the Vandalian social hierarchy. These courtier-like castes willingly prostrate themselves in the presence of their betters and are dependent on them for favors. "They lay flat on their faces," Symmes observes, to prove "how much they were obedient servants." Closer to the bottom of Vandalian society but above the Tawnies, are the teachers, philosophers, authors, and anyone who performs manual labor. These elements of society are barred from major social events, known as "in-si-pi-dité," or "dull affairs" in the Vandalian language. Only six topics of conversation are allowed at these events, ranging from the weather to ball music.[39]

Even though their conceit became attenuated over several issues of the *Red Book,* as the overuse of the Vandalian language grew tedious, Kennedy and Cruse had produced a remarkable piece of satire and seemed to enjoy writing every word of it. The two authors clearly owed a debt to Jonathan Swift, first for the sheer audacity of the Tawney bones idea, which is evocative of Swift's "Modest Proposal" essay (suggesting cannibalism as a means to reduce the number of poor children in Ireland), and second for inspiring the Tawnies themselves, who seem modeled after Swift's Yahoos (the grotesque and debased race in Part IV of *Gulliver's Travels*).[40]

It is also likely that, some eighteen years later, Edgar Allan Poe borrowed from "Journey to the Nether World" for his only novel, *The Narrative of Arthur Gordon Pym of Nantucket.* Poe's novel culminates in a journey to a land beneath Antarctica and contact with a humanlike but debased race of creatures there. While he may have read *Symzonia,* Poe's antipodeans bear no resemblance to creatures in that novel but are black to their teeth and despise the color white. Like Kennedy and Cruse, Poe may also have drawn from Swift. During his years in Baltimore, Poe likely would have been familiar with the *Red Book.* Kennedy became an important mentor to him, promoting the young writer to various publishers and helping him get a job at the *Southern Literary Messenger.*[41]

While its main satirical thrust was at the Deep South, one stimulus for the "Journey to the Nether World" may have originated closer to home. During the time Kennedy and Cruse were writing the *Red Book,* a vibrant traffic in slaves between Maryland and the Gulf Coast states was being conducted out of Baltimore. The largest slave trader, Austin Woolfolk, began running "Cash for Negroes" ads in city newspapers during 1815 and moved to Baltimore from Georgia in 1819. His major innovation was transporting slaves by packet ship from Baltimore to New Orleans instead of using the cheaper but slower "coffles" (chained columns of slaves) traveling overland. Woolfolk and other slave traders scoured the Maryland countryside for purchasable slaves and collected them in Baltimore before sending them south. He bought a large white house on Pratt Street, not far from his slave pen, and marched his slaves, usually a hundred or more at a time, to the wharves at night. Woolfolk alone shipped some 2,300 slaves out of Baltimore between 1815 and 1832. Frederick Douglass and Alexis de Tocqueville both mention him in their descriptions of the city.[42]

Many Baltimoreans were embarrassed by the activities of slave traders in their city. The *American* sought to exclude "Cash for Negroes" ads from its pages, and Mayor John Montgomery tried unsuccessfully to have the city council ban slave pens. Nonetheless, Woolfolk's business flourished, and he became a prominent member of the community. It is very likely that Woolfolk was Kennedy and Cruse's model "Tawney-Trader" and the impetus for their attack on the institution he served.[43]

Behind its thin allegorical disguise, the *Red Book* in its depiction of Vandalia replicates with surprising fidelity the proslavery argument emerging at the time. In his exchange with Captain Symmes, the Vandalian guide cites contemporary scientific belief, differences in physiognomy, and religious sanction to justify a racially based system of slavery. The guide goes on to provide a cool and facile rationalization for the high mortality rates generated by such a system and insists that such a system is entirely lawful. The brutal treatment of the Tawnies and the wealth amassed through their exploitation is no more than "honest industry." Having paid attention to both the content and tone of this argument, Kennedy and Cruse appear to have sensed its fundamental absurdity.[44]

Nor do the two writers give any quarter to slave-owning society. Not only does their satire highlight the deleterious effects of slavery on the master class, but it also points out the negative consequences accruing to the social strata below it. The absence of a work ethic and the lack of intellectual vigor in Vandalia strike at the reality of these deficiencies in much of southern society. So, too, the servile attitudes of nonelites toward the master class, while taken to ridiculous extremes in the *Red Book,* reflect the emerging power structure in many parts of the South. The *Red Book* satire would take its place in a critical continuum, stretching from Jefferson to Tocqueville, that called attention to the debilitating impact of slavery on white southern life. Kennedy would revisit the subject in *Swallow Barn.*[45]

By the second half of 1820, Kennedy and Cruse had exhausted much of their material for the *Red Book* and were showing signs of tiring. Much of the original wit and energy is missing from the periodical's later installments. Kennedy had turned his interest to politics and, in October 1820, was elected as a representative from Baltimore to the Maryland House of Delegates. By early the following year, Cruse wrote to Kennedy in Annapolis, proposing a tenth and final installment of the *Red Book.* He signed his letters "Horace."

When the valedictory installment appeared in March 1821, it consisted mostly of Cruse's poetry.[46]

It is unclear when and how Kennedy and Cruse finally disclosed their authorship of the *Red Book*. Whatever the public response, it was muted by the work's fading popularity. The two men remained close friends for the next decade. During the early 1830s, Cruse advised Kennedy on the character development and plotting of *Swallow Barn*. By then, Cruse had traded the law for journalism, becoming editor of the *Baltimore American* and later the *Patriot*. He perished in the cholera epidemic of 1832, his literary promise unfulfilled except for the *Red Book*.[47]

The details of Kennedy's entry into politics have been obscured by time. What is known, however, is that he worked hard at campaigning for public office, received some influential support along the way, and benefited from the fluid politics of the period. He often faced hostile crowds while campaigning but evidently won some of them over with his rousing oratory. On one occasion, he turned cries of "Down with him!" into approving huzzas. Importantly, Kennedy gained the endorsement of William Pinkney, one of Baltimore's most esteemed lawyers and a U.S. senator at the time. Pinkney had himself been a strong "stump" speaker during his earlier years and was always looking for fresh political talent. It probably did not hurt that Kennedy was courting Pinkney's daughter, Charlotte, and may have been engaged to her. (In the end, Charlotte chose to marry a man from New York.) Kennedy also had the backing of General Winder and William Wirt, who took a special interest in him as a promising intellectual and politician of the rising generation.[48]

His oratorical skills, personal charm, and political connections notwithstanding, Kennedy was only twenty-four when he ran for the state legislature and would probably not have gained his seat had it not been for the confusion of city and state politics after the Panic of 1819. At the municipal level, one of the "new men" of Maryland politics, John Montgomery, toppled the old guard in city government to become the mayor of Baltimore in 1820. At the state level, the long-overdue decline of the Federalists opened the House of Delegates to reform-minded Democratic-Republicans and a generation of younger politicians like Kennedy. While clearly positive for Kennedy, these changes did not inaugurate a new political order per se but rather signified a collapse of the old order. It would be 1827 before the Jacksonian Democrats introduced some ideological coherence into municipal and state politics. Until then, municipal elections would be decided by shifting interest-group coalitions, and state politics would be riven by chronic localism.[49]

Aside from enduring these unstable political conditions, both state and city faced social and economic problems in need of legislative action. The financial collapse of 1819 cried out for banking reform and the ensuing depression for some kind of debtor relief. Furthermore, the stagnating commercial sector demanded initiatives to improve the state's antiquated transportation system. Finally, the national debate over Missouri statehood and the future of slavery raised questions about Maryland's own slave laws and the management of its burgeoning free-black population.

John Pendleton Kennedy entered the old statehouse in early December 1820. The lower chamber's decrepit condition must have shocked him. Peeling paint, threadbare rugs, and broken desks attested to the long neglect and small maintenance budgets for such buildings at the time. There was one small stove, but someone had made off with the fender. During the months of December through February, when the House of Delegates met, the chamber was chilly and poorly ventilated.[50]

Still, as he mingled with the other seventy-two delegates, Kennedy must have experienced a mixture of curiosity and exhilaration. The variety of appearances and manners must have impressed him. The blunt speech and coarse clothing of the western delegates would have seemed out of place beside the polished diction and elegant dress of those from the southern Chesapeake. The representatives from northern counties looked and sounded more like Pennsylvanians than Marylanders. The so-called eastern and western shores of the state were so separated by the state's watery geography that each kept its own budget. Even more pronounced was the division between delegates from Maryland's northern agricultural counties, where farmers grew wheat and employed free labor, and those delegates from the state's southern counties, where growers planted tobacco and owned large numbers of slaves. Delegates from southern counties such as Calvert and Prince George, with half their populations enslaved, cared little about internal improvements, publically funded education, or poor relief for the workingmen of Baltimore. Such a factious collection of delegates, Kennedy would discover, made the passage of legislation difficult at best and often impossible.[51]

Another challenge was the heavy burden of routine, mundane business that clogged the legislative process. During most of its session, the House of Delegates was bogged down with numerous petitions for divorces, veterans' pensions, poor relief, and the admission of slaves into the state. Each petition had to be formed into a bill, assigned to a committee, read twice, voted on by the lower chamber, and passed on to the Senate for final approval. Additionally, the lower chamber dealt with road and bridge repairs, disputed elections of judgeships, the preservation of deer herds, and the eradication of crows.

Despite these obstacles, Kennedy entered the House of Delegates with optimism and a sense of purpose. No longer the critical bystander of the *Red Book,* he was now in a position to bring positive change to his troubled city and state. His first priority was debtor relief, a cause championed during the previous session by Thomas Kennedy (no relation), a delegate from western Maryland. Thomas Kennedy had worked hard to secure passage of a "stay of execution" bill, which restrained the state from immediately imprisoning debtors, placed minimum values on their salable property, and established an installment plan for repayment of their debts. It was against this background that the younger Kennedy proposed his own debtor legislation.[52]

There were several possible reasons why John Pendleton Kennedy joined the cause of debtor relief. Naturally, the support of Baltimore's workingmen might help ensure his future electoral success. Just as important, however, may have been the memory of his father's bankruptcy and the years spent at Shrub Hill. Only days after taking his seat, Kennedy introduced a bill calling for "the speedy recovery of small debts out of court." Two weeks later, he brought forward an ambitious bill to abolish imprisonment for debt in the state of Maryland. At the end of January 1821, Kennedy was on his feet again articulating a bill to spare debtors the loss of "bed, bedding, and wearing apparel," as well as other "necessary household items," up to a value of fifty dollars.

Both the bills to abolish imprisonment for debt and to settle small debts out of court went down to defeat in the lower house before they could be passed on to the Senate. However, the "bed and bedding bill," as it was called, was enacted into law in February 1821. Still, the bill faced strong conservative opposition in both houses. Fifty dollars worth of exemptions from seizure was a considerable sum in the 1820s and, so conservative thought ran, would lead to "abuse and mischief" by working people. The threat of seizure was "one of the most powerful stimulants to industry and frugality," conservatives argued, and actually benefited the working class. In the end, Kennedy's arguments prevailed and earned him the gratitude of Baltimore's working families.[53]

One of the few unifying sentiments among many of the delegates was their animosity toward Baltimore. This included those delegates from rural counties, who saw the town as contributing less to the state's coffers than it demanded, as well as those from towns such as Annapolis and Frederick, who were jealous of its commercial success. Once before, the powerful House Ways and Means Committee had attempted to take away the proceeds from Baltimore's auction tax. This 1 percent tax on the auction of foreign goods was vital to maintaining the town's port facilities and, in early 1821, again came under attack. In a long and impassioned speech, Kennedy accused those who would take away the city's revenues of "prejudices," "unnatural hostility," and "sinister dictates of sectional antipathies." He compared their attack with "the wily Greeks [who] would sack our Troy with smiling faces" and, more recently, with British troops before Baltimore "when they thundered at her gates." Kennedy went on to carefully analyze the town's finances and emphasize its economic and cultural importance to the state. He characterized Baltimore as "the great emporium of the state" and "the nurse of every liberal art and science." In the end, Kennedy's argument rescued the auction tax from extinction. During the days that followed, the young legislator earned plaudits from the *Baltimore Patriot* for his gallant defense of the town's finances. Not long after, he received a standing ovation as he entered one the town's main theaters.[54]

Because the Missouri Crisis formed the national backdrop of his freshman term, it was not surprising that Kennedy became involved in legislative debates over race and slavery. Within days of convening, the House of Delegates passed a firm resolve against any interference by Congress in the expansion of slavery to the territories. The legislature also rejected a memorial from the state's fledgling Colonization Society because the document's tone was considered abolitionist. Soon after, the legislature dispatched several complaints to neighboring Pennsylvania for allegedly harboring runaway slaves. As if roused from a slumber, delegates from southern Maryland began demanding tighter control of their state's free-black population. One proposed bill attempted to ban ownership of dogs and guns by free blacks, another to bar them from selling farm produce at public markets. One piece of legislation would have required free blacks to apply for certificates of "good conduct" from their local sheriff and submit proof that all property owned had been "honestly obtained." Fortunately for Maryland's free blacks, these bills either never came to a vote or were defeated in the lower chamber.[55]

Nonetheless, these debates over race and slavery would continue during Kennedy's three terms in the Maryland legislature. Although they were sometimes driven by events outside the state, these debates often revolved around purely local issues. One such issue was Maryland's antiquated and complex "Slave Importation Law." This law dated back to 1796 and required every Marylander wishing to bring slaves into the state to petition the legislature for permission to do so. Given the law's myriad of loopholes, these petitions were usually granted. For example, any resident of Maryland who acquired slaves outside the state through marriage or inheritance, or any new resident moving to the state, was allowed to bring slaves into the state. Most important, any resident of Maryland who sent slaves out of the state to work properties owned by that resident, or leased slaves to another property owner outside the state, could bring those slaves back at any time. In short, the Slave Importation Law allowed Maryland's largest slaveholders to periodically adjust their labor needs and earn lucrative incomes by sending their slaves out of state and returning them at will.[56]

By Kennedy's first term, the number of petitions to bring slaves into Maryland had increased beyond a manageable level. Each of these petitions had to be formed into a "special law" and voted on by both chambers of legislature. As a consequence, the Maryland Senate passed a bill repealing the Slave Importation Law and replacing it with a simpler, more streamlined "general law" that would obviate the cumbersome petition procedure. The proposed law would allow Maryland residents to bring slaves into the state strictly for their own use. Once in the state, these slaves could not be resold for any reason. Nor could they be manumitted by last will and testament. If such slaves were set free in this manner, they would be required to leave the state immediately. In spite of the need for something like it, the Senate bill was defeated when it reached the House of Delegates. Kennedy was one of the delegates who voted against it, and, in an hour-long speech, he explained why.[57]

In a newspaper article entitled "The Negro Bill," Kennedy's speech before the House of Delegates was reported in detail and quoted at length. The newspaper, probably the *Baltimore American,* was favorable toward Kennedy and described him as "demonstrating as warm a sensitiveness upon the subject of slavery, as could exist in the bosom of its greatest enemies." The tone of Kennedy's speech was mixed, at times drenched in the exaggerated sentimentality that typified the oratory of his day and at other times cautious and legalistic, in keeping with his chosen profession and political circumstances. While his primary goal was to explain his opposition to parts of the Senate bill, Kennedy broadened the scope of his speech to treat the issues of race and slavery in considerable depth.[58]

Slaves were "an unfortunate community," Kennedy began, and deserved the sympathy of all decent men. "They are a prosecuted and down trodden race," he continued, "whose nature, galled and chafed by the fetters which bind them to their fate, solicits from every man of feeling the most cordial sympathy." Still, though the slave's condition was regrettable, any laws designed to alleviate it needed to be "compatible with the general interest" and to "legislate for society as we find it." As if to put his more conservative colleagues at ease, Kennedy assured the legislature that the best that could be done for the slave was "mild and merciful legislation to cheer up his degraded nature and to teach him to smile amid his pain." In short, while he was an enemy of slavery in theory, Kennedy would refrain from any radical legislation to curtail the institution in practice.

Still, Kennedy had voted against the Senate's slavery bill. Although he favored simplifying the existing law to allow all Marylanders to bring slaves into the state for their own use, he opposed the requirement that those slaves manumitted by last will and testament leave the state immediately. Since slaves manumitted by deed were permitted to remain in the state, Kennedy felt that this part of the law was inconsistent and unfair. If this inconsistency could be corrected, he indicated that he would probably vote for the Senate bill.

But why, if he was truly opposed to the institution of slavery, did Kennedy favor a bill making it easier for most Marylanders to bring slaves into the state? He gave two reasons behind his thinking. The first was motivated by his professed sympathy for the lot of the slave: "If Maryland forever closed her gates . . . [and] Virginia and the states of the west imitate this policy, what is the consequence?" He answered his own question: "You drive the wretched African to the fens of Georgia, or the noxious Districts of Louisiana." Slaves condemned to the Deep South languished under "a barbarous system of agriculture" and suffered "all the tortures which cruelty and covetousness can inflict." If the Vandalia of the *Red Book* had any basis in reality, Kennedy appeared to believe, it was in the "sickly swamps and sultry regions of the south." Any slave permitted to enter Maryland would be spared "the severest horrors of slavery."[59]

Kennedy's second reason for supporting the bill was somewhat complicated. Not only would the slaves themselves benefit from more benign working conditions and more benevolent masters, but these slaves would also bolster the state's economic well-being. Noting the alarming increase in the number of Maryland farmers migrating to the West, Kennedy argued that slavery was critical in keeping agriculture viable in the state. Otherwise, no white man would continue to work the farms of Maryland as long as "the fertile regions of the western country open[ed] a resting place to his view." Admitting more slaves to Maryland would lower the cost of slaves to poorer farmers and would help older farmers work their fields more easily and profitably.

While he probably considered his economic logic quite sound, Kennedy may have sensed that there was a moral cost to this scheme. "If slavery be a sin, it is the sin of our fathers," he told his fellow delegates, "and heaven knows, we have suffered for it to the fourth and fifth generation, and will continue to suffer for it, to the twentieth." In other words, slavery would remain a fact of American life for several more centuries. It would only come to an end, Kennedy believed, when the white population became so dense that whites would be forced to compete with slaves for menial jobs. In that remote day, slavery would disappear naturally. Any tampering with this natural course of events would be "artificial" and, he implied, socially disruptive.

Nor did Kennedy believe that free blacks would ever be accepted into American life. Experience had clearly shown, he argued, that this population was "injurious" to society as a whole. Regardless of the privileges granted to them, free blacks would never be able to earn a livelihood among "more intelligent and active whites." Free blacks would inevitably become "dishonest, corrupt, and profligate—contaminating slaves with their vices and disturbing the peace of society with their crimes." Given such prejudicial views, it is surprising that Kennedy objected so strenuously to the manumitting clause in the Senate's bill. The clause's inconsistency with other manumitting laws seemed important to the lawyer in Kennedy.

Kennedy also gave a passing nod to the idea of colonizing free blacks outside the country. Regarding the Maryland Colonization Society and its affiliates in other states, Kennedy disapproved of their abolitionist tendencies but thought their goals of a geographic separation of the races and the establishment of a safe and receptive "asylum" for free blacks were worthy ones. Because he judged them to be "an unprofitable and worthless class," Kennedy believed that free blacks "should be separated altogether from a society in which they could enjoy no immunities."[60]

The attitudes contained in Kennedy's speech before the House of Delegates were the products of his time and place. Seen from his perspective, the brutal slave system of the Deep South not only seemed somewhat foreign but also provided a morally convenient foil for the more moderate expression of that institution in the borderland where he lived. Even with sectional tensions on the rise after the Missouri Crisis, Kennedy still felt comfortable condemning slavery in one part of the nation and condoning it in another.

Regarding the future of slavery and the eventual disposition of the free-black population, several factors probably influenced his thinking. Certainly, neither he nor any of his contemporaries could have predicted the accelerating rate of economic and social change that the nation would undergo in the decades to come. Since slavery had existed in North America for close to two centuries, there was no reason to believe that the institution would not continue for another century if left alone. In the meantime, the idea of colonization provided many Americans with the wistful hope that some free blacks could gradually be removed from the country. When slavery did eventually become obsolete, many white Americans seemed to think that the remainder of the black race would simply fade away. After all, Americans had already watched the continent's indigenous population rapidly vanish from the landscape in a way that seemed both inevitable and irreversible. The collapse of one race might portend the demise of yet another. For those whites convinced of their cultural superiority, such a course of events may have seemed natural or even preordained.

Although many of the attitudes contained in it may have been explainable, Kennedy's address before the House of Delegates was still a remarkably unstable piece of oratory. His sentiments were conflicted and his reasoning contradictory. His professed sympathy for black slaves seemed badly out of kilter with his deep disdain for free blacks. While he blamed slavery for the voluptuous habits of southern slave owners, he suggested that small farmers in Maryland turn their hard work over to slaves. Furthermore, the idea that the sins of slavery belonged exclusively to past generations, though commonly articulated throughout the slaveholding states, was a specious and morally bankrupt notion. In the end, the moral and humane considerations central to the issues of race and slavery confounded Kennedy's attempts to articulate his arguments and make them persuasive. These same considerations would plague Kennedy's politics and literary production for decades to come.

As Kennedy's first term drew to a close, efforts on the part of the House of Delegates to repair the Senate's slave bill faltered. Slaves continued to enter and leave the state according to the original law's complex and antiquated provisions. Following Kennedy's reelection in late 1822, however, the debate over the slave law was taken up again with renewed intensity. During the preceding spring, authorities in Charleston, South Carolina, uncovered what appeared to have been a slave revolt in the making. In the aftermath of what became known as the "Denmark Vesey conspiracy," named after a free-black carpenter who was accused of being the revolt's leader, Charleston authorities executed thirty-five slaves and free blacks and deported another thirty-seven to the Caribbean. By the time the winter session of the Maryland legislature convened, many of its delegates had read the gruesome newspaper accounts describing the cruel vengeance Vesey and his alleged conspirators had supposedly intended for local whites. Alarmed by what they read, a number of delegates called for another review of the state's Slave Importation Law.[61]

This time, the House of Delegates appointed a special committee to review the law and report back to the lower chamber with its recommendations. The committee was headed by James A. D. Dalrymple, a delegate from Calvert County, one of the largest slaveholding counties in Maryland. After a brief period of deliberation, the committee's conclusion was that no alterations at all should be made to the existing law governing the importation of slaves in order to, as Dalrymple articulated it, "give the utmost latitude to the importation of that species of population." In short, since the existing law benefitted Maryland's largest slave owners, Dalrymple and his downstate friends saw no reason to tamper with it.[62]

Upon hearing the committee's report, a heated debate broke out among the delegates over whether to accept or reject its recommendation. Although the details of that debate have been lost to the historical record, Kennedy was identified in several Baltimore newspapers as leading the opposition to the committee's report. Closing ranks behind him were his colleague Thomas Kennedy and a number of other delegates from Maryland's more northern counties. The subsequent vote by the House of Delegates narrowly rejected the committee's report, thirty-seven to thirty-four, and, by implication, its recommendation that the Slave Importation Law remain unchanged. Because the delegates from the state's southern counties voted overwhelmingly to accept the report and the delegates from the northern counties voted overwhelmingly to reject it, this amounted to a symbolic legislative contest for and against the status quo of slavery in Maryland. In the absence of a written record, one can only assume that the young Kennedy and those who voted with him wanted better control over the state's slave importations than the poorly codified and highly porous existing law provided. It can also be assumed that Kennedy still favored some kind of general law, roughly along the lines of the earlier Senate slave bill. He obviously felt strongly enough about the need to revise the existing law to challenge Maryland's powerful and entrenched slave-owning interests.[63]

It might have been expected that the rejection of the committee report would have led quickly to the passage of a new general law. However, this did not happen until 1823, after Kennedy had left the legislature. The new general law turned out to be more restrictive than the earlier Senate bill, only allowing slaves acquired through inheritance and marriage to be brought into the state. The selling of such slaves or their manumitting could only occur after they had been in the state for three years. In 1831, in the wake of the bloody Nat Turner slave uprising in neighboring Virginia, these restrictions would be tightened even further.[64]

Is it possible, then, to infer something more from the sum of Kennedy's participation in these slavery debates while he was serving in the Maryland legislature? One conclusion might be that the young Kennedy was at least suspicious of, and possibly hostile toward, large slaveholding interests. Certainly, his outright condemnation of the slave system in the Deep South and his forceful challenge to the large slave owners in his own state appeared to fit such a pattern. Like many of his legislative colleagues, Kennedy was too much of a lawyer to question the fundamental right of property in slaves either in Maryland or anywhere else. Yet, these same lawyerly instincts apparently caused Kennedy to challenge the poorly codified and often haphazard practice of slavery in Maryland. His strong opposition to the Dalrymple faction in the House of Delegates demonstrated Kennedy's clear determination to bring the institution of slavery under better regulatory control in Maryland. Very possibly, developments in the Deep South, which Kennedy viewed as detrimental to the slaves themselves as well as to the class of whites who owned them, had alerted him to the dangers of allowing large slaveholding interests to control politics in the borderland.

It would be reading too much into Kennedy's actions, however, to imply that he had any conception of how slavery would have to be modified to keep pace with the modernizing economy or might eventually be brought to an end. Rather, Kennedy's views on race and slavery were fundamentally unstable and complicated by occurrences like the Denmark Vesey conspiracy and later the Nat Turner uprising. Such mutable views on race and slavery contrasted sharply with Kennedy's surety of vision regarding other economic and social issues. The bedrock of this economic vision, fully in place before he entered politics, was his ardent nationalism. An astute observer of the country's economy, Kennedy was convinced of America's need for economic diversity, productive self-sufficiency, and a national transportation infrastructure. His promotion of commerce, especially through the construction of roads and canals, was bold and unwavering. His social vision emanated in part from his moral didacticism. Because he believed in the potential improvement of society, Kennedy championed a variety of public institutions, from public schools to universities to penitentiaries.

The fervent support by autonomous, individualistic social types like Kennedy for public institutions was not without irony. The irony stemmed from their drive for individual self-perfection, on the one hand, and their didactic impulse to make others conform to their way of thinking, on the other. Having worked through their own programs of self-improvement from *within,* these personalities supported institutions designed to impose moral and intellectual improvements on others from *without.* What is more, as a convinced Burkean, Kennedy saw these institutions as a way to inculcate in others the values needed for social and economic progress, especially as the more traditional mainstays of kin and community were fraying under the pressures of modern life. His faith in these institutions rested on his belief in the malleability of human nature and the state's right to intervene in its development.[65]

Predictably, education had a high priority on Kennedy's agenda. On his motion, the first committee was formed to establish a common school system in Maryland. Although his initiative was hobbled by conservative resistance, his advocacy and that of other progressive minds would eventually lead to the establishment of a common school system in Baltimore during the late 1820s. Though out of office by then, Kennedy took great pride in the part he had played in establishing the city school system.[66]

Kennedy's efforts on behalf of the University of Maryland were more successful in the short term. Formed by the merger of two smaller colleges in 1784, the university had suffered through a period of financial neglect. By the 1820s, its physical plant was deteriorating and its faculty understaffed. In his arguments before the legislature, Kennedy related the benefits of higher education to the functioning of democracy in the state. "The encouragement of literary enterprise and scientific labor," he explained, "deeply affect the character and best interests of a free state." Kennedy lamented that Maryland's young men were forced to leave the state to go to university and implied that Maryland itself was at risk of falling behind other states due to the poor quality of its higher education. Institutions of higher learning, he argued, "strengthen the energies of government by enlisting in their support a mass of intellectual force." After months of debate, Kennedy's funding bill for the university passed both houses of the legislature.[67]

Kennedy supported a number of institutions aimed at improving the lower orders of society as well. Like many of the state's institutions, the Maryland penitentiary was deeply in debt when Kennedy became chairman of the penitentiary committee. Part of his challenge was convincing his legislative colleagues that the penitentiary should be viewed as an institution for correction rather than punishment. Kennedy recommended that the minimum sentence for inmates at the penitentiary be three years because that was the time it took to train them in useful skills and ensure their "hope of amendment." Additionally, Kennedy called for the segregation of inmates who had progressed in their rehabilitation from those as yet unreformed. He also argued that "negroes and vagabonds" should be sent to institutions more suited to the unredeemable. Consistent with contemporary theories of prison reform, Kennedy was endeavoring to create within the walls of the state penitentiary a small-scale society of motivated inmates who, through strenuous labor and a sense of community, could one day be reintroduced into public life.[68]

These reforms were also intended to make the penitentiary more productive and profitable. After they had been in place for a year, Kennedy reported back to the House of Delegates. While the penitentiary debt was still considerable, he was confident it would soon be worked off. More encouraging was that almost three hundred inmates had been employed in the workshops at the penitentiary and had acquired, according to Kennedy's assessment, "habits of industry and a thorough knowledge of some useful trade." These moral and vocational improvements would allow these inmates "to obtain an honest living when their term of service shall expire."[69]

Having sought to renovate the character of the state's inmates and other victims of the depression, Kennedy turned his attention to repairing the damaged economy itself. This work was hampered by a prevailing skittishness among his fellow delegates regarding the incorporation of new businesses. Still, he was able to successfully shepherd several newly formed manufacturing companies, as well as a new bank, the Union Bank of Maryland, through the postpanic legislature. While some conservative voices called for the elimination of the banking system entirely, Kennedy placed tough strictures on bank directors regarding their ability to draw excessive salaries, receive favorable bank loans, and arrange preferential stock grants. Throughout his arguments, Kennedy stressed the importance of manufacturing in a diversified economy and the crucial role of banking in ensuring the free flow of capital.[70]

Many Marylanders also believed that internal improvements—the construction of roads, canals, and later railroads—were critical to the state's economic recovery. Nothing aroused Kennedy's passions more than this area of legislation. Nor, he would soon learn, was any other fraught with as much controversy and political risk at both the national and state levels. During the second decade of the nineteenth century, the federal government had funded the so-called National Road from Cumberland, Maryland, to Wheeling, Virginia (now West Virginia), on the Ohio River. One of its proponents in Congress, John C. Calhoun, famously predicted that projects of this type would "bind the Republic together." However, such nationalistic enthusiasm soon gave way to suspicions of federal power. In 1817, President Madison vetoed the "Bonus Bill," intended to pay for further infrastructure improvements, on constitutional grounds. After that, most internal improvements were relegated to the states. By the early 1820s, the State of New York had taken the lead with its hugely successful Erie Canal. This success unleashed an intense rivalry between the states known as "Erie Fever."[71]

Maryland had contracted a severe case of Erie Fever but faced unique problems due to the state's complicated geography and political localism. Such problems had doomed the earlier Potomac Canal, even with George Washington as its president and chief fund-raiser. So, too, the proposed crosscut canal between the Chesapeake and Delaware Bays, as well as a scheme to build a canal along the Susquehanna River, had ended in frustration and failure.[72]

With numerous petitions calling for internal improvements arriving from around the state and his own constituency clamoring for access to the "cornucopia" of the West, Kennedy accepted the chairmanship of the Internal Improvements Committee. He attacked the job with his usual determination. Kennedy clearly understood the needs of his city and state. The post-Napoleonic peace had "tranquilized" Europe, he told his fellow delegates, and killed off foreign demand for Maryland's agricultural products. In the new era of domestic growth, Americans had been "thrown back on their own resources." Each state was scrambling to exploit the country's internal markets, and Maryland needed to "keep pace with the zealous enterprises of its sister states."[73]

As an articulate but inexperienced legislator, Kennedy's rhetoric exceeded his management skills. Arguing that revival of the Potomac Canal would require "the wealth of an empire" and that the Delaware-Chesapeake crosscut canal lacked sufficient western orientation, Kennedy recommended a rejuvenated Susquehanna Canal to access the rich backcountry of Pennsylvania. Such a canal would deny Philadelphia that market and provide Baltimore manufacturers an outlet for their goods.[74]

It became immediately apparent that such a simple proposal could never satisfy a state divided by chronic localism. Downstate delegates insisted on a new Potomac Canal, while those from the Eastern Shore fought hard for the crosscut canal. Even the wards of Baltimore were divided between the Potomac and Susquehanna schemes. As confusion reigned, Kennedy lost control of the debate. After dissolving itself into a committee of the whole, the House of Delegates recommended that all three canal schemes be pursued, each to be paid for by residents along the various routes.[75]

In the course of the debate, Kennedy changed his own canal proposal from supporting one along the Susquehanna to one connecting Baltimore to the Potomac River near Georgetown, at the nation's capital. He also advocated cooperation on the project between Maryland and her neighbors, as well as the surrender of the state's sovereignty over some of its land in exchange for federal assistance. Kennedy's fellow legislators questioned his loyalty to the state for such suggestions. Frustrated by legislative indecision, the public also turned against Kennedy. The *Baltimore Patriot* claimed that his canal scheme had "the single object of diverting the whole Western trade into the lap of the District of Columbia." The *American* accused him of having "forgotten the city's interest." Someone spread the rumor that Kennedy's father had bought land along the proposed canal route, and at public rallies he was vilified as "Potomac Kennedy." His friends urged him to defend himself against these charges.[76]

When he finally answered his critics, it was in a long, rambling letter to the editor of the *Patriot.* Kennedy expressed surprise at the public's reaction to his canal policy and swore his loyalty to Baltimore. He reviewed the muddled history of the canal debate and tried to clarify his position. His letter was too little, too late. Canal building remained a high-profile issue over the summer of 1823, and attacks on Kennedy by his political enemies escalated. A series of articles in the *Patriot* entitled "From An American Farmer" accused Kennedy of bribery, corruption, and logrolling. These articles claimed he was "unworthy to breathe the air of Maryland." Rumors also circulated that Kennedy had been negotiating for a diplomatic job while serving in the state legislature. One of his critics managed to locate an obscure quote wherein Kennedy had commented that Baltimore's citizens were "not a reading people." All this was used against him.[77]

Kennedy's time in the Maryland legislature was as good as over. At the end of the summer, he announced that he would not run for reelection. He expressed his gratitude to the citizens of Baltimore for their past support. In the September election, seven candidates stood for Baltimore's two seats in the lower chamber. The two winning candidates avoided the issue of internal improvements altogether but, according to the *Patriot,* pledged to "defend the great commercial interest of Baltimore." Only one candidate supported internal improvements of any kind, and he finished dead last.[78]

When the Maryland legislature reconvened in the winter of 1823, its members were far too wary of canal politics to restart the debate that had driven Kennedy from office. It was not until 1828, after another shift in the political winds, that a brand new project called the Chesapeake and Ohio Canal finally broke ground. However, following a series of engineering setbacks, labor strikes, and an outlay of $11 million, this two-hundred-mile canal system connecting Baltimore with the Ohio River also proved to be a disaster. To make matters worse, the state began construction of the Baltimore and Ohio Railroad along much of the same route. The legislature refused to rationalize the two redundant systems for political reasons, mostly short-term electoral considerations. By the mid-1840s, Maryland would find itself on the verge of bankruptcy.[79]

Although he would have preferred a less ignominious withdrawal from state politics, Kennedy had become bored and frustrated with it by 1823. Because the legislature met for only three months of the year, Kennedy had been able to build up his law practice during his three terms of service. Valuable political connections made in Annapolis, as well as relationships formed with Baltimore's business community, helped him sign up new clients. Furthermore, his occasional trips to Washington, where he pleaded several cases, broadened his reputation as a talented lawyer and rising politician. On one of these visits, he had the opportunity to meet John C. Calhoun, recently appointed President Monroe's secretary of the army. At this point in time, Calhoun was still an ardent nationalist like Kennedy. They got along well and began a correspondence. Kennedy's longtime mentor William Wirt, now Monroe's attorney general, also proved to be a valuable connection in the nation's capital.[80]

As it turned out, the story spread by his political opponents that Kennedy had been offered a diplomatic post by the Monroe Administration was true. During the spring of 1822, Wirt had convinced Monroe to appoint Kennedy to head a diplomatic legation to the newly independent Republic of Chile, a job Wirt described as a "frolic for a year or so." Conflicted over whether or not to accept such a remote posting, Kennedy sought an interview with Monroe's secretary of state, John Quincy Adams. A difficult personality in the best of circumstances, Adams had spent most of his youth abroad, spoke several languages, and probably thought Kennedy was hopelessly naïve and inexperienced. When Kennedy asked Adams what instructions he might expect before embarking on his diplomatic mission, Adams responded "Instructions!" and, standing on his chair to reach a high pigeonhole, retrieved and handed over to Kennedy a drawing of the diplomatic uniform recently designed for the legation. This was all the guidance Adams would give him, and Kennedy declined the appointment. Calhoun reassured Kennedy that he had made the right decision.[81]

Kennedy also had romantic reasons for turning down this diplomatic post. On January 20, 1824, Kennedy married Mary Tenant, the daughter of a wealthy shipping merchant in Baltimore. The wedding took place at Thomas Tenant's mansion on Gay Street and was attended by Mary's family and the groom's colorful circle of young lawyers and budding literary talents. Peter Hoffman Cruse wrote a special poem to celebrate the happy occasion.[82]

Within the year, however, Kennedy's happiness turned to tragedy. In October 1824, Mary Kennedy died giving birth to a son. Tenant Pendleton survived less than a year. In his bereavement, Kennedy removed all references to these events from his personal papers. Two decades later, when the remains of his wife and son had to be transferred to a new cemetery, Kennedy recalled Mary with a sad and distant fondness: "She was twenty-two—a brief space wife, and still briefer mother—a woman of a kind and virtuous nature, true, just, and noble in character, with a spirit all devotion, cheerfulness and trust."[83]

No doubt, Kennedy's personal tragedy distracted him during the fall of 1824 from the four-way presidential race between John Quincy Adams, Andrew Jackson, Henry Clay, and William Crawford. It was the most exciting national election up to that time. If he gave the election any thought, Kennedy likely found Adams too quirky, Clay too ambitious, and Crawford too retrogressive. Calhoun, whom Kennedy liked and admired, was Jackson's running mate. Jackson himself was somewhat of a cipher, and, like most Americans at the time, Kennedy did not know much about his politics. If he voted at all, though, Kennedy probably supported Jackson.[84]

Jackson received the most popular and electoral votes in the election of 1824. However, because none of the four presidential contenders achieved a majority of electoral votes, a special election in the House of Representatives was required under the rules of the Constitution at that time. When Adams won in the House election with votes from the Clay faction and then appointed Clay as his secretary of state (and presumed heir apparent), Jackson and his outraged supporters accused them of having struck a "corrupt bargain." This disputed election and its questionable outcome sowed the seeds of a fierce political partisanship that would last for decades to come.[85]

Recently widowed and in the political wilderness, Kennedy may have pondered these unsettling events as he walked around Monticello during that hot July day in 1825. The Palladian-style main house stood on the crest of a hill and emanated a calm dignity. While not large, the house was centered amid a balanced system of walkways, terraces, and pavilions, reflecting the important social position of its owner. The formal arrangement of the house, gardens, and dependencies created a sense of harmony and order.[86]

Monticello must have seemed to Kennedy like a place out of another time. After all, the succession of presidents known as the "Virginia Dynasty" was gone forever. Gone, too, was the political order it had helped preserve for so long. It had been, Kennedy recalled, a time of "harmony and patriotic concert of good men." The nation had enjoyed "an immunity from party contention." As he watched an ill and exhausted Jefferson move slowly toward his chambers that day, Kennedy may have sensed that the nation was about to enter a new and more disorderly era.[87]

At the time of his Monticello visit, Kennedy had no way of knowing what form the rising political opposition would take after the disputed election of 1824. He could not have foreseen that Jacksonian Democracy would become a powerful counterforce to the economically progressive, socially interventionist, and nationalistic principles he espoused. "The rise of the opposition," he later remembered, "was like a dark cloud . . . a rumbling of distant thunder and angry flashes of lightening." In defense of these principles against Jackson and his followers, Kennedy would become a staunch champion of the new Whig Party.[88]

CHAPTER 3

The Whig in *Swallow Barn*

Swallow Barn—the plantation around which John Pendleton Kennedy constructed his 1832 novel of the same name—bore little resemblance to Monticello. Granted, the existence of a main house, numerous dependencies, and a nearby slave quarter underscored the hierarchical position of the master at each enterprise. But the setting and atmosphere of Swallow Barn contrasted sharply with Thomas Jefferson's mountaintop: "Swallow Barn is an aristocratical old edifice, that squats like a brooding hen on the southern bank of the James River. It is quietly seated with its vassal out-buildings, in a kind of shady pocket or nook, formed by the sweep of the stream, on a gentle acclivity thinly sprinkled with oaks, whose magnificent branches afford habitation and defense for an antique colony of owls."[1]

Time seems to have become the real master of Swallow Barn. There is a lost and abandoned feeling about the place: "The main structure is upwards of a century old, one story high with thick brick walls, and a double-faced roof, resembling a ship, bottom upwards; this is perforated with small dormant windows, that have such expression as belongs to a face without eyebrows." The main house at Swallow Barn consists of three sections, all constructed at different times and sitting "ill at ease" with one another. "These three masses compose an irregular pile," Kennedy writes. The most recent section rests like "an unlucky bark lifted by an extraordinary tide upon a sand bank."[2]

Not far from the main house sits an old barn, presumably the structure after which the plantation is named. It is "a huge, crazy, disjointed barn." Inside, "gaunt oxen" stumble about in the darkness, where "a sickly looking wagon protrudes its parched tongue, and droops its rusty swingle-trees in the hot sunshine, with the air of a forlorn ague." From outside, "a plough horse may be seen, peering through the dark window of the stable, with a spectral melancholy; his glassy eye moving silently across the gloom, and the profound stillness of his habitation now and then interrupted only by his sepulchral and hoarse cough."[3]

The jumbled layout and tumbledown condition of Swallow Barn is a far cry from the self-conscious balance and order of Jefferson's Monticello. Instead, Kennedy's fictional plantation seems the very symbol of incongruity and decrepitude. At times, his imagery evokes a sense of debilitating lassitude and even sickness about the place. Not only does his description of Swallow Barn cast doubt upon the Enlightenment pretensions of Jefferson and Virginia's ruling class—namely, their careful subordination of the natural environment around them and the rest of society beneath them—but Kennedy's language also seems intent upon disrupting the pastoral memory of the state's glory days.[4]

The perplexing tone that he uses to describe the novel's setting is just a sampling of what is to come. The haphazard structure of the story that follows, as well as the author's shifting perspective along its wandering course, only add to the modern reader's problems of interpretation. Two thin plot lines, one dealing with a seemingly senseless property dispute and the other concerning a bumbling love affair the reader never sees consummated, do little to unify a series of loosely related, occasionally bizarre interpolated tales. Like the main house at Swallow Barn, the novel itself can be described as having a layered, accretive, and ramshackle architecture. By the time it was finally completed in 1832, *Swallow Barn* had become a complex, disorganized, and, some might say, chaotic literary creation.

Not surprisingly, literary critics and historians have struggled to untangle *Swallow Barn*'s confusing content and conflicting messages. Much of their commentary has focused on Kennedy's puzzling ambivalence toward plantation society and its embrace of slavery. One scholar has called Kennedy an "Indian giver," lauding plantation society one minute and censoring it the next. Another scholar has described this ambivalence as a kind of "dual vision." Some of these critics and historians have attributed Kennedy's oscillating viewpoint to his divided parental heritage, others to a fractured sense of place, and still others to his shift in sectional loyalty during the novel's long gestation.

Scholars have also disagreed about how realistically Kennedy portrayed the Old Dominion in *Swallow Barn* and why he undertook the novel in the first place. One literary critic has accused Kennedy of being a proslavery intellectual, intent upon misrepresenting the southern plantation with its slave system as a pastoral utopia. While another critic has described Kennedy's novel as "free fantasy," several others have accepted it as a true and accurate depiction of the Old Dominion. At least one historian has argued that Kennedy was attempting to show the Old Dominion much as it had once been and that his novel was meant as an elegy to a bygone way of life. Other scholars have suggested that Kennedy wanted to ease sectional tensions by explaining southern attitudes and behavior as best he could to northern readers. Still others have maintained that Kennedy, like so many writers, was simply trying to work through his own conflicted feelings about the Old Dominion and its debilitating dependence on slavery.[5]

Most of these interpretations provide useful insights into Kennedy's novel, but none are robust enough to fully explain its odd construction and puzzling content. In the end, searching for some kind of unifying meaning in *Swallow Barn* or attempting to impose some organizing interpretation on it has proven to be a frustrating and fruitless task. It is more productive, however, to pursue a broader set of explanations for the novel's dissonance and incongruity—to include Kennedy's mindset during the novel's writing, the moral and politic tenets that influenced him, the literary models available to him, and the contextual events leading up to 1832, when the novel was published.

These explanations can be summarized as *character, style,* and *change.* The first of these, *character,* takes into consideration Kennedy's already well-formed social character and belief system by the mid-1820s, around the time he was beginning *Swallow Barn,* as well as his maturing political partisanship during the early 1830s, as he was completing the novel. The second area of inquiry, *style,* deals with the novel's narrative style. Kennedy believed this particular style would allow him to write about the Old Dominion, in spite of its controversial features and his personal connection to it, in a detached and controlled way. The third area of inquiry, *change,* addresses the historical developments that disrupted the narrative style and the rest of novel with it. This area of inquiry recognizes the importance of understanding the changing context when interpreting *Swallow Barn,* as well as of understanding the external forces that ultimately destabilized the novel.

Kennedy's character was well developed by the time he began conceptualizing his novel. His upbringing in the metropolis of Baltimore, with its good schools, libraries, and debating societies, had set Kennedy apart from those Americans still rooted in traditional kin and community relationships. On his own, Kennedy had pursued an intensive program of moral and intellectual self-improvement, guided by the Scottish moral philosophers and polite-style British writers, and then broadened this notion of improvement to encompass the collective betterment of society. In the Maryland legislature, he had supported a number of public institutions, from the state university to the penitentiary, in order to promote the moral and intellectual uplift of society at large.

Furthermore, Kennedy's wartime experiences had imbued him with an unshakeable sense of nationalism. This sense of nationalism and his faith in the proactive, interventionist role of government had made him a strenuous advocate of internal improvements. Such a position had run counter to the chronic localism of his native state and ultimately brought about his political demise. Likewise, Kennedy's ambivalent attitude regarding the institution of slavery had proven controversial in the divided political climate of the borderland where he lived.

In an effort to put the tragic loss of his wife and son behind him, Kennedy immersed himself in the vibrant urban life of Baltimore. In addition to building up his law practice, he wrote numerous articles for local newspapers, became an active promoter of the city's public library system, and joined the University of Maryland as its first professor of history. In 1826, Kennedy ran unsuccessfully for a seat in the U.S. House of Representatives. His opponents reminded the public of his role in the Potomac Canal debacle and questioned his commitment to Andrew Jackson.[6]

Given the intensity of his life in Baltimore, Kennedy's feeling of estrangement from his Virginia relatives was understandable. The more involved he became in the dynamic milieu of the city, the more Kennedy became aware of the growing divergence between the two cultures. If his views on internal improvements and social uplift had met with resistance in Maryland, such opinions contrasted even more sharply with the traditional patterns of thought and staid rural ways of the Old Dominion. In spite of the affection that he felt for his Virginia relatives, Kennedy had long regarded them as hopelessly provincial in their habits and thinking. By the time he began writing *Swallow Barn,* Kennedy had come to see himself as a "stray sheep" with respect to his mother's home place.[7]

By the mid-1820s, the Old Dominion had fallen on hard times. Agriculture, the economic lifeblood of the state, had never recovered from the collapse of land prices in 1819. Worse still, much of Virginia's soil remained exhausted and unproductive. In spite of considerable talk in regional periodicals and academic circles about the need for modern farming methods, nothing much was being done to address the worn-out condition of the state's struggling farms. Many members of the state's elite families, especially the younger generation, were leaving for more promising futures in the Southwest. From Kennedy's vantage point in Baltimore, the Old Dominion must have seemed moribund and retrogressive.[8]

Several scenes in *Swallow Barn* capture Virginia's depressed economic condition in the 1820s. Early in the novel, a description of the ruins of Jamestown, the state's former capital, sets a tone of abandonment, dilapidation, and decay. Later, the boarded-up commercial buildings at the landing near Swallow Barn, the setting of the colorful Fourth of July celebration, provide further testament to the state's stagnant economy. Just as telling is a passage describing the fields around Swallow Barn that Kennedy drafted but, for whatever reason, left out of the final manuscript. From the porch of the main house, he writes, one looks out on "a sickly crop of diminutive corn or some ragged rows of tobacco, and around which crept a consumptive and dislocated worm fence of withered chestnut rails where multitudes of lizards and ground squirrels amused themselves." While he occasionally tries to lighten his novel with quaint touches and nostalgic sweetness, Kennedy is unable to hide the fact that he regards the Old Dominion as an economy and a society in decline.[9]

Perhaps the most discouraging aspect of the Old Dominion was its political leadership. Rather than face the challenges posed by the nation's rapidly integrating transportation systems and the growing diversity of its modernizing economy, Virginia's most influential politicians urged their constituencies to stubbornly resist these developments and seek security in their old ways. While clearly out of step with the times, Jefferson's vision of a localized, agrarian republic retained an unbreakable hold on the minds of many Virginians. As *Swallow Barn* was taking shape, Virginia was increasingly falling under the sway of states' rights men and resurgent Old Republicans such as Philip Barbour, John Taylor of Caroline, and John Randolph. Kennedy alludes to these worrisome trends at several levels of society, from the hardening conservatism of Swallow Barn's master, Frank Meriwether, to the liquor-infused political debates of poor whites during the novel's rambunctious Fourth of July celebration.[10]

Kennedy's own political maturation took place during the late 1820s and early 1830s and left its imprint throughout *Swallow Barn.* At the time of his unsuccessful run for a seat in the U.S. House of Representatives in 1826 and for several years thereafter, Kennedy was a supporter of Andrew Jackson. As a veteran of the War of 1812 and a strong nationalist, Kennedy admired Jackson for his unwavering sense of patriotism and stunning victory at New Orleans. In preparation for the presidential election of 1828, Kennedy was appointed to the local Jacksonian "committee of correspondence." Still, neither he nor anybody else knew much about Jackson's policies prior to his election to the presidency. Jackson's political handlers had gone out of their way to reassure nationalists such as Kennedy that Jackson would be a supporter of internal improvements once elected. Furthermore, Jacksonian newspapers in Baltimore and elsewhere had made a point of stressing their candidate's nonpartisanship. Adams and Clay were vilified not only for their "corrupt bargain" in the previous election but also for being the real promoters of party faction. Kennedy appeared to accept these claims and accusations at face value.[11]

There were several other reasons for Kennedy's early support of Jackson. One was Kennedy's complicated relationship with Roger B. Taney, who in 1828 became the president of the Maryland central committee to elect Jackson president. (As a member of the committee for correspondence, Kennedy reported to Taney.) Although Taney's imperious personality differed markedly from Kennedy's more congenial one, the two men had been an effective team working on several important lawsuits for the Union Bank. Also, both were enthusiastic boosters of the University of Maryland, Kennedy as a faculty member and Taney as a trustee.[12]

Yet another reason for Kennedy's early Jacksonianism was his desire to capitalize on his reputation, established during his time in the House of Delegates, as a friend of the workingman. During this period of early industrialization, Kennedy and men like him still associated the "mechanical arts" with the larger idea of self-improvement. They had yet to distinguish between those they called "mechanics" and those they would later regard as factory workers. During the latter half of the 1820s, organized labor came into its own in Baltimore and became closely allied with the party of Jackson.[13]

Although he would vote a straight Jacksonian ticket as late as the local election of 1829, Kennedy would break ranks with the party of Old Hickory less than a year later. On May 27, 1830, President Jackson vetoed the Maysville Road Bill. Kennedy and others who had helped elect Jackson as a supporter of internal improvements were shocked. The bill would have appropriated federal funds not only for the Maysville Road in Kentucky but also for a much anticipated turnpike from Frederick, Maryland, to Washington, D.C. The latter project was widely expected to boost Maryland's flagging economy and help open new markets to the West. While Jackson's Maysville Road veto served as a way to curry favor with states' rights men and Old Republicans, whose allegiances were leaning toward Vice President John C. Calhoun, its political cost was to accelerate the coalescence of anti-Jackson forces in places where internal improvements were popular.[14]

Kennedy expressed his frustration and anger in a journal entry after the veto: "Jackson's Maysville message especially the veto is the most absurd state paper I ever read, and will consign him to oblivion." He went on to explain that he had been approached by local supporters of Henry Clay but still regarded him as too much of a party man. Yet, as Kennedy considered his political options, he reluctantly admitted that Clay's positions on internal improvements, a protective tariff, and other issues related to the national economy were closer to his views than Jackson's had been.[15]

Although his commitment to the emerging anti-Jackson coalition was tentative at first, Kennedy was poorly constituted to sit on the political sidelines. Soon he became engaged in attacking the Jacksonians and their Old Republican allies with a determination more in keeping with his nature. Even though he had started *Swallow Barn* as a loyal Jacksonian, Kennedy would finish his novel as a nascent Whig. As his partisanship hardened, Kennedy found it impossible to keep politics from invading *Swallow Barn.*

In order to trace the origins of the novel's style, it is necessary to step back several years. It is not entirely clear when Kennedy began thinking about writing a plantation novel, or precisely when he drafted the first passages of what might be called the Ur-*Swallow Barn.* There is ample evidence, however, that he started to conceptualize his ideas for the novel several years before October 1829, when his first journal entries were recorded. To begin with, Kennedy probably read Washington Irving's *Brace Bridge Hall,* the fictional template for *Swallow Barn,* shortly after its American publication in 1822. During 1825, Kennedy's parents moved to "The Bower," the presumed model for the Swallow Barn plantation and a place Kennedy occasionally visited. Most important, he had a great need to occupy himself after the deaths of his wife in 1824 and son in 1825.[16]

It is difficult to know how Kennedy dealt with the death of his wife and son, as he destroyed most of his papers from prior to 1825. One can only assume that he sought the comfort of friends and family, the distraction of legal work, and very likely the escapism of novel writing. His best friend and former *Red Book* collaborator, Peter Hoffman Cruse, worked in a neighboring law office and was a constant presence during this time. Cruse accompanied Kennedy on several research trips to Virginia for *Swallow Barn* and, along with other friends, provided Kennedy with a steady stream of advice on the novel.[17]

Understanding Kennedy's state of mind after the loss of his wife and son helps explain why he chose to write about the Old Dominion. After all, Kennedy had already conducted preliminary research on what would become his second novel, *Horse-Shoe Robinson.* (He had actually met the aging revolutionary hero and protagonist of that novel on a business trip to South Carolina in 1819.) However, the prospect of writing about the Old Dominion must have seemed more appealing. Not only was the setting familiar to him, but writing about it would evoke memories of a happier time in his life. By recalling his carefree summers in the Old Dominion as a young boy and describing its scenery and characters in his novel, Kennedy might escape from his despondency.[18]

The problem for Kennedy was how to write about the Old Dominion in a way that balanced his nostalgic fondness for the place with his low opinion of the state on almost every other measure. Like most American writers of his generation, Kennedy had been trained in the neoclassical literary style, once hugely popular but somewhat dated by the mid-1820s. This neoclassical style had retained its intellectual currency in parts of the mid-Atlantic and South even after it had succumbed to romanticism in the rest of the country. While rendered by a writer like Joseph Addison with erudition and aplomb, the neoclassical style in the hands of someone like Jonathan Swift was capable of biting wit and sharp satire. Kennedy and Cruse had deployed that keen-edged, acerbic version with devastating effect in the *Red Book.* Subjecting the Old Dominion to such a style might sweep away the nostalgic haze and dreamy lassitude of life there and expose the grim reality beneath it.[19]

The recent works of Washington Irving suggested a way around this problem. Irving was another of Kennedy's literary elders and someone with whom he would form an enduring friendship after the publication of *Swallow Barn.* More than a decade earlier, Irving had not only thoroughly mastered the neoclassical style but also transplanted it to the New World without any apparent loss in satirical power. Reading his frolicking and hyperbolic *Knickerbocker's History of New York,* published in 1809, one is reminded of the unrestrained satirical passages of Swift's *Gulliver's Travels*. Irving's vicious satire of Thomas Jefferson, in the guise of William the Testy, as well as other parodies of America's most-revered figures and events, quickly captured the attention of the reading public and made Irving a literary celebrity.[20]

Within a decade of this triumph, however, Irving's circumstances had changed and his mood with it. Irving had relocated to Liverpool, England, to work in a branch of the family export business, only to become stranded in that dismal city when the business suddenly went bankrupt. He had never fully recovered from the loss of what appears to have been his only love interest, Matilda Hoffman, some years before, and a continuing stream of news about the deaths of friends and family members drove him into a deep melancholy.[21]

In an effort to shed his melancholy and support himself in England, Irving produced two books, *The Sketch Book* (1820) and *Bracebridge Hall* (1822). In these books, he made the important transition from the aggressive satirical humor of the neoclassical style to a more good-natured adaptation of it that, once fully developed, seemed very much his own. This new style relied on gentle mockery of the truly ridiculous, artfully constructed farce, and occasional touches of fantasy to entertain readers. Most important, this new humorous style lost its didactic edge and seemed more congenial to multiple perspectives. Such an approach allowed Irving to describe the foibles and idiosyncrasies of the British squirearchy, as well as the vanishing folk ways of the rural village, with a kind of amused affection, endearing him to readers in his host country. Irving's resulting popularity, this time on both sides of the Atlantic, lifted his flagging spirits.[22]

It would be a mistake, of course, to treat Irving's novels as completely spontaneous productions. He had arrived in England at the height of the romantic movement and was heavily affected by it. In his border novels, Sir Walter Scott had done more than any other writer to bring together antiquarianism, regionalism, and other intellectual influences and to give romanticism its extraordinary vitality and power. Irving included numerous references to Britain's chivalric past in his two novels, including scenes having to do with falconry, Morris dancing, and vestiges of courtly love. In his special prose style, Irving was able to simultaneously parody and pay homage to England's "good old feudal times."[23]

In addition, Irving bathed his two novels in the soft hues of pastoralism. Harkening back to Oliver Goldsmith as well as earlier writers, Irving imparted to British rural life a kind of moral dimension. Country life possessed "a moral feeling that seemed to pervade it," Irving writes in *The Sketch Book.* He implies that strong cultural and social forces emanate, at times almost magically, from the soil itself. There was, Irving suggests, "a hereditary transmission of home-bred virtues and local attachments that speak deeply and touchingly to the moral character of the nation."[24]

In the wake of his own personal tragedy and recent political defeat, Kennedy must have found the genial style and cheerful disposition of Irving's prose a welcome palliative. But, even more important, Irving offered Kennedy a safe yet entertaining narrative style with which to describe plantation life in the Old Dominion. Just as Irving's inquisitive sketch artist, Geoffrey Crayon, ambles about the British countryside gathering impressions of daily life, Kennedy's fictional traveler, Mark Littleton, wanders through the Old Dominion, satisfying his curiosity in the same way. "The undercurrents of country-life are grotesque, peculiar and amusing," Littleton declares in the introduction to *Swallow Barn,* "and it only takes an attentive observer to make them an agreeable book by describing them." Like Crayon, Littleton is a connoisseur of detail, a collector of commonplace images, with no purpose other than setting them down in their peculiar charm and amusing oddity.[25]

In its earliest manuscript form, Kennedy's plantation novel was faithfully Irvingesque. The plantation manor bore the whimsical but improbable name of Hoppergallop House and its master the obvious tag-name of Frank Oldstock. At this point in the novel's development, the characters were so thinly sketched, so stereotypical of what might be expected in a Virginia novel, that they were no more than caricatures. Initially, Kennedy devoted his efforts at developing the physical description of his fictional plantation and finding the proper location for it. Eventually, he settled upon the Tidewater area, though much of the novel's setting would be based on the western part of the state and, more specifically, on the plantation to which his parents had moved, "The Bower."

In addition to its safe and genial narrative style, Irving's *Bracebridge Hall* supplied a rough plot structure, a convenient cast of characters, and a number of usable story elements for Kennedy's novel. Kennedy had only to transplant Simon Bracebridge, the master of Bracebridge Hall, to the Old Dominion; transmute his loyal retainer, Old Christy, into a faithful Virginia slave; and reassemble the social hierarchy of the British village on the banks of the James River. Drawing on his considerable literary background, Kennedy would add occasional digressions reminiscent of other authors that he admired, such as Jonathan Swift, Henry Fielding, and Oliver Goldsmith. Finally, he would base parts of the novel on his own experiences in western Virginia and elsewhere.[26]

There was one critical difference between Kennedy's proposed plantation novel and Irving's British-based model. Kennedy had a personal connection to the Old Dominion, while Irving had no such relationship with the society that he depicted in *Bracebridge Hall.* In fact, Irving's emotional separation from his subject matter was instrumental in achieving the light, genial style that he used to describe it. Kennedy lacked the authorial distance from his source material needed to replicate Irving's detached narrative style.[27]

By 1830, Kennedy had decided on a "new plan" for his novel. After completing several research trips to the Tidewater area and in response to suggestions from his literary friends, he began introducing a greater degree of verisimilitude to his characters and place names. At the urging of his friend Peter Cruse, Frank Oldstock was given the more realistic name of Frank Meriwether. Hoppergallop House became Swallow Barn. At the same time, the novel became more politicized. Based on reports from his Uncle Phil Pendleton about the changing condition of Virginia politics, Kennedy began fleshing out the conservative political views of Frank Meriwether. Kennedy also declared his intention to use dialogue between poor whites living near Swallow Barn in order to "illustrate the vulgar opinion of the question of states' rights." Finally, he allowed the subject of race into his narrative as a major theme. Specifically, he expressed the desire to show "the character of the old negroes of the low country." As a result of these changes, his new plan began diverging markedly from the arm's length treatment that Irving had used to portray British country life. Irving had paid only marginal attention to Britain's yeoman class, ignored the subject of politics entirely, and scrupulously avoided the kind of incendiary issues Kennedy was taking up by exploring race and slavery.[28]

Kennedy's new plan for his novel turned out to be a Pandora's box. His decision to make his portrayal of the Old Dominion more realistic and to introduce such volatile issues as states' rights and slavery into his novel—while trying to maintain the genial, detached narrative style that he had borrowed from Irving—would create unbearable tensions throughout *Swallow Barn.* Mark Littleton's ambivalent commentary would prove ill suited and at times ingenuous when describing the harsh reality of plantation life. Although supposedly a northerner who has heard prejudicial things about the Old Dominion, Littleton intends to go there and see for himself: "One ought to travel before he makes up his opinion. There are two sides to every question, and the world is right or wrong; I'm not sure I know which." This disconnection between the novel's narrative voice and its subject matter would only grow more awkward as *Swallow Barn* was forced to absorb the influence of unfolding events and weather a rapidly changing historical context.[29]

In his journal entries of 1830 and 1831, Kennedy recorded the progress of his new plan for *Swallow Barn,* interspersed with commentary on various events and developments during this time. It is therefore easy to determine how change began to disrupt his narrative. For example, he grew increasingly upset with the class antagonisms and public disorder that were beginning to dominate his native Baltimore. With some justification, he attributed these unsettling developments to the forces unleashed by Andrew Jackson's landslide election in 1828. Voter turnout in urban centers such as Baltimore had quadrupled since the previous presidential election, and, once set in motion, the popular forces that had helped elect the new president were not easily controlled. Organized labor remained highly energized after the election and frequently took to the streets with its grievances. Increasingly, these disturbances were aimed more at venting frustration than achieving political goals. In his journal, Kennedy took umbrage at the "power of the mob" and expressed disgust at what he perceived as the demagoguery of manipulative politicians who, he believed, were intent on "creating distraction between the lower and higher orders of society." Kennedy's distaste for such demagoguery and his low regard for those elements of society receptive to it found their way into *Swallow Barn.*[30]

Several tumultuous developments of the 1830s touched Kennedy more personally. One of these was the growing debate over the protective tariff. After Congress passed highly protective tariffs in 1824 and 1828, the tariff issue became intensely politicized. Southern planters and Jacksonian free traders lined up against northern manufacturers and their protectionist allies. So egregious was the tariff of 1828, labeled the "Tariff of Abominations" by its opponents, that residents of South Carolina proposed "nullifying" federal authority to collect import duties at the state's ports. The so-called nullification movement spread rapidly throughout the South. It gained prestige and intellectual vigor when John C. Calhoun, former nationalist turned states' rights champion, published a pamphlet entitled *The South Carolina Exposition and Protest,* explaining how to challenge the federal government over the tariff. In his journal, Kennedy condemned the nullification movement as "rebellion" and called for its leaders to be suppressed by force.[31]

But the tariff debate affected more than Kennedy's offended sense of nationalism. On February 5, 1829, Kennedy married Elizabeth Gray, the daughter of Baltimore industrialist Edward Gray. While the marriage would prove a lasting love match, one of its consequences was the close and profitable relationship between Kennedy and his new father-in-law. Suddenly, the protective tariff became a family affair.

Edward Gray had emigrated from Northern Ireland in 1794 and, largely through his own talent and ambition, had become a highly successful textile manufacturer on the nearby Patapsco River by the time of his daughter's marriage. Gray was extremely wealthy, had no sons, and liked Kennedy. Recognizing his new son-in-law's polemical skills and economic nationalism, Gray quickly recruited him as a publicist for his pet cause, the maintenance of a high protective tariff. Some scholars have exaggerated Gray's influence on Kennedy. After all, Kennedy had been a strong economic nationalist and a proponent of a high protective tariff before entering the Maryland legislature. Without Gray's encouragement, however, Kennedy probably would not have devoted himself so assiduously to the tariff issue. Not only did Gray cover the printing cost of Kennedy's tariff pamphlets, but he also rewarded his son-in-law with cash bonuses for those that were well received.[32]

The tariff was a complex subject, exactly the kind that someone with Kennedy's skill at argumentation and broad grasp of facts could sink his teeth into. As he became more knowledgeable about the tariff, Kennedy joined a select circle of protectionist writers that included Philadelphia's Mathew Carey, whose firm would publish *Swallow Barn,* as well as Baltimore's Daniel Raymond and Hezekiah Niles. More important, Kennedy's protectionist writing attracted the attention of Henry Clay, the Kentucky senator and leader of the anti-Jackson coalition in Congress. Some years before, Clay had codified his platform of economic nationalism into a kind of doctrinal shorthand known as the "American System." A high protective tariff was an important component of this system. Just as he was shaping the narrative of *Swallow Barn,* Kennedy's activities as a tariff writer and lobbyist were drawing him into the orbit of Henry Clay and a select group of politicians who would become the nucleus of the Whig Party.[33]

Published in early 1830, under the pseudonym "Mephistopheles," Kennedy's most successful tariff pamphlet took aim at the free trader Churchill C. Cambreleng, a member of the U.S. House of Representatives from New York City and chairman of the House Commerce Committee. In a recent House speech, Cambreleng had attacked the tariff and called for adoption of a free-trade policy. In his response, Kennedy dismissed free trade as a "beautiful abstraction." He accused Cambreleng of blatant political pandering, in his attempts to lure southern nullifiers into the Jacksonian camp, and of selfishly promoting his native city as the "carrier" of British goods, at the cost of the nation's economic development. Marshalling an impressive array of protectionist opinion and statistical data, Kennedy demolished Cambreleng's case for free trade and, with it, the Jacksonian mantra for federal nonintervention in commerce. "Mephistopheles" was reprinted by a number of pro-tariff publications, including the *New York Herald* and *Niles' Weekly Register.* Kennedy's pamphlet was vigorously debated between opposing newspapers in the weeks that followed.[34]

Kennedy did not limit himself to statistics alone. In florid prose, he described how factories were proliferating across America, now that a high tariff protected them from predatory British traders. Manufacturing was even making its way into the South, Kennedy observed, into what he called the "anti-tariff desert of Virginia." Those communities touched by manufacturing had awakened as if from a prolonged sleep and were enjoying the blessings of prosperity. "Villages have sprung up under its influence; the waste has been turned into a garden," Kennedy wrote, "the unoccupied and profitless population of the country, have found labor and reward at their hands, and the most happy and joyous changes have occurred in the condition of thousands of helpless families." While clearly carried away by the idea of mechanizing the countryside, Kennedy was nonetheless calling attention to what he considered the retrogressive economic policies and industrial backwardness of the South and, more pointedly, the Old Dominion. These views, so far from Jefferson's agrarian ideal and Irving's pastoral glorification of rural life, would be echoed in the pages of *Swallow Barn.*[35]

The issue of slavery also touched Kennedy personally during this period. At some point in late 1829 or early 1830, his father gave him a slave named Sam, about whom little is known. Kennedy intended to educate Sam and then set him free. Within a year, however, he had become deeply disappointed with Sam, accusing him of being "a liar, thief and rascal." Kennedy returned Sam to Virginia, with instructions to sell him to anyone willing to take him, and swore never to own another slave.[36]

While he never elaborated on the events that caused his falling out with Sam, Kennedy did say that he "could not keep him in the family." For all we know, Sam's transgressions may have been minor but were greatly magnified by Kennedy's presumptions about his loyalty, not to mention his apparent misconception that slavery was a quasi-familial institution. If so, Kennedy's expectations and disappointments were typical of many slave owners at the time. Not only did they control the lives of their slaves in almost every aspect, but many slave owners also lived in close proximity to their slaves and developed personal relationships with them. As a result, many slave owners believed that their paternalistic treatment and occasional kindness toward their slaves were being reciprocated with genuine loyalty and devotion. If for some reason slave owners discovered that this was not true, their disappointment could be profound and the retribution meted out to their slaves terrifying.[37]

The problems inherent in the master-slave relationship would haunt *Swallow Barn,* from the novel's depiction of slave characters like Old Carey, to its treatment of masters like Ned Hazard and Frank Meriwether, to its handling of the catastrophic Nat Turner uprising at the novel's conclusion. Kennedy would struggle throughout the novel to mediate between his pastoral treatment of slavery and the horrific truth that defined the institution.

So, if it was so awkwardly designed and so thoroughly disrupted by external events, why should anyone bother to read *Swallow Barn?* After all, William Wirt described the novel as having "very little incident." However, Wirt may have missed the point. Being practically devoid of any plot, Kennedy's novel was remarkable because the most important events and developments of the day crowded onto its pages. Kennedy's opinions—whether having to do with Jacksonian politics, plantation society in the Old Dominion, or the overarching issues of race and slavery—attached themselves to the novel's superficial surface. With its farcical love story of Ned Hazard and Bell Tracy and its seemingly pointless Apple-pie Branch boundary dispute, *Swallow Barn* was a kind of tabula rasa upon which Kennedy transcribed more important stories about his life and times.[38]

What is more, this capacious and malleable novelistic design allowed Kennedy's fixed cultural beliefs and hardening political partisanship easy entry into the narrative sweep. Nearly every aspect of the novel became colored with either Kennedy's self-perfected, didactic social character or his nascent Whiggery. His construction of Ned Hazard, the heir apparent of Swallow Barn and frustrated suitor of Bel Tracy, serves as a perfect example. In many ways, Hazard seems to be modeled after Kennedy. He is similar in age and physical stature and, like the author, ruggedly handsome and flamboyant in dress. Like Kennedy, Hazard is athletic—proud of his boxing skills and horsemanship—and he possesses a natural charm that attracts others to him. He is not positively influenced by a father, having lost him early in life. Likewise, the adolescent Kennedy dismissed his father as a failure and apparently never sought his advice.[39]

There are other similarities between author and protagonist. For example, Hazard's boyhood reminiscences, especially his expressions of fellowship with black playmates, closely resemble Kennedy's account of his early summers in western Virginia. Hazard's memories include time at Mr. Crab's academy and youthful frolics like the author's. What is more, Hazard has spent a year in South America, dabbling in revolutionary politics and, after almost losing his life, has returned cured of at least some of his romantic illusions. Kennedy had been tempted by a diplomatic post in the same region but had resisted that adventure in favor of other options. Hazard's military service in the southern hemisphere is a somewhat quixotic adventure, as was Kennedy's service during the War of 1812, but, like Kennedy, Hazard is shaped by the experience.[40]

Even more interesting is to compare Hazard's time at Princeton College, described by Kennedy as "the great resort of southern students," with the author's own experience at Baltimore College during his Shrub Hill years. Given his family's Presbyterianism and place of residence, Princeton would have been the logical collegiate path for Kennedy. Until his family fell into financial hardship, he probably expected to go there. At that time, Kennedy referred to his father's business failure as a fortunate turn of events, because it conditioned the young Kennedy to improve himself and succeed in the face of adversity. Still, it would have been difficult for him not to envy more privileged youths or be curious about what life might have been like at Princeton.[41]

Ned Hazard is one of those privileged youths, not only able to attend Princeton but equipped with a lavish allowance. True to his name, however, Hazard finds Princeton fraught with pitfalls. Unlike Kennedy, who had systematically addressed his personal failings and assiduously applied himself to his studies while attending Baltimore College, Hazard is all "bluster and bravado" and "recklessness" at Princeton, visiting village taverns too frequently, womanizing too freely, and gambling well into the night with fellow southerners. He even engages in several duels. In the end, Hazard is expelled from Princeton, making "a ship wreck of his fortunes" and "an inglorious return" to Swallow Barn. In Kennedy's telling of it, Ned Hazard's time at Princeton is an example of how quickly and easily a life can be squandered.

While certainly a didactic tale, this is not the story of Cud, Kennedy's chronically mischievous schoolmate. In Ned Hazard, Kennedy gives his readers an extremely likeable character, whose amicability and merriment endear him to nearly everyone. Adults, children, blacks, whites, and even dogs follow him everywhere. Mark Littleton is immediately drawn to him. "He can accommodate himself to all kinds of society," Littleton observes. Yet, Kennedy notes, there is something missing behind the bright, laughing eyes of this young cavalier. "His mind is a fantasy land," Kennedy writes. Hazard's attempts at deep thought yield no more than a "ludicrous pensiveness." At times, there seems to be "an undercurrent of sadness" about Hazard, as if he is somehow aware of his shortcomings. In spite of his superficial good qualities, his penchant for romantic illusion and his impetuous behavior reflect a shallow and undisciplined character.[42]

Perhaps, Kennedy's nuanced and somewhat sympathetic portrait suggests that *Swallow Barn*'s young cavalier is a partially inverted self-portrait of the author, a kind of road-not-taken version of Kennedy's own story. Or, Kennedy may have been concerned about the younger members of his generation who were growing up in the Old Dominion. After all, he had three younger brothers living there during the time he was writing the novel. It is also possible that he had simply given up on the younger members of Virginia's planter class and, in spite of his efforts to treat them with bemused detachment, could not contain his criticism of them.[43]

In the end, Hazard becomes so freighted with Kennedy's didacticism that he is incapable of carrying the plot of *Swallow Barn* much beyond the farcical courtship of Bel Tracy. Any political pronouncements or weighty thoughts about the future of the Old Dominion are left to Hazard's uncle and the master of Swallow Barn, Frank Meriwether. Nonetheless, in what is arguably the novel's most memorable scene, the great banquet at Swallow Barn celebrating the settlement of the Apple-pie boundary dispute, Kennedy chooses to focus his attention on Hazard: "And there, too, above all, was Ned Hazard, an imp of laughter, with his left arm dangling over the back of his chair, and his right lifting up his replenished glass on high, to catch the sparkling beams of light; his head tossed negligently back upon his shoulder; and from his mouth forth issuing, with an elongated puff, that richer essence than incense of Araby: his dog Wilful, too, privileged as himself, with his face recumbent between his master's knees. Such are the images that gladden the old-fashioned wassail of Virginia."[44]

As the most esteemed member of the community around Swallow Barn, Frank Meriwether serves as the bellwether figure of Kennedy's novel. While Ned Hazard is a part of the ascending generation of Virginia's elite, Frank Meriwether represents the predominant generation of the state's planter class, whose opinions and influence are setting the political and cultural tone of the Old Dominion. For this reason, Irving's country squire, Simon Bracebridge, whose only interest seems to be foxhunting and whose antique manners make him somewhat of an anachronism, is too much of a stock character to serve as the model for Meriwether.[45]

Instead, Kennedy turned to Philip Pendleton, his mother's brother and his favorite uncle, as a model on whom he could fashion a more well-rounded character for Meriwether. From as far back as the summer of 1814, when Kennedy had described his exploits at the Battle of Bladensburg to his uncle, the two had kept up a lively correspondence. They exchanged information and opinions on a variety of subjects, including local politics and national events. Kennedy sent Pendleton a copy of the "Mephistopheles" tariff pamphlet, which, according to Kennedy, his uncle read "with great satisfaction." On several occasions, Pendleton traveled to Baltimore to visit his nephew.[46]

Pendleton's appearance, manners, and position in the community likely went into the construction of Meriwether. However, Meriwether is much more insular and opinionated than his real-life counterpart ever was. While at times "contemplative" and even "philosophical," Meriwether is proudly provincial and totally self-convinced in his views. Kennedy describes him as an "ardent admirer of the genius of Virginia" and someone whose ideas are fixed by an "utter impregnability of belief." Meriwether disdains city life, never travels further than Richmond, and places little value on what he calls "mercantile interests." What is more, he has become increasingly suspicious of what he sees as "deep-laid combinations" in the nation's capital, largely bent upon subverting the rights of Virginians. For these reasons, Meriwether has recently cancelled his subscription to the moderately nationalistic *Richmond Whig* and replaced it with the *Enquirer,* a newspaper much friendlier to the opinions of Old Republicans and fervent states' rights men like himself.[47]

Meriwether regards with great unease most internal improvements and technical innovations, especially those having to do with transportation, which he feels threaten the sovereignty of the Old Dominion. At one point, he questions the merits of the steamboat: "This annihilation of space, sir, is not to be desired. Our protection against the evils of consolidation," he argues, "consists in the very obstacles to our intercourse." On another occasion, Meriwether cites the opinion of his old friend, Splatterthwaite Dubbs of Dinwiddie, who opposes repairing the state's road system. When asked why, Dubbs explains that "the home material of Virginia was never so good as when her roads were at their worst." While highly exaggerated in *Swallow Barn,* Kennedy may have heard similar opinions during his visits to the Old Dominion or while serving in the Maryland legislature.[48]

As an economic nationalist, Kennedy took exception to these views and went to great lengths to show how irrational they were. Throughout *Swallow Barn,* Kennedy draws a clear distinction between what he considers his own logical political and economic ideas and the more emotionally based "sentiments" of men like Meriwether. "Though in their opinions they may be mistaken," Meriwether observes of his fellow Virginians, "in their sentiments they are never wrong." In Kennedy's view, these so-called sentiments were symptomatic of outdated, traditional attachments to kin and community and, more important, the root cause of the state's debilitating provinciality and stubborn resistance to change. Kennedy describes Meriwether's hopelessly recalcitrant neighbor, Isaac Tracy, as guided almost entirely by sentiments. Whether having to do with his seigniorial pride, his obsessive defense of property, or some superfluous point of honor, Tracy's sentiments repeatedly overrule his logic.[49]

In order to devalue such sentiments, Kennedy chooses to demonstrate their intellectual paucity in a raucous tavern scene, where the "sediment of the population" has gathered for the evening and is engaged in "diatribes with violent gestures." Serving as Kennedy's narrator, Mark Littleton describes what happens next. The tavern keeper navigates his way through the intoxicated crowd like a "wily politician," attending to his thirsty patrons but careful not to take sides in their heated disputes. When finally forced to declare his views on a particular subject, the tavern keeper seeks refuge in his sentiments: "It isn't my business to break with customers, or be setting up against them. What signifies opinion this way or that! But, sentiments is another thing! Let any man ask me my sentiments!—that's all; Thar's no flinch in me, you may depend upon it!" Having learned the difference between opinions and sentiments, Littleton retires for the night.[50]

Not only were sentiments devoid of logic, Kennedy believed, but they were also so inexact and malleable that they could be used by those with power and influence to manipulate whole communities. This was especially true in rural Virginia, where people were often uneducated or poorly informed and deferred to a small, elite group for guidance on important issues. The story of how Frank Meriwether's sentiments regarding the sovereignty of the Union, expressed in front of a few farmers and employing the biblical metaphor of Aaron's rod, are picked up and spread through the community illustrates this danger. Kennedy appears to have based this episode on an exceptionally strident speech made before Congress by Philip Barbour, a radical Old Republican from Virginia, in opposition to the Survey Bill of 1826. Because he considered its funding for internal improvements both unconstitutional and a threat to states' rights, Barbour compared the bill to the "rod of Aaron."[51]

Initially, only a small group overhears Meriwether utter his sentiments. Among them are the local farmers, Mark Littleton, and Swallow Barn's schoolmaster, Mr. Chubb. "Mark me, gentlemen," Meriwether warns them, "you and I may not live to see it, but our children will see it, and wail over it—the sovereignty of this union will be as the rod of Aaron; it will turn into a serpent, and swallow up all that struggle with it." This recondite statement of Meriwether's sentiments quickly takes on a life of its own. Elated to have been privy to such insight, Mr. Chubb quickly shares it with his pupils. He instructs them "to keep a lynx-eyed gaze upon the serpent like ambition which would convert the government at Washington to Aaron's rod, to swallow up the independence of their native state."[52]

Within days, the whole community around Swallow Barn seems to be in a state of excitement over Meriwether's words. Even the old slave Carey calls out rather ominously to Hazard, "Look out, Master Ned! Aaron's rod a black snake in Old Virginny!" A few days later, Meriwether himself happens upon two carpenters discussing his thoughts in a similarly garbled fashion. Disregarding what had been lost in transmission, Meriwether is gratified that his sentiments have been so broadly acknowledged and have contributed to a "wholesome tone of feeling amongst the people."[53]

Although he clearly enjoyed constructing this episode, Kennedy was genuinely worried about the tenor of such sentiments. He blamed them for the economic stagnation of the Old Dominion and the antipathy of its people toward federal authority. He brings these concerns together in the novel's Fourth of July celebration, in a chapter entitled "The National Anniversary." Both the timing and the location of the Fourth of July celebration are important. Exploring popular expressions of disunity at such an event infuses the episode with irony. So, too, the event's dismal setting undermines any reason for celebration. Where Irving had exalted in the vibrancy of the English village, with its variety of artisans and abundance of shops, Kennedy chooses a dilapidated landing on the James River, not far from Swallow Barn, as the site of the event. There are few villages or large towns in the Tidewater area, Kennedy tells his readers, "where men may meet and devise improvements or changes in the arts of life." Such knots of humanity are critical for commerce, Kennedy explains, and they also foster institutions of human improvement.[54]

The very nature of the landing, not to mention its deplorable condition, highlights this deficiency. Even in their heyday, such places had been the most basic kind of entrepôts, devoted more to the exchange of goods than their production. Such places served the large plantations scattered about the countryside and were never meant to be real communities. At one time, the landing in the novel was operated by an ambitious Scottish merchant. He built a large warehouse, extended the wharf, and gathered about him complementary enterprises. But even this frail endeavor has fallen victim to the decline of tobacco prices, and what remains is desolation. There is a small, decrepit hostelry and a few derelict buildings, most with collapsed roofs and boarded-up windows. Even these sad remnants are threatened by rampant patches of Jamestown weed, thick stands of bulrushes, and impinging tidal muck from the river.[55]

Before relating the Fourth of July episode, Kennedy digresses into a seemingly irrelevant flight of pastoralism. In a pattern repeated throughout the novel, he juxtaposes his description of the deplorable condition of the landing with a passage extolling the natural beauty of the Tidewater area. This frequent shift in focus has fascinated and puzzled modern critics of *Swallow Barn.* Mindful that he was writing a novel and not a moral tract, Kennedy may have tried to soften his didacticism with these pastoral digressions. Or perhaps he simply wanted to provide a natural backdrop for his tale. After all, such natural descriptions appealed to northern readers curious to learn more about the South, as well as southern readers who shared Kennedy's admiration for their region's scenic charms.[56]

Looked at closely, however, Kennedy's pastoralism seems more qualified, more critical than it appears on surface. In his description of the James River, for example, he implies that those living on its banks have been subsumed, possibly even seduced, by their natural surroundings. The landscape there is "soft," "indolent," and "voluptuous." The river is described as a "bosom" at its widest point. Although it shimmers magnificently at sunset, it is no more than a "beauteous waste." Everything floating on it seems "fixed as by a spell." A somnambulant haze hangs about the landing, "as if nature had retreated into this drowsy nook, and fallen asleep over its own image." In short, Kennedy seems to connect the enervating atmosphere of the Tidewater area with the lassitude of its inhabitants, as if they have surrendered to the will of nature and retreated from more purposeful pursuits.[57]

By the time the group from Swallow Barn arrives at the landing, the Fourth of July celebration is underway. The celebrants gathered there are mostly "rough-looking rustics" and "lank and sallow watermen," most of whom have been drinking for some time and are making ribald jokes and arguing loudly about politics. One of the more elevated voices is that of Sandy Walker, a sunburned waterman and proprietor of the nearby hostelry. He and another member of this motley assemblage, "a greasy gentleman in a blue coat, out at the elbows, with a nose lustrous with living fire," are locked in debate over a fine point of constitutional law.

The issue being debated, with "more vehemence than perspicacity," is whether Congress can build a road across someone's property: "Can't Congress," Sandy postulates, "supposing they were to pass a law to that effect, come take a road of thairn where they mind to, through any man's land?" Such a road might even "go through your house, sir," he warns, "Sweeping your bed right from under you." If the federal government had enough power and money to build a canal over the Allegheny Mountains, Sandy asks, what good were states' rights anyway? The answer from his red-nosed opponent is that the states can easily nullify such federal intrusions. "Nullify!" Sandy responds. He calls the group's attention to what General Jackson did to the Creek nation when it stood in his way. As president, Jackson would deal with nullification in the same manner, Sandy counters. After all, he was already behaving "just the way Bonaparte went on." This exchange arouses the group, and other views are offered up for consideration. "What is the use of states," another rustic poses, as he slices himself a large quid of tobacco, "if they are all to be cut up with canals and railroads and tariffs?" "We hav'nt *fout* and bled for our liberties," adds another, "to have our posterity and their land circumcised." In the end, the exhausted debaters begin making their way home, leaving these vexing issues unresolved.[58]

Like much of *Swallow Barn,* the landing episode is wrapped in political context. What is more, it is remarkably prescient. In the dialogue between Sandy Walker and his fellow celebrants, for example, Kennedy suggests that the rudest notions of nullification are becoming dangerously comingled with states' rights sentiments in the Old Dominion. Since Calhoun's pamphlet *The South Carolina Exposition and Protest,* the founding document of the movement, had been published in 1828 and distributed throughout the South, nullification had become widely discussed. Kennedy had followed this development closely and features it in the landing episode. Even more impressive, he anticipated a major crisis over nullification almost a year before it actually occurred. The South Carolina Nullification Convention and President Jackson's subsequent threat to use military force against that state did not take place until late 1832, nearly a year after Kennedy completed his novel.[59]

The mention of General Jackson and the Creeks during the landing episode refers to Jackson's defeat of that tribe at the Battle of Horseshoe Bend in 1814. Indirectly, however, Kennedy wants to remind his readers of President Jackson's Indian Removal Bill of 1829. This bill dispossessed the Creek, Cherokee, Chickasaw, and Seminole tribes of their lands in Alabama and Georgia and forced their removal west of the Mississippi. This legislation was opposed by many reformers, who saw it as unjust and immoral, and by many political observers who interpreted Jackson's disregard for the Supreme Court's ruling in favor of the tribes as imperious and illegal. Kennedy's mentor William Wirt represented the tribes before the Supreme Court, eventually arguing successfully for them. Outrage at Jackson's Indian policy and his refusal to abide by the high court's decision would cause many moral reformers to move into the anti-Jackson coalition.[60]

The comparison of the president to Bonaparte calls attention to what Kennedy saw as Jackson's increasingly arbitrary behavior. Many shared the fear that Jackson's command style as a military leader was corrupting the nation's highest office. If history was any guide, many believed, such a development could threaten the survival of the republic. This fear would be instrumental in melding the heterogeneous anti-Jacksonian forces into a viable political opposition.

In his early notes for *Swallow Barn,* Kennedy declared his intentions to illustrate the "vulgar opinions" of the rural inhabitants of the Old Dominion. This was not particularly difficult because most readers of *Swallow Barn* in the 1830s recognized Sandy Walker and his drinking companions as social types and understood what they were talking about. What educated, informed reader of the novel could assign any credence to states' rights doctrine, nullification theory, or the various objections to internal improvements when espoused by such a debased representation? In short, it was Kennedy's strategy to leverage the historical embeddedness of his readers to strengthen his political and moral arguments.[61]

In Kennedy's hands, the lower echelons of rural Virginia seem debased to a man. One literary historian has noted that all the poor whites in *Swallow Barn* are "men in decline." Irving's poor but honest yeoman farmers and village artisans have no equivalents in the novel. Nor are the more honorable back-country types of James Fenimore Cooper to be found there. Such characters would have to await Kennedy's second novel, *Horse-Shoe Robinson.*[62]

In his characterization of Miles Rutherford, for example, Kennedy reverts to the same censorious tone he had used to chastise his errant classmate Cud. In one of *Swallow Barn*'s more memorable scenes, Rutherford, an intemperate bully, challenges Ned Hazard to a fistfight. This confrontation takes place at a small crossroads, similar to the landing in both its ramshackle condition and as a gathering place for what Kennedy ironically describes as "that industrious, thriving and reputable class of comers who laudably devote their energies to disputation, loud swearing, bets and whisky,—a class which, to the glory of our land, is surprisingly rife in every countryside."[63]

Hazard proceeds to make short work of Rutherford, much as Kennedy bested the scrappy, truant Cud in their schoolyard days. Although Rutherford has received a good education, he has been misled into believing "that the care by which a good name is won and preserved is useless virtue, and that self-control is a tax which only men of inferior parts pay for success." Such disregard for the kind of self-improvement and moral perfection to which Kennedy attached so much importance can have only one consequence. Rutherford has fallen into intemperance and debauchery, making a "total wreck of [his] worldly hopes." Rutherford's story, Kennedy cautions his readers, is a "history which is often told of men, and varied only in the subordinate incidents which color the common outline."[64]

One of the bystanders watching the altercation is Hafen Blok. While less mean-spirited than Rutherford, Blok represents yet another wretched country type who appears several times in *Swallow Barn.* At one point, Bel Tracy tries to turn the uncouth Blok into a kind of medieval troubadour or minnesinger, with laughable results. Elsewhere in the novel, Hazard and Littleton come upon Blok checking his traps and drinking alone in a nearby swamp. Kennedy describes Blok as a poacher and petty thief who has lost what little standing he had in the community due to "his increasing propensity for drink." Landless, unemployed, and dependent on backdoor charity, Blok has been forced to the fringes of society by his intemperance. Because he lives in a swamp, Blok is no better than a slave.[65]

Many moralistic future Whigs such as Kennedy were convinced that intemperance *was* a form of slavery. Like chattel slavery, strong drink robbed men of their free will and subverted their better natures. During the 1820s and 1830s, in part because of the social and economic instability of the period, Americans drank three times more hard liquor than they do today. The curse of intemperance could strike anyone, sending its hapless victim to the bottom of society. The country lawyer, Taliaferro Hedges, better known around Swallow Barn as Toll Hedges, is such a work in progress.[66]

Appearing first in the novel's county court episode, Hedges deports himself as a marginally effective defense attorney, popular with the jury because of his rough manners and sarcastic wit. His character, Kennedy observes, falls somewhere between "a wag and a brawler." Hedges's clothes have a slept-in look, and his eyes are red from a night of carousing. Later, during a banquet at Swallow Barn, Hedges becomes an embarrassment. He has "imbibed too much boisterousness of the bar room." Hedges tells stories that are too bawdy for mixed company, and his laughter can be heard a hundred yards from the house. In spite of his distant relationship to Meriwether, Kennedy predicts that Hedges's behavior will not be condoned for long and that his undisciplined ways will doom him. "The course of intemperance," Kennedy declares, "gravitates by fatal degrees downward."[67]

Alcohol abuse was seen as a widespread and chronic problem by the 1830s. By that time, over a million people were engaged in temperance reform. The American Temperance Society had been formed in 1826 and was the largest organization of its kind in the nation. While it is unclear whether Kennedy was a member, he was a moral interventionist and concerned about intemperance.

In fact, his attention to the evils of drink in *Swallow Barn* anticipated a rash of popular fiction related to the problem, some highly didactic and some merely sensationalist, that continued for decades. Evangelical Whigs such as Lyman Beecher and Theodore Frelinghuysen, as well as more secular members of the party such as Horace Greeley and Kennedy, would ensure that temperance reform became an important part of Whig culture.[68]

Though a serious problem, intemperance alone had not condemned poor whites in the Old Dominion to their degraded condition. Rather, their intemperance, poverty, and ignorance resulted from a larger problem—namely, that there was little economic role for poor whites in an agricultural economy where a small, elite class owned most of the land and relied almost exclusively on slave labor. This problem was exacerbated by the scarcity of towns where a free population might find more diverse employment and by the political dominance of an elite class determined to preserve the economic and social status quo.[69]

That Kennedy understood these dynamics in the early 1830s is difficult to dispute. After all, his take on poor whites in *Swallow Barn* is quite explicit. He is unflinching in his description of their condition as degraded and debilitated. Furthermore, he establishes Frank Meriwether's dominance over his plantation and its environs early in the novel. Kennedy implies that Meriwether is just one of several masters in the area who share a common ideology. But Kennedy goes further in a chapter entitled "Traces of the Feudal System," in which he assigns blame for most of the state's socioeconomic problems to "the gentlemen of Virginia." This aristocratic class, Kennedy explains, is "scattered about like the chiefs of separate clans, and propagate opinions in seclusion, that have the tincture of baronial independence." These men are "surrounded by their bondsmen and dependents; and the customary intercourse of society familiarizes their minds to the relation of high and low degree." Though couched in a feudal metaphor, Kennedy accurately describes the two-class white society of the Old Dominion, with its unbridgeable hierarchical separation and overwhelming dependence on chattel slavery.[70]

Kennedy goes on to describe the Old Dominion as the "purest form of a republic," where the laws and customs of the state ensure "a certain fixedness." The introduction of any "foreign alloy" into the population of the state and any "popular commotions" in its politics are systematically resisted. So, too, the growth of towns and "changes and improvements" in the public infrastructure are actively discouraged. The Old Dominion presents, Kennedy ironically suggests, "a tolerable picture of feudal munificence." In short, it is a historical anachronism and, if the plantation barons have their way, will remain so.[71]

Given that *Swallow Barn* is so replete with them, Kennedy's use of feudal allusions has provoked a variety of interpretations by those who have studied the novel. These run the gamut from benign to extreme, with some saying that Kennedy intended no more than light-hearted mockery of southern manners and others accusing him of taking a proslavery stance. Naturally, this debate has also touched on the question of how enamored the South actually was with the so-called chivalric myth at the time of the novel's writing and during the decades before the Civil War.[72]

Given that they are an integral part of Irving's *Bracebridge Hall*—and that Kennedy borrowed many of them nearly intact—the chivalric elements and feudal allusions that permeate *Swallow Barn* definitely trace their provenance to the earlier work. Irving had shown how gingerly the eccentricities of the British squirearchy could be handled in a faux-feudal context. Such a patina of lingering feudalism also adds an elegiac tone to his narrative. Even after debunking any claim by Britain's landed aristocracy that the feudal past was "a gay delirium" and suggesting that "those days were never," Irving still packed *Bracebridge Hall* with medieval references. Kennedy avails himself of a number of them. For example, Bracebridge Hall itself contains a portrait gallery that chronicles the owner's ancient lineage and a library that is stocked with romantic tales. The main houses at Swallow Barn and the nearby Brakes are similarly constituted. Irving's Lady Lillycraft, whose mind is "stuffed with love-tales of all kinds," serves as the model for Frank Meriwether's spinster sister, Prudence. In the fields around Bracebridge Hall, the antique sport of falconry is practiced as it has been for centuries. Irving's description of it, which includes a falcon's unexpected escape from its handler, provided Kennedy with the inspiration for his own falconry episode, wherein Bel Tracy's avian ward, Fairbourne, flees from her control.[73]

Though neither subscribed to elite notions of feudal inheritance, both Irving and Kennedy were forced to acknowledge the popularity of romantic novels, especially those of Walter Scott. It is also clear that both authors found the romantic register, once entered, somewhat addictive. At the beginning of Kennedy's novel, the slow, discursive ride out to Swallow Barn by Mark Littleton and the venerable ex-bondsman, Scipio, evocative of the mounted philosophical exchanges between Don Quixote and Sancho Panza, anticipates the author's intention to make use of such romantic material. In the pages that follow, Kennedy refers to plantation houses as "great castles," to male members of the planter class as "knights" and "cavaliers," and to slaves as "dependents" and "young serfs." Kennedy's lengthy digression on the life of Captain John Smith, as Littleton peruses the library at Swallow Barn, represents the author's most indulgent, and irrelevant, engagement with this kind of material. Given these romantic allusions and other narrative characteristics, *Swallow Barn* can be read as a tentative transition novel from the neoclassical to romantic style. Kennedy would commit himself more fully to the romantic style in his later novels.[74]

Walter Scott's romantic novels were extremely popular in the South, as they were in other parts of the nation. However, the degree to which Scott's works contributed to separatist sentiment in the antebellum South and the role that the so-called chivalric myth eventually played in secession are open to debate. Some historians have argued that the South, after abandoning the highly rational and emotionally restrained mindset of the Enlightenment, embraced romanticism in the post-Revolutionary period with exuberance. These historians have maintained that, because slavery complicated the South's spiritual development, the fervor provoked by the religious awakening that swept the region in the early 1800s was partially redirected to romanticism. As the South became more alienated from the North, which had a more commercially successful and morally assertive culture—so this thinking goes—southern intellectuals turned their attention to the Middle Ages. Concepts of male honor, courtly love, and chivalric deportment were seen as better suited to the region than the material bent and stiff manners of the bourgeois North.[75]

Though its importance has been exaggerated, the notion that a particular version of romanticism found a place in the southern mind has some validity. However, there are serious questions of degree and timing. Certainly, there was a shift from the cold rationality of the Enlightenment to more emotive forms of artistic expression in the South. So, too, this transition was complicated by slavery. Nonetheless, the South did not take to romanticism as quickly as some historians have suggested. Many writers in the South were slow to abandon the neoclassical literary style. Furthermore, the works of Walter Scott did not achieve the broad and lasting popularity in the South that many have assumed.

As late as the 1830s, the region was still culturally divided and intellectually diverse.[76]

Where romanticism did find a foothold was in the Old Dominion. Several so-called Virginia novels written in the 1820s celebrated plantation life and alluded to an Old World, "cavalier" connection among the state's elite families. Kennedy is known to have read one of these novels, *Edge-Hill, or, The Family of the Fitzroyals,* written by James Ewell Heath and published in 1828. As an editor of the *Southern Literary Messenger* in Richmond for a time, Heath stressed the need for a regional literary style and was partial to southern romanticism in particular. Nonetheless, these early Virginia novels do not appear to have influenced Kennedy's own plantation novel and were only moderately popular with the reading public.[77]

Historians have speculated as to why Virginia in particular embraced the idea of a feudal inheritance among its gentry and the chivalric pretensions associated with it. However tenuous these claims may have been, settlement patterns during the colonial period provided the Old Dominion with the best pedigree in the region for them. More important, Virginia's economic and political declension during the first quarter of the nineteenth century was among the most precipitous of any southern state. Formally a cradle of the Revolution and the birthplace of presidents, Virginia had become an economic and political backwater by the 1830s. The state's feelings of insecurity and its need for renewed self-esteem were among the most poignant in the South, and the creation of the cavalier myth and its attendant trappings served to restore some of the state's lost pride.[78]

What neither Kennedy nor anyone else could foresee in the 1830s was the part that southern romanticism, with its claims to an Old World connection and a cavalier heritage, would play in the construction of a sectional identity before the Civil War. Preposterous though these illusions were, they eventually became part of the justification for secession. To what extent these ideas of ethnic separateness, appearing in newspaper editorials and literary journals, resonated with the southern public is difficult to know.[79]

Given this background, it is no surprise that a number of literary historians have wrongly placed *Swallow Barn* in a southern romantic continuum that begins with the arrival of Walter Scott's works in the South, continues through the Virginia novels of the 1820s, and culminates in Kennedy's novels and those of his contemporary William Gilmore Simms, the prolific romantic author from South Carolina and avowed proslavery separatist. However, Kennedy is badly out of step in this literary procession. Not only was he an urban-centered, borderland author, but his plantation novel was derivative primarily of Washington Irving, not Scott or the early Virginia novelists. Nor can Kennedy's views on slavery or secession be likened to those of Simms. That Kennedy drew from Scott as well as other English writers, and that he was aware of the cavalier pretensions of the Tidewater elite, is not in question. In fact, the Old Dominion's feudal illusions served as a catalyst for Kennedy's transplanting Irving's Old World squirearchy, depicted in *Bracebridge Hall,* with its antique customs and charming eccentricities, to *Swallow Barn*'s New World setting. The feudal metaphor Irving used so effectively to gently mock Britain's landed aristocracy was meant to provide Kennedy with the stylistic cover needed to subtly critique the Old Dominion's planter elite.[80]

But as often happens in *Swallow Barn,* Kennedy lost control of this narrative device. Where Irving had employed the feudal metaphor to maintain a light, genial touch, Kennedy was unable to hide the fact that he regarded the outmoded beliefs and insular pride of Virginia's planters as responsible for the state's economic backwardness and retrogressive politics. In Kennedy's hands, the quaint habits and odd foibles that nourished Irving's depiction of the ruling class became symbols of hopeless provinciality and stubborn resistance to change. Where Irving had balanced multiple perspectives, Kennedy created an undercurrent of confusing ambivalence. In the end, readers of *Swallow Barn* are not sure what is serious and what is farce. Nor is it always clear where Kennedy, speaking from the vacillating standpoint of Mark Littleton, is coming from.

Kennedy best connects romanticism in the Old Dominion with the antiquated beliefs of its planter class in his characterization of Isaac Tracy and his daughter Bel. Their residence, the Brakes, is architecturally unchanged from its colonial days, with its woodwork carved into "gorgeous forms of ancient pomp" and stone fireplaces sculpted into "noble monuments of ancient hospitality." Every day, Isaac Tracy dresses in his antique clothes before a huge mirror ringed with "twisted snakes, each swallowing his own tail." Both in dress and deportment, Tracy is unbending in his adherence to "ancient custom." He is prideful and arrogant in the extreme, an attitude that projects a "contemptuous defiance of feudal dignity." "The crust of his prejudices," Kennedy observes, fits Tracy "like a suit of mail."[81]

Totally infatuated with her romantic conceit, Bel Tracy has almost come to believe that she lives in the fourteenth century. Her condition is partly the fault of her indulgent father, who has spoiled her and imbued her with a "severe and exaggerated sense of personal respect." What is more, Bel has recently decided that she possesses "some peculiarly aristocratic drop of blood inherited from some over-stately grandam, reappearing at the surface after a lapse of a century."[82]

Once he has a feeling for it, Kennedy goes out of his way to conflate the Old Dominion's embrace of chivalry with the state's apparently willful and universal backwardness. Romanticism becomes an all-embracing metaphor for Virginia's retrogressive behavior and reactionary attitudes. For example, Kennedy compares the seemingly senseless Apple-pie boundary dispute between Tracy and Meriwether to the "ancient days of bull-headed chivalry." Similarly, Meriwether's ceremonial procession from Swallow Barn to the county court, where he presides over the state's antiquated legal system, is likened to a kind of "Crusade," with the master and his retinue marching forth as if "on the sandy plains of Syria." While describing Ned Hazard's cavalier antics at Princeton, Kennedy launches into a diatribe about how the romantic notions of Virginia's young men run counter to scholarship and learning: "Engrossed thus, like states of the dark ages, in cares of love, war and politics, it is not to be wondered at, that the arts and sciences have fallen into some disesteem." Life in the Old Dominion harkens back to the feudal era, Kennedy continues, "when barons fought for lady love,—swaggered, and swore by saints,—and frightened learning into the nests of monks."[83]

Based upon Kennedy's telling of it, romantic sentiments seem to have swept through the Old Dominion like cholera. Neither men nor women have been spared. Ned Hazard is so maddened by love for Bel Tracy that he is ready to return to the Andes and upon "reaching the heights of Chimborazo . . . engrave with his sword the name of the cold Bel upon the ice of the glacier." The country lawyer and dilettantish poet Singleton Swansdown has excited the passions of romantically inclined schoolgirls and rural spinsters like Prudence Meriwether with his pamphlet of rhymes, "The Roumaunt of Dryasdale." Although these poems are no more than a "delicate effusion of superfine sentiment," Kennedy predicts that Swansdown will one day "reflect credit upon the literature of the South."[84]

But it is the women in *Swallow Barn* who seem most afflicted with these romantic sentiments. Like Bel Tracy, Prudence Meriwether mourns the passing of the golden age of chivalry and is fully committed to reviving it in the Old Dominion. She has become an avid reader of romantic literature, mostly Scott since she disapproves of Byron's immorality, and has taken to sketching scenes of the feudal past on her strolls through the grounds of Swallow Barn: "knights, and old castles, and pensive ladies—madonnas and cloistered nuns, the teeming offspring of an imagination heated with romance and devotion." Given her literary bent and artistic abilities, Prudence is regarded as somewhat of a prodigy by the unlettered locals.[85]

Some historians have referred to the aura of dignity and respect that Prudence Meriwether and Bell Tracy are endeavoring to create as the "cult of the lady." Whereas northern women were less isolated during this period and had more opportunities to modernize their thinking, many privileged women in the South turned to reading romantic novels. Southern men were complicit in encouraging heightened notions of innocence and purity in these women, especially those who might be prospective wives. As a consequence, exaggerated forms of gallantry became the social norm. In spite of its flattering overtones, such treatment afforded southern men a degree of control over their women and, with it, their role in southern society.[86]

The process of courtship became highly complicated in the antebellum South because of inflated notions of propriety, various romantic embellishments, and the art of coquetry. Southern belles often discouraged marriage proposals and even rejected multiple offers from frustrated suitors as part of the courting ritual. The courtship of Bel Tracy by Ned Hazard parodied this ritual by taking it to ridiculous extremes. Most southern readers probably understood the humor in this parody and found it entertaining. Northern readers, especially young women, were also interested in the subjects of love and courtship and contributed to *Swallow Barn*'s popularity as a novel.[87]

In its treatment of women, *Swallow Barn* is more than a novel of manners. Kennedy develops the characters of Prudence Meriwether and Bel Tracy in some depth. In doing so, he reveals his own changing views of women. Although Prudence is based on Irving's Lady Lillycraft, who also engages in novel reading and charitable work, Kennedy endows her with more human interaction, livelier conversation, and fuller expression of her thoughts and feelings. Rather than just listing her good works in the environs of the plantation, which include founding three Sunday schools and several tract societies, Kennedy probes Prudence's motivation for this work. In doing so, he seems to be testing out his own acceptance of women operating outside their domestic sphere. As a resident of the borderland, Kennedy was probably less exposed to female-dominated benevolent societies than his northern cohorts were. His exploration of Prudence's charitable work shows that he was slowly becoming accustomed to these bold, new female ventures.[88]

The origins of Bel Tracy are obscure. Her character may be based on one of Kennedy's cousins in western Virginia or someone he met on a visit there. During the summer of 1828, Kennedy wrote from Martinsburg to his fiancé Elizabeth Gray, "They have belles and beauties here, and coquettes too, and scores of flirtations. I mean to write a chapter upon 'country belles,' and am looking about for subjects." Bel Tracy may be one of these coquettes.[89]

The passage on "country belles" in *Swallow Barn* turns out to be a didactic one, reminiscent of Kennedy's earlier writings on the susceptibility of women to luxury and fashion. He argues that a rural setting is best for raising virtuous young women and that they should be kept as close to home as possible. "There is nothing more lovely than the picture of an artless girl, tranquilly gliding onwards to womanhood," Kennedy rhapsodizes. Such a creature should receive her "first lesson from the lips of a mother" and henceforth "her only lore taught her at the fireside." When defining such a young woman's sphere of activities, Kennedy speaks of "*her* world" (emphasis Kennedy's) and urges that it be restricted to those "objects with which she [is] familiar; and her ramblings limited to the ancient neighborhood, like the flights of a dove in its native valley."[90]

Based on this passage alone, Kennedy comes off as more of a conservative Jacksonian, relegating women to their traditional place, than a nascent Whig, acknowledging their broader role in society. Coming early in *Swallow Barn,* however, this passage may represent a kind of benchmark for his changing perspective on women over the course of the novel. Certainly, his characterization of Bel Tracy belies such a fixed and outdated model for womanhood. Bel is anything but an "artless girl." She doesn't even have a mother to nurture and instruct her at home. At times, she is so forceful that she seems almost masculine. At one point, she proposes that the Apple-pie boundary dispute be settled in a game of dice. She then throws like a seasoned gambler against Ned Hazard. On another occasion, Hazard observes that Bel's horsemanship is every bit as good as his own. Where Prudence Meriwether's efforts to recreate the chivalrous past in the Old Dominion are intellectual, Bel's endeavors toward the same end are physical. Whether transforming Hafen Blok into a minnesinger or training her pet hawk in the art of falconry, Bel shows a determination to shape *her* world according to her design.[91]

Bel Tracy's character represents a significant step for Kennedy toward the creation of Mildred Lindsay in *Horse-Shoe Robinson.* Like Bel, Mildred is an assertive and motherless young woman. In Mildred, however, patriotism and bravery replace Bel's romantic conceits. More important, this novelistic development signals Kennedy's evolving view regarding the part women should play in society. This change would prove almost as important for Kennedy's engagement with broader Whig culture as his identification with the needs and aspirations of the common man. Although unable to vote, reform-minded and politically engaged women would constitute a vital component of the emerging Whig movement.[92]

It is reasonable to ask what influence the strong-willed Nancy Pendleton Kennedy had on her son's views of women. While he considered her unwavering loyalty to the Old Dominion a sign of provinciality, Kennedy nonetheless admired his mother's commanding personality. He credited her with holding her family together after his father's business failure. Kennedy thought enough of his mother's advice to visit her during the summer of 1828 and discuss his plans to marry Elizabeth Gray. One can only speculate where the best qualities of Nancy Pendleton are scattered among the women of *Swallow Barn* and Kennedy's later novels.[93]

Not all of the female characters of Kennedy's novel are as well drawn as those of Prudence Meriwether and Bel Tracy. The mistress of Swallow Barn, Lucretia Meriwether, for example, is described in a cursory way. Still, what Kennedy gives his readers is more or less historically accurate. Like many successful plantation mistresses, Lucretia Meriwether fulfills the exhausting double role of being a refined and devoted wife while managing the extended household that is the center of plantation life. She is up before the rest of Swallow Barn, "infusing an early vigor into the whole household." Her first concern is for the "youngsters of her numerous family, both black and white." Her domestic responsibilities consist of everything from supervising the kitchen staff to putting up winter stores to doling out medicine for sick slaves. Everything runs smoothly because Lucretia has reduced the management of Swallow Barn to "a perfect science." Yet, by evening, she is beautifully attired and seated at her harpsichord, the pride of her admiring but indolent husband.[94]

Here Kennedy departs from what is generally known about plantation mistresses. According to Kennedy, Lucretia Meriwether has set up a textile industry on the grounds of Swallow Barn. So many spinning wheels are at work around the place that they can be heard at some distance when the breeze is right. "In these laboratories," Kennedy writes, "the negro women are employed in preparing yarn for the loom, from which is produced not only a comfortable amount of clothing for the working people, but some excellent carpets for the house." Lucretia's industriousness is due to her passion for "the protection of manufacturers," Kennedy explains, and her success at finished-goods self-sufficiency has made her "the very priestess of the American System."[95]

The inclusion of Lucretia's textile enterprise in *Swallow Barn* is an awkward one. Kennedy may have wanted to deliver on the claim in his "Mephistopheles" pamphlet that, in response to higher tariffs, manufacturing was making inroads in the South. If so, Lucretia's spinning mill was more wishful thinking than broad reality. It is also possible that Kennedy was paying homage to Henry Clay, soon-to-be leader of the Whig Party and inventor of the "American System," a term that embodied the party's nationalist economic program. Support for domestic industry and higher tariffs to protect it were key components of Clay's system.

So devoted was Clay to his system that he tried it out at his Ashland plantation, not far from Lexington, Kentucky. Clay integrated hemp farming and rope manufacture on the grounds of his plantation and, because the quality of his rope was inferior to imports, made sure a high tariff was passed into law to protect his production. What made Ashland well known by 1830, however, were the contributions of Clay's wife Lucretia. During her husband's long absences in Washington, she taught herself agriculture and learned how to manage the plantation herself. Not only was her advice sought by local farmers, but she turned Ashland into a thriving and profitable enterprise. Naïve though it may have been, the inclusion of Lucretia Meriwether's spinning mill in *Swallow Barn* may have reflected Kennedy's optimism that the South would one day realize these same economic successes.[96]

For all their forward thinking about the American economy, nascent Whigs like Clay and Kennedy remained socially conservative. In spite of their unbounded optimism, they believed a nation's progress needed to be steady but gradual. It should never be allowed to disrupt the underlying fabric of society. While he tested new manufacturing methods and diversified production at Ashland, Clay also tripled the number of slaves working there. This represented a compromise between innovative and traditional approaches and was not a problem for Clay.[97]

For most nascent Whigs, Henry Clay embodied gradualism and compromise. Not unlike Kennedy, Clay had mastered his early, uncontrolled character through personal compromise. Some who knew him claimed Clay *was* a compromise. With respect to the issue of slavery, for example, he had condemned the institution as "an evil" and continued to believe it would die out long term. Clay had played a central role in the Missouri Compromise of 1820, whereby the status quo of slavery was preserved in both the South and its most likely area of western expansion. This sectional compromise was credited with saving the Union and earned Clay the sobriquet of "The Great Compromiser." In his Distribution Bill of 1833, he came surprisingly close to securing federal funding for African colonization, only to see his efforts defeated by President Jackson's veto. Two years later, Clay assumed the presidency of the American Colonization Society. To social conservatives like Kennedy, Clay's approach to the issues of race and slavery embraced the right pace and policy.[98]

By modeling the mistress of Swallow Barn after that of Ashland, Kennedy did not mean to imply that Frank Meriwether was anything like Henry Clay. Yet, Kennedy makes a point of differentiating Meriwether from his ultraconservative neighbor, Isaac Tracy. Furthermore, it is Meriwether who almost singlehandedly designs a compromise to end the ancient boundary dispute between Swallow Barn and The Brakes.

It is tempting to read the Apple-pie Branch boundary dispute as an amusing satire on litigious neighbors and their lawyers. Certainly, the real estate at issue is nearly worthless. According to Mark Littleton's description of it, the Apple-pie Branch is no better than "a garden of wankopins and snake-collards" and should be "relinquished by unanimous consent to skunks and muskrats." However, it becomes clear that, though foolish in substance, the Apple-pie dispute transcends the question of material value. Isaac Tracy is obsessed with gaining clear title to the Apple-pie Branch. "There was something at the bottom of the dispute," Kennedy explains, "that belonged to his character." The dispute has dragged on for several generations and now stands in the way of Ned Hazard's plans to marry Bel Tracy. Even the area's old sibyl, Mammy

Diana, comments on the divisive effect of the dispute on the two neighboring families.[99]

As a resident of the borderland, Kennedy recognized that such a disagreement seldom traced to a single issue and was almost always exacerbated by emotion. The nullification movement in South Carolina, for example, had arisen out of a complex of frustration and fear but was now fixated on the tariff issue. So, too, resistance to internal improvements in the Old Dominion reflected more general fears of federal encroachment, as well as resentment over the state's loss of national prestige. One can only guess what sources of tension lie behind Isaac Tracy's fixation on the Apple-pie Branch.[100]

Kennedy was clear, however, about how to resolve such disagreements. The story of the Apple-pie settlement is about compromise or, in the spirit of Henry Clay and other emerging Whigs, compromise backed by the rule of law. To begin with, resolutions of this kind require that special attention be paid to the emotions of the aggrieved party. Toward this end, Frank Meriwether engages the services of a respected country lawyer, Philpot Wart. Although Meriwether intends to relinquish his rights to the Apple-pie Branch, he coaches Wart on how to best approach Isaac Tracy. "We must accommodate ourselves to the peculiarities of our neighbors," Meriwether cautions, "and pray be careful that you give no offence to his pride, by the course you pursue."[101]

The figure of Philpot Wart is loosely based upon Kennedy's mentor William Wirt and stands out as one of the most colorful characters in *Swallow Barn*. Even when discussing the simplest subjects, Wart employs as much legal Latin as he can. Some small thing that has not yet taken place is a "potential remotissima," something not yet in existence is "in nubibus." While his habit of seeing everything through a legal prism makes him a bit of an oddity, Wart's dry humor and knack for storytelling allow him to get away with this legal banter.[102]

More important is Wart's approach to the law, which conforms to emerging Whig legal theory at the time. Conservative jurists such as Wirt and Rufus Choate resisted parsing the law into too many cases and sought to emphasize its overall authority. Such lawyers strove to establish a Burkean respect for the law rather than delve into Lockean explanations for its legitimacy. Choate said that he wished to draw "a mysterious veil" over the law in order to enhance the public's veneration of it.[103]

Kennedy describes Philpot Wart as having similar perceptions of the law and how it should operate. Wart has read "little law later than Coke and Littleton," and "too much particularity" perplexes him. Wart has "no need of looking into cases," Kennedy explains, because he understands "the currents of the law, and knows where they must run." Wart proceeds to "mystify the case" before Isaac Tracy; he not only obfuscates his argument before the old man but also provides the Apple-pie settlement with the imprimatur of legal interpretation needed to make it final and lasting.

Meriwether's willingness to compromise and his careful reading of his neighbor's sensitivities, coupled with the aura of legal authority brought to the settlement by Wart, finally put the long-standing boundary dispute between the two families to rest. The Apple-pie Branch is awarded to Tracy, and the boundary between the two plantations restored to, as Wart phrases it, "status quo ante bellum." "It is a great thing," Meriwether remarks with pride, "to pacify these boundary disputes." Certainly, everyone involved in the settlement seems impressed by the enabling power of compromise. "If it were the right season," Wart observes, "I think we should be likely to look over more boundary lines than the one to-day."[104]

Few scholars who have studied *Swallow Barn* have attached much importance to the Apple-pie boundary dispute. It has generally been seen as purposefully trivial so as to be in accord with the novel's lighthearted take on life in the Old Dominion. However, while this may have been Kennedy's *original* intention, this interpretation does not go far enough in explaining what sort of meaning the author, influenced by events during the writing of the novel and his growing political convictions, attached to the *final* rendering of the episode. As with so much of the novel, the historical context that gradually enveloped *Swallow Barn* and the increasing pull of Whig culture on its author eventually subsumed Kennedy's genial narrative approach and freighted it with deeper meaning.[105]

In his earliest manuscripts, Kennedy described Frank Meriwether as not only "generous and hospitable" to his neighbors but also "kind to his slaves." The Apple-pie settlement further establishes the master of Swallow Barn as a relatively enlightened member of the Old Dominion's planter class. However, it is easy to overestimate the role that Kennedy originally intended for Meriwether. He was probably meant to serve as an admirable representative of his class but not necessarily as a spokesman for it, especially on the controversial issues of race and slavery. Only at the end of the novel, when external events force Kennedy to address these issues, is Meriwether thrust into the role of spokesman and quasi-apologist for the institution of slavery.[106]

Rarely does the grim reality of the master-slave relationship find its way into Kennedy's novel. Still, there are two occasions when it manages to penetrate, or nearly penetrate, his narrative. One involves Ned Hazard's great-uncle some years before. Old Hazard, as he was called, constructed a milldam and gristmill on the slowly meandering Apple-pie Branch. On the day of the mill's inauguration, however, before the old man's assembled neighbors, the mill wheel stopped dead after only two hours of operation. Sensing the obvious before his master did, Hazard's head slave commented that "the mill's run out of water." After being told to hold his tongue, the slave added softly, "It's a two-hour mill." Hearing this, Hazard turned "blood-red with anger" and struggled to control his temper. In his final manuscript, Kennedy wrote that Hazard "would have attacked him with a stick," but he removed these words prior to publication.[107]

At another point in the novel, Mark Littleton notices that the slave children at Swallow Barn seem especially wary of him. He soon learns that they think he might be a "Georgia man," there to purchase Meriwether's surplus slaves and ship them to the Deep South. A visit from such a slave trader to a plantation would have been very likely at the time of *Swallow Barn*'s writing. Following the decline of the tobacco economy, Virginia planters had developed a lucrative business supplying excess slaves to the cotton-growing states. Across the Upper South, this internal slave trade broke up an estimated one in three slave marriages and separated half of all slave children from a parent. Kennedy would remove this reference from the 1851 version of the novel.[108]

For most of *Swallow Barn,* Kennedy relegates slaves to the background of the narrative. He repeatedly calls them "domestics," "dependents," "retainers," or simply "working people." What is more, there are surprisingly few descriptions of slaves actually working on the plantation. Granted, Kennedy describes some household chores being attended to by slaves. But, more often, he depicts slave children at play and older slaves simply lounging about. Able-bodied field hands, performing hard physical labor, are simply missing from Kennedy's narrative. Furthermore, the subject of slavery never enters into the heated political discussions that take place in the drawing rooms of plantation houses or the ruder public forums described in the novel. Neither the suspected conspiracies in Washington nor the federal intrusions in local affairs are ever connected to the issue of slavery. Only at the end of the novel, when external events force him to, does Kennedy make slavery the subject of open discussion. For most of *Swallow Barn,* the institution of slavery appears to be a kind of invisible force, a silent but reliable engine, that makes privileged life in the Old Dominion possible but is seldom observed in operation or much talked about.[109]

In the main body of the novel, the only discussion of slavery as an abridgement of human freedom is an oblique one. It takes the form of an Irving-inspired, mock-chivalric parable involving Bel Tracy and her trained hawk, Fairbourne. Bel is attempting to replicate the art of falconry in the fields near The Brakes. Her friend Harvey Riggs warns Bel that her trust in Fairbourne is misplaced and that her pet might try to escape. "There are creatures," Riggs cautions her, "that prefer the open world to your hand, strange as it may seem." Bel protests that "nothing that I have tended so kindly would dessert me." Fairbourne makes his escape, of course, leaving Bel and her companion to ponder the event's larger significance. Possibly reflecting his own disappointment with the slave-owning experience, Kennedy has Riggs declare that Fairbourne "belongs to an ungrateful tribe, and is not worth reclaiming." Seemingly chastened by the experience, Bel confesses that "There is some virtue in fetters . . . when milder means fail."[110]

Just as he softens his criticism of the Old Dominion's political and economic backwardness with numerous feudal allusions, Kennedy employs pastoralism to integrate slavery into the context of plantation life. By eliding references to blacks and their humble dwellings with other landscape elements, he creates the impression that slavery belongs to the natural order of things. Often, his interweaving of these elements is practically seamless.

> A short distance from the mansion, a brook glides at a snail's pace towards the river, holding its course through a wilderness of laurel and alder, and creeping around islets covered with green mosses. Across this stream is thrown a rough bridge, which it would delight a painter to see; and not far below it an aged sycamore twists its roots into a grotesque framework to the pure mirror of a spring, which wells up its cool waters from a bed of gravel and runs gurgling to the brook. There it aids in furnishing a cruising ground to a squadron of ducks who in defiance of all nautical probability, are incessantly turning up their sterns to the sky. On the grass which skirts

> the margin of the spring, I observe the family linen is usually spread out by some sturdy negro women, who chant shrill ditties over wash tubs and seem to live in ceaseless warfare with little besmirched and bow-legged blacks, who are never tired of making somersets, and mischievously pushing each other on the clothes laid down to bleach.[111]

But, yet again, Kennedy's pastoralism is flawed by some disquieting notes. Just as his description of the James River hints at the lassitude of those living along its banks, his portrayal of black children playing by the spring is subtly freighted. On one level they are simply playful, but on another they are mischievous and ill disciplined. Nor is the description of them as "besmirched" and "bow-legged" particularly flattering.

In fact, the description of these black children points up one of the most disturbing aspects of *Swallow Barn* for modern readers—namely, the racially disparaging language and, at times, outright mockery of blacks throughout Kennedy's novel. This negative descriptive treatment is extended to slaves and free blacks alike and commences before Mark Littleton's arrival at Swallow Barn. Mirroring Kennedy's own low opinion of free blacks, Littleton describes young black males at night behaving boisterously in the streets of Richmond: "And, at intervals, strutting past [was] a careering, saucy negro, with marvelous lips, whistling at the top of his bent."[112]

Like many white residents of the borderland, Kennedy regarded free blacks as a degraded and anomalous element of the population. While serving in the Maryland legislature, he characterized free blacks as a dishonest and worthless class and suggested that they be separated from white society, possibly through African colonization. Though Kennedy is not known to have been a member of the American Colonization Society, his friend John Latrobe was a ranking officer of the Baltimore chapter. Furthermore, Henry Clay, the future president of the society and Kennedy's soon-to-be political mentor, had thrown his considerable stature behind the cause of removing blacks entirely from American soil. In a widely published speech to the society during early 1830, Clay identified whites and blacks as "incongruous elements of the population" and called for their "total and absolute separation, by an extensive space of water or land."[113]

On the ride out to Swallow Barn, Mark Littleton is accompanied by an old free black man named Scipio. Speaking through Littleton, Kennedy describes this old man in terms that reveal a great deal about the author's perceptions of race.

> His name was Scipio. His face, which was principally made up of a pair of lips hanging below a pair of nostrils, was well set off with a head of silver wool that bespoke a volume of gravity. He had, from some aristocratic conceit of elegance, indued himself for my service in a cast-off dragoon cap, stripped of its bear skin, a ragged regimental coat, still jagged with some points of tarnished scarlet, and a pair of course linen trousers, barely reaching the ankles, beneath which two bony feet occupied shoes, each of the superficies and figure of a hoe, and on one of these was whimsically buckled a rusty spur.

Littleton is pleased with Scipio's "antique grace." Scipio conducts himself with a "deferential courtesy and formal politeness" that, Littleton admits, greatly enhances his estimation of the old man's "breeding." Still, Littleton considers Scipio's style of horsemanship, like the clothing the old man wears, too showy. "He bounced up and down in his saddle," Littleton observes, "with an ambitious ostentation of a groom in the vigor of manhood." Furthermore, Littleton's positive response to Scipio's attempts at conversation "awoke his [Scipio's] vanity." Littleton refuses to be fooled by Scipio's posturing, however, and dismisses most of what the old man says as "undoubtedly picked up from some popular orator."[114]

Even though it is difficult to generalize about racial prejudice in any period, the descriptive pattern Kennedy uses in his treatment of blacks, beginning with old Scipio and continuing throughout the novel, typifies a set of racial views widely espoused in the author's time and place. These racial views were a kind of complex, consisting of historical perceptions of blacks reaching back centuries, as well as more recent notions derived from pseudoscientific theory and popular American culture. Although consisting of many parts, this complex of racial prejudice was powerful enough to convince many antebellum whites that the black race was congenitally inferior to them in both intelligence and refinement and, therefore, incapable of improvement.[115]

The descriptive pattern that Kennedy employs with regard to black characters in *Swallow Barn* almost always begins with a disparaging critique of their physical appearance. Kennedy usually focuses on the physiognomy but often describes other body parts as well. In the case of old Scipio, for example, Kennedy describes him more or less from head to toe. By emphasizing Scipio's nose and lips, Kennedy quickly reduces the old man's face to a distorted caricature of his race. In spite of his dressing up to serve as Littleton's guide, the old man's exposed ankles and bony feet are compared to common tools of the field. Kennedy often juxtaposes disparaging physical descriptions of his black characters with what he depicts as the cast-off nature and mock elegance of their attire. Also, he frequently uses his black characters' dialogue to illustrate what he considers their inept mimicry of white speech and thought. Scipio's garbled profundities are typical of this narrative device. The overall intent is to show that black attempts at imitating the appearance and behavior of whites is comical and even ludicrous.[116]

Certainly, Kennedy's classical education had made him aware that slavery was often color-blind in earlier eras. Yet, as a student of history, he would also have known that slavery was increasingly associated with sub-Saharan peoples in later European and Arab cultures. A number of European philosophers that Kennedy had probably read, among them David Hume, Immanuel Kant, and Voltaire, wrote about what they considered the intellectual inferiority and lagging cultural advancement of the black race. Furthermore, the seventeenth-century discovery of new primate species on the African continent had reinforced preconceptions of blacks as primitive and animal-like. Kennedy and Peter Hoffman Cruse's descriptions of the Tawnies in the *Red Book,* creatures so grotesque that they do not appear to be fully human, may have been inspired by such discoveries. Other authors writing before and after Kennedy, from Jonathan Swift to Edgar Allan Poe, drew heavily on these exciting but poorly understood discoveries in their works. Even Thomas Jefferson, in one of the most notoriously racist passages of his *Notes on the State of Virginia,* associated blacks with what he called "Oranootans." Kennedy compares blacks to monkeys so often in *Swallow Barn* that the reader wonders whether he is in jest or serious about such a connection.[117]

Most historians agree that racism was on the increase in the United States at the time of *Swallow Barn*'s writing. Its influence seems to have permeated every stratum of white society. The poorest immigrant groups saw both free blacks and urban slaves as competition in the workplace. Because they were more or less defenseless, blacks were frequently attacked at work sites and in the streets of cities like Baltimore. By the late 1820s, the Democratic Party began to exploit these tensions with anti-black rhetoric. In doing so, the Democrats brought newly arrived Irish immigrants into their ranks. During this period, minstrelsy also began its phenomenal rise in popularity. This new musical form, with its "blackened-up" white entertainers shuffling across urban stages in outright mockery of blacks, struck a common chord with both poor and better-off white theater goers. At the same time, pseudoscientific theories such as phrenology lent new legitimacy to America's callous racial attitudes.[118]

Living as he did in the urban milieu of Baltimore during the 1820s and 1830s, Kennedy was influenced by these developments, many of which found their way into *Swallow Barn* and racialized its text in ways that startle modern readers. Phrenology was just one example of how this process occurred. This strange, quasi-scientific discipline had its roots in so-called French and English Materialism, which discounted environmental influences on the human brain and emphasized its physical makeup instead. Phrenologists were trained to analyze the swells and bumps on the surface of the human skull in order to assess an individual's strengths and weakness. German pioneers had already identified twenty-two cranial "organs" and mapped them on the human skull by the time phrenology reached the United States in the 1820s. By the end of the decade, phrenologists were displaying their signs on the main streets of most American cities, colleges and universities were including phrenology in their curricula, and penal institutions were using this new capability to evaluate the deviances of their inmates. By the 1830s, one respected journal in the South claimed that phrenology was no longer laughed at by educated men but had "assumed the majesty of science."[119]

As a believer in the concept of faculty psychology, Kennedy was naturally drawn to phrenology. It is possible that he learned about this new study from Professor George Calvert, who taught "mental philosophy" at the University of Maryland during the time that Kennedy was an instructor of history there. Calvert also gave public lectures on the subject of phrenology, in which he utilized a collection of human skull casts representing the various races of man. This was common practice in such presentations, since phrenology had drifted into the realm of "ethnological science" before reaching the United States. Lectures and periodicals frequently juxtaposed the skull types and facial features of Africans, Asians, Native Americans, and Caucasians with observations regarding the races' intelligence and other mental faculties. Calvert occasionally borrowed skull casts from the Baltimore Phrenological Society, where Kennedy was an active member. On several occasions during 1830, Kennedy hosted gatherings of twenty-five or more members at his home and, according to his journal, "passed the evening *phrenologically*" (emphasis Kennedy's).[120]

Kennedy approaches most of the black characters in his novel phrenologically as well. One of the slaves at Swallow Barn, Young Beelzebub, is described as "a flat-nosed pigmy" with "a mouth distended from ear-to-ear." Another, Old Jeff, has "bolster-lips" with a "lugubriously lengthened visage." During the great banquet scene at Swallow Barn, Kennedy focuses on the faces of the house slaves serving Meriwether's guests. "The visages of the whole group," Kennedy observes, "wore that grave, momentous elongation which is particular to the African face, and which is eminently adapted to express the official care and personal importance of the wearer."[121]

Kennedy's phrenological beliefs also influenced his views on racial advancement. If the intellectual capabilities and other faculties of a race were defined by physical appearance, then these mental attributes would logically be fixed for generations, perhaps forever. Kennedy comes closest to addressing this critical question in the novel's great banquet scene. With his typical ambivalence toward such questions, Kennedy initially hints at some evidence of civilizing progress among Meriwether's slaves, at least in terms of their deportment and manners; it is easy to tell the raw field hand from the venerable house servant. In the end, however, Kennedy dismisses such evidence as a mere "satire" upon all human vanity and posturing. He then proceeds to mock such pretensions on the part of Swallow Barn's staff.

> A bevy of domestics, in every stage of training, attended the table, presenting a lively type of the progress of civilization: the veteran waitingman being well-contrasted with the rude half-monkey, half-boy that seemed to have been for the first time admitted to the parlor; whilst, between these two, were exhibited the successive degrees that mark the advance from the young savage to the sedate and sophisticated image of the old-fashioned negro nobility. It was equal to a gallery of caricatures, a sort of scenic satire upon man in his various stages, with his odd imitativeness illustrated in the broadest lines. Each had added some article of coxcombry to his dress; a pewter buckle fastened to the shirt for a breast-pin; a dingy parti-colored ribbon, ostentatiously displayed across his breast; with one end lodged in his waist coat pocket; or a preposterous cravat girding up an exorbitantly starched shirt collar, that rivaled the driven snow, as it traversed cheeks as black as midnight, and fretted the lower cartilage of a pair of raven-hued ears.[122]

This unrestrained mockery of blacks, who are presumed to imitate white appearance and behavior, took its inspiration largely from minstrelsy. The humor that made minstrelsy so popular was based upon the same premise. Blackened-up white entertainers exaggerated the supposed foppery of black dress and the alleged ludicrousness of black deportment. Dialogue was written and body movements choreographed to communicate ignorance, vanity, and laziness. Outlandish wigs and makeup were used to create foolish, comical stereotypes of the black race.[123]

The first of these black stereotypes was Jim Crow. His character was supposedly based on an old, crippled black man of the same name whom the so-called father of minstrelsy, Thomas Dartmouth Rice, encountered shuffling along the streets of either Cincinnati or Baltimore in 1828. Transposing the old man's shuffle into a set of dance steps and melding Irish ditties with black vernacular and banjo tunes, Rice concocted a new musical form that was an immediate sensation and within a year was being performed before white audiences from Pittsburgh to Philadelphia.[124]

Kennedy was never above participating in the popular culture of his day. He was an avid theatergoer from his earliest years and stood in line with everybody else to see the famous "Siamese Twins" when they visited Baltimore. He would have had difficulty avoiding what became known as the "Jim Crow Extravaganza," when it was being performed in Baltimore and Philadelphia during the late 1820s and early 1830s. In fact, a reference to Thomas Rice's lead character found its way into *Swallow Barn.* At one point in the novel, Meriwether's guests gather around to hear the old slave Carey sing and play the banjo. Kennedy explains that "the old man [was] not a little proud of his minstrelsy." One of the guests requests that Carey play "Jim Crow." Carey cannot accede to this request, of course, because he does not know the song. However, Kennedy evidently did.[125]

The character of Carey presents larger problems than this for his creator. Of Kennedy's black characters, Carey is by far the best developed but does not always seem to be under the author's control. At times, Carey's behavior seems inconsistent with his status as a slave and fluctuates between obsequiousness and rebelliousness. Very possibly, Kennedy miscalculated when he decided to model Meriwether's old slave after Simon Bracebridge's faithful huntsman, Old Christy. Irving's character is looked up to by the other servants at Bracebridge Hall and plays a large part in raising the estate's thoroughbred horses.

Old Christy is, according to Irving, a "professor of equitation" and can be argumentative with his master on the care of these animals or questions relating to their pedigree.[126]

Similarly, Carey considers the blooded horses at Swallow Barn to be "his children" and frequently holds forth on the most obscure details of their lineage. Carey brooks no challenge to his expertise in the care of these animals. Because of his knowledge and expertise, Carey occasionally argues with his master. This habit, Kennedy explains, "begot a familiarity in the old negro which is almost fatal to Meriwether's authority." At one point in the novel, when Meriwether tries to instruct Carey on something having to do with feeding the horses, Carey counters with, "Who sot you up, Master Frank, to tell me how to fodder that 'ere cretur, when I as good as nursed you on my knee?" On another occasion, Carey interrupts Meriwether midsentence to correct him on some fine point of equine history. In the scene where he sings and plays his banjo for the guests at Swallow Barn, Carey goes so far as to poke fun at Ned Hazard's bumbling courtship of Bel Tracy. When Hazard tells him to stop, Carey places his hand over Hazard's heart and responds, "Ah! That makes you sore there, master Ned Hazard."[127]

Throughout *Swallow Barn,* Carey seems to operate in a strange middle ground between independence of spirit and servitude. And, while Kennedy may have intended to portray Carey as a "trickster" slave, it is also possible that his handling of Carey is simply unstable. Carey's behavior fluctuates too wildly between rebelliousness and obsequiousness. After watching Carey poke fun at Ned Hazard, for example, Mark Littleton observes that the old slave sings and plays in a way that "signified his obedience to our orders." After being rewarded for his performance by Harvey Riggs, Carey exclaims, "God bless you, master Harvey, and young masters all!" After one of his arguments with Carey, Frank Meriwether remarks to Mark Littleton that the old slave is "a faithful old cur, too, that licks my hand out of pure honesty." In spite of Carey's frequent assertions of independence, Kennedy repeatedly describes the old slave as "in his place" and, at one point, as "the perfect shadow of his master." During much of the novel, Carey is shown dutifully fulfilling his orders, whether serving at Meriwether's table, cleaning out the family carriage, or tending to some other task assigned to him. Against this backdrop of faithful servitude, Carey's bursts of contentiousness seem daring and even dangerous.[128]

And, yet, in subtle and unintended ways, the figure of Carey disrupts Kennedy's placid portrait of plantation life. During the great banquet scene at Swallow Barn, Carey assumes a haunting presence. As Kennedy allows a soft pastoral haze to invade Meriwether's dining room, obscuring most of the gathered company there, the old slave stands out not just as the unswerving servant he is commonly taken for but as someone at once more noble and slightly foreboding.

> The dining room had for some time past been gradually assuming that soft, mellow, foggy tint which is said by painters to spread such a charm over an Indian-summer landscape. The volumes of smoke rolled majestically across the table, and then rose into the upper air, where they spread themselves out into a rich dun mass, and flung a certain witchery over the scene. The busy riot of revelry seemed to echo through another Cimmerium and the figures of the guests were clad in a spectral obscurity. Motionless, exact and somber as an Egyptian obelisk, old Carey's form was dimly seen relieved against the light of a window, near the end of the table; all the other domestics had fled, and the veteran body-guard alone remained on duty.[129]

As little under his control as Carey, Kennedy's own racial attitudes evade precise definition. Although rooted in powerful historical and contemporary beliefs, these attitudes were unstable at their margins. At times, his prejudice seems tempered by positive memories of black children from his boyhood or by some more recent exposure to dignified adult slaves or free blacks. Perhaps, Kennedy had known someone like Carey, whose racially stigmatized appearance masked but could not conceal the fundamental humanity beneath it.

These unstable racial attitudes are mirrored in the behavior of Ned Hazard. Recalling his time at Mr. Crab's academy in western Virginia, Hazard confesses to having felt a "vagabond fondness" for his black playmates in the area. After leaving the academy, Hazard remembers these playmates as "some of the best friends I have ever parted with." Years later at Swallow Barn, Hazard is in the habit of regaling mixed groups of children with his adventure stories and, when acting out some fearsome detail, describes how they "nestled up together like a group of black and white cherubim." Yet, this same Ned Hazard can be uncaring and callous toward the plantation's black children, as when he organizes them into a degrading entertainment for some bored houseguests. In one of the most disturbing scenes in Kennedy's novel, these poorly clad children grovel amid a pack of dogs for a few tossed coins. Furthermore, while he seems to get along with almost everyone most of the time, Hazard can speak insultingly to Swallow Barn's more adult slaves. He seems comfortable calling the teenage slave Ganymede a "black rascal" to his face and telling Carey, after the old slave has completed a particular task, "Now old gentleman, you have done your duty, so creep back to your kennel." In short, Hazard's attitudes are probably not too dissimilar from those of Kennedy and, when dealing with black characters of any age, are notable for their instability.[130]

Kennedy concludes *Swallow Barn* with a tour of the plantation's slave quarter, referred to in the novel as the "Quarter." This conclusion is entirely consistent with Irving's narrative architecture, which ends with a visit to a gypsy encampment near Bracebridge Hall. Once inside the encampment, Geoffrey Crayon comments on the "sunshiny existence" of the gypsies and envies them for their freedom from "ordinary cares and anxieties." He thinks of the gypsies as "fairies and witches" but is put off by their constant begging for money. Similarly, Mark Littleton notes that the slaves in the Quarter are free from "care and vexation" and prefer lounging about because of their "love of sunshine." He observes that the younger slaves wear a "comic air of deviltry" and notes how many of the older slaves ask for money and other favors.[131]

Still, Kennedy felt the need to supplement Irving's narrative framework with additional material. With this in mind, he returned to his neoclassical roots and, more specifically, to Jonathan Swift's *Gulliver's Travels.* In the final part of that tale, Swift describes Gulliver's visit to a desert island inhabited by two different races, the Houyhnhnms and the Yahoos. Although the former inhabit the bodies of horses, they are highly intelligent and cultivated. The latter, though resembling humans in overall form, move in "the manner of monkeys" and are "the most unteachable of animals." The Yahoos are brown-skinned, have "frizzled" hair, and live in crude huts separated from their betters, the Houyhnhnms.[132]

Taking his lead from Swift, Kennedy routes Meriwether's party through a scenic meadow filled with the plantation's most prized, purebred horses, before visiting the slave quarter. These most beautiful of animals recognize Meriwether and, frolicking playfully around his party, nuzzle the visitors with almost humanlike affection. These animals possess lineage no less noble than that of their owner and, in Kennedy's rendering of them, serve as an equine metaphor of Virginia's elite society: "Altogether, it was a scene of boisterous horse-play, well-befitting the arrogant nature of such licentious, high-blooded, far-descended and riotous young nobility."[133]

Predictably, Kennedy juxtaposes Meriwether's scenic horse pasture and its beautiful beasts with a picture of the Quarter, which is as squalid in its living conditions as its inhabitants are wretched in appearance. Suddenly, the pastoralism that has up until now softened the impression of slave life in the novel falls away. The Quarter consists of scattered "hovels," rudely constructed out of untrimmed logs and mud with "little regard for neatness." The "inmates" of these crude dwellings are mostly children and old men. The children, Kennedy notes, come "in all varieties of grotesque nature from the most knock-kneed to the most bandy-legged." The old men are even more crooked-limbed and pathetic, "with faces shortened as if with draw-strings, noses that seemed to have run to nostril, and with feet of the configuration of mattock." It appears that Kennedy was well along in the construction of this grotesquery, when word of the Nat Turner rebellion caused him to rethink the end of his novel.[134]

The Nat Turner rebellion began at two o'clock on Monday morning, August 22, 1831, when a handful of slaves entered Joseph Travis's farmhouse, not far from the small town of Jerusalem, the administrative seat of Southampton County, Virginia. Turner struck the first blow, wounding but not killing his master. His fellow conspirator Will finished off Travis and then dispatched the farmer's wife and son. Turner took his first life closer to dawn, when he struck down Margaret Whitehead in a nearby field, as she was trying to escape from the rebels. By nine o'clock in the morning, Turner's forces numbered about forty slaves, all armed and mounted. Not until noon was a local official in Jerusalem able to dispatch a rider to Petersburg, some fifty miles away, with an urgent request for help. But, by that time, Turner and his men had invaded approximately fifteen households and slaughtered around sixty white people, most of them women and children.[135]

During that month of August, Kennedy and his wife were vacationing in Berkeley County, Virginia, some two hundred miles north of Jerusalem. In addition to visiting friends and family, Kennedy was trying to finish his novel. Given the poor condition of roads in the state, the first news of the Turner rebellion probably took three or four days to reach him. It would have arrived in the form of distorted but alarming word of mouth.[136]

The first newspaper reports on the rebellion appeared two days after the event and were sketchy, cautionary, and somewhat disbelieving. Not until the end of the week were large numbers of white victims being reported. But, even then, the *Richmond Enquirer* still suspected some kind of exaggeration and stated, "No one has dreamed of any such event in any part of Virginia." However, the *Norfolk Herald,* a newspaper located closer to the scene of the slaughter, reported that at least twenty-five families had been destroyed and that "General Turner" had been routed with about forty of his men. The same newspaper warned ominously that "great indeed will be the dessert of these sable-hearted Africans."[137]

Even though the Nat Turner rebellion lasted only thirty-one hours, it took more than a week for most Virginians to grasp the full extent of the carnage that had been meted out on both whites and blacks in the area around Jerusalem. After several cavalry units converged on the area and armed locals were aroused, more than 120 blacks were killed either because they were thought to be in league with Turner or purely as retribution. At the end of August, a so-called court of oyer and terminer was convened in Jerusalem and sentenced another thirteen blacks to be hanged. Dozens more suspects awaited trial in makeshift jails. Amazingly, Turner himself remained at large.[138]

During the last week of August, rumors circulated that the slave rebellion had not been confined to the area around Jerusalem and that further outbreaks of violence might still occur. Possibly for this reason, Kennedy sold the team and gig with which he and his wife had been touring Virginia and returned to Baltimore by stagecoach. The Kennedys arrived there on the first day of September. Kennedy made no mention of the Turner rebellion in his journal. In fact, he made no journal entries between September 1 and November 19, 1831. On the latter date, Kennedy wrote, "Ever since my return from Virginia until about the 20th of October I was steadily engaged in the second volume of Swallow Barn." On New Year's Eve, 1831, Kennedy's single journal entry read "Finished Swallow Barn."[139]

It is unclear, however, exactly when Kennedy ceased to work on *Swallow Barn.* His brother Andrew did not deliver a transcript of the novel to the Philadelphia publisher, Carey and Lea, until the beginning of February 1832. Negotiations over the terms of publication, conducted by Peter Cruse, took another month, after which Cruse left what appears to have been a final manuscript with Carey and Lea. Kennedy received daily proof sheets from then until the publication of *Swallow Barn* during the middle of May 1832.[140]

This protracted schedule allowed Kennedy ample time to reflect on the dramatic events following the Turner rebellion in the concluding pages of *Swallow Barn.* The first of these events was the capture of Turner on October 30, 1831.

Prior to being tried and hanged, Turner was interviewed by a local lawyer named Thomas C. Gray. After being used as evidence in the trial, the transcript of the interview was rushed into publication. Entitled *The Confessions of Nat Turner,* Gray's pamphlet contained a considerable amount of background on Turner as well as details about the planning and conduct of the slave uprising. Published in late November 1831 by the Baltimore firm of Lucas and Deaver, Gray's *Confessions* went on to sell somewhere between forty to fifty thousand copies.[141]

In his *Confessions,* Gray positioned Turner to serve both as a scapegoat for southern slaveholders and a hero for northern abolitionists. On the one hand, Turner was described as a literate and abstemious slave who claimed to have been divinely inspired. On the other, he was a "complete fanatic," capable of "fiend-like barbarity." What is more, Gray's account hovered somewhere between fact and fiction. It was attacked as contrived and stylized. Some of Gray's facts were wrong, and his rendering of Turner's speech seemed too articulate for a slave. Yet there was enough of Turner's voice in *Confessions* to make it irresistible reading. The importance of Gray's work, then, was not only its wide readership but also its depiction of Turner as a half-real, half-fictionalized character. None of this was lost on Kennedy as he was completing *Swallow Barn.*[142]

Gray's disturbing portrait of Turner added to the maelstrom of public debate following the Southampton uprising. If he accomplished nothing else, Turner showed white southerners that they needed to take their slaves more seriously. The men Kennedy depicted lounging around the grounds of Swallow Barn and Thomas Rice mimicked shuffling about on stage could kill. In this way, the Turner rebellion was transformative. It impelled whites in Virginia and elsewhere in the South to look more closely at blacks living among them and make some decisions about their future relationship.

"Who are these people?" one member of the Virginia legislature asked. A Richmond newspaper editor answered that the state's slaves were nothing short of "monsters" and compared their ferocity to that of blood-thirsty wolves falling upon a flock of sheep and Indians decimating white settlements on the frontier. "The death-like apathy of the negro," another journalist observed, had suddenly been illuminated for what it really was. These were "not an ignorant herd of Africans" but rather "an active and intelligent class." One newspaper editorial urged immediate legislative action for the safety of future generations of white Virginians. "This dark population is growing upon us," the writer warned. He prayed that his grandchildren would not have to "brave the storm."[143]

Others disagreed with this assessment of the state's race problem and what should be done about it. They maintained that Turner was an aberration. Such a catastrophe could be avoided in the future, these voices argued, with legislation curtailing black education and religious assembly. "Our slave population is not only a happy one," one planter insisted, "but is contented, peaceful and harmless."[144]

The main forum for this debate was the Virginia House of Delegates, called into special session by Gov. John Floyd in response to the Southampton uprising. This session commenced in early December 1831 and lasted three months. It was broadly hoped that some meaningful legislation addressing the state's race problem would result. After all, Governor Floyd himself seemed to favor some form of gradual emancipation. So, too, did many non-slave-owning delegates in the western part of the state. Furthermore, members of a younger, more liberal generation of Virginians such as William Roane, the grandson of Patrick Henry, and Thomas Jefferson Randolph, the grandson of Thomas Jefferson, had recently won seats in the legislature. In anticipation of something eventful, spectators packed the galleries of the state house in Richmond, a building designed by Jefferson. Local newspaper coverage was close and continuous. The entire South became fixated on the proceedings.[145]

The ensuing discussions regarding race and slavery were frank and wide ranging. Slavery was identified as an "evil" by some of the delegates, not for the cruelties it imposed on slaves but for its effect on the work ethic and morals of whites. Slavery had destroyed Virginia's yeomanry and artisan class, these delegates argued, and had retarded the state's economic progress. Early in the session, Thomas Jefferson Randolph presented a plan for compensated emancipation followed by African colonization. The plan would be postponed until 1840, be self-funding, and rid Virginia of its black population by 1860. The state's two major newspapers endorsed the plan.

In spite of these encouraging signs, the deeply embedded conservatism of the Old Dominion's slave-owning class and the obstructive influence of its states' rights men frustrated any attempts at reform. Shortly before the beginning of the session, John C. Calhoun visited Governor Floyd. Calhoun appears to have convinced Floyd that emancipation ran counter to the interests of the South. In his opening address to the legislature, the governor made no mention of emancipation, placed responsibility for Virginia's economic problems on the protective tariff, and blamed northern abolitionists for the Southampton insurrection. During the session that followed, the House of Delegates defeated three antislavery motions, including the Randolph plan. In late January 1832, the legislature narrowly agreed to a statement calling for some future consideration of emancipation, once public opinion could be more thoroughly tested. The only measures it eventually passed had to do with better policing of blacks, tighter restrictions on their education and religious practices, and a watered-down budget for the colonization of free blacks.[146]

There would be no further discussion of emancipation in the Old Dominion. Delay, the refuge of the compromisers who held the swing votes in the legislature, proved fatal for the antislavery movement. Virginia's proslavery forces needed little time to reset their doctrine and close off further debates. Before the year was over, at Governor Floyd's request, Thomas R. Dew, a professor at William and Mary College, codified this new doctrine in his *Review of the Debates of the Virginia Legislature.* Among Dew's main points were that any plan for emancipation and removal of Virginia's slaves was impractical and that there was no evidence that slavery exerted deleterious effects on either white morals or the state's economy. Virginia's flagging economy, according to Dew, was the fault of the tariff. Slavery, he insisted, had been forced on Virginia during the colonial period, and nothing in either the Old or New Testament called for ending it *once introduced.* Slavery was as good as permanent and would last at least a hundred years. Furthermore, slaves were a legitimate form of property, protected by both state and federal law. Most important for the proslavery cause, however, was Dew's assertion that slavery was good for the slave. History had shown, he insisted, that slavery was "perhaps the principle means of impelling forward the civilization of mankind." Because it recast slavery as historically defensible and morally justifiable, Dew's *Review* became a watershed document for the southern proslavery cause.[147]

Although Kennedy's *Swallow Barn* reached booksellers a few months before Dew's *Review,* both responded in different ways to what had happened in the Old Dominion. While the authors shared some similarities in viewpoint, they differed on the important questions of slavery's fundamental legitimacy and long-term viability. Unlike Dew, Kennedy was not a Virginian and had no intellectual commitment to slavery. Nor did he have a material stake in the institution. Rather, Kennedy lived in an economically diverse, urban center of the borderland and hoped for a timely, orderly transition by Virginians, as well as by his fellow Marylanders, out of slavery. Unfortunately, like most Americans at the time, Kennedy had no idea how and when such a feat could be accomplished.

Forced by recent events to deal more explicitly with the issue of slavery, Kennedy needed to integrate a discussion of it into *Swallow Barn* and, more important, decide what to say about it. Given the novel's narrative flow and late stage of development, Frank Meriwether's tour of the Quarter with Mark Littleton offered the best opportunity to take up the subject. Littleton prepares the ground for Meriwether's exposition by describing Swallow Barn's slaves as "comfortable and contented" and their master as an "intelligent slave holder." According to Littleton, Meriwether is such a "kind and considerate master" that he won't entrust his slaves to an overseer. Meriwether visits the Quarter often, dispensing gifts and necessities to alleviate the slaves' wants and increase their comforts. He is in the habit of paying his slaves for certain commodities raised in their gardens and conducts a kind of "high court of appeal" to settle disputes among them. Impressed with these enlightened practices, Littleton asks Meriwether for his thoughts on slavery.[148]

"This topic," Meriwether responds, "has grown to possess a fearful interest of late." What worries him most, however, is not the substance of the slavery debate but its effect on Virginia's slave population. Consistent with the belief that the recent uprising, and slave discontent in general, has been provoked from sources outside the Old Dominion, Meriwether condemns such efforts to "inflame the ignorant minds of these people." As to whether slavery as it exists in Virginia *is* an evil, Meriwether hedges. He admits that slavery "is theoretically and morally wrong" but adds that "it may be made to appear wrong in all its modifications." After all, slavery was forced on Virginia during a much earlier period and was done so "without our agency." In the present circumstances, Meriwether explains, Virginia's slaveholders are discharging a kind of sacred duty to their slaves: "the only duty that is left to us is to administer wholesome laws for their government, and to make their servitude as tolerable to them as we can." In other words, the state's slave owners have been placed in their roles involuntarily and are meeting their obligations as best they can.[149]

"As to the evils they suffer," Meriwether observes, "I do not believe in them." The slave population of the state neither works particularly hard nor lacks the basic comforts of life. "They are required to do less work than any other laborers in society," Meriwether argues, and "in *their* estimation of comforts [are] more comfortable than the tillers of the soil of other nations" (emphasis Kennedy's). In a convoluted line of reasoning, Meriwether goes on to explain that, because slave owners do not perform much physical work themselves, they are "inclined to regulate their demands upon others by their own standards."[150]

No less strained is Meriwether's handling of slave punishment. To start with, he holds that his fellow slave owners are "men of kind and humane tempers." Of course, Virginia's slaves must occasionally be punished for misdemeanors, like offenders in any society. The only difference, Meriwether insists, is "the mode of inflicting punishment." Whereas a criminal in New York is sent to prison in chains by the authorities, an errant slave in Virginia is whipped by an overseer. Even though the extent of the punishment is probably the same, Meriwether points out, the slave owner is vilified by northerners for his alleged cruelty. Before leaving the subject of slave punishment, Meriwether does raise the possibility of legislation to protect slaves from abusive owners. Still, he foresees little need for these laws in his own neighborhood.[151]

As for the future of slavery, Meriwether predicts its eventual end but stipulates that any initiatives in that direction must come from slave owners. "Whenever emancipation of slaves, or the abolition of slavery, is to be required," he cautions, "the requisition must come from the slave-holding states themselves." For Virginians, he adds, the issue of slavery is not an "abstract question" but one with serious social and economic consequences. "Our lives, fortunes, families—even our commonwealth—are put at hazard of this resolve." For these reasons, "violent removal" and "general emancipation" are not workable solutions to the slavery problem. However, if a way can be found to abolish slavery, he declares, "I would do it."[152]

At this critical point, Meriwether's exposition breaks down. Having nowhere else to go, Kennedy seeks cover behind the chivalric veil that has masked the grim reality of slavery throughout the novel. In a loose and jocular tone, Meriwether says he wants to establish a "feudatory" at Swallow Barn. He likens the slaves who would live there as a "class of privileged serfs," enjoying "manorial jurisdictions" over their lands. These slaves would pay him an annual tithe but govern themselves according to their own code of laws. Such a feudal system, he explains, worked well "in parts of Germany." When Littleton asks Meriwether if a slave like Carey would trade his current privileges for those of such a system, the two men enjoy a hearty laugh.[153]

Kennedy realized, of course, that recent events in the Old Dominion were no laughing matter. Newspaper descriptions of white retribution on the state's slaves following the Turner uprising were horrific. One Richmond paper deplored the "barbarity" of vengeance on innocent blacks. In Baltimore, *Niles' Weekly Review* described widespread slave "executions" without trial. No one knew what toll armed whites had already taken, and extremists were calling for a campaign of "extermination."[154]

With these events as backdrop, Kennedy introduced the story of the good slave "Abe" near the end of *Swallow Barn*. The seemingly random insertion of the story is not what makes it so awkward. After all, it is only one of several interpolated tales Kennedy drops into the novel from out of nowhere. Rather, it is the jarring shift in Kennedy's attitude toward blacks, his sudden and unexpected sympathy for them, which causes the story to feel so out of place. It is as if the humanity buried in the wretchedness of his black characters has broken free and commandeered Kennedy as its literary servant.

> My purpose is to bring to the view of my reader an exhibition of natural forms in which the passions are displayed in those lowest and humblest of the departments of human society, and to represent truly a class of people to whom justice has seldom been done, and who possess many points of character well calculated to win them a kind and amicable judgment from the world. They are a neglected race, who seem to have been excluded from the pale of human sympathy, from mistaken opinions of their quality, no less from the lowliness of their position.[155]

The story of Abe appears in a chapter entitled "A Negro Mother." By relying on Littleton's firsthand observations and retelling of what Meriwether has previously explained to him, Kennedy tries to push the novel's narrative voice onto Littleton. As a first-time visitor from the North, Littleton is depicted as an objective, credible observer of plantation life. This narrative guise collapses, however, as Littleton analyzes the "negro character" in too much depth and subtlety for a newcomer. Clearly, the nuanced prejudices that undergird the chapter belong to its author.

In calling attention to "one of the most remarkable features in these negro clans," for example, Kennedy (speaking through Littleton) notes that most blacks are rooted to the land on which they have grown up. This "strong attachment to the places connected with their earlier associations," Littleton observes, is "what in phrenology is called inhabitiveness." When explaining the unwavering devotion of Abe's mother, Lucy, to her delinquent son, Kennedy attributes such apparently mindless loyalty to the "unreasoning instincts of the animal sway of the human mind, in its uneducated condition." Lucy's tireless industry and clever resourcefulness in preparing Abe's clothing before he goes off to sea are indicative of this same instinct. "She provided for him, as for a sickly child," Kennedy writes at his most saccharine, "what little delicacies her affluence afforded; and, with a furtive industry, plied her needle through the livelong night, in making up, from scanty materials at her command, such articles of dress as might be found or fancied useful to him, in the uncertain changes that awaited him." Even through Kennedy regards these admirable aspects of Lucy's character as largely instinctive and somewhat overwrought versus white norms, he nonetheless implies that they signal an underlying stratum of humanity within her.[156]

In describing Lucy's devotion to her wayward son and her slide into madness following his disappearance at sea, Kennedy employs a cloying sentimental tone found nowhere else in *Swallow Barn.* Likewise, the exchange between Meriwether and Lucy is overwrought with tears and tender words of comfort. Kennedy uses the visit to Lucy's cottage to elicit the reader's sympathy for Lucy's pathetic condition and to demonstrate Meriwether's remarkable kindness to her. After all, the history of Lucy and Abe, melancholy though it is, would not have been possible without the benevolence of their white masters. Years before, Walter Hazard had repaid the wartime loyalty of Abe's father, Luke, by training Luke and Lucy's children as skilled artisans and house servants at Swallow Barn. By the time Meriwether had taken over the plantation, their youngest son, Abe, had become a lawless slave in the neighborhood. It was Meriwether who sent Abe to sea rather than selling him South. Once rehabilitated, Meriwether expected Abe to return to Swallow Barn. "Walter Hazard could never bear the idea of disposing of any of his negroes," Kennedy explains, "and when Meriwether came to the estate, he was even more strongly imbued with the same repugnance." Clearly, Kennedy thought that respecting the integrity of the slave family in the novel might help disarm some of slavery's harshest critics. More generally, his sentimental portrayal of these intertwining families, one white and one black, is meant to show how a kind of interracial mutuality allows the slave system, despite its imperfections, to work.[157]

Such a portrayal of race relations on the plantation was, of course, an illusion. To make it even remotely plausible, Kennedy had to abandon the gentle, satirical style with which he began the novel and turn to the exaggerated sentimentality of the Lucy episode and the romantic fantasy of the story of Abe. Without such a stylistic shift, Abe's extraordinary feats and, more important, his motivation to perform them would not have a modicum of credibility.[158]

Kennedy makes it clear that Abe is an exceptional slave. According to Kennedy's description, Abe is blessed with "uncommonly symmetrical proportions for the race to which he belonged" and is missing "the flat nose and broad lip of his tribe." He is shrewd, passionate, and courageous, possessing a restlessness that rejects the "monotonous avocations" of slave life. As a slave with a romantic heart, Abe's restless inclinations led him astray. Surrounding himself with "profligate menials" from neighboring plantations, Abe and his "band of out-lying negroes" sequestered themselves in a nearby swamp and "annoyed the vicinity by nocturnal incursions of the most lawless character." Compared to the tranquility of the novel's foregoing narrative, only marginally disrupted by Carey's occasional impertinences, Abe's blatant transgressions severely undermine Kennedy's portrait of the pastoral plantation.[159]

There can be little doubt that Abe is meant to be a counterpoint to Nat Turner. Given the overwhelming nature of the events that happened as he was finishing his novel, Kennedy felt compelled to respond to the Turner rebellion. The good slave Abe is Kennedy's narrative foil for Turner. With a handful of black mariners, Abe, in a redemptive act, rescues a crippled brig caught in a deadly gale on the Chesapeake. Whereas Turner's men had taken dozens of white lives on their brutal rampage, Abe and his slave crew sacrifice themselves to save a group of white sailors. Before departing on his fateful mission, Abe declares before his master "I always obey orders!"[160]

Though he expressed little concern for blacks throughout most of his novel, Kennedy believed that whites in the Old Dominion needed to take a calmer, more balanced view of them after the Turner uprising. In order to make his case, Kennedy must adjust his own prejudices to convey a more positive view of the slave. To help him do this, Kennedy remolds Abe's carriage and physiognomy to seem less stereotypical and gives him a romantic nature in order to excuse his delinquencies as a slave. Even so, Kennedy's praise for Abe's accomplishments seems reluctant, ingenuous, and, at times, back-handed. For example, Abe's success as a sailor is due to the way life at sea "works marvelously upon the heedless and irresponsible temperament of the negro." Similarly, Kennedy credits Abe's courage to "that spirit of rivalry that belongs to even the lowest classes of human beings." Where he cannot bend his prejudices to the narrative, Kennedy buries them in romantic sentiment and epic hyperbole.[161]

One of the white sailors watching Abe depart on his mission remarks, "That negro has a great deal of good and bad in him—but the good has the upper hand." In the end, Kennedy asks Virginians to take a similar view of their slaves. For every Turner living among them, Kennedy seems to be saying, there might be an Abe. Although driven by the wrenching events of recent months and carefully hedged, such a concession is remarkable, coming from Kennedy. What is more, Kennedy provides an extraordinary epitaph for Abe and his crew near the end of the novel. Both its content and tone contrast sharply with what has gone before.

> I might stop to compare this act of an humble and unknown negro upon the Chesapeake with the many similar passages in the lives of heroes whose names have been preserved fresh in the verdure of history, and who have won their immortality upon less noble feats than this; but History is a step-mother, and gives the bauble fame to her own children, with such favoritism as she lists, overlooking many a goodly portion of the family of her husband Time. Still, it is a gallant thing, and worthy of a better chronicler than I, to see this leader and his little band—the children of a despised stock—swayed by a noble emulation to relieve the distressed; and (what the fashion of the world will deem a higher glory) impelled by that love of daring which the romancers call chivalry—throwing themselves upon the unruly waves of winter, and flying, on the wing of the storm, into the profound dark abyss of ocean, when all his terrors were gathered in their most hideous forms; when the spirit of ill shrieked in the blast, and thick night, dreary with unusual horrors, was falling close around them; when old mariners grew pale with the thought of the danger, and the wisest counselled the adventurers against the certain doom that hung upon their path:—I say, it was a gallant sight to see such heroism shining out in an humble and unlettered slave of the Old Dominion.[162]

By its publication in May 1832, *Swallow Barn* had grown into a sprawling, disjointed novel full of puzzling inconsistencies and contradictions. In the end, the novel foundered as a coherent literary work because its detached and genial style, largely borrowed from Washington Irving, was incompatible with

Kennedy's didactic nature, ingrained racial prejudices, and emerging Whig partisanship. Furthermore, the tumultuous events that occurred during the writing of *Swallow Barn*—the rise of Jacksonian democracy, the emergence of the nullification movement, and, most significant, the outbreak of the Turner rebellion—badly disrupted the course of Kennedy's narrative.[163]

Still, the loose structure and disparate content of *Swallow Barn* allowed literary reviewers to find whatever they wanted in its pages. One of the novel's critics, writing for the prestigious *North American Review,* recognized Kennedy's neoclassical roots and suggested he devote his talents to the pursuit of "polite literature." While the *Baltimore American* thanked Kennedy for avoiding the "excesses" and "extremes of excitement" of the romantic novelists, the *New York Review* singled out the chapter on Abe and Lucy for its "pathos and power." The story of Abe, the latter critic wrote, was "not surpassed by anything that had yet appeared in the literature of our country."[164]

Several reviewers saw *Swallow Barn* as groundbreaking for American letters. They were especially impressed with the novel's generous use of domestic source material. Up to this time, only Washington Irving, James Fenimore Cooper, and a few other writers had drawn their inspiration from the country's unique social culture and magnificent landscape. With this in mind, the *Baltimore American* applauded Kennedy's attention "to characters which we recognize as familiar and constant, to manners such as we know them to be, and, above all, to scenery and customs of our country." In a similar vein, the *New York Review* observed that *Swallow Barn*'s distinguishing feature was "its pure Americanism."[165]

Given his vantage point from the borderland and the divisive political events occurring around him, Kennedy seemed less interested in elevating the country's patriotism than preserving national unity. In a letter written in early 1832 to his publisher Henry Carey, Kennedy expressed hope that *Swallow Barn* would help rebuild national solidarity. In his reply to Kennedy, Carey reiterated the same desire for the novel. "If it should produce such a feeling as you desire," Carey wrote, "you will have rendered a great service to the nation. Each portion of the Union looks with a feeling of dislike towards the other, when it requires only to know them better to see the admirable qualities in every portion. The Yankee dislikes the Virginian and the Virginian despises the Yankee, when a stranger would find good reason to admire both." The best way to reduce sectional tension, both Kennedy and Carey seemed to be saying, was to promote better understanding between the sections and encourage patience and compromise regarding the issue of slavery.[166]

Not everybody agreed with Kennedy and his publisher on these issues or reviewed *Swallow Barn* favorably. The *New England Magazine,* for example, came away from the novel convinced that the author meant to "show up" the Old Dominion's planter class with his satire of it. Virginia planters were, the magazine concluded, "conceited, pompous, ignorant and dogmatic" and "the most ordinary, trifling, useless generation the world ever saw." Frank Meriwether, the magazine observed, had little better to do than "to receive visits, to attend courts, and to watch the multiplication of his horses and negroes." For those predisposed to think the worst of them, Kennedy's novel was a damning indictment of Virginia's slave owners.[167]

One of the most puzzling reactions to *Swallow Barn* came from William Wirt, Kennedy's mentor, to whom the novel was dedicated. In a May 1832 letter to his friend and confidant, Dabney Carr, Wirt expressed his embarrassment at the novel's dedication and severely criticized the work. This "*sort* of novel," Wirt said, was written in a "light, trifling, fantastic style—but not deep . . . solemnizing." It seems Wirt had lost his sense of humor by the time *Swallow Barn* appeared. He was over seventy and would be dead in two years. He had spent most of his life building a reputation in his adopted state of Virginia, currying favor with its elite families, and dreaming of one day owning a plantation. Certainly, Kennedy's satire of life in the Old Dominion, not to mention his outright mockery of the state's political and economic institutions, did not sit well with Wirt. Nor did the character of Philly Wart, while affectionately rendered, flatter a man who took himself so seriously. Because Wirt expressed himself to Carr in confidence, it is unlikely Kennedy ever knew his mentor's low opinion of *Swallow Barn.*[168]

The majority of the public who read Kennedy's novel did so for entertainment. For them, he includes a postscript tying up the novel's loose plot-ends. Ned Hazard and Bel Tracy are finally married. Isaac Tracy suffers from boredom now that there is no Apple-pie dispute. As expected, Toll Hedges descends further into dissipation. Philly Wart is elected to the state legislature. Yet, the larger issues that Kennedy struggled with over the course of the novel, those dealing with race and slavery, defy such tidy resolution. Granted, there are *indications* of what might be done about them. The principle of compromise is amply celebrated in the Apple-pie settlement, and Lucretia Meriwether's textile works suggest the possibility of southern industrialization. Even though his ideas for abolishing slavery are altogether fantastic, Frank Meriwether at least acknowledges its moral wrong and predicts that it will end one day. Even Abe's removal from Swallow Barn by sea hints at some future colonization scheme.[169]

Still, *Swallow Barn*'s inconclusiveness regarding the problems of race and slavery haunts the novel. This inability to arrive at an even partial resolution was attributable to Kennedy's precarious location in the borderland and his nascent Whiggery. Though fundamentally opposed to slavery, Kennedy's morally didactic and economically progressive impulses were hampered by his deeply ingrained racial prejudices and social conservatism.

Ironically, at the moment of its birth, Whig culture was already signaling the fatal indecisiveness that would cause its demise in just two decades. Nowhere is this more apparent than in *Swallow Barn.* Kennedy would sidestep the issues of race and slavery in his next two novels but would return to them in the 1851 edition of *Swallow Barn,* just as the Whig Party and its revered principle of compromise were collapsing.

CHAPTER FOUR

Tippecanoe and *Horse-Shoe* Too

After weeks of unusual rain and chill, the Fourth of July, 1840, was splendid. Church bells rang, cannons boomed, and Baltimoreans gathered outdoors to celebrate the holiday. The more sedate citizenry made its way to the rural crossroads of Greenwood, where the Temperance Society and the Sunday-School Association sponsored a joint picnic. Those desiring more exciting fare attended one of several "military movements," where the Independent Greys, Maryland Cadets, or German Guards showed off their precision drills. Most ardent Democrats and Whigs celebrated separately, the former at Fair Mount and the latter at Bladensburg. At both locations, celebrants gave speeches, drank toasts, sang songs, and listened to the reading of the Declaration of Independence.[1]

Newly extended railroad spurs and faster steamships allowed some townspeople to venture further afield, to more inland venues or those across the Chesapeake Bay. John Pendleton Kennedy took the steamship *Maryland* over to Cambridge on the Eastern Shore. He then rode by carriage with a few other Whig operatives to the small community of Barren Springs, not far from Vienna. In a large open field, more than a thousand people had assembled to hear a marathon debate between the Democrats and the Whigs. The two parties were hotly contesting the presidency, as well as seats in Congress and the local legislature, in the forthcoming November elections. The atmosphere at the event was part patriotic festival and part sporting event. Excitement ran high. "We spoke until dark," Kennedy wrote his wife Elizabeth, "alternating—we getting the decided advantage over our adversaries." After arguing Whig doctrine for hours before a noisy crowd, Kennedy said he was "as hoarse as a frog."[2]

Although it also took place on the Fourth of July, the debate at Barren Springs differed in important ways from the one depicted in the landing episode of *Swallow Barn.* Kennedy described the Whig speakers at Barren Springs as nothing short of "eloquent." By the summer of 1840, he and other Whig leaders had honed their arguments. In their view, President Andrew Jackson's misguided policies regarding the tariff, the currency, and banking had caused the Panic of 1837 and a depression that still plagued the nation. Even worse, Whigs argued, Democratic abuses of executive power and patronage had undermined the health of the Republic. The Whigs promised to sweep away what they claimed was the corrupt and incompetent administration of Martin Van Buren, Jackson's successor, and replace it with morally based, economically progressive, and "disinterested" political leadership.

Still some aspects of the Barren Springs debate were evocative of the landing episode in *Swallow Barn.* By the summer of 1840, Whig rallies had developed a reputation for being raucous, boisterous events. The Barren Springs debate was no exception. An event of its size attracted men little better than Sandy Walker and Miles Rutherford. Because they voted, such men were welcome in the ranks of the Whig Party. Party leaders, while they may have had a few eloquent moments at Barren Springs, usually eschewed high-toned rhetoric and chose themes that appealed to the common man. The party's repeated references to Jackson's seemingly authoritarian behavior and to Van Buren's reputedly aristocratic tastes resonated with these voters.[3]

Kennedy's political and novelistic writings during the 1830s and early 1840s provide unique insights into this developing political culture. These writings explain how the Whig Party co-opted the democratizing spirit of American politics from the Jacksonians and went on to win the watershed election of 1840. The Whig Party's fruitful engagement with the common man was symbolized by its presidential candidate William Henry Harrison, who underwent a process of social leveling to become "Old Tippecanoe," the rugged Indian fighter who had allegedly lived most of his life in a log cabin. In his second novel *Horse-Shoe Robinson,* Kennedy delineates his protagonist of the same name, an honest but illiterate Revolutionary soldier, in similar fashion. So, too, the novel anticipates the Whig Party's recruitment of women into its cause. The novel could easily have been named for its resolute heroine, Mildred Lindsay. In his third novel, *Rob of The Bowl,* Kennedy projects deeply held Whig beliefs regarding social order and wise governance onto the town of St. Mary's in colonial Maryland. In Kennedy's hands, St Mary's becomes a kind of Whig utopia. Both *Horse-Shoe Robinson* and *Rob of The Bowl,* published in 1835 and 1838, respectively, bear the unmistakable imprint of Kennedy's Whiggery. By the election of 1840, better known as the "Log-Cabin Campaign," Kennedy's political and literary pursuits become comingled in *Quodlibet,* his devastating satire of Jacksonian Democracy.[4]

His second and third novels also reflect Kennedy's borderland perspective. The setting of *Horse-Shoe Robinson* is the internecine middle ground of Virginia and the Carolinas during the Revolutionary War. Similarly, *Rob of The Bowl* takes place during the early religious confrontations between Catholic and Protestant Marylanders. Standing astride the two great rival sections, Kennedy understood better than most writers the tensions inherent in such contested geography, past and present.

Remarkably, Kennedy's literary and political careers took off simultaneously. Within a few weeks of *Swallow Barn*'s publication, Kennedy dined first with Henry Clay and then with Washington Irving. Although he had used the pseudonym Mark Littleton, Kennedy was widely recognized as the author of the strange new novel about the Old Dominion. During a visit to Philadelphia, Kennedy noted with satisfaction that everyone was "making a great parade" about *Swallow Barn.* During gathering at James Madison's Montpelier estate, the ex-president questioned Kennedy's friend John Latrobe about the novel's author.[5]

But it was his engagement with the tariff that propelled Kennedy into national politics. A year and a half after the publication of his "Mephistopheles" tariff pamphlet and six months before the appearance of *Swallow Barn,* Kennedy addressed the Friends of Domestic Industry in New York City. This important tariff convention took place in late October 1831 and drew over five hundred delegates from as far away as Pittsburgh. Powerful manufacturing interests and their tariff allies were reacting to the demands by southern states' rights men and northern free-trade Democrats for tariff reductions. It seemed possible that the federal government might accede to these demands.[6]

The most vehement opponents of the tariff were the South Carolina "nullifiers." By 1831, the nullification movement dominated the state's politics and was gaining national attention. Led by radicals such as Governor James Hamilton and Congressman George McDuffie, the movement had elided itself with other regional causes such as opposition to internal improvements and, after the Turner rebellion and Virginia slavery debate, the defense of slavery. Under pressure from his home state, Senator John C. Calhoun issued his Fort Hill Letter, declaring his support for the radical nullifiers and sacrificing any future chance at the presidency. As the nullifiers grew more strident, Congress and the Jackson administration signaled a willingness to reduce those duties the nullifiers found most onerous.[7]

Kennedy delivered several major addresses before pro-tariff industry groups during the 1830s. His presentation to the Friends of Domestic Industry was quite typical of them. In predictable fashion, Kennedy drew on his sense of nationalism in calling attention to the country's still vulnerable defenses. He recalled the nation's disastrous lack of preparedness during its second war with England. "Our armies went to the frontiers clothed in the fabrics of the enemy," he reminded his audience. The country had survived that contest but might not be so fortunate next time. Unless it built up its industrial infrastructure, Kennedy warned, the United States might "cease to be an independent nation." Just as predictably, he noted that such an industrial infrastructure was needed to create a diversified economy and generate a vibrant internal commerce, which, in turn, would unite the sections of the country in "bonds stronger than any political ties." Ironically, Calhoun had made the same argument for internal improvements a decade earlier.[8]

Kennedy described such a diversified economy in glowing terms. If achieved, it would have an immense hygienic effect on the nation's well-being. It would allow intensive commercial reciprocation between its various sectors. Urban manufacturing centers would purchase foodstuffs and raw cotton from agricultural areas. In exchange, domestically manufactured tools, textiles, and other finished goods would be shipped back to farms and plantations. All classes of labor would find gainful employment. As this exchange became more integrated and harmonious, internal commerce would bring the nation together in mutual economic interests and ensure economic and political independence for generations to come.[9]

For nascent Whigs like Kennedy, this idealized economic equilibrium was not too different from the perfectly balanced social character into which they had endeavored to mold themselves. Bringing the nation's economy into such harmonious working order would be like gaining control of one's own mental faculties in order to realize their full potential. It was only natural for Kennedy to project his personal strategy for self-improvement on to the nation's economy.

The great enabler of this fully diversified economy was, of course, domestic manufacturing. As in his "Mephistopheles" pamphlet, Kennedy described how manufacturing brought new life to moribund villages and animated economically stagnant areas of the country. "A rapid increase in population, dwellings, culture, of the comforts of life and of the value of property, wherever manufactures prevail," he declared, "bespeak their capacity to diffuse happiness and wealth." For economic progressives like Kennedy, industrialization possessed an irresistible attraction because of what they saw as its almost magical transformative power.[10]

Unquestionably, Kennedy's faith in American industry and his advocacy for its protection were genuine and heartfelt. After all, he had railed against the "invasion" of British goods in his "Swiss Traveller" essays and vigorously supported the incorporation of local manufacturing enterprises in the Maryland House of Delegates. Moreover, his involvement with his father-in-law's cotton-spinning factory deepened Kennedy's commitment to manufacturing and its protection. Edward Gray had benefitted enormously from the tariffs of 1824 and 1828, which imposed high duties on imported cotton cloth and more or less guaranteed his prosperity. Not only did Kennedy serve as Gray's legal counsel and tariff publicist, but he also looked after the factory when Gray was away for extended periods. During one of these absences, Kennedy wrote his father-in-law that "The mill runs on first rate." While at times naïve about the promise of manufacturing, Kennedy seems to have had a firsthand knowledge of the factory floor.[11]

Of course, not everyone living in the 1830s agreed with Kennedy's paean to industrialization. Many greeted the so-called Age of Machinery with suspicion and fear. In America's crowded industrial centers, labor agitators voiced concerns about the poor working conditions and low wages of factory workers. In Boston, Seth Luther pointed out that underage factory workers were being denied an education and that female mill operatives were being exploited by being made to work long hours for low pay. In New York, Thomas Skidmore complained that factory workers could not make enough to feed their families. In New York and Baltimore, the Workingmen's Party grew strong enough to challenge the Democratic establishment. By 1833, the Baltimore branch of the Workingmen's Party had its own newspaper and elected two delegates to the state legislature.[12]

Agrarians from the South added their voices to this anti-industrial chorus. Many Old Republicans echoed Thomas Jefferson's plea that "our work-shops remain in Europe." These agriculturally oriented conservatives were not only suspicious of the entrepreneurial ethos of America's rising industrialists but also resentful of northern economic influence over their region. Taking their lead from the radical nullifiers, these southerners were among the most vocal advocates of low tariffs and free trade with England. The irony of all this was that it had largely been the tripling of cotton exports during the early 1830s, to over $70 million annually, that had paid for America's great leap in factory building. In short, the bankers and shippers of New York City had creamed off enough profit from southern planters to finance the growth of northern industry.[13]

For most Americans, however, the pace and scope of the nation's industrialization was so impressive that it was easy to overlook its social costs. Even President Jackson, visiting the Merrimack Company during his 1833 tour of New England, was so taken with the technical innovations he was shown that he paid scant attention to the female operatives working nearby. Others simply denied there were any social costs connected to the country's industrial development. During an 1830 Fourth of July celebration at the Lowell factory, Massachusetts governor Edward Everett claimed that America's industrial revolution bore no resemblance whatsoever to the "infernal mills of Europe." American capital and labor, he declared, constituted "one great party, one comprehensive society." Between the two, Everett boasted, there existed a "holy alliance."[14]

In his address before the Friends of Domestic Industry, Kennedy went out of his way to defend the dignity of the factory worker. "We have no class in America corresponding with the operatives, the human machines, of Europe," he told his listeners. "Labor is not with us," he continued, "the mere instrument of capital." Rather, the industrial worker was "an intelligent, active, principled partner and sharer in the increase of wealth." Fulsome praise for the American worker was becoming a major component of industrial promotion and would soon find a place in emerging Whig doctrine.[15]

Kennedy reserved his most powerful rhetoric for those he believed posed an imminent threat to American manufacturing. "Aversion to manufactures has engendered, of late, bitter local prejudices in parts of the States in which they do not flourish," he warned his audience. He rejected the imputation by southern free traders that the morals of northern manufacturing towns were lower than those of other communities. Furthermore, southern demands for lower tariffs were hypocritical, he insisted, given the high levels of protection the section enjoyed on commodities such as indigo and sugar. More serious still, the threat of nullification might derail the nation's developing economy and posed a danger to the Union. In Kennedy's view, nullification equaled treason.[16]

Much as he would in his second novel, *Horse-Shoe Robinson,* Kennedy implied that the southerners were repeat offenders in their betrayal of American interests in the face of British military and economic hegemony. "It is the cotton-growing States," Kennedy declared, "who would subvert this prosperity and lay us *once more* before the power of our rival" (emphasis added). Congress should ignore southern intimidation and uphold the protective tariff. Failure to do so would expose American industry to "the overwhelming force of English capital and skill." In short, Kennedy's animus toward South Carolina rivaled that which he felt for Great Britain, and he equated southern attitudes toward national security in the 1830s with the section's wavering loyalty during the Revolution.[17]

At the conclusion of his address, Kennedy paid special tribute to the economic nationalism of Henry Clay. Kennedy reprised what he had told his audience under the rubric of Clay's "American System." Still, although he had long admired Clay and often quoted him, Kennedy had never met the man face-to-face. That would happen when the Friends of Domestic Industry voted to send Kennedy to the nation's capitol. Once there, he would argue for the tariff in the capacity of what today would be called a "lobbyist."[18]

Kennedy arrived in Washington during February 1832, while the tumultuous Twenty-second Congress was in session. Both inside and outside the nation's capital, the country seemed to be coming apart. During the previous year, President Jackson had taken the unprecedented move of dissolving his cabinet over the "Peggy Eaton Affair" (also known as the "Petticoat Affair"), a ridiculously overblown social scandal that had turned political. The scandal had involved Jackson's secretary of war, John Henry Eaton, Eaton's new wife Peggy, and the couple's alleged premarital relationship. Because she reminded Jackson of his deceased and similarly maligned wife, Rachel, he had strenuously defended Peggy Eaton before Washington society. Nonetheless, most of town's elite had treated her coolly. Calhoun, Jackson's vice president, had been the greatest loser in the affair, largely because of the apparent snubbing of Peggy Eaton by his wife and the machinations of Martin Van Buren, the secretary of state at the time. Calhoun had taken his revenge as president of the Senate by blocking Van Buren's nomination as minister to Great Britain. This bitter note set the tone for the contentious and vituperative debates that followed over the protective tariff, funding of internal improvements, rechartering of the national bank, and other issues before Congress.[19]

Outside Washington, federal authority was under siege as never before. The state of Georgia was threatening to ignore the Supreme Court's ruling against the expulsion of the Cherokee people, and the Jackson administration was unwilling to intervene. Without the president's support, the highest court in the land would be rendered impotent. More serious still, the South Carolina nullifiers were moving closer to defying federal authority in the collection of duties at Charleston. "Never have I seen any period of the Republic," Henry Clay observed, "when the future was wrapped in more doubt."[20]

Adding to these tensions, 1832 was a presidential election year. Both the Jackson administration and the congressional opposition were vying for political advantage in the run-up to the November voting. Henry Clay and Daniel Webster, the two titans of the Senate, were intent upon passing as much of their nationalist economic agenda as possible before the election. Clay would shepherd the tariff through Congress, while Webster would manage the rechartering of the Bank of the United States. Clay was also trying to pass his Distribution Bill, an ambitious bundle of legislation calling for the sale of federal lands to fund internal improvements, education, and, most controversial of all, the colonization of free blacks. While Kennedy cared about all of this legislation, his specific charge from the Friends of Domestic Industry was the maintenance of a high protective tariff.

Kennedy was introduced to Clay at the Supreme Court during mid-February 1832. Clay had known Kennedy's father and inquired whether he was still alive. Clay invited Kennedy to dinner a week later, where he met members of Clay's inner circle. They included Senators Edward Everett of Massachusetts, Theodore Frelinghuysen of New Jersey, and Willie P. Mangum of North Carolina. Soon after, Kennedy added Webster to his list of contacts. In his discussions with these men, Kennedy offered information and advice about the tariff. Having reprinted his address to the Friends of Domestic Industry in pamphlet form, he supplied copies to anyone receptive to his arguments. Kennedy wrote his wife that he enjoyed "instructing the great men what to say."[21]

It is impossible to know how much influence Kennedy had in the Tariff of 1832. Clay managed most of the negotiations in the back halls of Congress. Furthermore, ex-president John Quincy Adams, joining the House of Representatives for the first time and honored with the chairmanship of the Committee of Manufactures, took an active role in shaping the final tariff. Known as the "bill of compromise," the new tariff lowered average duties from 45 to 25 percent and reduced federal revenues by almost $5 million. Importantly for the South, the duty on the cheap woolens worn by slaves was brought down from 45 to 5 percent. While the majority of southerners voted for the bill, representatives from Virginia and South Carolina did not. They objected to the fact that tariffs on iron products and cotton textiles, the articles on which Kennedy's efforts were mostly focused, remained highly protective. In the end, Kennedy and his allies in Congress had done their job well.[22]

Other parts of the nationalist agenda did not go as smoothly. Clay's controversial Distribution Bill got bogged down and was postponed until the next session. Worse still, President Jackson vetoed the bill rechartering the Bank of the United States. In doing so, he converted his opposition to the bank into the central issue of the upcoming election. In his veto message, Jackson depicted the bank as the symbol of wealth and privilege, unconstitutional in theory and unfair to the common man in practice. The anti-Jackson coalition had decided to recharter the bank two years earlier than required, believing that Jackson would never veto it in an election year. Instead, he made the election of 1832 a referendum on the bank and turned the tables on his political rivals.[23]

In the November presidential election, the antiadministration forces were hopelessly divided. Henry Clay stood as the candidate of the National Republicans. Kennedy's mentor William Wirt headed the ticket for the newly formed Antimason Party. Still, even if they had been united, these two factions stood little chance against the Democrats. Adding potent antibank rhetoric to their superb grassroots organization, the party of Jackson outdid their campaigning of four years before. The Democrats staged torchlight parades, hickory-pole raisings, and massive barbecues in support of their candidate. In party-controlled newspapers and speeches before local "Hickory Clubs," Democrats hailed their candidate as the only man brave enough to defeat the British at New Orleans and bold enough to slay the "Monster Bank."[24]

Still, putting these factors aside, the failure of the opposition to coalesce and run a more effective campaign in 1832 is puzzling. After all, most of the principles and beliefs that would define the Whig Party were in place. They filled antiadministration speeches in Congress and were etched into the minds of Clay, Webster, and those who supported economic nationalism, moral uplift, and limitations on executive power. Even the name "Whig"—with origins going back to the American Revolution and seventeenth-century opposition to the British Crown—was being used in anti-Jackson newspapers around the country. As Jackson's behavior seemed to grow more autocratic, the Whig name gained traction among those who opposed him.[25]

Even though their cultural framework and, arguably, their name existed in 1832, antiadministration forces were completely disorganized. One problem was the reluctance of the elitist National Republicans to court lower-class Antimasons as political allies. The latter movement had arisen from the antiestablishment social milieu and overheated spiritual atmosphere of upstate New York, known as the "Burned-Over District." This same area had spawned such religious creeds as Mormonism and Millerism. With some justification, the worthies around Clay and Webster viewed these political upstarts as bizarre in origin and quirky in style.

Nonetheless, the Antimasons were passionate foes of the Van Buren machine in New York State, known as the "Albany Regency." Moreover, after watching Van Buren and his crack cadre over the years, the Antimasons had learned how to campaign hard and win elections. In the election of 1832, they captured an astonishing 8 percent of the popular vote. Wirt even took Vermont. In short, the Antimasons were the logical allies of the National Republicans.[26]

Another problem for the National Republicans was their refusal to embrace the new "party style" of American politics. As the popular vote expanded during the 1820s and 1830s, what was called "King Numbers" came to rule the game. By not engaging the broadening voter franchise, the National Republicans had fallen behind their more astute rivals. To make matters worse, many National Republican leaders harbored "anti-party" convictions, considering political parties to be unpatriotic and morally wrong. After the election of 1832, however, even Clay, who had been obdurate about partnering with the Antimasons, confessed, "I want aid—all the aid that can be given." What may have changed his mind was that the anti-Jackson factions had done surprisingly well in local elections across the country. Together the National Republicans and the Antimasons had reduced the Democrats' majority in the U.S. House of Representatives and won control of the Senate. Acknowledging these results, Clay sought to rally the anti-Jackson forces around the issue of executive tyranny and revive what he called "the campaign of 1777."[27]

Kennedy was much more despondent. During September 1832, his friend and *Red Book* collaborator, Peter Hoffman Cruse, died of cholera. Kennedy was also shocked at Jackson's reelection by such a wide margin. When he had seen the president earlier in the year, Kennedy had described him as an "old lion," expecting him to retire peacefully after one term. Instead, because of his shrewdly staged "Bank War," Jackson had gained new life and brought the country, in Kennedy's view, to "the verge of absolutism." For Kennedy, who had endeavored his entire life to bring his mental faculties into balance, Jackson's impulsive, violent, and seemingly irrational behavior was completely anathema. In his journal, Kennedy called Jackson an "old dotard" and an "imbecile."[28]

Along with these calamities came terrible news out of South Carolina. Ignoring the recent compromise tariff, a special convention in Charleston had voted to defy federal authority and issue an ordinance of nullification. The dark side of Kennedy's love of the Union was his paranoia about its possible dissolution, and this news set off a chain of events in his imagination. "Convention at S. C. has just passed the ordinance of nullification," he wrote in his journal during early December 1832. He recorded his predictions.

1. They will secede from the Union.
2. That it will henceforth become a question of secession and not nullification. That the states of Virginia, N. Carolina, Georgia, Alabama and Mississippi will sustain them in their right to secede. That these states will form a coalition which will be too powerful for the Union.
3. That the Union will be dismantled.
4. That there will be three governments—a northern, a western and a southern.
5. That this will be brought about by war and bloodshed.
6. That the Republican system will be modified in these new governments and will be organized more upon the plan of military aristocracies.
7. That the state of Virginia will be dismembered, and the upper portion of it united with Maryland.[29]

It was in this state of despair and agitation that Kennedy began his second novel, *Horse-Shoe Robinson.* "I am writing at present at the most hurried and imperfect form," he confessed after a few chapters. In a different mood than when taking up *Swallow Barn,* Kennedy was writing not as a means of escapism but with urgency and purpose. In spite of its gloomy backdrop, Kennedy seemed excited by the task before him. After all, his publisher, Carey and Lea, had told him that *Swallow Barn* was selling briskly, and most reviews were positive. Kennedy was delighted when his publisher forwarded a letter from James Fenimore Cooper, who praised *Swallow Barn* as a "very clever work" and called its author one of the country's "ablest" writers.[30]

Kennedy had every reason to believe *Horse-Shoe Robinson* would outsell his first novel. The tremendous success of Cooper's Revolutionary War novel *The Spy,* published in 1821, had unleashed a flood of historical romances. That the country had just marked the fiftieth anniversary of that struggle spurred on this trend. Cooper had shown that the genre of historical romance, originally inspired by the novels of Sir Walter Scott, could not only take root in American soil but find fresh vitality there. More than any other writer, Cooper had established America's *literary* independence.[31]

Like many budding Whig intellectuals, Kennedy believed a domestic literature was vital to instill patriotism in the American citizenry. As early as "The Swiss Traveller," he had emphasized the importance of "remembrance"—heroic stories passed from generation to generation—to create a national consciousness. In his preface to *Horse-Shoe Robinson,* Kennedy noted that the last widows of the heroes who had fought in the Revolutionary War were slipping from the pension rolls. He urged that the stories these heroes had told their wives be written down for the good of the nation's "fraternity."[32]

By "fraternity," Kennedy meant the Union and the shared loyalty that made it cohere. That loyalty could never be taken for granted. In his preface, he declared his intention to describe "the condition of things in the south during the very interesting period of the 'Tory Ascendency.'" By choosing to write about the southern theater of the Revolutionary War, where the commitment to independence had been so tenuous, Kennedy would show how divided loyalties there had once before jeopardized the nation's existence. Now, as he contemplated the nullification crisis and its dangerous implications, Kennedy not only would explore the morality of the war for independence, as Cooper had done in *The Spy,* but would remind the public that the survival of the Union depended on recovering that morality. As a consequence, his novel would be more nationalistic and didactic than Cooper's had been.[33]

Cooper's *The Spy* served as a model for Kennedy's second novel, although not nearly to the degree that Irving's work had influenced *Swallow Barn.* For example, one important innovation Cooper brought to the retelling of the American Revolution was a realism regarding its internecine nature. Kennedy expands on this by exploring an even broader spectrum of commitment to independence in the Carolinas. For Kennedy, these degrees of commitment owe little to happenstance. Rather, individual strength of character and moral clarity determine a particular character's devotion to the Revolution. What is more, when he wishes to emphasize these qualities, Kennedy abandons realism for the romantic style. As a result, *Horse-Shoe Robinson* blends the grim reality of civil war in the Carolina backcountry with the passionate emotions and daring deeds characteristic of romanticism. This narrative approach allows Kennedy to define the first stirrings of American patriotism according to his own moral principles and dramatize them using the full power of the romantic style.[34]

It is likely that Cooper's main character in *The Spy,* Harvey Birch, served as a partial model for Kennedy's rugged protagonist, Galbraith "Horse-Shoe" Robinson. Both characters come from the lower levels of society, have colorful manners of speech, and are skilled in disguise. Just as likely, Natty Bumppo, the backwoods hero of Cooper's "Leatherstocking Tales," also influenced the character of Robinson. Both are "loners," knowledgeable in the ways of the forest, and comfortable living on the fringes of society. Still, there were so many frontier types in the popular literature of the 1820s and 1830s, often referred to as "ring-tailed roarers," that Kennedy could have chosen from a number of sources. In fact, Robinson's massive build, "bullet proof" constitution, indomitable fighting skills, and uncanny ability to outwit his enemies make him more like these exaggerated prototypes than Cooper's heroes. One critic of Kennedy's novel has called Robinson a "shape shifter and trickster." Kennedy claimed to have met the real-life Robinson during a legal trip to North Carolina in 1819. While one scholar has questioned this claim, a person fitting Robinson's description appears to have fought in the southern theater of the Revolution and retired to Alabama, where he died in 1838.[35]

Another novel, less known than any of Cooper's, helped shape *Horse-Shoe Robinson.* Kennedy read James Ewell Heath's *Edge-Hill* when it first appeared in 1828 and praised it to a friend while working on his second novel. Though lacking Kennedy's talent for characterization and scenic description, Heath contributed several ideas to the narrative structure and dramatis personae of *Horse-Shoe Robinson.* One of these ideas is the ideological schism between father and daughter over the Revolution, which anticipates an important plot element in Kennedy's novel. In both books, the daughter and her love interest are patriots and the father a Tory, and the father's manipulation by the British is central. Historical figures interact with fictional characters in *Edge-Hill* and *Horse-Shoe Robinson,* with Banastre Tarleton, the infamous Tory irregular, making an appearance in both. Most interesting of all, Heath briefly introduces a patriot named Sergeant Trueman, "whose bodily strength," Heath tells his readers, "was as sinewy and powerful as his spirit was dauntless." Heath kills Trueman off in a firefight halfway through the novel, but he is around long enough to excite speculation as to whether he prefigures Horse-Shoe Robinson.[36]

One possibility is that *both* Heath and Kennedy had heard about the real-life campaigner but only Kennedy had met him. Perhaps, Heath's marginal use of this massive and daring personage in *Edge-Hill* inspired Kennedy to exploit him more centrally in *Horse-Shoe Robinson.* Kennedy's decision to do so produced a superbly crafted character and led to the novel's popular acclaim. Still, the relationship between the two characters raises interesting intertextual questions and shows how nineteenth-century novels often built on previous ones to achieve their literary ends.[37]

The action of Kennedy's novel takes place in a broad, forested swatch of Virginia and Carolina backcountry, after the fall of Charleston to the British in early 1780 and the region's subversion by Tory influence. Kennedy superimposes his story on actual events, which were dominated by brutal partisan warfare across much of the area. Kennedy adheres closely to the fluctuating course of the conflict and introduces historical figures such as Francis Marion, Banastre Tarleton, and Lord Cornwallis into the narrative. At the conclusion of the novel, Kennedy brings most of his fictional characters together at the Battle of King's Mountain, a decisive victory for the patriots en route to Yorktown.

The storyline revolves around Sergeant Galbraith "Horse-Shoe" Robinson's mission to deliver Major Arthur Butler to a patriot command somewhere in the South. In spite of Robinson's efforts, Butler is captured by Tory irregulars, led by the cutthroat freebooter Hugh Habershaw and wily British agent James Curry. There follows a series of elaborate schemes and daring adventures by Robinson and Mildred Lindsay, to rescue Butler—that Mildred is Butler's wife remains a secret until the end of the novel. At times, Mildred's efforts to gain her husband's release threaten to usurp Robinson's central role. A major subplot concerns Mildred's troubled relationship with her aristocratic father, Philip Lindsay, who has fallen under the influence of a loyalist agent, James Tyrrel. (He is actually a British captain named St. Jermyn, which is also not revealed until the end of the novel.)[38]

The wilderness through which Robinson and Butler must travel is rampant with loyalist sympathizers. "It was the misfortune of South Carolina during the revolution," Kennedy writes, "to possess a numerous party less attached to the union or more tainted with disaffection than the inhabitants of any other state." Why, after the fall of Charleston, had there been a "singular rapidity of conquest of the whole province"? Granted, there had been a paucity of republican principles in the state. But the real source of South Carolina's coolness toward the Revolution, Kennedy insists, can be traced to the state's trade with Great Britain. "They did not quarrel with the assumption of Great Britain to regulate their trade for them," he observes. "Being a colony of planters whose products were much in demand in England, neither regulations of their trade nor the restrictions upon their commerce were likely to be so adjusted to interfere with the profitable expansion of their labors." Then as now, Kennedy infers, South Carolina was more attached to its own economic interests than to the national enterprise.[39]

Because they are moving through an area of ambiguous political allegiances, Robinson and Butler exercise caution toward those they meet. Whenever the two riders pause on a hilltop and survey the sparsely populated wilderness below, they can distinguish those farms belonging to good patriots from those with loyalist sympathies. In addition to a person's appearance and deportment, Kennedy tells his readers, the condition of one's home speaks volumes about one's character and moral principles. "By looking at a man in his own dwelling," he writes, "and observing his domestic habits," one can make such judgments. "If his household be well ordered . . . and there be no slovenly inattention to repairs," the owner of such a dwelling is "one who will not have his virtue tainted." Since equating Manly's tidy homestead with his spotless and patriotic character in "The Swiss Traveller," Kennedy had lost little of his discernment in such matters.[40]

The comparison between Wat Adair's farm and Allen Musgrove's mill is a case in point. Adair's property is a scar on the land. His poorly worked fields show "thriftless and slovenly tillage." The area around his dilapidated farmhouse is "spotted with stumps," and a stand of girded trees nearby rises like a "huge grove of skeletons." The only signs of life are a "bevy of little negroes" and a pack of unruly hunting dogs. No one can pass by such a place "without a sense of disgust at the disfiguration of the landscape."[41]

The interior of Adair's cabin is no better. All is filth and disorder. Adair's wife is "care-worn and joyless," prematurely aged, surly in temperament, and burdened with too many children. Adair himself is thin, dark complected, and stoop-shouldered. His carriage lacks symmetry, and he walks with an uneven gait. His face "expressed cunning rather than hardihood," Kennedy writes, "habitually alternating between the manifestations of waggish vivacity and distrust." Having abandoned farming for the meager income of hunting and trapping, he occupies the lowest echelon of frontier society.[42]

In one of the novel's more disturbing scenes, Adair skins a trapped wolf alive, much to the horror of Robinson and Butler, who are powerless to intervene. Adair has no principles unrelated to his own survival. In his own words, Adair "must play a little double, just to keep out of harm's way." In Kennedy's view, Adair lacks the moral grounding to differentiate between the loyalist and the patriot sides in the war and resist the lure of material gain for his allegiance. When asked by a neighbor whether he has any scruples about working for the British, Adair responds that the patriot cause is heading "down hill" and, regarding the question of conscience, declares, "There ain't no such thing going on in these days." Firmly in the pay of the British, Adair arranges for the capture of Butler and, if not for the mercy of Robinson, would be hanged for treason at the end of the novel.[43]

Compared to Wat Adair's farm, Allen Musgrove's mill is a study in contrasts. On one side of Musgrove's neat cottage lies "cultivated ground neatly enclosed in fences." The other side is "shaded by a cluster of trees which had been spared from the native forest." A flock of geese are clustered about the mill trace, and a group of children stand transfixed by the turning of a large mill wheel. There are no slaves around the establishment. Mill workers can be identified by their "whitened habiliments" as they devoutly go about their jobs. The entire scene excites "pleasant thoughts of rural business and domestic content."

Not surprisingly, Musgrove bears little resemblance to Adair physically, professionally, or morally. Although showing some "traces of age," Musgrove's frame is "still muscular and his bearing erect and steadfast, denoting firmness of mind." As an enterprising miller, Musgrove represents a kind of proto-industrialist of his day. His industriousness is complemented by an intense religiosity, and the Bible exerts a guiding influence over his family. Musgrove reads frequently from the scriptures and says the blessing before every meal. During a visit from Butler and Robinson, the family, its employees, and guests sing hymns together, converting the place into a temple of faith and industry.

Musgrove's wife is frugal and devout. She and her husband are migrating toward the patriot cause and believe it will succeed. Together they have raised an exceptional daughter in Mary Musgrove, who, in spite of her rustic education, is already deeply committed to the Revolution. In love with a patriot soldier, John Ramsay, Mary declares herself ready to "forego all maidenly scruples and bravely perform her duty, come what may." By the end of the novel, the Musgrove family's religious faith and commitment to the Revolution will be severely tested but sustained. Allen Musgrove's mill is burned to the ground by marauding Tories, and Mary loses her lover in a bloody skirmish.[44]

As war ravages the Carolina backcountry, Widow Dimrock's roadside inn is one of the few sanctuaries, possibly due to its proximity to the estate of loyalist Philip Lindsay. Here again, Robinson and Butler detect the same simplicity in Dimrock's way of living, including her sensible attire, that defines those who support the patriot cause. Desperate wartime shortages and the shared need for resourcefulness, Kennedy observes, have the effect of "putting the opulent and the needy to a certain extent upon the same footing."[45]

Bringing Americans together across class barriers and social divides—in a sense, putting them "upon the same footing"—had been Kennedy's desire since the heady days of Bladensburg. In "The Swiss Traveller," he argued that the Revolution had created a sense of nationhood by encouraging "simplicity of manners" and "moderation of desire." These classical republican sentiments had been reiterated in the *Red Book.* Hardship and deprivation had produced a sense of collective purpose and an upwelling of native virtue. Not only would this desire for social harmony help define Kennedy as a Whig, but it would become the central theme of his next novel, *Rob of The Bowl.* During the writing of *Horse-Shoe Robinson,* the nullification crisis and divisiveness of Jacksonian politics intensified these feelings. As a result, though it was set against a background of internecine struggle, Kennedy's second novel contains numerous instances of social coalescence and shared patriotic ethos arising from the independence movement.[46]

Examples of this idealized social coalescence—at times romanticized into a kind of indigenous nobility of character—recur throughout Kennedy's second novel. At one point, after a surprisingly recondite assessment of the military situation by Widow Dimrock, Robinson praises her homespun sagacity. She has, Robinson declares, "spoken with as much wisdom and circumspection, mought come out of the mouth of e'er a lady in the land—high born or low born—I don't care where the other comes from." Similarly, Robinson compliments Mary Musgrove on the remarkable poise she displays for a country girl, characterized by her "modest and natural courtesy." Likewise, Kennedy notes that Mildred Lindsay's ardent patriotism has a spontaneous quality about it and that her ability to inspire others with her feelings has little to do with her fine education or ladylike upbringing. Rather, it is her "familiar bearing" and "natural eloquence" that appeal to those who meet her.[47]

Of course, it is Horse-Shoe Robinson who serves as Kennedy's most powerful embodiment of this broadly denominated American nobility, this native dignity that seems to thrive so naturally on American soil. While a man of an "altogether rougher mold" than the gentlemanly Butler, Robinson cuts an impressive figure in his powerful and rough-hewn way. Over six feet tall and massively built, Robinson's limbs are nonetheless "sinewy and remarkable for their symmetry." His gait is long and exhibits a free stride. "Nature had carved out in his person," Kennedy observes, "an athlete whom the sculptors might have studied to improve the Hercules. Every lineament of his body indicated strength."[48]

But Kennedy makes it clear that Robinson's physical power is derived from his strength of character. That Robinson is illiterate and converses in a "Doric form of speech" are of little significance, Kennedy emphasizes, when one considers "that real delicacy of mind that lies at the bottom of a kind nature and inhabits the shaggy breast of the rustic, at least as full as it lodges in the heart of the trim worldling." One glance at Robinson shows there is nothing suspect or hidden from view in his character. There is, Kennedy writes, "a radiant, broad good nature upon his face." Robinson's eyes express a "shrewd, homey, wisdom . . . inviting friendship and trust."[49]

For Kennedy, Robinson stands for something quintessentially American. Most important, he is direct and forthright in a way that the British can never be; he serves as a perfect foil for the duplicity and underhandedness of British agents like James Tyrrel and James Curry. In one of the novel's memorable scenes, Robinson catches Curry asking around Dimrock's inn about Butler. Robinson takes exception to Curry's devious methods: "It's the custom in our country . . . to larn a little about the business of every man we meet; but we do it by fair, out-and-out question and answer—all above board, and we hold in dispise all sorts of contwistifications, either by laying of tongue-traps, or listening under eaves of houses." Since their languages and cultures are so far apart, Curry has no idea what Robinson is talking about.[50]

Because of his physical strength and combat seasoning, Robinson is indispensible to Major Butler. Partly, this is because Butler is out of his element in the Carolina backcountry. His fine education and "gentle breeding" make him seem of the Old World and, at times, inept in frontier warfare. Butler spends most of the novel incarcerated by the enemy. In the final pages, Robinson delivers Butler to Mildred amid the swirl of battle on King's Mountain. "He swung Butler from his horse," Kennedy describes, "with scarce more effort than he would have used handling a child." Clearly, men like Butler needed the help of men like Robinson.[51]

So, too, did the Whig Party. By the time of *Horse-Shoe Robinson*'s writing, the leadership of the anti-Jackson forces realized that good men of common standing were indispensible if the new party wanted to win in the rough-and-tumble politics of the 1830s. By closing ranks with the more plebian Antimasons, which the National Republicans did in 1833, the anti-Democratic opposition replaced its polished rhetoric and patrician image with a scrappier, earthier brand of politicking capable of broader reach. By focusing on Jackson's alleged executive tyranny, portraying him as "King Andrew The First" in one famous illustration, the National Republicans helped combine the antiprivilege, antiestablishment culture of Antimasons with the nationalistic economic principles of Clay and Webster. Soon this coalition began fielding a new breed of spokesmen, such as Ohioans Tom "Wagon Boy" Corwin and John "The Buckeye Blacksmith" Bear, as well as the unlettered ex-Indian fighter and Tennessee backwoodsman, Colonel David Crockett. These exuberant stump speakers took full advantage of the popular vernacular and dealt with populist themes that appealed to men cut from a rough mold with little education. Many of these backwoods orators were not so different from the hero of Kennedy's second novel, either in terms of their humble background or colorful, colloquial style of speech.[52]

Kennedy provides evidence that Robinson represents not just the common man but the honorable artisan or noble mechanic, whom the author often extolled in his tariff speeches. After all, Robinson was a blacksmith before taking up arms. After winning independence from Britain, Kennedy explains, men like Robinson have secured that independence through progress in the mechanical arts. Drawing on the romantic style, Kennedy portrays Robinson as an almost Promethean figure. The novel's hero assumes an "iron form" and radiates the hot, protean energy of American industry. At one point, Robinson refers to his hardened condition as something elemental, as if he were the product of his own anvil. His entire body has "been hammered in these here wars like an old piece of iron," he declares, "that's been one while a plough coulter, and after that a gun-barrel, and finally run up with others into a piece of ordnance—not to say that it moughtn't have been a horse shoe in some part of its life, ha! ha! ha!"[53]

Of course, such romantic hyperbole allows Kennedy to handle the character of Robinson at arm's length. Like the good slave Abe in *Swallow Barn,* Robinson is often rendered in terms so exaggerated as to be unreal, terms that enable Kennedy to deal in a limited way with the actual issues associated with the character he is describing. In the case of Robinson, such treatment allows the class nature of America's early industrial development to go unaddressed. Nor had Kennedy ever intended that the leadership of his party, not to mention that of the nation, be turned over to men like Robinson. While most Whigs desired social harmony between classes, they believed it depended on what they saw as the natural hierarchy of society. Kennedy is careful to show that, in spite of his remarkable boldness in battle, Robinson's position in society remains humble. He rides beside Major Butler in "respectful silence" and observes all the "habits of subordination" expected of a sergeant. Kennedy would explore these notions of obedience and subordination more fully in *Rob of The Bowl.* For now, however, Kennedy made it clear that a man like Robinson is just as praiseworthy for his obedience and sense of duty as for his battlefield valor. After delivering Butler to Mildred at King's Mountain, Robinson tells her, "take him ma'am. I promised myself today I'd give him to you, and now you've got him." Soon after, Robinson disappears from the novel. In his conclusion, Kennedy explains that Major Butler and Mildred Lindsay are happily married and Mary Musgrove is living with them, but, by this time, the real hero of the novel is forgotten.[54]

This treatment of Robinson does not mean that Kennedy was ingenuous in his concern for the common man. To the contrary, Whigs like Kennedy actively solicited the support of society's lower orders and took a deep interest in their moral condition. Kennedy's didactic judgments regarding the household management and moral deportment of Wat Adair and Allen Musgrove exemplify this interest. Furthermore, the very conception of Robinson's character pays homage to the common man and his role in America's future. From a literary perspective, however, Robinson's disappearance at the end of the novel is consistent with his mythic, larger-than-life status as a romantic hero. Authors such as Kennedy and Cooper faced a problem of how to accommodate their rough, raw frontier heroes in the increasingly refined, bourgeois society of the 1820s and 1830s. Men like Robinson and Natty Bumppo never marry and rarely form strong attachments to others. Since such characters live on the periphery of society and are only called upon to perform their extraordinary exploits during times of crisis, there is not much left for Robinson to do at the end of Kennedy's novel. In short, it is time for the heroic but humble Robinson, like the good slave Abe before him, to move on.[55]

Kennedy's second novel also pays homage to women, many of whom played a part in the Revolution and were involved in the reform movements of the 1830s. He had been perplexed about the role of women for some time. In "The Swiss Traveller" and the *Red Book,* he expressed concern regarding their susceptibility to luxury and fashion. At the same time, he acknowledged their moral influence as wives and mothers. In *Swallow Barn,* he created the strong-willed Bel Tracy but constrained her to frivolous pursuits. He also explored in limited depth the good works of Prudence Meriwether.[56]

What is surprising about Kennedy's treatment of women in his first and second novels is not that it changes but that it changes so much. Between novels, his take on women shifts from superficial and skeptical to substantive and positive. Mary Musgrove is just one example. Her development as a coheroine to Mildred Lindsay suggests that there were many heroic women engaged in the Revolutionary struggle. What is more, Mary Musgrove's inclusion shows that the patriotic spirit and the moral basis for the Revolution ran across class and was not limited to better-off, well-educated women like Mildred Lindsay. At great risk to herself, Mary Musgrove warns Major Butler that her uncle, Wat Adair, has betrayed him to the British. Disguised as an apple seller, she also delivers a letter to the British courtroom that saves Butler from execution. For her part, Mildred Lindsay travels hundreds of miles through the wilderness to find her husband, enduring numerous hardship and meeting Tarleton, Cornwallis, and Marion along the way. The antebellum reader preferred having the moral character of a novel's main figures demonstrated rather than described. By allowing Mildred Lindsay and Mary Musgrove to participate in the action of his novel, Kennedy made their characters more credible than if he had he simply described them as moral exemplars.[57]

Just as impressive is the way Kennedy repeatedly challenges the initiatives of his female characters with male skepticism and condescension, only to expose the error of such judgements. "It is my opinion, ma'am," Robinson tells the Widow Dimrock, "the best thing a woman can do in these here wars is to knit; and leave the fighting of it, to us who haven't faces to be spoiled by bad weather and tough times." Yet, it turns out that Dimrock serves as an important link in the patriots' communication network. Having jokingly called Mary Musgrove "a staunch little petticoat sodger," Robinson later acknowledges her courage on several occasions. So, too, Butler at one point apologizes to Mildred for sharing some bad news from the battlefront with "one so sensitive as yourself." Yet, it is largely through Mildred's efforts that Butler is rescued from the British. Her father, Philip Lindsay, goes further to diminish her confidence as a supporter of the patriot cause. "We may thank the gods that they gave you a petticoat instead of a soldier's cloak," Lindsay declares, "and placed you at the head of a breakfast table instead of a regiment." With characteristic self-assurance, she responds that she "would not altogether disgrace the cloak now, woman that I am, if the occasion requires me to put it on."[58]

It is difficult to know why Kennedy devoted so much of his second novel to strong women. It certainly ingratiated him with the large and growing number of female readers. He had admired his mother's "degree of command" in the family and looked up to his schoolmistresses, Mrs. Coffee and Mrs. Priestly, for their assertiveness and athleticism. But historical developments also influenced his take on women. By the 1830s, women had assumed an important role in public life. During the Second Great Awakening, women sometimes introduced their husbands to the conversion experience and led them into evangelical churches. This did not happen to Kennedy, but it did to his mentor William Wirt. Reaching out from their churches, women broadened their sphere of moral influence and good works to temperance associations, Bible societies, Sunday school unions, and even the African Colonization Society. Kennedy likely encountered female organizers in the Baltimore chapter of the latter organization, since women were active in it and Kennedy delivered at least one lecture there in the early 1830s.[59]

The burgeoning benevolent societies of the 1830s placed women in unique positions of moral authority. For this reason, the Whig Party welcomed women into its ranks. In fact, the benevolent societies served as natural conduits into the party. Several of these societies were led by prominent Whigs such as

Henry Clay, president of the American Colonization Society, and Theodore Frelinghuysen, president of the American Tract Society and American Bible Society. At election time, Whig women sewed banners for party parades, cooked bread for picnics, and swelled attendance at rallies. On Sundays, pulpits controlled by these women disseminated Whig doctrine. Eventually, women writers sympathetic to the party's cause, most famously Sarah Josepha Hale and Catherine Beecher, developed what one historian has referred to as "a feminine version of Whiggery" and another has called "the party's innovative gender ideology." All in all, Whig women brought an invaluable moral endorsement to the party's crusading spirit. One Whig newspaper editor was impressed enough to write, "From Maine to New Orleans our mothers, sisters, and daughters are now, as in the days of the Revolution, all Whig."[60]

Kennedy lauds the role of Revolutionary women in *Horse-Shoe Robinson.* "The fervor with which the American women participated in the cares and sacrifices of the revolution," he writes, "has challenged the frequent notice and warmest praise of its chroniclers." Among the novel's characters, Mildred Lindsay best captures the female heroism of that struggle. Like Bel Tracy in *Swallow Barn,* Mildred Lindsay is an excellent horsewoman and is intelligent, confident, and articulate. However, unlike Bel, Mildred has been summoned to a loftier cause. She embraces the principles of the Revolution which, Kennedy explains, imbue her with the "devout self-dedication of a religious obligation" and an "unvarying current of resolution that shrank from no perils." In a word, it is Mildred's "resolution" that drives her and much of the novel's action forward. "I will not blench now, in the last struggle," she swears before Robinson, "though the perils thicken around me."[61]

While most of Kennedy's novel is devoted to Mildred's search for her husband, her relationship with her younger brother Henry is more indicative of how the author envisioned the role of women during the Revolution and his own time. It falls to Mildred to convert Henry to the patriot cause over the objections of their Tory father. Since Philip Lindsay has recently been widowed, the contest for Henry's loyalty is between Mildred and her father. Mildred wins this ideological struggle because of the "warmth of her principles" and her ability to "sway the minds of mankind." Kennedy seems to be saying that, as a woman, Mildred exercises a degree of moral authority over her brother against which her father stands little chance of success.[62]

Once she brings him over to the side of independence, Mildred takes charge of Henry's character building and military training. Because of her "somewhat masculine character," she is up to the task. Unlike her brother (and Kennedy in his youth), Mildred has no fear of the dark. In order to purge this defect from her brother, she forces Henry to perform midnight sentry duty alone in the woods. Mildred also drills Henry in the military arts to fortify his bravery and make him battle ready. So powerful is Mildred's sway over her brother that Kennedy hints at an odd gender exchange between the two siblings, where Henry seems like a "girlish boy" and Mildred a "boyish girl."[63]

One cannot help speculating whether, in exploring the relationship between Henry and Mildred, Kennedy was confronting his own conflicted feelings for his mother. During his early childhood, Kennedy's mother tried to toughen his constitution with freezing bathwater, and she later coldly dispatched him to fight at Bladensburg. The failures of a weak father, a cavalry officer not unlike the often inept Major Butler, only complicated Kennedy's parental orientation. Possibly, Kennedy not only dealt with these personal issues in the novel but also found a place for his rebalanced understanding of gender roles in the framework of Whig culture.[64]

Much of the novel takes place at Dove Cote, Philip Lindsay's estate in the foothills of the Blue Ridge Mountains. Though American born, Lindsay spent his youth in England and married an heiress before returning to Virginia. At Dove Cote, he and his wife indulged their "comfort-seeking fancy" and lived in "voluptuous ease." Despite the beauty of its natural setting, Dove Cote's architecture is over-embellished and its grounds pretentiously landscaped. Gravel pathways, scythed lawns, and special plantings are among the "artificial establishments of the spot." Inside the house, the deep nap of Turkish carpeting silences the visitor's footfall, so as not to disturb Lindsay in his library. Given his aversion to republican simplicity, it is no surprise that Lindsay is a Tory.

These attempts to improve upon nature are not all that is wrong at Dove Cote. As a lover of ancient books, Lindsay's pursuit of knowledge has taken an unnatural turn. "The ply of his mind was toward Metaphysics," Kennedy observes, "the Gnostic mysteries . . . phantasmagoria of Judicial Astrology." Instead of following the "truer philosophers and more approved and authentic teachers," Lindsay has indulged in an "unhealthy appetite for the marvelous and the mystical." Although he understands the dangers of such investigations, he has collected a library of dark and fearful texts and has allowed the "most volatile fancies" and "awful agencies of the spiritual world" to subvert his logical faculties.[65]

Recently widowed, estranged from his children, and bewildered by the politics of his neighborhood, Lindsay searches his arcane volumes to explain destiny's unpredictable course. What secret forces, he wonders, "compel the animal existences of this earth . . . or the fever of the human brain." Sequestered late in his library during a terrible storm, Lindsay surrenders to the "fanciful and distempered philosophy" of his unsanctioned texts and slips into delirium. "The needle of his mind trembled upon its pivot," Kennedy writes, "and began to decline towards a fearful point." "Have not men heard the strange whispers in the breeze—the voice of warning?" Lindsay cries. "Have not they felt the fanning of the wing that bore the secret messenger through the air? Have they not seen some floating fold of the robe as it passed by? O God!—have they not seen the dead arise?" Seeing the specter of his deceased wife beckoning to him from the lawn below, Lindsay falls unconscious from the strain of his frenzied imagination.[66]

In his description of Lindsay's dark ruminations, Kennedy avails himself of the gothic style. Originating in England, this style represented the dark side of romanticism and was preoccupied with haunted castles and the horrors of the dungeon. In its American form, the gothic style dealt less with ruined castles and more with disturbances of the mind. It was less architectural and more psychological. While a few American writers were predominantly gothic—among them Charles Brockden Brown and Edgar Allan Poe—others employed the gothic style more sparingly, often to dramatize their characters' cultural contradictions. Kennedy used it primarily to demonstrate Lindsay's deviant intellectualism and misguided allegiances.[67]

The account of Lindsay's distemper operates on several levels. On one level, it allows Kennedy to debunk the spiritualism and pseudoscientific thinking popular at the time of the novel's writing. These beliefs and theories were widespread because scientific understanding lagged behind industrial progress, and religious fervor often accommodated them. Hydropathy, homeopathy, and mesmerism, flourished during the 1830s and the decades that followed. Swedenborgianism, which described the afterlife in glowing terms and encouraged communication with the dead, was instrumental in the rise of spiritualism.[68]

On another level, the pitiable example of Philip Lindsay enables Kennedy to show how the pursuit of knowledge alone, with no forethought as to its practical ends and no structure in its acquisition, is not only fruitless but dangerous. As a student, Kennedy had struggled because of a "want of structure" and a "tendency toward more imaginative speculation." At times, it had been an overwhelming, "kaleidoscopic" experience for him. Eventually, his more disciplined scholarly approach enabled him to avoid the kind of intellectual pitfalls and promiscuous diversions that undo Lindsay.[69]

Finally, the sad experience of Philip Lindsay demonstrates how morally blind and vulnerable to the influence of others the ill-conceived and haphazard acquisition of knowledge can make a person. Lindsay is oblivious to the principles of freedom and independence for which men are dying around him. Although well read and worldly, he is unable to grasp the basic precepts of the patriot cause that the unlettered and provincial Galbraith Robinson sees so lucidly. Furthermore, given the unstable state of his mind, Lindsay has "no defense in temper or worldly skills" against the intrigues of the British agent James Tyrrel. In the end, Lindsay's misplaced political loyalty is attributable to his dark scholarship and its unbalancing of his mental faculties.[70]

Though tragically misguided, Philip Lindsay is not an evil man. At the end of the novel, he acknowledges his errors as he lies dying on King's Mountain. No other Tory in the novel is allowed such moral latitude. For Kennedy, anyone else serving under the "hateful banner" of England is on the wrong side of a sharply divided moral contest.[71]

Even Lord Cornwallis admits to Mildred Lindsay that rebel hangings have become an "every-day tale" inside his camp. Under his command, Colonel Patrick Ferguson and Banastre Tarleton are permitted to "gratify their own thirst for blood in the most revolting barbarities." Tory irregulars are "the wildest crew of devil babies who ever stole cattle or fired a haystack." These frontier bullies cannot be "handled like Christians" and must be disciplined with a "good taste of the cat." Following their murderous rampages, their first demand is for strong drink. Their campsite, with its broken bottles, drained flasks, and shallow-dug graves, gives evidence of their gross and sensuous natures.[72]

Juxtaposed to this loathsome enemy are men like John Ramsay, who sacrifices his life to save Butler and whose rustic funeral is used by Kennedy to consecrate the patriot cause. As John Ramsay's body is lowered into the ground, his father tells his surviving son to "remember your brother has met his death fighting these monsters, who hate the very earth that nurses liberty." However, Allan Musgrove cautions the mourners not to debase the cause of independence by seeking revenge for its own sake. The patriots must pursue their "lawful war" and leave vengeance to God. Otherwise, the moral force of the Revolution will be lost.[73]

Throughout *Horse-Shoe Robinson,* Kennedy refers to John Ramsay and his fellow patriots as "Whigs." Although Americans often used the term to describe themselves during the Revolution, Kennedy uses the Whig name so frequently that several scholars have commented on it. Since the Whig Party was founded in April 1834, a year before the publication of *Horse-Shoe Robinson,* Kennedy had time to see that the name of the new party was peppered throughout the novel. By doing so, Kennedy implied a continuity between the Revolution and the Whig movement. This was consistent with Whig thinking. Implicit in the party's choice of a name was the idea that the Whigs were initiating a kind of second American Revolution, one that would free the nation from the tyranny of Andrew Jackson and restore the vision of the Founders. Over the next two decades, Whig leaders would claim such political provenance and ideological linkage in their speeches. *Horse-Shoe Robinson* was a harbinger of this rhetorical convention.[74]

Blending fact and fiction in a tumultuous finale, Kennedy ends his novel with the Battle of King's Mountain, a major patriot victory on the road to Yorktown. Once opposing forces are joined, the battle becomes a "thick haze" from which "huzzas" and "feeble groans" emanate. Patriots and loyalists "mingle hand to hand . . . rage [having] replenished the men." At one point, Robinson catches sight of his old foe James Curry and crushes his skull with a rifle butt. "The grudge is done," Robinson declares. Mildred watches from the nearby woods, wishing she could "be in the midst of yonder crowd of angry men." For her, the day is bittersweet. She is reunited with Butler but watches her father die after asking forgiveness. "It was ordained," Lindsay tells her. "I have unwisely struggled against my doom."[75]

Published in June 1835, *Horse-Shoe Robinson* was a resounding literary success. Kennedy's new publisher, Lea and Blanchard, sold out its first three thousand copies that summer and printed a like number in the fall to satisfy popular demand. In 1836, the novel exhausted a similar run and appeared as a dramatic production on the New York stage. *Horse-Shoe Robinson* would be reissued almost two dozen times over the coming years and was adapted for the stage a second time. While the title character became fixed in the minds of

Americans, Kennedy's financial benefit was modest. He earned less than two thousand dollars for his literary efforts.[76]

Most newspapers and journals praised Kennedy's second novel for its successful blending of fiction and historical fact. Only Cooper had carried off this literary experiment as convincingly. Whereas some critics had regarded *Swallow Barn* as adhering too closely to Irving's work, the originality of Horse-Shoe Robinson's character, especially his rustic language and convivial manner, overshadowed any debts its creator may have owed to Cooper. In a letter to Kennedy thanking him for the novel's dedication, Irving correctly predicted that the "honest Horse-Shoe will be a decided favorite with the public."[77]

There was less controversy around Kennedy's second novel than with *Swallow Barn*. Journals as regionally diverse as the *New York Review* and the *Southern Literary Messenger* complimented Kennedy on his literary nationalism and inspirational treatment of the Revolutionary period. That he had shifted his focus away from slavery and made blacks nearly invisible in his second novel contributed to these universal plaudits. Slavery was an issue that most readers were eager to forget and, at least for the moment, *Horse-Shoe Robinson* allowed them to do that.[78]

Still, Kennedy's second novel was heavily contextualized and freighted with politics. For these reasons, Edgar Allan Poe's review in the *Southern Literary Messenger* is most interesting. Poe had gotten his place at the publication with Kennedy's help, through a connection with its owner, Thomas White. A businessman above all else, White believed that, in order to achieve national circulation, a southern literary journal needed to avoid party politics and deal gingerly with the issue of slavery. As White's editor, it was Poe's job to perform this balancing act.[79]

Poe began by praising Kennedy's novel for its originality, especially the character of its indomitable patriot sergeant. Interestingly, Poe did not mention the novel's similarities to James Heath's *Edge-Hill*, even though he worked with Heath at the *Messenger* and considered him a talented writer. Possibly, Poe had not read Heath's novel or simply chose to focus on what was unique about *Horse-Shoe Robinson*. One such aspect was Kennedy's delineation of his female characters, especially the "ardent, eager, the simple-minded, the generous and devoted Mary Musgrove!" These portraits had succeeded, Poe declared, where attempts by most other authors to describe such characters had failed.

Whether Poe understood Kennedy's allusions to the nullification movement behind the tale of Tory ascendency is unclear. With respect to South Carolina, Poe commented awkwardly, "this state evinced more disaffection to the confederated government than any other in the Union." On a purely historical level, Poe took issue with Kennedy's anti-British bias. "Perhaps too scrupulously rigid poetical justice," Poe suggested, is meted out to the British and their loyalist allies in the novel. Poe had not fought in the War of 1812, of course, and did not share Kennedy's preoccupation with protection against British trade. Poe had also spent five years in England as a youth.

While he liked the character of Robinson, Poe asked why Kennedy had not made Major Butler the hero of the story. As a West Point man and somewhat of an elitist, Poe could not see why Kennedy had inverted the country's social hierarchy and military chain of command. Given characters like Robinson and Mary Musgrove, Poe believed the novel would be "eagerly read by *all classes of people* (emphasis added)." While a friend of Kennedy, Poe was no friend of broad-based democracy.[80]

Kennedy had met Poe as the result of a literary contest sponsored by Baltimore's *Saturday Visitor* magazine. Along with James Miller, a successful doctor and member of the local literati, and their mutual friend John Latrobe, Kennedy served as a judge for the contest. "We met one pleasant afternoon in October 1833," Latrobe recalled. As the junior member of the group, Latrobe was in charge of opening the envelopes and reading the submissions, while his two colleagues "filled their glasses and lit cigars." The three judges awarded Poe's short story "MS. Found in a Bottle" the first prize of fifty dollars. Kennedy was so impressed with Poe's talent that he passed several of the young writer's short stories on to Henry Carey in Philadelphia. Kennedy also helped Poe land his job at the *Southern Literary Messenger,* where Poe quickly became editor. While *Horse-Shoe Robinson* could stand on its own merits, Poe's gratitude certainly influenced his review of the novel.[81]

Kennedy and Poe corresponded for over a decade. Even as he began to succeed as a writer, Poe was always short of money and suffered from bouts of depression. Kennedy occasionally assisted him with small sums and tried to help him through his melancholy. "Write me immediately," Poe pleaded in late 1835. "Convince me that it is worth one's while, that it is at all necessary to live." Responding that he was sorry Poe had been "invaded by these blue devils," Kennedy included a page of avuncular advice on how a young man of Poe's "age and temper [could] master these adversary forces." Kennedy's counsel seemed to help for a time, and Poe thanked him for his "frequent and effectual assistance and kindness." Still, Poe's behavior remained unstable and his requests for money unrelenting. In late 1845, he would ask Kennedy for a fifty-dollar loan to keep the *Broadway Journal,* which Poe had just taken over, financially afloat.[82]

"Poor Poe!" Kennedy wrote in his journal four years later when Poe died. Kennedy described him as "an original and exquisite poet." He had welcomed Poe to his table, promoted his work, and found him employment. Along with a handful of others, Kennedy's support sustained Poe long enough for him to produce a unique corpus that enriched the national literature. Though it would be years before Poe's brilliance was widely recognized, Kennedy saw it early and mourned its loss. "He is gone—a bright but unsteady light has been awfully quenched."[83]

Kennedy hardly needed a successful second novel to raise his stature as a man of letters in Baltimore. Sometime in 1831, he had established the "Monday Club," a group of several dozen influential members of the community who met weekly to discuss literature, philosophy, science, and other topics of interest. This club and ones like it in other cities served as stopping places for visiting luminaries from around the country and abroad. As the founder of the Monday Club and one of its most successful members, Kennedy became an axis around which much of the city's intellectual life revolved.[84]

During the summer of 1833, Kennedy and his friend Josias Pennington bought a lot on Baltimore's prestigious Monument Square. After building a townhouse there, Kennedy and his wife played host to many of the town's notable visitors. Among the writers to dine or lodge with the Kennedys were Washington Irving, William Thackeray, Harriet Martineau, and, of course, Edgar Allan Poe. Irving, who seemed congenitally itinerant, grew fond of the Kennedys and often visited for weeks at a time.[85]

During the two and a half years it took to finish *Horse-Shoe Robinson,* Kennedy continued to travel in support of the tariff and became increasingly involved in national politics. During the first months of 1833, as the nullification crisis was peaking, Kennedy visited the nation's capital several times. The political situation there was again in a state of disarray. President Jackson had issued his "Proclamation" against the nullifiers, soon to be known as the "Force Bill," but his vice president, Martin Van Buren, believed its language was too strong. Instead, Van Buren favored the Democrat-sponsored compromise tariff, or "Verplanck Bill," working its way through Congress. Meanwhile, Daniel Webster rushed to back Jackson and became an overnight favorite at the White House. For his part, John C. Calhoun was desperate to end the crisis; he had helped create the situation but then had lost control of it to radicals in his home state. Whatever Calhoun's course, he could not be seen caving in to his archenemy Jackson or hated rival Van Buren.[86]

The only player who had not weighed in was Henry Clay. As the nullification crisis worsened, Clay sniffed opportunity. At the urging of southern sugar interests and a few northern manufacturers, Clay initiated contacts with Calhoun's inner circle. The meetings between Clay and Calhoun took place during late January or early February 1833 and resulted in a tariff agreement between the two old rivals.[87]

Not only did Clay outmaneuver Webster, but he surprised Kennedy, who had met individually with Clay and Calhoun a week or so before. Kennedy knew nothing about the negotiations between the two until informed by Calhoun that it was a fait accompli. "Calhoun told me he was willing to arrange matters with the tariff, but not with Jackson," Kennedy wrote in his journal. "He told me moreover that he and Mr. Clay had conversed over the subject and had agreed the terms." Kennedy expressed disbelief to Calhoun—who had always insisted that discriminatory duties were unconstitutional—that the South Carolinian was ready to agree to them now. Calhoun responded that such flexibility "was absolutely necessary to insure the success of the compromise for which he was very anxious."[88]

Kennedy was upset about the terms of the Clay-Calhoun agreement and about not being consulted by either man beforehand. But, while he criticized Clay for indulging the nullifiers, Kennedy admitted that the agreement had "saved us from recourse to army." Still, Kennedy believed that South Carolina would never be satisfied longer term and that the peace would not hold. He also believed that Webster, who had defended the tariff against the nullifiers, would emerge from the crisis as the winner.[89]

While his long-term misgivings would prove correct, Kennedy was wrong about the political fortunes of those involved in the crisis. On February 11, 1833, Clay interrupted a debate in the Senate on the Force Bill to announce his compromise bill. In his speech the following day, Clay pleaded for the benefits of peace rather than the horrors of war. The nation wanted "no civil war, no family strife," he declared. "We want no sacked cities, no desolate fields, no streams of American bloodshed by American arms." When Clay finished, Calhoun rose and pledged his support for the compromise bill. In a nearly unanimous show of relief, the Senate floor and galleries broke out in applause, embraces, and tears.[90]

While he emphasized the tariff as a means of raising revenues in his Senate speech, Clay never surrendered the principle of protectionism. Even though the new tariff would be 20 percent on all goods, implying a lack of discrimination, it would not go into full effect for almost a decade. What is more, Clay forced an amendment into the final bill calling for "home valuation" of all protected articles. This meant that the tariff would be calculated ad valorem according to the market price at the port of entry, thereby increasing the duties on all imported articles short term. Another amendment rescinded the tariff reduction on cheap woolens given to the South the year before. In short, American manufacturers suffered minimal reductions in the tariff and ended up with a more favorable bill than the Democrats had proposed.[91]

Congress passed the new compromise tariff and the Force Bill at the end of February 1833. Jackson signed both at the beginning of March. In order to keep Clay humble, Jackson pocket-vetoed a second attempt at a distribution bill, which Clay had again shepherded through Congress. With it went the last chance for federal funding of African colonization. South Carolina subsequently rescinded its Ordinance of Nullification but, in an empty gesture of defiance, "nullified" the Force Bill. Always the abstract thinker, Calhoun ignored the details of the new tariff and, along with Clay, harvested the honors of the peacemaker. Jackson garnered praise for defending the Union but at a terrible cost to his party. States' rights men across the South began leaving the Democratic Party. Initially attracted to Calhoun, most would join the Whigs.[92]

Few could resist Clay's charms for long, and Kennedy's dissatisfaction with him was short lived. Possibly, Clay sought Kennedy's expertise during the tariff bill's amendment process. If so, the two men repaired their relationship during that collaboration. If not, then it was their joint speaking engagement at the American Institute Fair in New York during October 1833 that brought them together in sympathy and belief. The main event at the American Institute Fair was, in Kennedy's words, "a very beautiful exhibition of manufacturers" at the city's capacious Masonic Hall. The exhibition covered everything American made, from steam engines and rotary pumps to clocks and trusses. A recently patented steam bedbug exterminator attracted considerable attention. Following the opening of the exhibition, an overflow crowd of three thousand convened at the Chatham Street Chapel to hear Clay and Kennedy speak.[93]

Clay and Kennedy sat next to each other in the front row and were introduced as the event's featured speakers. In their addresses, both men praised the American System and, with each mention of it, drew bursts of applause. In his own speech, Kennedy explained how industrial advances were transforming the economic landscape of the nation and the productivity of its citizens: "Value is given to the production of the forest, the field, and the mine . . . The hunter, accustomed to waste half of his life in idleness upon the sunny hill-side, or to gather a precarious and scanty support from the desultory pursuit of game, is converted into a feeder of sheep, or the proprietor of a thriving mill." While publication of *Horse-Shoe Robinson* was still in the future, such descriptions anticipated the contrasting images of Wat Adair and Allan Musgrove.[94]

Of course, not every American wanted what men like Kennedy and Clay thought best for them. Some preferred the idleness of the sunny hillside to the darkness and clatter of the mill. Many Jacksonians felt these moral and economic interventionists threatened man's basic freedoms and individual rights. In his address before the American Institute, Kennedy took aim at the radical editor of the *New York Post,* William Leggett, who had demanded that these meddling politicians and reforming do-gooders "Let us alone!"[95]

Ever since his time in the Maryland legislature, Kennedy had advocated a strong role for the state in everything from internal improvements to social engineering. In a bold rejection of this laissez-faire doctrine, Kennedy argued before the Chatham Street audience that the collective community and, in its highest institutionalized form, the *state,* knew what was best for the individual. "Individual astuteness may be a safe guide in individual concerns; but it will never shape or control the circumstances of the state," he declared. If anything, Kennedy's statism had hardened in response to the extreme laissez-faire doctrine and dismantling zeal of radicals such as Leggett.[96]

After the Chatham Street event, a select group of manufacturers, politicians, and city officials dined at a fancy Broadway restaurant. Kennedy toasted Clay's speech, and Clay graciously reciprocated. The two men also spent time together at the American Hotel before Clay's sendoff from the Courtland Street dock on the final day of the fair. The steamboat *President* was decorated for the occasion, and hundreds gathered to catch a glimpse of Clay. It is not known whether Kennedy accompanied him back to Washington. Nonetheless, a bond between the two men had been sealed.[97]

No record has survived regarding what Clay and Kennedy talked about at the American Hotel. During the second half of 1833, Clay held a number of discussions around the country, some with Antimasons in the North, some with states' rights men in the South, and others with Democrats alarmed by Jackson's radical economics and imperious behavior. Still lacking, however, was a galvanizing issue to unite these disparate groups as a viable opposition. As it turned out, Jackson presented them with such an issue around the time that Clay and Kennedy were together in New York. Jackson began removing federal funds from the Second Bank of the United States and going about it in a way that brought opprobrium on himself and his party.

Jackson had, of course, vetoed the bank's rechartering in 1832. Still, radicals like William Leggett hated the bank and wanted to annihilate any vestige of it before its charter expired in 1836. Jackson shared with these radicals the fear that Nicholas Biddle, the bank's president, might use the institution's wealth and influence to extend its life. When Jackson first suggested removing federal funds from the bank, no one in his cabinet other than Amos Kendall and Roger Taney supported the idea. Congress also rejected the scheme by a large margin. Jackson then set about using the power vested in his secretary of treasury to accomplish his plan, first switching out Louis McLane for William Duane, and then Duane for Taney, at last finding someone who would execute it.

Taney began removing federal funds from the bank in October 1833, with three major consequences. The first was a severe contraction of commercial credit by Nicholas Biddle in response to the attack on his bank. This credit contraction caused business failures on a scale not seen since the Panic of 1816. The second consequence was a "motion for censure" against Jackson for circumventing the will of Congress and manipulating the cabinet to implement his plan. This rebuke to the president was organized by Clay and passed the Senate during March 1834. The third consequence was the creation of a system of "pet banks" by Taney. These were state banks, friendly to the Jackson administration, into which the funds removed from Biddle's bank were deposited. As the number of pet banks proliferated, opponents of Jackson's program argued that they were a new form of patronage. Worse still, rumors began circulating about financial abuses at several of the pet banks.[98]

One of the most notorious pet banks was the Union Bank of Baltimore. Its president, Thomas Ellicott, had always been jealous of the Second Bank of the United States, and his bank was the only one in the city to support removal. Furthermore, Ellicott was a friend of Taney, who was both a stockholder and legal counsel of the Union Bank. Ellicott was a hard-dealing giant of a man, who never let business ethics stand in the way of personal gain.

Kennedy also had a long-standing relationship with the Union Bank. He had supported its incorporation while in the Maryland legislature and served as legal counsel with Taney. Once the Union Bank became a pet bank, a clash between Kennedy and Ellicott was inevitable. During a bank meeting in which Kennedy criticized the removal program, Ellicott instructed Kennedy to keep his politics to himself. Replying that he was fed up with the "usurpations of General Jackson and his disregard for the Constitution," Kennedy severed his ties with Ellicott and the Union Bank.

This was a wise move by Kennedy. Ellicott had used his advanced knowledge that the Union Bank was to become a pet bank to enrich a circle of friends around him with bank stock. Through a holding company, Ellicott had also invested Union Bank capital in an elaborate scheme to expand the Bank of Maryland into the western part of the state. When Biddle's credit contraction caused a run on the overextended Bank of Maryland, not even Ellicott could save it from bankruptcy. When the incestuous relationship between the two banks became known, there was a similar run on the Union Bank. The ensuing financial debacle required an emergency visit by Taney to Baltimore and untold sums of federal money to ameliorate the situation. Public hearings on the defunct Bank of Maryland lasted two years and, because the bank held the savings of so many middle- and lower-class depositors, were followed by five days of rioting when the hearings ended. Ellicott was publicly disgraced by the affair, and his friendship with Taney ended.[99]

Certain aspects of Jackson's removal program made it the perfect rallying point for antiadministration forces. First, the program had been controversial from the start. A large number of Democrats, who had earlier backed the president's bank veto, thought removal was unnecessary and reckless. Removal split the party as no issue had before. Second, the economic impact of Biddle's credit contraction in response to removal was sharp and widespread. Economic distress occurred up and down the economic ladder, affecting wealthy investors as well as common wage earners. Finally, even though Biddle received his share of blame for the crisis, Jackson bore the most responsibility for initiating and doggedly pursuing removal. Not only had he ignored the advice of his cabinet and the objections of Congress, but his actions throughout seemed to fit a pattern of imperious and, some believed, tyrannical behavior.

Most important, Jackson's opponents no longer needed to argue the issue of the bank's rechartering, an issue that had lost them the recent presidential election and made them appear economic elitists. Instead, the opposition could focus upon Jackson's alleged executive usurpation, disregard for the legislature, and manipulation of the cabinet. Those who believed Jackson had abused the powers of the presidency during the removal episode now joined those states' rights men who thought he had overstepped these powers during the nullification crisis. Similarly, the Antimasons found fresh justification for their populist, antiestablishment outrage in the blatantly partisan and scandal-ridden pet bank debacle.[100]

Ever since the appearance of the 1832 cartoon of "King Andrew The First"—showing Jackson comfortably outfitted with crown, scepter, and ermine robe, holding his veto message aloft and trampling on the Constitution with his slippered foot—the idea of a Whig opposition had gathered momentum. In response to the president's Force Bill, several states' rights newspapers began referring to themselves as "Whigs." In his April 1834 Senate speech censuring Jackson, Clay likened antiadministration forces to earlier British Whigs who had opposed the dictatorial policies of their king. Shortly thereafter, James Watson Webb, editor of the *New York Courier and Enquirer,* urged the coalition against Jackson to officially adopt the Whig name. Similarly, Isaac Monroe, editor of the *Baltimore Patriot,* compared anti-Jackson forces to Revolutionary patriots. "So sure as the Whigs of the Revolution opposed arbitrary powers," Monroe wrote, "so sure will the Whigs of this day and this community oppose it." With better coordination among its parts, a viable issue around which to rally, and a relevant name to go by, the concept of a Whig opposition was gaining traction and acceptance. What had started as a series of parliamentary coups against the president was fast becoming the great political rivalry historians would one day call "the second party system."[101]

Even though they were quick to exploit the opportunity Jackson's removal program offered them, most Whigs were genuinely worried about the enlargement of presidential power occurring at the center of the Democratic administration. For nationalists and states' rights advocates alike, the preservation of a "balanced" system of government was a political priority. Ideas about the separation of powers and mixed government had defined the Whig tradition as far back as Tudor England. Seventeenth-century British writers, such as James Harrington, and so-called country-party men had articulated these beliefs. Later, they were taken up by subversive pamphleteers during the American Revolution and then by conservative authors of *The Federalist*. These ideas formed the core ideology of men like Daniel Webster, Henry Clay, Edward Everett, and other American Whigs. Webster would draw upon Harrington's *Oceana* in his most famous speeches. These ideas were reinforced by the concept of faculty psychology, where the notion of mental equilibrium was likened to balanced government. Such theories of individual governance translated logically to the body politic. Regardless of how many Whig adherents understood these traditions and interpretations, most recognized that balanced government offered the most effective safeguard against executive tyranny.[102]

During the spring of 1834, these Whig precepts found their way into the debate over Jackson's removal program and his conduct in its implementation. The Senate's motion of censure against Jackson and his written "Protest," or rebuttal, to the Senate three weeks later became opposing positions from which these constitutional principles were argued. Not surprisingly, Kennedy chose this format for his keynote address at the Maryland Whig Party's inaugural rally on April 23, 1834.[103]

The rally took place in Monument Square, not far from Kennedy's townhouse, and was an immense gathering even by Baltimore standards. By early afternoon, the square was filled to capacity. The enthusiastic throng spilled into the adjacent streets. Kennedy led off by accusing Jackson of trying to silence the Senate, a representative body of the people. His "Protest," Kennedy declared, was "an unwarranted interference between the senators and their constituencies." While Jackson had the right to select his own cabinet, Kennedy continued, its members were not "*his* agents, subject to *his* control." Rather, Kennedy argued, members of the Cabinet were "officers of *the law,* responsible to *the law,* and subject to no man's dictation" (emphasis Kennedy's).[104]

With respect to the removal program, Kennedy labeled Jackson's actions and justification for them "executive usurpation" and "dangerous dogma." The executive branch did not have exclusive authority over public money, Kennedy insisted, and only Congress could decide the placement of such money, whether in a bank, federal depository, or some other agency. Though on shaky constitutional ground regarding Jackson's handling of his cabinet, Kennedy was able to show that Jackson had overstepped his authority in the removal program. By attempting to exercise powers not delegated to him by the Constitution, Kennedy warned, Jackson was undermining the foundations of the republic.

So, what was to be done? It was the duty of the people of Maryland, Kennedy declared, drawing upon the "great and glorious Whig principles," to resist Jackson's injurious encroachments on their freedoms and liberties. To that end, Kennedy announced, the "STATE WHIG SOCIETY" formed and designated Reverdy Johnson, a distinguished former Jacksonian, as its chairman. To a cheering crowd, other notables were named to the party's organizing committee. In Maryland, at least, the Whig Party was ready for battle. Maryland Whigs attacked hard in the fall, hammering away at Jackson's economics and the hardships they had caused the state and nation. In the resulting landslide, Whigs swept the House of Delegates and captured four of eight congressional seats. They added another congressional seat the next year but failed to break the Democratic grip on Baltimore.[105]

Nationally, building a new party proved more challenging and early successes more ephemeral. In states like Maryland, where a strong National Republican Party had existed and administration policies had damaged the economy, Whigs achieved impressive victories. Also, in New York and Ohio, National Republicans and Antimasons came together quickly and seamlessly. In other places, battening together disparate anti-Jackson forces took more time. In the South, states' rights men were slow to cooperate with the new party. Men like John Tyler of Virginia and Willie P. Mangum of North Carolina could only do so much to promote Whig unity. In Louisiana, Illinois, and Indiana, where it took governorships in fall 1834, the party benefitted more from the factional rivalries among its opponents than from its own appeal. Within months of its founding, the Whig Party began losing vitality. Whereas they had captured almost 60 percent of congressional seats contested before September 1834, the Whigs took only 40 percent during the rest of the year and a paltry third of them in 1835.[106]

The problem was that the Whigs had no time to build on their initial successes. The financial panic caused by Jackson's removal program and Biddle's credit contraction, while sharp and painful for the nation, was over quickly. A robust recovery followed, led by a boom in cotton exports. During the 1830s, the value of cotton production in the United States tripled, creating a multiplier effect throughout the economy. Government land sales quadrupled because of the demand for cotton acreage in the South and for farmland to grow foodstuffs in the West. At the same time, eastern manufacturers expanded their capacity to make clothing, tools, and farm equipment. The need for improved transportation caused a resurgence in canal and railroad building. By mid-decade, Kennedy's vision of a thriving, diversified economy was being realized, albeit under the aegis of a Democratic administration. The British author and visitor to the United States, Harriet Martineau, thought nothing could end the boom short of an "earthquake."[107]

That earthquake arrived in the form of a sharp economic downturn in spring 1837. The ensuing financial panic brought on a depression of unprecedented depth and length. It would last well into the 1840s. The same factors that had produced the prior boom were responsible for its reversal. During the years of high cotton and land prices, the number of banks doubled and cash in circulation increased dramatically. Since the boom was export driven, international capital and trade flows played an important part. Britain had lent huge sums to fund land speculation and transportation projects, in addition to flooding the American market with consumer goods.

During the economic expansion, the Jackson administration lost control of its pet banks and their reckless printing of banknotes. In desperation, Jackson issued his Specie Circular during the summer of 1836 requiring federal land purchases be paid for in gold. When the Bank of England, uneasy about specie exports to the United States, raised interest rates at the same time, the American economy began to suffocate from a lack of credit. When cotton prices collapsed in early 1837, the American economy fell too.[108]

The collapse came too late to benefit the Whigs in the presidential election of 1836. Just as debilitating, however, was the party's continuing failure to organize nationally. The Whigs refused to hold a national convention before the election and fielded three presidential candidates in different parts of the country. One of these, Hugh Lawson White of Tennessee, did well in the South, apparently benefitting from the fact that Van Buren's running mate, Richard M. Johnson, lived with a mulatto mistress. Another Whig candidate, Daniel Webster, refused to vacate the contest and was reduced to running only in Massachusetts. Finally, William Henry Harrison did well in the South and the West but could not overcome the disadvantages of his party's three-pronged ticket.

Henry Clay chose to sit out the race in 1836, frustrated with his party's muddled election strategy and distracted by the illness of his only daughter, who died at the end of the year. Van Buren squeaked out 50.9 percent of the popular vote and won the electoral college by 170 versus 124 for his various opponents.

As the Whigs sifted through the ashes of defeat, they found some solace in Harrison's performance. This attractive hero of the Battle of Tippecanoe had never been a National Republican and, unlike Clay and Webster, carried no political baggage. Harrison had captured a large number of newer voters with no party loyalties and in search of fresh political options. He seemed the strongest choice for 1840. Clay's future would be left up to the party kingmakers.[109]

What is more, the depression that arrived with such force in 1837 tarred the Democrats with economic mismanagement and doomed Van Buren to a turbulent, one-term administration. His laissez-faire attitude toward the depression and its many victims seemed more hard-hearted and irresponsible the longer it dragged on. "Has he no mercy for the country?" the *National Intelligencer* asked. "No wish to alleviate the distress?" While a disaster for the nation, the collapsing economy restored the political raison d'être of the Whig Party and would serve as its springboard for the election of 1840.[110]

Kennedy had begun working on his third novel, *Rob of The Bowl,* in August 1835. Though the economy was still vibrant, he was concerned about the haphazard economic policies of the Jackson administration and what seemed to be an unraveling of the nation's social fabric. He questioned the inconsistency between the administration's hard money rhetoric and its unrestrained issuance of paper money. As he began his third novel, he pasted several newspaper articles in his journal about the Specie Circular and scrawled over them "The Gold Humbug." In the same pages, he described the rioting by the Baltimore workingmen who had lost their savings in the Bank of Maryland collapse. These riots convulsed the city for nearly a week, and dozens of people were hurt in showers of rocks and brickbats. Kennedy noted that the rioters had demolished several townhouses belonging to the bank's directors.[111]

He was not alone in his concern over the rising level of civil disturbances. *Niles' National Register* published statistics showing a spike in mob violence during the years 1834 through 1836. Public violence occurred for every conceivable reason. In Charlestown, Massachusetts, a convent was burned to the ground after Lyman Beecher delivered an anti-Catholic sermon. In nearby Boston, an antiabolitionist mob nearly killed William Lloyd Garrison. In Alton, Illinois, Elijah Lovejoy was murdered during an attack on his abolitionist press. In Hagerstown, Maryland, Irish canal workers battled for days over low pay, and, in New York City, Whig and Democratic voters traded blows so violently that the state militia had to be called in.[112]

With the onset of the depression, misery was added to violence. Massive unemployment set in as failed businesses disgorged workers at an alarming rate. In August 1837, over five hundred New York City men answered an advertisement for spade workers at $4 per month plus board. Every class of society felt the sting of economic collapse. By mid-1839, Philip Hone, an aristocratic diarist in the city, wrote that he had lost two-thirds of his wealth and both his sons were out of work. Another wealthy New Yorker, George Templeton Strong, described the general breakdown: "working men thrown out of employ by hundreds daily. Business at a stand; coal mines in Pennsylvania stopped and no fuel in prospect for next winter." As class tensions grew more acute, Strong suggested the nation was heading for "political convulsion and revolution."[113]

As the depression deepened, the Van Buren administration floundered. Its hands-off ideology precluded meaningful action to help the ailing economy. The president and radical Locofocos blamed the nation's economic ills on "moneyed power," "stock jobbers," and the alleged evils of paper money. The business community and their political allies placed responsibility on Jackson's dismantling of the banking system and the implementation of his hard-money policies. The American Institute, where Kennedy and Clay had recently spoken, condemned the compromise tariff of 1833 for exposing the nation's economy to predatory British merchants. Still others blamed the great British financial houses for inflating the country's economy and encouraging excessive consumption. "All we undertake to do," Hone observed, "is predicated on the chance of borrowing from John Bull." As in previous depressions, newspaper editorials lectured the public on the immorality of excessive consumption and vilified "luxurious habits from abroad."[114]

As a student of history and lecturer on the subject at the University of Maryland, Kennedy normally regarded such events as part of a longer historical pattern of upward growth rather than as isolated incidents. Like many Whig intellectuals, he tended to view the slow progress of the nation's development optimistically. And, yet, there was a dark side to Whig history that began to assert itself as the depression wore on. America's rising social tensions, increasing political factionalism, and worsening economic crisis were reminders that the course of empires had usually been cyclical, with periods of economic and cultural achievement followed by descent into anarchy and barbarity. Such a life-cycle model had been elaborated by Adam Ferguson, the eminent historian of the Scottish Enlightenment and, in Kennedy's time, by American Whig historian, William H. Prescott. His book on the Spanish empire, *The History of Ferdinand and Isabella,* investigated the seeds of Spain's decline from greatness and was published in the first year of the American depression. During the same year, the Whig landscape artist, Thomas Cole, exhibited a series of paintings entitled *The Course of Empire.* The paintings depicted a magnificent city rising from a bucolic landscape, flourishing during its moment of greatness, and then falling into decadence, social chaos, and ruin. Similarly, the Whig jurist, Rufus Choate, wrote that a nation could only *delay* its demise by paying assiduous attention to its vital institutions and cultural underpinnings. These Whig intellectuals expressed their underlying fears that nations, like individuals, were prone to aging and decay.[115]

These melancholy thoughts swept over Kennedy as he walked the barren fields that had once been the town of St. Mary's, the former capital of seventeenth-century Maryland and the setting for *Rob of The Bowl.* This once vibrant community had been reduced to a few scattered shards and bleached ground beneath his feet. Gone were the sounds of life in St. Mary's, the playful din of young children and the gruff exchanges of worthy burghers at street corners. And what of that race of people who had hunted in these fields even earlier? What traces of their existence called out for some feeble acknowledgement? "They are gone!" Kennedy cries out despairingly at the beginning of his novel.

> Like shadows have these men of might sunk on the earth. They, their game, their wigwams, their monuments, their primeval forests,—yea, even their graves, have flitted away in this spectral flight. Saxon and Norman, bluff Briton and heavy Suabian inherit the land. And in its turn, well-a-day! Our pragmatical little city hath departed. Not all its infant glory, nor its manhood's bustle, its walls, gardens and bowers,—its warm housekeeping, its gossiping burghers, its politics and its factions,—not even its prolific dames and gamesome urchins could keep it in the upper air until this our day. Alas, for the vaulting pride of the village, the vain glory of the city, and

the metropolitan boast! St. Mary's hath sunk to the level of Tyre and Sidon, Balbec and Palmyra! She hath become trackless, tokenless.[116]

So, why did Kennedy feel compelled to resurrect the town of St. Mary's, long obliterated and forgotten by the 1830s, in his third novel? The answer touches on his literary impulse as a historical novelist and his compulsion as a Whig moralist, witnessing what he saw as the cultural declension of his own time and imagining a better society in the past.

Kennedy's historical research for *Rob of The Bowl* was unprecedented for its time. He spent weeks at the state archives in Annapolis, examining crumbling records from Lord Baltimore's governing council and other documents from the 1670s and 1680s. He painstakingly reconstructed the story of the failed Protestant rebellion by Josias Fendall and John Coode against Lord Baltimore's Catholic government. Many of the novel's characters, such as Baltimore's dashing but impetuous nephew, George Talbert, and other members of the council are based on historical persons. So too, the great estates in the novel, namely, "Rose Croft" and "Notely Hall," are modeled on actual residences. Kennedy even incorporated minor events from the period into his story to enhance its feeling of authenticity and strengthen its factual context.[117]

Like other writers of historical romances, Kennedy felt the need to enhance the spare descriptions of those who lived in the past in order "to clothe them in the flesh and blood of human brotherhood" and portray their time as "a world of living figures." As he imagined it, seventeenth-century St. Mary's was an Old World Cavalier culture transplanted to the untamed shores of the Chesapeake Bay. Many of its residents retained their European habits and manners. Some still spoke with heavy accents, signaling their origins. To create this sense of historical distance for his readers, Kennedy drew on his knowledge of Elizabethan drama. One of the novel's main characters, the portly wit and captain of the town guard, Jasper Dauntrees, is modeled after Shakespeare's Falstaff, and Dame Dorothy, mistress of the Crow and Arrow Tavern, where Dauntrees and his cronies do their drinking, appears to be derived from Mistress Quickly, who appears in several of Shakespeare's plays. While the young hero of the novel, Albert Verheyden, is probably original, he is thinly drawn compared to the novel's other characters. The same can be said of the beautiful young heroine, Blanche Warden. In both cases, Kennedy's efforts to embellish them with chivalrous speech and behavior impedes their development as characters.[118]

The novel's namesake, Rob of the Bowl, may have been inspired by Irving's *Money Diggers*. This pathetic but hardened recluse, who navigates his legless torso using a bowl-like contraption strapped beneath him and makes his living smuggling, stands out as one of the oddest figures in literature. Other characters such as Garret Weasel and Arnold de la Grange, both "wet companions" of Dauntrees, as well as Richard Cocklescraft, the villainous British pirate and Rob's partner in crime, round out the novel's colorful cast.

The chief criticism of *Rob of The Bowl* has been that it lacks a central character. One could argue, however, that Kennedy meant St. Mary's itself to be the central character of the novel and that the town's cast of characters brings it to life. Neither of his previous novels, both set in rural locations, allowed Kennedy to describe a real community and to examine the social fabric that gives it coherence. With his idealized portrait of St. Mary's, Kennedy is able not only to describe a harmonious society as it might have been in the past but to suggest how such a society could be recreated out of the social discord of his own time. While sensitive to historical facts, he renders his picture of old Catholic Maryland in the light of his experiences as an American in the 1830s. What is more, the resulting portrait is filtered through the author's finely ground moral lens; St. Mary's could be renamed "Whigville."[119]

From their earliest days on the river that gave the town its name, the people of St. Mary's have watched "the wilderness put forth blossoms of security and comfort." By Lord Baltimore's time, a small garrison has been established at St. Mary's. The harbor is guarded by a stone fort, its brass cannons positioned like "watch dogs against the horizon." No less important is the fortitude of the people. "The deep, unconquerable faith in religion and the impassioned instincts of Anglo-Saxon devotion," Kennedy writes, "were breathed by household groups in customary household terms."[120]

The town's orderly plan gives prominence to the institutions that inculcate these values in its citizens. At one end of the main square sits the State House, side-by-side with the tools of governing authority, "a sturdy and tight jail," "pillory and stocks," and a "ducking stool, that hung over a pool of sufficient depth for the most obstinate case that might occur." At the other side of the square stands the Catholic Church of St. Ignatius. On days when mass is held, troops of town elders, young men, and maidens make their way there "in orderly steps." Inside the church, the tall figure of Father Pierre, arrayed in his black tunic and towering over them, dispenses spiritual leadership and moral guidance to his parishioners. Though popular with the community, his sudden appearance on the street "subdued the gayety of the crowd." The young women of St. Mary's, including Blanche Warden, seek out "the valuable instructions of Father Pierre."[121]

Following Father Pierre's example, Christian charity and mercy permeate the community. Those more privileged go about their good works with "scrupulous regularity." Lord Baltimore's sister, Lady Maria, is the most zealous promoter of these activities, as she "visited the sick, fed the hungry, and clothed the naked." Such impulses of Christian charity have virtually eliminated class tension and bind St. Mary's society together. Compassionate sentiments drift down to its lowest orders. Everyone, for example, treats the village idiot, Wise Watkin, with sympathy and kindness.

While the institutions of church and state exert a unifying influence on St. Mary's, Lord Baltimore, referred to as "The Proprietary," is instrumental in setting the harmonious tone of community life. He has endeavored to impress upon the native peoples of the region the "pacific temper" of the community and "treat with the Indians upon friendly bargain and sale." What is more, Lord Baltimore has "erected his government upon the basis of perfect religious freedom." Because of its tolerance, St. Mary's has become not only a refuge for those of his own faith but "an asylum to all who might wish for shelter in a land where opinion should be free and conscience undisturbed." Given the callous treatment of native peoples and religious intolerance in his own time, Kennedy's description of the St. Mary's proprietorship seems tinged with elegiac wistfulness.[122]

There is also a prevailing "air of competence and comfort" about St. Mary's. The job of ensuring that the provincial purse is kept full enough to provide for the protection of the community falls to Anthony Warden, known as "The Collector." Warden sees that customs duties are collected at the port and is renowned for his dedication and honesty. Both the character of his daughter and the appearance of his estate attest to Warden's exemplary nature. Although she is the town's reigning beauty, there is no one more humble and devout than Blanche Warden. Everything about Warden's estate, Rose Croft, from its straight pathways and orderly parterres, serves as an infallible index of his "purity of mind."[123]

As Kennedy looks back on it, old Catholic Maryland seems to him "the most wisely planned and honestly executed scheme of society which at that era, at least, was to be found in the annals of mankind." He yearns for a return to such an organic community, where social classes harmonize with one another to form a unified whole. In St. Mary's, a visitor can easily distinguish someone's standing in society by their dress and deportment. "The divisions of society were not more authentically distinguished," Kennedy writes, "than in the embroidered velvet of the man of wealth, and the plain serge, worsted, or leather of the craftsman." Still more important is how the lower classes of society conduct themselves. Before the great dance at Rose Croft, for example, every member of the community fulfills their allotted role in preparing for the event. Cooks labor over the evening's delicacies, seamstresses sew ladies into their gowns, and gardeners trim hedges so tightly that "not a straggling leaf shall you see upon it." As the honored guests arrive, Willy of the Flats, the town fiddler, cries out, "hands to your caps lads, and wenches sink!"[124]

Whereas he had used the chivalric mode to mock the pretensions of plantation life in *Swallow Barn,* Kennedy employs it in *Rob of The Bowl* to glorify the hierarchical society of St. Mary's. It is as though the earliest immigrants to Maryland not only have brought their Cavalier culture with them from the Old World but have succeeded in reviving its feudal origins in their New World setting. Kennedy embellishes his novel with chivalric language, courtly manners, rich costumes, formal gardens, and, near the end of the novel, an elaborate festival with knightly combat on the village green. Lord Baltimore's physical appearance and dignity attest to his "stateliness and feudal importance," while his ardent supporter, George Talbot, exhibits "the firm stride and dauntless carriage of a belted and booted knight of chivalry." Lady Maria takes a "feudal pride" in her good works, and Blanche Warden is described as "a fresh and blooming maiden." Blanche's lover, Albert Verheyden, woos her with his lute playing, hawking skills, and chivalric verse recited in the original French. At one point, even the crippled Rob rides quixotically into St. Mary's with his bowl "hanging by a strap like a shield at his back."[125]

While his indulgence in the chivalric mode can be explained by the popular, Scott-inspired literary conventions of his day and is accommodated by the antiquarian setting of his tale, Kennedy's religious views of early Maryland are harder to understand. If unaware that Kennedy was a Protestant, the reader of *Rob of The Bowl* would think its author a devout Catholic. "The gentle solicitude with which the ministers of that ancient faith watch and assist the growing zeal of its votaries," Kennedy writes, "the captivation of its venerable ceremonies, and the familiar and enduring tone in which it addresses itself to the regard of its children, sufficiently account for the sway over so large a portion of mankind."[126]

As a storytelling device, Kennedy's portrayal of Catholic Maryland as a New World religious exotic contributes to the uniqueness of his novel. More fundamentally, however, he seems genuinely impressed with the "discipline of the Romish church" as a unifying institution. Compared to mainstream Protestantism, rent by revivalist schisms and eroded by new sects and cults during the 1820s and 1830s, American Catholicism seemed stable and unified. Furthermore, by describing Lord Baltimore's Maryland as a beacon of religious tolerance, Kennedy may have hoped to mitigate rising levels of anti-Catholic prejudice in Maryland and elsewhere. Even though he was of Scotch-Irish Protestant descent and a member of the Presbyterian Church, Kennedy felt considerable sympathy and kinship with Irish Catholics. Kennedy was a member of the Hibernian Society of Baltimore and years later would eschew membership in the anti-Catholic Know-Nothing Party, much to his political detriment.[127]

In spite of its wise government and reputation for tolerance, old Catholic Maryland was not without problems. Since he is writing a didactic history, Kennedy proceeds to delineate these problems and show how they contributed to the passing of such a prosperous and harmonious society. Not surprisingly, he goes about this with a close eye on his own times. In his view, the most dangerous threat to good government, in his own and Lord Baltimore's day, was political faction. Like many Whigs, an antiparty strain tinctured Kennedy's conception of politics. In part, this was because the Whigs were so convinced of their own beliefs that they were incapable of acknowledging rival points of view. Also, more than a decade of Jacksonian party politics, during which the use of patronage and the so-called spoils system was seen by many as having corrupted the country's political process, tended to reinforce these convictions. Still, true antiparty convictions had a long history going back to America's early years and, before that, to British Whig thought. According to such thought, political interest groups could settle their differences through negotiation and compromise, a process that, if properly managed, would result in a kind of ecumenical majority in legislative government. Ironically, Kennedy and many of his fellow Whigs came to see themselves as nonpartisan. In doing so, they regarded professional party men as no better than self-interested schemers.[128]

The problem of faction serves as the political backdrop for Kennedy's story of colonial Maryland. The problem preoccupies Lord Baltimore's council meetings and erupts in an attempted coup d'etat by the Protestant faction, barely suppressed by George Talbot, Jasper Dauntrees, and other forces loyal to Baltimore. In recounting it, Kennedy gives the Protestant insurgents no rhetorical quarter. Having no legitimate grievances to excuse their disloyalty, he describes them as "church brawlers," "vaporing bullies," and "factious stirrers of discord." He characterizes the Protestant leaders Josias Fendall and John Coode as "rapacious malcontents" who threaten to bring down Baltimore's enlightened government with their "wily propensity for mischief."

What motivates Fendall and Coode, Kennedy explains, are the spoils of political office. Both men are "thirsty leeches" who crave material gain from the "emoluments of post." Coode has set his sights on the potentially lucrative collectorship, Anthony Warden's office, and "gloated upon it with the gaze of a serpent." If the Protestants get their way, men like Warden, "who have won a home by valor and patient, wise endurance" will be disenfranchised by these undeserving conspirators.[129]

While Fendall and Coode pose a threat to the peace and tranquility of St. Mary's, Captain Richard Cocklescraft is the ultimate disturber of community. "There is nothing but riot and reeling from the time the skipper is expected in port until he leaves it," Dauntrees observes. British by nationality and a former pirate by trade, Cocklescraft has sailed the world under several flags and amassed a bloody resume. From his ship, *Olive Branch,* he has hailed and plundered many a naïve vessel at sea, and he and his ferocious crew have reduced several towns the size of St. Mary's to ashes.[130]

Because he is without principles, Cocklescraft is politically flexible. Once he becomes involved in St. Mary's politics, he espouses the Protestant cause to advance his fortunes. He is quick to recognize the benefits of replacing Anthony Warden with John Coode, sure to be a more compliant customs collector. Recently, Cocklescraft has turned to smuggling for a living. Posing as an honest merchant, he has built up a thriving business by circumventing duties at the port of St. Mary's. Cocklescraft, Rob, and their band of cutthroats conduct their illicit trade in an abandoned and allegedly haunted structure known as the "Black Chapel," symbolically located across the St. Mary's estuary from Father Pierre's house of worship. Although aware of his reputation, a number of St. Mary's citizens do business with Cocklescraft. He and Rob deal mainly in wines, liquor, and luxury goods, "costly stuffs, and tissues of exceeding richness, such as cloth of gold, velvets of Genoa, arras and tapestries." At one point, Dauntrees chides Garrett Weasel, the owner of the Arrow and Crow Tavern, for selling smuggled spirits.[131]

Cocklescraft also has designs on Blanche. "Her dress was characterized by simplicity," Kennedy writes. "No jewel or gem contributed its luster to grace her person . . . [or] consorted with the virgin purity or artless character of the wearer." Misreading her simple taste and upright character, Cocklescraft gives her an elegant cloak. Of course, Blanche spurns his offering, bluntly telling him, "I am unused to such gaudy trappings, and should not be content to wear such a cloak." Rejected and furious, Cocklescraft makes plans to abduct Blanche under cover of darkness.[132]

Cocklescraft's British origin and his aversion to paying customs duties had their inspiration in Kennedy's tariff advocacy and criticism of British trade practices. In Kennedy's view, British merchants not only threatened America's fledgling industries but perverted public morals with imported luxuries. As far back as his "Swiss Traveller" essays, Kennedy had warned that women were especially susceptible to these temptations. Cocklescraft's gift to Blanche is an example of how such subversions are meant to trap innocent female prey.

One of the strangest interpolated episodes in Kennedy's third novel is the arrival in St. Mary's of Dr. Claus Debor, better known as the "Dutch Doctor." This itinerant purveyor of patent medicine, announced by a trumpeter as he enters the town dragging his kit of pharmacological wonders, is probably a caricature of President Van Buren. "He was a little, sharp-featured portly man," Kennedy writes, " in a white periwig, cream colored coat and scarlet small clothes: of a brisk gait, and consequential air, which was heightened by the pompous gesture with which he swayed a gold-mounted cane full as tall as himself." This "travelling healer of disease" got his start in Albany, New York, in the employ of the colonial governor there, and now peddles his magical cures throughout the land. "Not withstanding his broad accent," Kennedy observes, "he spoke with a ready fluency that showed him well skilled in that voluble art by which, at that day, workers of wonderful cures and possessors of infallible elixirs advertised the astonishing virtues of their compounds." By the time of Kennedy's third novel, Van Buren's short stature and natty style of dress, as well as his shrewd politicking and allegedly aristocratic taste, had become subject to Whig ridicule. So, too, did Van Buren's hard-money nostrums for the ailing economy seem to men like Kennedy little better than alchemy.[133]

As he had done with *Horse-Shoe Robinson,* Kennedy concludes *Rob of The Bowl* with a flourish of action and revelations about its characters. As it turns out, Albert Verheyden is Rob's long-lost son. Upon discovering this, Rob repents his past and helps rescue Blanche from the clutches of Cocklescraft. Blanche and Albert are reunited but not before Cocklescraft takes Rob's life. As the crippled man expires, Father Pierre grants him absolution. Kennedy allows Cocklescraft to escape from St. Mary's, possibly signaling an intention to bring him back in a sequel.[134]

Unfortunately, this was not to be. *Rob of The Bowl* was published in fall 1838. Kennedy's publisher, Lea and Blanchard, printed four thousand copies, but sales were sluggish, partly due to a worsening economy. Kennedy's strange tale, with its exotic setting and antiquarian flavor, also went up against more conventional stories published the same year by James Fenimore Cooper, Robert Montgomery Bird, and William Gilmore Simms. Furthermore, the novel's praiseworthy treatment of Catholicism was out of step with the rise of nativism during the period. One reviewer in the *Gentleman's Magazine,* while praising the novel as an "able work," noted that certain of its characters suffered from a "lack of power" and that an "excess of dialects" made parts of it tedious. Nor would the passage of time be kind to Kennedy's third novel. *Rob of The Bowl* would be reprinted only eight times until 1907, after which it faded from the country's literary memory.[135]

Even though John Latrobe claimed it had been "struck off in a heat," Kennedy's third novel had taken longer than *Horse-Shoe Robinson* to complete. Possibly, it took longer because Kennedy had to do historical research for the novel, but it was more likely that he was too busy with his legal work and political activities to find time for writing. During 1835, Kennedy was admitted to practice before the U.S. Supreme Court, and, in 1837 and 1838, he stood for a seat in the U.S. House of Representatives. The first time he was narrowly defeated, and the second time he won.[136]

Given his hard work for the Whig Party of Maryland, including taking a strong hand in its founding, Kennedy was the obvious candidate to break the Democratic grip on the city's congressional representation. He lost his initial run in the fall of 1837 by less than two hundred votes out of twelve hundred cast. It had been a scurrilous campaign in which his opponent, Isaac McKim, attacked Kennedy with everything from his political past and tarred him as a "novelist" who, by nature, had little sense for practical matters. However, when McKim suddenly died in office the next spring, Kennedy was again nominated and won handily. He had not held public office for fifteen years and was the first Whig to represent his native city in Congress. From Washington, Kennedy wrote his uncle Philip Pendleton, "I wish you could get one glimpse of Henry Clay's face as it was yesterday when he came down to my room and dined with me."[137]

While he was delighted to see the affable and energetic Marylander receive his political reward, Clay was also in desperate need of Whig support in the House. During the previous session, the Whigs, outnumbered in the Senate, had failed to block passage of President Van Buren's Sub-Treasury Bill. This legislation called for the separation of the banking system from the federal government through the creation of an "independent treasury." This idea had its origins with William Gouge, the guiding philosopher of the hard-money Democrats. Van Buren's plan would establish a sub-treasury branch in every major city. These sub-treasury branches would no longer accept state banknotes but only specie and newly issued Treasury notes. With this cumbersome piece of legislation, Van Buren hoped to satisfy both the hard-money and paper-money wings of his party. To further complicate matters, Calhoun attached a last-minute amendment to the bill requiring all payments into the sub-treasury branches be made exclusively in specie after 1840. By upstaging Van Buren, Calhoun wanted to reap political credit from hard-money Democrats and states' rights faction. With Calhoun's amendment attached, the Sub-Treasury Bill passed the Senate and went to the House for debate as Kennedy took his seat in June 1838.[138]

In his maiden speech there, Kennedy attacked the Sub-Treasury Bill head-on. He ridiculed the "phantasmagoria" of hard-money theory and cited recent economic events as proof of its folly. He urged the administration to "cast aside its experiments, devices and jejune expedients" and address the real needs of the economy. Kennedy called the Sub-Treasury Bill pure legerdemain. He pointed out that New Yorkers thought its passage would expand the amount of paper money in circulation, while its supporters in South Carolina and Virginia believed it would put paper money on the path to extinction. By pointing out these perceptual inconsistencies, Kennedy hoped to drive a wedge between the paper-money and hard-money factions of the Democratic Party and wreck Van Buren's legislation.

In reaction to Calhoun's support for the Sub-Treasury Bill, Kennedy took aim at South Carolina in his speech. "South Carolina," Kennedy reminded the House, "has gone in pursuit of strange gods—she has fallen into the spiritual sins of false doctrine, heresy and schism; she has become mischievously sophisticated, bewildered with political metaphysics." Of course the proposed separation of the federal government from the banking system and the parceling out of supervisory authority to the localities appealed to South Carolina. Virginia's behavior was little better, Kennedy went on. The worthy gentlemen of that state had become so suspicious of the dangers posed by national commerce, and so narrow in their view of the Constitution, that they were now "mere naked divorce men." Both South Carolina and Virginia, Kennedy warned, threatened "the circle of trade" that bound the nation together, and, if not opposed, would "leave the different geographical sections of the country no longer useful to each other in their dealings." Such attitudes, he predicted, "would lead irresistibly to separation."[139]

In his first two novels, Kennedy had hinted at aspects of what he said in his diatribe against Virginia and South Carolina. Here were echoes of Frank Meriwether's exaggerated fears of interstate commerce and Philip Lindsay's bizarre metaphysics and confused loyalties. But the House debate was no place for such nuance and subtlety. Kennedy continued to bore into the fragile logic of the administration's policies. How was the country supposed to recover from the pet-banking debacle and hard-money missteps that had ruined the economy? Wouldn't the centrifugal tendencies being encouraged by Van Buren's banking legislation work against an economic recovery? How exactly would credit be transferred from New York to New Orleans with each state "sovereign as respects the question of banking?"[140]

Kennedy and opponents of the Sub-Treasury Bill were remarkably successful in blocking its passage. The bill was subjected to slashing debate in the House during 1838 and 1839 and was defeated whenever it came to a vote. When the Democrats finally managed to pass the bill in January 1840, their victory was short-lived. A Whig majority repealed it a year later.[141]

Kennedy unleashed a second oratorical attack on the Democrats during February 1839. He began by cataloguing the statesmen who had either abandoned President Jackson or been purged by him. Casting the administration in the dark hues of a Shakespearian tragedy, Kennedy asked, "Where is Berrien, Branch, Ingham? Where is Duane, McLane, and other friends of the chief?" Those who remained had either been corrupted by their complicity or were feckless and unable to lead the country out of its economic dilemma. This paucity of talent explained how, after destroying the Second Bank and removing its funds, the administration had ensured that these funds were "scattered far and wide with a profuse indulgence." Such profligacy, Kennedy observed, had encouraged a frenzy of lending competition between the pet banks, stimulated unprecedented land speculation across the country, and encouraged unrestrained consumption by the public. "Trade, traffic and adventure spurned their old and sober channels," he recalled. "The farmer turned from his plough, and the mechanic from his tools to become lords of boundless acres and founders of towns and cities. People became extravagant in their habits of expense and rioted in the imagination of riches infinite," Kennedy explained.

Then, like a drunkard stumbling upon a temperance tract, Kennedy continued, Jackson had picked up William Gouge's "book of banking horrors" and suddenly changed course. Infected with "hard money madness," Jackson had imposed the Specie Circular, requiring massive importations of gold from abroad. Not long after this "famous abortion," the nation's bloated, confused, and exhausted economy had descended into depression. "The idea of political consistency never entered into the President's head," Kennedy concluded.[142]

But how had Jackson and his party survived this succession of economic blunders and policy reversals? Why had these "wild and visionary theories," these "heavings and spasms of capricious power," failed to bring the Democrats down? The answer, Kennedy averred, was far more nefarious than the impetuous and fickle behavior of their leader. Jackson owed his survival to what Kennedy called "coherence of party." Years before, Jackson and his political friends had recruited "an army of party-zealots," whom they nourished on "spoils" and schooled in "subserviency." There were squadrons of these spoilsmen, he told the House, who were kept in line by "the force of party dictation" and Jackson's "dictatorial authority." These men were kept in "perpetual motion" and had to be nimble to navigate the "quick sand" of changing policy. Their only goal was to promote "the mischievous popularity of the Executive" and, in doing so, advance their own careers.

In this tightly controlled party system, Kennedy argued, nothing was what it seemed. Defending the party's shifting policies required "an organized plan of misrepresentation." After flouting the will of the people with his vetoes and intimidation of Congress, Jackson had bestowed the name "Democracy" on his party. More recently, President Van Buren had peddled his Sub-Treasury Bill as a panacea to both hard-and soft-money Democrats, adjusting his story depending on which group he was addressing. Kennedy called the party's newspaper, the *Globe,* an "engine of slander." It was trying to paint the Whigs as allies of "Abolition," a charge he vehemently denied. Party demagogues were spreading this falsity high and low, from the "tippling shop" to the floor of the Senate. The entire party, he concluded, "lived and moved, and had its being in the Universal, Inextinguishable, Everlasting LIE."[143]

Kennedy would have continued these attacks on the Democrats had he not lost his House seat in the fall of 1839. He may have become complacent about his constituency. Baltimore Democrats had held power too long to be denied it by the untimely death of Isaac McKim and their underestimation of Kennedy's popularity. Taking no chances in 1839, they generated a massive voter turnout, four times that of the previous year, and swamped Kennedy's reelection campaign. Of five thousand votes cast, he lost by only four hundred. Denied the House floor to continue his attack on the opposition, Kennedy had no choice but to reach for his pen.[144]

The defeat shocked Kennedy, but he soon realized that the critique he had leveled at the Democratic Party in the House had cost him the election. He had, in fact, been attacked by an "army of party-zealots" and suffered the consequences of their unfounded slander and manipulation of the electorate. In a long journal entry following his defeat, Kennedy analyzed how the Democratic Party chieftains had mobilized the lower classes of society with "cheap flattery" and the promise of easy rewards "from the public coffers and public employment." These party leaders had used every trick to "rouse the passions, flatter the prejudices and blind the perception of the masses they lead." Taken together, these insights served as the premise for Kennedy's political satire *Quodlibet.*[145]

Unlike the well-governed community of St. Mary's, the town of Quodlibet has been totally corrupted by politics. Yet, most of its citizens are happy with their lot because the town has grown enormously prosperous since "The Removal," the year after which all events are dated in the Quodlibetarian calendar. By designating Jackson's removal as "Year 1" and by calling his political operatives "Jacobins" throughout *Quodlibet,* Kennedy associates the excesses of Jacksonianism with those of the French Revolution.[146]

The story of this booming little borough is narrated by Simon Secondthoughts, the local schoolmaster and secretary of the "Grand Central Committee of Unflinching New Light Quodlibetarian Democrats." Nicknamed "Sober" by his friends, his name was inspired by President Van Buren's oft-quoted statement, that "The sober, second thoughts of the people is never wrong." Throughout his narrative, Secondthoughts endeavors to put the best face on the confusing and questionable activities of the local Democratic Party. This is because he once tutored the town's esteemed Democratic congressman, Middleton Flam, and regularly enjoys a plate at Flam's table. Secondthoughts eloquently describes his relationship with Flam as "embalmed in the unction of my gratitude." While sticking mainly to politics, Secondthoughts occasionally describes the town's bucolic setting in lyrical prose. After such lapses, he asks his readers to "excuse his poetical orgasms."[147]

Intended to portray a microcosm of Jacksonian culture, *Quodlibet* also served as a mocking commentary on 1830s Baltimore, with its frenetic commerce, corrupt banking practices, and spoils-fed Democratic politicians. Not only is Quodlibet's topography similar to that of hilly, watery Baltimore, but certain characters in the story are modeled after some of the town's prominent figures. For example, Nicodemus Handy, the head cashier at the Copper-Plate Bank of Quodlibet, is fashioned after Thomas Ellicott, president of Baltimore's Union Bank. Eliphalet Fox, Democratic editor of the *Whole Hog,* closely resembles James H. Cox, editor of the *Baltimore Republican.* Elliot had been responsible for Kennedy's separation from the Union Bank and for that bank's demise, and Cox had hectored Kennedy during much of his political career. Finally, Middleton Flam, whose father is described in the story as a Hartford Convention Federalist, bears a likeness to Benjamin Chew Howard, the silk-stocking Democrat who defeated Kennedy in his 1839 congressional race and whose father had been an arch-Federalist. Once he got into it, Kennedy found *Quodlibet* an excellent way to settle scores around town.[148]

The story line of *Quodlibet* begins after Jackson's removal and distribution of funds to the pet banks, one of which is Handy's Copper-Plate Bank. The story continues through the Sub-Treasury debate in Congress and the hard-soft money schism in the Democratic Party. It concludes with the Whig presidential victory in 1840. Kennedy's recounting of these events—supplemented with partially fictionalized letters from Treasury Secretary Roger Taney, speeches by Presidents Jackson and Van Buren, and selected *Globe* articles—while interesting to Kennedy's contemporaries, places a heavy burden on today's readers. Similarly, *Quodlibet's* satirical style, harkening back to the neoclassical and reminiscent of the *Red Book,* requires patience by modern readers to reap its humorous payoff. Finally, time has obscured many of the more parochial references in the story. Still, in spite of these hurdles, *Quodlibet* provides a rare, on-the-ground look at the important election of 1840. Kennedy's description of shifting party allegiances and the ideological tensions driving them, while exaggerated for humorous effect, are rendered in the vernacular of the day.[149]

Any reader of *Swallow Barn* might predict how Kennedy would demonstrate the degraded state of Jacksonian politics in *Quodlibet.* The author relocates the likes of Sandy Walker and Miles Rutherford from the countryside to the urban barroom as Flanigan Sucker and Ben Inky. He even recasts the impartial tavern owner from his first novel as Jesse Ferret, who, like his literary predecessor, insists that "a Publican should have no side" vis-à-vis the opinions of his patrons and, when pressed for his views, falls back on his "sentiments." Ferret's tavern, "The Hero," serves as the venue for the story's most animated political discussions. Party leaders such as Agamemnon Flag and Theodore Fog seem incapable of practicing their craft anywhere but "the hot atmosphere of the cock-tail and julep manufacturies." During a rare absence from the barroom to attend a campaign rally, Fog becomes so intoxicated that he can hardly speak. His addled condition is of no consequence, Secondthoughts explains, because Fog has "all the thirstiest men in the Borough under his thumb."[150]

Unlike in *Swallow Barn,* however, Kennedy provides readers of *Quodlibet* with more than passing glimpses of these rough-natured, politically involved men. Their fuller treatment allows him to show how confused they have become because of the constantly changing and contradictory messages provided by their leadership. "I never could keep any principles upon account of the changes," Jesse Ferret complains.

> Before a plain, simple man can cleverly tell where he is, everything has wisked away in the contrary direction. One year we are "all tariff," and the next "down with it as an abomination." Here we go for "canals and railroads!"—crack the whip, and we are all t'other side . . . Here, t'other day,

> this here Sub-Treasury was monarchy and revolution to boot, and treason outright; and now, what it *is,* every man's afeared to say—some's for, some's against—some's both, and it's all in a state of amalgamation, perplexity and caterwauling unaccountability. What with between specy circular, anti-masons, pocketing of bills (Lord knows what that means), vetoes, distribution, fortifications, abolition, running down of Indians and running up of accounts, politics has got into a jumble that a Philadelphia lawyer couldn't steer through.[151]

While sympathetic to Ferret's quandary, Secondthoughts believes it serves as a warning for such men "against the folly of ever allowing themselves to have any individual opinion." The better course, he tells Ferret, is "the perfect surrender of himself to the cause of his party." With leadership like Middleton Flam, there is no reason to agonize about the changing course of events or the party's shifting interpretation of them. "We are, at all hazards, real Flam men," Secondthoughts insists. "As a principle, our New Light Democracy is all out and out Flam."[152]

Changes in party direction are of no importance to Flam. He believes the party should never commit to anything and that commitment is antithetical to freedom. "There is no reproach in the fact that we neither build, legislate, think nor determine for the next generation," Flam declares. "We oppose Vested Rights, Charted Privileges . . . we oppose Tariffs, Internal Improvements, Colleges and Universities, on the broad democratic ground, that we have nothing to do with Posterity. Posterity will be as free as we are. Let it take care of itself." In short, laissez-faire doctrine for Quodlibetarians means doing absolutely nothing about anything.[153]

Nor can Theodore Fog, even after his radical "True Grits" have hived off from Flam's "New Lights," disagree with Flam about the need for political flexibility. Fog makes no excuses for President Jackson's shifts in policy. "Well, sirs, he *did* change—What of it? Is Democracy like the laws of the Medes and the Persians?" he asks at a True Grit rally. "Is the great sublime truth which vivifies the patriot's heart, resuscitates his ambition and sparkles in the human breast, like a stone at the bottom of a well for toads to sit on? . . . Is not democracy itself the march of intellect? And does not marching consist in change of place? I hear you all answer, Aye, aye, aye!"[154]

Of course, Kennedy was just as critical of the Democrats' duplicitous rhetoric as he was of their doctrinal inconsistency. In *Quodlibet,* the master of truth bending is, not surprisingly, Middleton Flam. His followers stand in awe of his semantic manipulations. Whereas the Flam family seat was formerly called "Quality Hall" and was situated on "Poplar Flats," he renames his mansion "Equality Hall" and its location "Popular Flats." After making these simple but meaningful alterations, Flam realizes that "Words are Things." Pondering this awhile, he declares, "I might say *better* than Things." In Quodlibetarian politics, he decides, "a name is half the battle." If, for example, "We wish to destroy the Bank; we have only to call it a Monster: We desire to put down the opposition, and keep the offices amongst ourselves; all that we have to do is set up a cry of Aristocracy. If we want to stop a canal, we clamor against Consolidation."[155]

Secondthoughts revels at what he perceives as the "sublime system" of Democratic politics. "The beauty of this unrivalled philosophy," he observes, "consists of the harmony with which it reconciles past time with the present, with which it dovetails discordant principles." And, yet, Kennedy allows doubt to penetrate his narrator's partisan filter. The True Grits—Kennedy's fictional surrogate for the radical Locofocos, who split the party in the late 1830s—have deserted Flam's New Lights. What is more, the True Grits have begun attacking the town's merchants, no matter how humble their line of trade, as "Money Power." Theodore Fog, leader of the True Grits, declares that, "for every *one* merchant you lay on his back, you gain *five* True Grits on your side." He urges his followers to brand every merchant "a Rag Baron, a Ruffled Shirt, [or] a Scrub Aristocrat."[156]

Men like Abel Brawn and Neal Hopper, Quodlibet's blacksmith and miller, respectively, have been loyal Democrats most of their lives and are astonished to find themselves under attack. "Who are the rich they are talking about?" Abel asks. "Is industry a sin in this land, that when it has earned a little something for a wet day, the man who has thriven by it must be held up as an enemy to his country?" As industrious and thrifty members of the merchant class, these men realize they are in the wrong party.[157]

The debate over the sub-treasury exacerbates the split between the New Lights and True Grits. Confusion reigns as to "whether the Sub-Treasury is to kill or cure the banking system." The party's credibility begins to evaporate in the heat of rhetorical excess. After Handy's Cooper-Plate Bank collapses and he flees to Europe, the True Grits label his bank "a Whig-Rag Factory." As the Whigs turn the power of words against the Democrats—this time "LOG CABIN" and "HARD CIDER"—Secondthoughts urges the party to find new and more powerful words for its counterattack. "Abolition is the best hobby we have since the death of the Monster," he declares.[158]

The Whig juggernaut described in *Quodlibet* began at the party's December 1839 convention in Harrisburg, Pennsylvania. Once delegates chose William Henry Harrison and John Tyler to head the Whig ticket, someone coined the slogan "Tippecanoe and Tyler Too." A few days later, James Cox's *Baltimore Republican* inadvertently supplied even more potent imagery. An editorial in that Democratic newspaper suggested that the elderly Harrison be given a barrel of hard cider and pensioned off to a log cabin. Because Van Buren had been accused of living extravagantly in the White House while the rest of the country suffered, the Whigs pounced on these imputations of their candidate's humble origins and simple taste as a way to differentiate him from the president. Now, from New York to Illinois, antiadministration newspapers juxtaposed Harrison's alleged simplicity with the elite image of Van Buren. The *Albany Evening Post* declared that the "The Log Cabin is a symbol of nothing Van Burenism knows, feels, or can appreciate." Within months, the Whigs had rolled out an impressive array of campaign paraphernalia, which included coonskin caps, cider mugs, log-cabin songbooks, and even mobile log cabins for parades and rallies. Before the Democrats could counter it, the Log-Cabin Campaign was sweeping everything before it.[159]

Kennedy wrote the final chapters of *Quodlibet* while on the road campaigning for Harrison and the Whig Party. Kennedy seems to have been everywhere in Maryland, from Monument Square in Baltimore to Barren Springs on the Eastern Shore. He also spoke to large Whig gatherings in Pennsylvania and Virginia. As he completed the last pages of his satire and wrote home to his wife describing the campaign, life and literature merged into a single account. The overlapping descriptions in his letters and satire were replete with torchlight parades, booming canons, minstrel music, barrels of beer, endless speeches, and huzzahs from massive crowds. The night before a rally in Chester, Pennsylvania, Kennedy wrote his wife that he expected to have to compete with "rope dancing, sword swallowing and fire eating." Nonetheless, he promised, "I will make *such* a speech!"[160]

Quodlibet was published by Lea and Blanchard in September 1840. Kennedy did not attach his name to the work, but residents of Baltimore traced it to him. Only 1,500 copies were printed, and the work was not particularly successful. Kennedy believed that the public was too caught up in the election itself to bother with his satire. However, he was pleased when Baltimoreans recognized those locals who were its targets.[161]

From his perspective in the borderland, Kennedy felt that the Whig cause was bringing the nation together. With a rugged westerner and a polished Virginian, on its ticket, the party appeared to have united two great sections of the country. With a victory in the fall and a popular mandate, the Whigs would soon have their protective tariff, internal improvements, and national bank—programs that would restore prosperity and ensure the safety of the Union.[162]

The Whigs achieved a tremendous victory. Harrison won 234 electoral votes versus 60 for Van Buren. The popular vote was 53 to 47 percent. The Whig Party captured majorities in both houses of Congress. With nearly 80 percent of eligible males going to the polls, voter participation was higher than it had ever been. Exalting in the magnitude of their win, Kennedy and his fellow Whigs had no idea how short-lived their jubilation would be.[163]

CHAPTER 5

Return to *Swallow Barn*

After a day of speech making and interviews with office seekers, William Henry Harrison was finally able to relax at Kennedy's townhouse on Monument Square. Baltimore was one of his last stops en route to Washington, where, during the first week of March 1841, he would be sworn in as the nation's ninth president. Even though the dinner party included his entourage and numerous local dignitaries, Harrison had time to talk with Kennedy's wife Elizabeth, her sister Martha, and their father Edward Gray. All of them, including Kennedy, found the old general animated and charming. After the party broke up, Kennedy recorded his impressions of the incoming president: "He's 68 years old tomorrow, and uncommonly vigorous and flamboyant for a man of his time in life."[1]

Not everybody agreed with this assessment. After meeting with him the previous November, Henry Clay wrote to a friend that Harrison looked "much broken" and "weather beaten." In addition to campaigning harder than presidential candidates had done up to that time, Harrison had been worn down by the deluge of job applicants following his party's victory. In spite of their protestations regarding Democratic patronage, Whigs who had contributed to the party's landslide were eager to reap their rewards. Although there were nearly two thousand federal jobs available, even this number seemed insufficient to satisfy the scramble for office. Kennedy felt some of this pressure himself. "Great contest for office!" Kennedy wrote in his journal. "I have become the medium of communication between the City of Baltimore and the Gov't. in relation to nearly every appointment."[2]

The rivalry between Daniel Webster and Henry Clay further complicated the allocation of public jobs. Once Harrison announced he would serve only one term, the two rivals began positioning themselves for the next election. Webster, as Harrison's designated secretary of state, was building his power base inside the new administration, while Clay, as Senate leader, was extending his influence outside it. Both men wanted to place as many of their supporters in office as possible. Even Kennedy became a pawn in this great game when, during a visit to the Senate, Webster offered him the newly created position of undersecretary of state. The job entailed managing the diplomatic corps and standing in for Webster at diplomatic events, and it paid an annual salary of $3,500. Explaining his intention to run for a House seat in April, Kennedy tactfully declined the offer. His loyalty to Clay likely influenced his decision.[3]

By Inauguration Day, March 4, 1841, after attending many ceremonial dinners and dealing with endless queues of office seekers, Harrison was exhausted. On the platform over the East Portico, not far from Kennedy's seat, the new president—without a topcoat to protect him from the damp, chilly weather—delivered a long address. "It was of awful length (taking one hour and twenty minutes), well spiced with Greeks and Romans, but sound and striking in its sentiments," Kennedy recalled. There followed a "perfect carnival" of inaugural balls, parties, and more dinners, some of which Harrison felt compelled to attend. The new president probably contracted pneumonia during this long, inclement, and physically wearing day.[4]

On March 22, 1841, Kennedy met with the president at the White House to discuss patronage appointments. The meeting was pleasant, and Harrison invited Kennedy to return for dinner at five o'clock. Since the dinner was small, apparently just the president and several other guests, Kennedy had a chance to observe Harrison closely. In his journal, Kennedy made no mention of his health.[5]

Only ten days later, however, many Americans were deeply worried about the president. What is more, no one had paid much attention to Harrison's vice president and potential successor, John Tyler, of Virginia. At the Whig convention in Harrisburg, Tyler had seemed to fit the party's needs. Had Clay been the presidential candidate, there would have been no reason to place another southerner on the ticket. But Harrison's Indiana background made the situation different. "William Henry Harrison is the commander of the ship and John Tyler is the first mate," the *Niles' National Register* gushed. "Both of them have been tried and found faithful and experienced navigators." Like other early assessments of Tyler, the *Niles'* article was naïve in the extreme. Tyler was not a Whig at all and had only joined the party, after passage of the Force Bill, out of hatred for Jackson. Tyler's Whig principles had never been tested, and, on closer examination of his politics, he seemed likely to navigate the ship of state in a whole new direction.[6]

"He is a reputed abstractionist of the worst school of Virginia," Kennedy wrote in his journal regarding Tyler, "against the Bank, protective duties, internal improvements, distribution of the proceeds of the land, in fact against everything useful." Kennedy had vilified these Virginia gentlemen in his first House speech. They were, he said, so enamored of "moot constitutional points," so caught up in "the spirit of dissertation and debate," that they had become lost in their own abstractions. They adhered to the same insular attitudes and antiquated beliefs Kennedy had parodied in *Swallow Barn.* If Harrison did not survive, the likes of Frank Meriwether, or worse, would be installed in the nation's highest office. "God help us!" Kennedy exclaimed.[7]

On April 4, 1841, exactly one month after his inauguration, Harrison died. "The town is in the deepest gloom—the bells tolling, the flags of shipping at half mast," Kennedy wrote. Other than attending Harrison's funeral, however, he had little time to mourn the president's passing. He was preoccupied with efforts to regain his House seat. Either because he had mishandled some local patronage issue or because Webster's job offer had been leaked to his enemies, Kennedy encountered difficulty winning his party's nomination. Once he had cleared that hurdle, he expected to defeat his Democratic opponent easily. Instead, the opposition mounted a tough and scurrilous campaign, one he characterized as "the usual amount of vulgar vituperation from that type of Locofocoism." Kennedy won by less than eighty votes out of fifteen thousand cast. He took his House seat at the end of May 1841, in time for the extra session called by the late president to deal with the nation's struggling economy. With majorities in both houses of Congress, the Whigs were in a strong legislative position. The great question was Tyler.[8]

The extra session of Congress lasted all summer. Given the chairmanship of the Committee on Commerce, Kennedy figured prominently in the struggle with the new president. From his position inside the administration, Webster tried to preserve the relationship between Tyler and the Whigs in Congress. For his part, Clay sought to implement the full array of Whig programs, to reaffirm congressional prerogatives, and to undermine the new president's authority. While Tyler's Whig apostasy doomed the extra session from the start, the rivalry between Webster and Clay also contributed to its failure.

The extra session was a failure on almost every measure. Although the Sub-Treasury Act was repealed and the tariff increased, the land-sale distribution bill, bankruptcy legislation, and new federal loan scheme ended up as poor, watered-down renditions of well-intentioned Whig programs. However, it was the struggle over the newly proposed national bank, meant to replace the sub-treasury, which caused the final break between Tyler and the Whig Party.[9]

The first national bank bill, engineered by Treasury Secretary Thomas Ewing, required the states to approve the establishment of bank branches within their boundaries but, once established, gave the bank branches broad discounting powers. After some legislative tinkering by Clay, this bill passed both houses of Congress but was vetoed by Tyler in mid-August. A second bill was designed to limit the national bank's discounting powers exclusively to bills of exchange, an idea suggested by Attorney General John Crittenden. It was passed by Congress but vetoed by Tyler in early September. In both cases, those members of Tyler's cabinet and those congressmen who had tried to develop a bill acceptable to the new president felt betrayed by his vetoes.

To make matters worse, Tyler gathered around him a "kitchen cabinet" of Virginians more constitutionally strict than he was. Known as the "Virginia Cabal," or the "Impractables," this group included Abel Upshur, Nathaniel Beverly Tucker, and Thomas Dew. They were supported in Congress by fellow Virginian Henry Wise. After Tyler's second veto, every member of his cabinet except Webster tendered their resignations. Their complaint had to do with the president's bank vetoes and his reliance on these shadow advisors.[10]

A Whig caucus soon met to read the president out of the party. A dozen congressmen were chosen to prepare a public statement, and Kennedy was asked to write it, which he did, with, as he described it, "some words from Mr. Clay."[11]

The "Whig Manifesto," as it was called, began by reviewing the Whig programs passed into legislation during the extra session to rescue the economy from the mistakes of past Democratic administrations. The document then turned to Tyler. As "one professing to be a member of the Whig party," Tyler had initially implied his support for Whig economic programs, and, in the interest of cooperation, the party had tried to address the president's "constitutional scruples" whenever they arose. However, Tyler's opposition to a national bank was really meant "to lead to new political combinations," Kennedy asserted. He accused Tyler of deceitfully allying himself with forces known to oppose Whig principles. As a consequence, the Whig Party was ending its "unnatural relationship" with the president.

The Whigs printed twenty thousand copies of their manifesto and distributed them throughout the country. Whig newspapers condemned Tyler as a traitor to the party, calling him "The Executive Ass" and "His Accidency." Some towns burned him in effigy. Deeply offended by Kennedy's document, Tyler sent him a personal note telling him to stick to writing "romance." Tyler's son, who had admired Kennedy's literary skills, snubbed him on the street in Washington.[12]

The failure of the Whigs to achieve their goals during the extra session cost the party at the polls. Beginning in fall of 1841 and for the rest of the Tyler's time in office, the Whigs lost control of state governorships and legislatures. While they retained a thin majority in the U.S. Senate, they lost control of the House during this period. Fortunately, Kennedy held on to his own seat. The Whigs did not lose many voters to the Democrats. Rather, newly recruited Whigs expressed their disappointment by simply not voting. To make matters worse, Tyler unleashed a "reign of terror" on Whig political appointees, wrecking the party's patronage system. Every week, newspapers announced an important postal or customs job going to a Democrat or states' rights friend of the president.[13]

Kennedy's unbroken service in the House of Representatives spanned the period from May 1841 until October 1845, when he eventually lost his seat. Such continuity was unusual during a time when House seats changed hands more often than they do today. During most of this period, Kennedy rented a set of rooms on Washington's Third Street for himself, his wife Elizabeth, and her sister Martha, from whom Elizabeth was inseparable. These lodgings were shared with House members Robert C. Winthrop and Millard Fillmore, and their wives. A scholarly Brahmin from the Bay State, Winthrop regarded Kennedy as an equal in social status and erudition. He tolerated the less refined but more ambitious Fillmore, who represented New York State and would eventually become president. Winthrop introduced the powerful New England manufacturer, Abbot Lawrence, to the group. However, it was Kennedy who attracted visitors such as John Quincy Adams, Philip Hone, and Charles Augustus Davis to the Third Street rooms. A wealthy New York businessman, Whig wire-puller, and dedicated diarist, Hone wielded a rapier wit and seldom suffered fools. Also possessed of a sharp wit, Davis had written his own satire of Jacksonianism, entitled *The Letters of Jack Downing, Major*. These friendships proved important sources of advice and influence while Kennedy was in Congress and later in the statesman phase of his political life.[14]

The actual job of congressional representative could be both exhilarating and stressful. Much as he had done upon entering the Maryland House of Delegates two decades earlier, Kennedy described the inhospitable but intoxicating atmosphere of the forum where he did business.

> The Hall has a most unnatural vagueness in it for every sense; you hear nothing distinctly; you see nothing accurately. There is a great tomb-like, ill-timed, disconcerting reverberation over your own words from the vault above you; a most diabolical buzzing from sundry corners as if fifty dead kings were mocking you. The speaker, in your eyes, is a little man in a distant perspective, enveloped in drapery; you are perfectly sure he does not hear you; and his great eyes, which for politeness' sake he fixes upon you, glow like one of Fuseli's specters from out of damask curtains. Then, in the House itself, there is no sympathy; no nod of approbation to say—"I understand you," except from two or three civil Whig friends . . . every Locofoco has left the House except one—a grinning, malignant sentinel, to take notes and answer you. He sits close by, with a snaky eye fixed upon you and a livid face—livid from hatred; and every now and then laughs scornfully, seizes his pencil, ducks down and writes like the devil for thirty seconds, and rises up again with the most infernal smile, as much as to say, "I have got you."[15]

Committee work added a terrible burden to the job of a House member. Nonetheless, given his strong work ethic and penchant for detail, Kennedy's chairmanship of the commerce committee was unusually productive. His committee generated a large volume of reports on currency reform, reciprocal trade agreements, copyright law, African colonization, and other subjects. Of these, the report on African colonization was the most unusual. It was in response to a memorial from the Maryland Colonization Society, headed by Francis Scott Key. In his report, Kennedy reviewed the history of Liberia and the Cape Palmas colonies on the west coast of Africa. There were about 900 black Americans living at Cape Palmas, which had been funded by a $100,000 grant from the Maryland legislature after the Turner rebellion. Kennedy's report recommended that a federal agent be assigned to the two colonies in order to make treaties with local tribes and purchase land for future settlements. While he succeeded in having this recommendation reported as a joint resolution,

Kennedy was unable to keep it from being tabled due to intractable southern resistance.[16]

In terms of legislative successes, Kennedy could point to his support for the Tariff Act of 1842 and his efforts to fund Samuel Morse's telegraph. The tariff of 1842 increased duties on a wide range of articles by roughly 20 percent. Passed with the aid of Pennsylvania Democrats, the tariff was vetoed twice by President Tyler. Only when convinced that it was needed for federal revenue did Tyler finally sign it. Because he had first come to Washington as a champion of domestic industry, Kennedy was pleased with his part in raising the tariff to a more protective level.[17]

Samuel Morse had sought help from Congress to fund his telegraph during the late 1830s. However, after the economic collapse of 1837, most politicians were wary of such fantastic schemes. In early 1843, Morse was back, and Kennedy's committee reported out a $30,000 bill to get Morse started. When Kennedy tried to bring the bill to a vote, he was mocked and shouted down by several southern members. Delighting in their own wit, they amended the bill to include funding for mesmerism and Millerism. They enjoyed a good laugh as the bill went down to defeat. Undeterred, Kennedy was able to get the telegraph bill passed by a narrow vote a few weeks later. After approval by the Senate and Tyler, Morse began stringing a telegraph wire from Washington to Baltimore. On May 23, 1844, he transmitted a simple message—"What hath God wrought"—between the two cities. While Kennedy never mentioned the project in his journal or letters, Morse called his role in the development of the telegraph crucial. In hindsight, the telegraph was one of the era's greatest internal improvements. It annihilated space and brought the country together as nothing before had.[18]

In March 1842, Henry Clay resigned from the Senate in preparation for the presidential election of 1844. He asked Kennedy, now acknowledged as the Whigs' chief ideologue, to write a history of their party and put the best possible face on the lackluster extra session. Kennedy began "The Defense of the Whigs" by arguing that the party had frequently been "misunderstood and misrepresented." He rejected the notion that it owed its landslide victory in 1840 to "noise and pageantry," as well as that the party had failed during the extra session because of factionalism within its ranks and a lack of "constancy" in its principles. Responding to instructions from Clay, Kennedy placed responsibility for the party's shortcomings squarely on President Tyler.[19]

But Kennedy had a more ambitious plan for this unusual document. He intended nothing less than a rewriting of Anglo-American political history and a bold investigation into the origins of the Whig and Democratic parties. In so doing, he would elevate the Whigs above the unhappy moment of the extra session and position them in a historical continuum of political progress moving inexorably toward victory in 1844. Consistent with his penchant for reducing nuanced moral issues and complex political situations to their simplest dichotomies, Kennedy began by defining the centuries-long struggle for representative government as a contest between two rival parties, one "chiefly distinguished as friends of Executive Power" and the other as "enemies of that Power and noted for their distrust of it." Throughout history, Kennedy argued, the party of executive power had shown "a motive to reward subserviency [and] convert public servants into political minions." The enemies of that party, which he called the party of "Representative Legislature," had never been motivated by "personal ambition, vanity or selfishness." That was because "it has no person, but is an aggregate of many persons and many minds." Nor, Kennedy maintained, did the party of representative government have "patronage to gratify a love of making dependents" or "motive to flatter man's pride or stimulate any man's usurpation."[20]

These two great contending parties dated back to Stuart England, where they were called the Country and Court parties, or the Whigs and Tories. "We had our Whigs and Tories," Kennedy reminded his readers, insisting that the Whigs of 1688 and 1776 were the legitimate "ancestors" of his own party. Thus, the historical continuity that Kennedy had implied in *Horse-Shoe Robinson* was made explicit in "The Defense of the Whigs." Just as the British Whigs had to defend their liberties after the Revolution of 1688, the founders of the American nation faced internal challenges to popular government after independence. The Federalists, Kennedy explained, "identified with the supporters of Executive Power" and, even after being disgraced at the Hartford Convention, harbored "an ancient grudge" and remained "watchful as lynxes" for a return to power.[21]

The period from 1816 through 1829 had been an idyllic period in the nation's history, Kennedy continued. Thanks largely to President James Madison and his two successors, Whig principles had reigned pure and supreme. The "havoc of war [was] slowly but surely repaired," and there followed "a progressive increase in every element of the national happiness." This enlightened leadership strengthened the national bank, established a protective tariff, and promoted internal improvements. Kennedy's own sense of nationalism had been awakened during this time, and now he claimed its legacy for his party. "The Whigs stand emphatically upon the Madisonian platform," he declared.[22]

In explaining how this political Shangri-la had come to an end, Kennedy resorted to historical sleight of hand, the extrapolation of half-truths, and outright fabrication. The Federalists, he maintained, had returned to power in the guise of Jacksonian Democracy. The chief strategist in this political reincarnation had been Aaron Burr. He and his fellow conspirators had identified Andrew Jackson as a figure of great public magnetism but malleable enough to control. Jackson was "not an educated man," Kennedy reminded his readers, and the ex-Federalists soon "took possession of his ear and insinuated themselves into his confidence." There were other warning signs about Jackson, of course. "There was a danger in his temper . . . [and] in his stern self-will nursed in camps . . . that filled his atmosphere of command."[23]

Given how long the Federalists had retained power in Maryland and how many of them—men like Roger Taney, Virgil Maxcy, and Benjamin Howard—had been early supporters of Jackson, there might have been a modicum of truth to this historical reconstruction. More likely, though, Kennedy invented it in order to claim the Madisonian platform for his own party and explain why the Democrats had changed so radically under Jackson. Since the Democrats were always accusing the Whigs of being ex-Federalists, Kennedy decided to simply reverse the charge.[24]

In constructing his historical dichotomy, Kennedy had little difficulty locating Jackson on the side of executive power. According to Kennedy's telling of it, Jackson's Federalist handlers had filled the president with "monarchial" pretensions. He had hurled "the Kingly veto, like Jove's thunderbolt," shown "contempt for all highest judicial decisions," and demonstrated "reproof of the Legislative Power." As an example of his Napoleonic ego, Jackson had declared himself "the direct representative of the American people!"[25]

In the latter part of "The Defense of the Whigs," Kennedy finally got around to defending the Whigs' performance during the extra session of Congress. He focused on Tyler's two bank bill vetoes. On both occasions, Tyler had misled those attempting to craft a bill acceptable to him. The first time, Tyler claimed he had not read the bill, even though he had had it for almost two months. "He had not read it!" Kennedy exclaimed. The second time, Tyler fell back on what he called the "sanctity of his office" and the need to protect the

American people from "infraction by a majority of Congress." "Such laborious wanderings out of the way," Kennedy wrote, describing Tyler's bewildering logic, "such intrepidity of indirection, such unprofitable perverseness." Had Tyler, like Jackson before him, finally succumbed to the "immoderate intoxication of unexpected power"? Or had his circle of "peculiar friends" from Virginia and his "new Democratic allies" swayed him? Perhaps this "High Priest of Abstraction," this "freak of political ambidexterity," belonged among that party's "incongruous fragments" with their "opposite and heterogeneous views." Perhaps Tyler's ideological wanderings would cease now that he had joined the ranks of these "Old Democrats and Federalists."[26]

Clay liked "The Defense of the Whigs" so much that he wanted it produced in a cheaply bound volume and distributed to every Clay Club. With the help of Horace Greeley, the Whig editor of the *New York Tribune,* Harper and Brothers printed several thousand copies. However, Kennedy was disappointed with the quality of the pamphlet and complained that Harper did not advertise it. As with *Quodlibet,* it is difficult to know how often the "Whig Manifesto" and "The Defense of the Whigs" found their way into newspapers, speeches, conversations, and other media. Although it had suffered losses at both the state and local levels during the Tyler years, the Whig Party was probably in better health than those elections suggested. Many lapsed Whig supporters were beginning to realize what an impediment Tyler had been for the party, and, as the economy gradually recovered, they credited the Whig-sponsored Tariff of 1842 for its improvement. Furthermore, the Whig Party seemed clearer about what it stood for. Rather than select an "available" candidate as they had with Harrison in 1840, the Whigs would run Henry Clay, who embodied the party's principles, in 1844. Kennedy's writing likely contributed to this renewed sense of integrity and purpose.[27]

Whigs' hopes were further bolstered by the growing disarray within the ranks of the Democratic Party. Whereas the division over hard- and soft-money policies had badly disrupted the party, the question of Texas annexation threatened to fracture it completely. The party's presumed presidential candidate in 1844, Martin Van Buren, opposed the admission of Texas into the Union, as did his large political following. However, the expansionist wing of the party strongly encouraged President Tyler and his new secretary of state, John C. Calhoun, to sign an annexation treaty with Texas. While many expansionists were proslavery southerners, some were patriotic northerners who belonged to the "Young America" movement. These chauvinistic northern Democrats trumpeted their cause under the rubric of "Manifest Destiny."[28]

Whigs were more uniformly against Texas annexation and the war with Mexico that it would likely provoke. Those Whigs with religious affiliations hated war on moral grounds. Others saw war as a breakdown of social order and a threat to commerce. Although he had been a hawk during the War of 1812, Henry Clay now saw war as the ultimate failure of negotiation and compromise.[29]

On April 27, 1844, Henry Clay issued his "Raleigh letter," declaring himself against Texas annexation. Clay argued that any claim to Texas had been given up in the 1819 treaty between the United States and Spain. He also worried about potential discord between free and slave states if such a large territory were brought into the Union. Worst of all, a costly and bloody war with Mexico would likely ensue. "Annexation and war with Mexico are identical," Clay warned. Since Van Buren issued a similar statement the same day, some historians have argued that two candidates met and agreed to jointly oppose annexation. More likely, the timing of their statements was coincidental.[30]

Unbeknownst to Clay at the time of his Raleigh letter, the process of bringing Texas into the Union was well underway. President Tyler had sent a secret treaty agreement that his administration had negotiated with Texas to the Senate in early April 1844. In a surprising move, Calhoun, Tyler's recently appointed secretary of state, had attached a copy of his "Pakenham letter" to the treaty documents. Written as a warning to the British minister to the United States, this letter positioned Texas annexation as a proslavery initiative. Calhoun's letter not only made a case for the extension of slavery into Texas but also included a dissertation on the inferiority of the black race. Although the Senate deliberations over the treaty were meant to be secret, Benjamin Tappan, an antislavery Democrat from Ohio, became so enraged by Tyler's secret negotiations and Calhoun's letter that he leaked both to the press. With the country in an uproar and the Senate in disarray, Kennedy decided to write his own Texas letter.[31]

While reiterating several points from Clay's Raleigh letter, Kennedy took a much stronger stance against Texas annexation than his mentor had. Kennedy attacked the terms "re-annexation" and "improvident cession of 1819" used in Tyler's treaty documents that were sent to the Senate. Tyler's distortion of diplomatic history was no better than "wretched sophistry," Kennedy declared.

Ignoring prior treaty agreements would be an "offense against the laws of nations," he added, going on to call Tyler "our Polonius President" for negotiating the treaty behind Congress's back.[32]

Worst of all, Kennedy accused Tyler and his southern friends of a "nefarious scheme" to form "a new Confederacy of which it shall be a prominent feature that no free State shall come into the League." It had become fashionable for southerners to talk about slavery as a "blessing," Kennedy reminded his readers, but Maryland and many other states did not share this view. The annexation of Texas would provoke a greater crisis than Missouri statehood had two decades earlier. Was Texas annexation worth risking the Union? Was it worth the cost of blood and treasure to be spent in a war with Mexico? Kennedy closed with a plea for both major parties to resist Tyler's attempts to "kindle a war fever" and send Americans to die in "the pestilence of the Gulf."[33]

Kennedy's Texas letter took his indictment of the South to a new level. Whereas his novels and speeches had suggested that southerners' abstract thinking and recalcitrant behavior might inadvertently lead to separation from the Union, his Texas letter accused them of *conspiring* to form a new nation with slavery as its "fundamental element." What is more, he took exception to the assertion that slavery was a "blessing." This idea had been planted in southern minds by Thomas Dew after the Turner uprising and the Virginia slavery debates. Now Dew was a member of President Tyler's kitchen cabinet and was plotting with his fellow southerners to take slavery into Texas. Facing the cabal of Tyler, Calhoun, Dew, and others of their persuasion in positions of federal power—and discovering that Texas annexation was nearly a fait accompli—Kennedy threw off all restraints in condemning what he saw as the boldly expansionist and overtly separatist ambitions of the South.

Kennedy's letter was picked up by a number of northern newspapers and praised as a lucid assessment of the perils and pitfalls of Texas annexation. John Quincy Adams declared Kennedy's antiannexation arguments the best he had read. When it was voted on by the Senate during early June, the Texas annexation treaty was defeated thirty-five to sixteen. Most Van Buren Democrats joined the Whigs. Tyler would later succeed in bringing Texas into the Union as a state using a joint resolution of Congress and a simple majority vote. However, under the statehood option, Tyler was unable to address the important issues of boundary determination and debt resolution. Kennedy took pride in helping defeat Tyler's more comprehensive annexation treaty.[34]

Still, navigating the Scylla and Charybdis of sectional politics became increasingly difficult for Border Whigs. Henry Clay needed to treat the subject of slavery carefully, especially after the Democrats abandoned Van Buren as their presidential candidate and nominated James K. Polk on a platform of Texas annexation. During July 1844, Clay issued his "Alabama letters," attempting to trim his position on annexation. It may have been the worst mistake of his political life. Clay's language sounded foolish and prevaricating and satisfied no one. Northerners suddenly saw him as just another slave owner accommodating the South, and southerners detected no new assurances about protecting their peculiar institution. For those who had admired him, Clay's "constancy" seemed to waver. For those who had always seen him as a "gamester," the Alabama letters confirmed his image of possessing cunning without principles.[35]

The Alabama letters were not the only reason the Whigs lost the election of 1844. The Democratic Party ran a more effective campaign. Although he was America's first "dark-horse" presidential candidate, Polk was a grassroots organizer with a keen sense of campaign strategy. His careful handling of the tariff issue in Pennsylvania, for example, was everything Clay's treatment of Texas annexation was not. Polk's "Kane letter" duplicitously implied to Pennsylvania voters that he would keep tariffs high if elected. Furthermore, the Democrats were more energetic in mobilizing voters. Democratic organizers ventured deep into immigrant neighborhoods and explained the importance of Texas annexation to poor, land-hungry voters. To make matters worse, new causes entered the political arena and eroded the Whig franchise. The rise of the antislavery Liberty Party cost the Whigs New York State and, very possibly, the entire election. Similarly, the emergence of nativism drew off Whig voters in several northern states. The choice of the Protestant do-gooder Theodore Frelinghuysen as Clay's running mate offended Catholics but failed to attract nativist voters because the Whigs made no promises of immigration reform.[36]

For all of his mistakes, Henry Clay came within a hair's breadth of winning the election of 1844. Out of almost 2.7 million votes cast, Clay lost by just over 38,000. While his loss of 105 to 170 in the electoral college was more substantial, Clay failed to win six states by very small margins. As often occurs in close contests, the Whigs accused their opponents of foul play. The normally even-tempered Greeley ranted in the *Tribune* that New York Democrats had plied the city's poor laborers with liquor to get their votes. "Is there not illumination, revelry and extra blue rum at Five Points," Greeley raged, "and in nine tenths of the three thousand drunkard manufacturies in our city?" Worse still, there was evidence that the Democrats had marched recently arrived immigrants, mostly Irish Catholics and Germans, to the polls en masse. Clay himself believed that he might have won "if the recent foreigners had not all been united against us." In a letter that appeared in Greeley's *Tribune,* Kennedy argued that the true will of the electorate had been "outweighed by voices *un*American." While he believed the nation should continue to provide "all hospitality to the stranger," he called for "a modification of the Laws of Naturalization."[37]

Not only was the election of 1844 one of the closest in American history, it was also one of the most consequential. The Democratic victory would lead to a rollback of the tariff, the establishment of the independent treasury, war with Mexico, territorial expansion, and the long-term consequences of these actions. But in the wake of defeat, the Whig Party's most immediate concern was its own future. Some dispirited members of the party predicted its imminent demise. Others questioned whether the party could carry on with the same principles and the same name. Kennedy believed that it could. In the February 1845 issue of the *American Review,* he reminded Whigs that they were still one of the nation's "great political *parties*" and urged them to retain their principles of "*constitutional* government" and the "name of WHIG." Gone, it seemed, was any vestige of Kennedy's antiparty sentiment.[38]

As the Polk administration got under way, the Whigs began to behave more like a national political party. As the new president proceeded to dismantle Whig economic programs piece by piece—first with the Walker Tariff, then the Independent Treasury, and finally the defeat of the massive rivers and harbors bill—the Whigs converted these assaults into political capital in off-year elections. Better coordination at a national level and more astute local strategies won them over half of the congressional seats contested in 1846 and several gubernatorial races. By late 1847, however, the Whigs were once more running out of steam. They had predicted that the economy would collapse under Democratic mismanagement. Instead, a potato famine in Ireland and crop failures across Europe caused agricultural exports to soar and the overall economy to thrive. When the Whigs turned their oppositional rhetoric from the economy to the Mexican War, their new line of attack proved problematic.[39]

Officially declared in May 1846, the Mexican War generated an outpouring of patriotism while raising questions about its legitimacy and morality. It became entangled with the issue of slavery's extension during the summer of 1846, when the freshman Democratic congressman from Pennsylvania, David Wilmot, attached an amendment to President Polk's "$2 million bill," a bill intended to fund a possible Mexican peace treaty. The so-called Wilmot Proviso would prohibit slavery in any territory acquired from Mexico except Texas. It not only doomed Polk's $2 million bill but, more importantly, provided a rallying point for antislavery forces. Although it divided both major parties along sectional lines, the Wilmot Proviso damaged Whig unity most. Henceforth, southern Whigs found it difficult to campaign against the conduct of the war or to support conditions on the territorial spoils expected from it.[40]

Further complicating the political landscape was the rise of nativism. Although nativist sentiments were as old as the Republic, Protestant ministers had stepped up their attacks on the Catholic Church during the 1820s and 1830s. With the onset of the Irish potato famine in 1846, and political and economic stress elsewhere in Europe, the number of immigrants arriving in America rose to unprecedented levels. Newly arrived immigrants were blamed for lowering the wages of workers, ruining the quality of urban life, and degrading American culture. By the late 1840s, the so-called American Republicans were calling for tighter restrictions on immigration and were winning municipal elections in Philadelphia and New York City.[41]

With its large Catholic community and burgeoning immigrant population, Baltimore became a hothouse for the growth of nativism. Local Protestant ministers were virulent in their attacks on Catholics from the pulpit and published numerous pamphlets condemning the Church of Rome. Sensing that nativism would draw off Whig voters, local Democrats did all they could to encourage the formation of a viable nativist party. Unimpressed with the fledgling movement, Kennedy dismissed the Baltimore nativists as "new fangled and very ridiculous."[42]

Kennedy underestimated their disruptive force, however. Very likely the new party cost him his House seat in October 1845. Kennedy lost to his Democratic rival by a margin roughly equivalent to the nativist vote. His defeat was the first of many the Whigs would suffer from nativist incursions.[43]

Part of Kennedy's problem during the election was his health. For years he had suffered from skin disorders, including psoriasis of the lips and attacks of eczema. The salves and ointments his doctor prescribed seemed to exacerbate his condition. More recently, a bad fall from a horse had injured his hip and confined him to bed for months. He was also plagued with frequent colds and during the summer of 1845 battled typhoid for several weeks.[44]

Having just turned fifty-one, he was beginning to slow down physically and welcomed his respite from Congress. He also wanted to resume his literary pursuits. South Carolina novelist William Gilmore Simms had recently dedicated his novel *Count Julian* to Kennedy. In a letter thanking him, Kennedy wrote, "I am no better than a laggard in the glorious path where you have become a leader." In search of a new literary endeavor, he agreed to take on the writing of William Wirt's biography, a job both John Quincy Adams and Washington Irving had declined. "Mr. Wirt was a very intimate and kind friend of mine," he explained. Little did he realize how unorganized Wirt's papers were and how tedious it would be to mold them into a coherent narrative. The project would take him more than three years.[45]

In search of better health, Kennedy, his wife, and his sister-in-law Martha made frequent visits to the spas of Berkeley County, Virginia, and Sharon Springs, New York. Kennedy used the trips north to stay in touch with Whig colleagues like Robert Winthrop, Abbot Lawrence, and Daniel Webster. Through Winthrop and Webster, Kennedy was introduced to other powerful New England Whigs such as Nathan Appleton and Harrison Grey Otis. During visits to Virginia, Kennedy reconnected with more southerly Whigs like John Berrien and John Crittenden.[46]

Kennedy's expanding literary circle was no less impressive. Using his diplomatic contacts in Washington, he arranged several meetings with Charles Dickens during his American tour. Kennedy made the acquaintance of Henry W. Longfellow at Philadelphia's Wistar Club and met historian William H. Prescott while visiting Winthrop in Boston. During the spring of 1845, Kennedy traveled to Otsego, New York, to meet James Fenimore Cooper. While picnicking with the Coopers, Kennedy and the party were drenched by a thunderstorm and ended up at Cooper's home, dressed in spare, ill-fitting clothes. Kennedy described the event as a kind of "masquerade" at Otsego Hall, listening to Cooper tell stories while their clothes dried by the fireplace.[47]

In the strangest development of his political career, Kennedy returned for one session to the Maryland House of Delegates. After first declining the opportunity, he accepted it with the idea that it would ensure his nomination for the House race in October 1847. Maryland was in deep financial trouble and needed someone with Kennedy's stature and experience to guide it back to financial health. The state had accumulated nearly $15 million worth of debt pursuing costly and redundant internal improvement projects and was virtually bankrupt. A Democratic administration had ceased paying bond interest in 1842 and, by doing so, had destroyed the state's credit.

Arriving in Annapolis during December 1846, Kennedy was immediately elected house speaker and proceeded to organize his various committees. With the help of the Whig governor, Thomas Pratt, and the party's narrow legislative majority, Kennedy was able to pass the Resumption Law, which authorized interest payments beginning in 1848. The irony of the situation was that Kennedy had returned to the Maryland House of Delegates to clean up the same kind of internal improvements debacle that had, more than two decades before, caused his ignominious exit from that body. His mission completed, Kennedy returned home at the end of the session.[48]

Based on his service in Annapolis and the support of Governor Pratt, Kennedy was nominated by the Whig Party to run for the U.S. House in the fall of 1847. By the time of the election, the country was preoccupied with the Mexican War. The war's largest engagement, the Battle of Buena Vista, had been fought in February 1847 and had turned General Zachary Taylor into a national hero. Yet, more than seven hundred Americans had died in the war, and the country remained sharply divided over its legitimacy. Daniel Webster and Henry Clay had each lost a son in uniform, and the latter statesman characterized the conflict as "this most unnecessary and horrible war." Kennedy had lost all traces of his youthful jingoism. While he praised the heroism of American soldiers, he was deeply troubled by the moral questions raised by the Mexican War. "There is the highest appreciation of the gallantry of the army, and in its success," he wrote in his journal, "but this is a distinct sentiment from that which touches upon the question of the war."[49]

Kennedy believed most Baltimoreans shared his feelings about the war and promised to speak his mind in the fall election. He declared the country "sick of this carnage" and demanded an end to the "bloody work" in Mexico. He blamed President Polk for provoking Mexico and deceiving the American public about the war's causes. Naturally, the Democrats attacked Kennedy viciously for not supporting the war. He responded that Democratic rhetoric was no better than "gross and vulgar sentiment that begets this beastly appetite for war." In a badly divided community, Kennedy overplayed his opposition to the war.[50]

Election Day, October 7, 1847, was a day of torrential rainfall and unprecedented flooding in Baltimore. Local rivers rose over eighteen inches, damaging homes and factories. Voting was disrupted for all but the most determined political operatives. Maryland Whigs took four out of the six House seats, but Kennedy failed to win his. He was distraught at his loss and claimed fraud. Rumors circulated that the Democrats had spent $30,000 to defeat him and that more party members had voted in his district than lived there. In the days before the election, Kennedy had noticed "a large accession of voters thrown into the district—strangers, vagrants, persons whom no one knew anything about." He called for "a good registry law."[51]

After two failed attempts, Kennedy had little chance of winning back his House seat. Nor would he be nominated for a run at the Senate. Maryland's Whig Party was divided between Senator Reverdy Johnson's "Court House clique" and those party members like Kennedy who supported the state's other senator, James Pearce. Although his career as a congressman was at an end, Kennedy's political life was far from over. What he lacked in local clout he made up for with his circle of powerful Whig friends in other states and his prestige as an author. In short, Kennedy assumed the status of elder statesman and began to influence party affairs as an éminence grise.[52]

After surveying the national scene, Kennedy decided that Zachery Taylor, the hero of Buena Vista, was the only Whig who could win the presidency in 1848. "Clay is too old—now seventy one. It would be useless to make another effort with him," Kennedy reasoned. "And Zachery Taylor, old Rough & Ready, will be President Agreed! We cannot have an honester and wiser man, nor a truer Whig—I go with him with all my heart." Although he had never met the man and knew nothing of his principles, Kennedy recognized that, as a slave owner, Taylor was acceptable to the South and that his military achievements would appeal across party lines. Furthermore, as the nation's economy continued to improve, Whig programs like the tariff, the bank, and internal improvements were losing resonance with voters.[53]

During the run-up to the election of 1848, Kennedy's health kept him away from most speaking engagements and limited him to wire-pulling behind Taylor's nomination. Kennedy worked closely with Kentuckian John Crittenden, who served as Taylor's unofficial campaign manager. By July 1847, Kennedy had swung the Whig Central Committee of Maryland over to Taylor. To do this, he fought off an incipient "No Party" movement in support of Taylor and a bumbling attempt by Reverdy Johnson to form a Whig-Democratic fusion ticket.[54]

As Border Whigs, Kennedy and Crittenden were instrumental in solidifying support for Taylor in both the North and South. The two men had to wean more traditional Whigs away from Henry Clay while keeping maverick Whigs and other groups from drafting Taylor as a nonpartisan candidate. In order to accomplish this delicate shift in allegiance and maintain at least some vestige of party integrity, Kennedy and Crittenden met often with northern party leaders such as Winthrop, Appleton, and Fillmore, as well as southern leaders like Berrien, Willie Mangum, and Thomas Butler King.[55]

These and other efforts on his behalf resulted in Taylor's nomination on the fourth ballot at the Philadelphia Whig Convention during June 1848. However, the nominating process was unusually bitter and divisive for the party. When the balloting was over, many party members were not sure what kind of Whig they had nominated. In his letter to Philadelphia newspaperman George Lippard, for example, Taylor stated flatly, "I am not a party candidate." Then, a few weeks later, in one of his so-called Allison letters, Taylor declared that he was a Whig and, consistent with party principles, intended to let Congress govern without his interference. By this time, most Whigs were delighted to get at least a hint of where their candidate stood politically.[56]

Preoccupied with national unity, Kennedy ignored this blurring of Whig principles and the tepid tone of the campaign. To many Whigs, the campaign of 1848 seemed lackluster and cautious versus those of 1840 and 1844. What is more, the Whigs ran different campaigns in the North and the South, especially with regard to the issue of slavery and its extension into the conquered Mexican territory. Taylor's careful hedging on these volatile issues and his appearance of nonpartisanship attracted large numbers of disaffected Democrats. Other Democrats followed Van Buren into the Free Soil Party. In 1848, the slump in voter turnout and the effect of third parties hurt the Democrats more than the Whigs. Taylor managed handily to beat his Democratic rival, the unpopular Lewis Cass.[57]

Although the election had been characterized more by apathy than enthusiasm, Kennedy was delighted with Taylor's victory and hailed it as "a second and wholesome Whig ascendency." The weather on Inauguration Day was nearly perfect, and the military parade down Pennsylvania Avenue was splendid. Riding next to Taylor in his barouche was Kennedy's friend Winthrop and in the next one the president-elect's running mate, Millard Fillmore, also a Kennedy friend. The lavish balls that night celebrated the Whig restoration, though it would turn out to be a superficial and troubled one.[58]

By the spring of 1849, Kennedy could be doubly proud of his accomplishments. Not only had he contributed to the Whig presidential victory, but he had finished his biography of Wirt. In September, Lea and Blanchard published *Memoirs of the Life of William Wirt* in two volumes. The work sold out quickly and went through five more printings. One reason for its success was that no one had written much about the Monroe and John Quincy Adams administrations, in which Wirt had served as attorney general. Another reason was that Wirt had not been dead long and still held a prominent place in the public memory. A number of reviewers praised the book, further burnishing Kennedy's reputation as one of the country's leading authors and intellectuals.[59]

Most modern readers find the *Life of William Wirt* dull and ponderous. Adhering to the style of nineteenth-century biographies, Kennedy constructed his work by stringing together hundreds of Wirt's letters and connecting them with a thin narrative. What is more, Kennedy superimposed his own moral and political views on the story of Wirt's life and altered many of his subject's letters to suit this purpose. One shortcoming of the *Life of William Wirt* is its failure to capture the congenial, often playful side of Wirt's personality, something those who knew him commented on. This was somewhat odd, given that Kennedy had modeled the convivial Philpot Wart in *Swallow Barn* on Wirt. That he paid very little attention to Wirt's considerable literary successes, consisting of two novels and a biography of Patrick Henry, is more understandable. Kennedy never played the role of literary critic during his life.[60]

Although he resisted eulogizing his subject, Kennedy held Wirt up as an exemplar for younger generations. As often happens when a highly accomplished didactic enters elderhood, Kennedy was critical of many young people he met during the late 1840s. On one particular occasion, he observed that the young men and women of Baltimore laughed too much and seemed ill at ease in genteel company. They had "no standard of manners by which they might study what is requisite for elegant intercourse, and the consequence is a marked want of ease and accost." These young people were "very deficient in education and appear to care very little about learning anything," Kennedy observed.[61]

Wirt's biography was intended as instructional literature for a generation seemingly unsure of itself and uninterested in the pursuit of learning. Orphaned as a child and raised by an aunt, Wirt had been a model of a self-made man and gone on to become one of the most revered intellectuals of the Early Republic. From his youth, Wirt dedicated himself to his education and sought out mentors to guide his campaign of self-improvement. Wirt absorbed Joseph Addison, Laurence Sterne, and the other neoclassical authors. Through his "methodized study," Wirt mastered Greek and Latin. After his schoolmaster Mr. Hunt took him to the county court to watch the proceedings there, the young Wirt began reading Blackstone and committed himself to study law. Not satisfied with his attainments in the legal profession, Wirt went on to distinguish himself as a novelist. He capped off his career by serving as attorney general to Presidents Monroe and John Quincy Adams. During large portions of his biography, Kennedy seems to be writing as much about his own campaign of self-improvement and accomplishments as about Wirt's.[62]

In Kennedy's hands, the colorful side of Wirt's character is expunged and replaced with a blander version of the man. In a letter allegedly written to his daughter Elizabeth, Wirt credits the workings of faculty psychology for his self-mastery and equipoise. "Genius," Wirt explains to her, was no more than a "fever of the brain." Left unrestrained, it is also a dangerous thing. "You will find it rising from the grave like a vampire" one minute, and the next "reclining on the bank of a river and weeping with idiot sorrow." Then, in the flash of a second, genius will be "rushing with maniac fury up the slopes of Mont Blanc." The only way to tame such bedlamite impulses is to balance genius with common sense. While "genius may fill the sails till the canvass cracks," Wirt advises his daughter, "put common sense at the helm." Even in simple conversation, genius and common sense have to be combined, "genius supplying the *impetus* and common sense the *tact*."[63]

At times, Kennedy endows Wirt with a didacticism more bourgeois than homespun republican. To another daughter, Laura, who was moving with her husband to a new town, Wirt asks, "Do you wish to make your husband and yourself *popular?*" His advice to her is to "Dress as plainly as possible, and to conform as closely as possible to the manners of the place." Overly fine clothes and haughty behavior are antisocial, he explains, and "will excite envy, criticism, malignity, quarrels and contempt."[64]

In addition to its didactic burden, the *Life of William Wirt* is heavily freighted with Kennedy's political beliefs. The metanarrative he had developed in "The Defense of the Whigs"—that after the second war with England there occurred an efflorescence of Whig principles that were then swept aside by Federalist-controlled Jacksonians—runs through the biography. During the postwar period, the "conciliatory temper" of Madison and Monroe had enabled them to "break up the old array of parties" and to bring about an "adjustment of differences" between contesting interests, Kennedy writes. In Congress, "the genius of compromise" had prevailed to resolve the Missouri crisis.[65]

With the ascendency of Jackson, however, "the serpent of discord had been hatched." The Jacksonians assumed "an organized form—became compact, eager, intolerant and even vindictive." In the Supreme Court, Wirt defended the right of the Cherokee people to their lands against the aggressions of the Jackson administration and the state of Georgia. In Wirt's view, the breaking of the Indian treaties was Jackson's most egregious act, "a disgrace which the waters of time can never wash away."[66]

Kennedy closes his biography with a plea for sectional understanding. After a trip to Boston, Wirt allegedly wrote to a friend in 1829 that Bostonians were among the kindest and most warm-hearted people he had ever met. "Would to Heaven the people of Virginia and Massachusetts knew each other better," Kennedy quotes Wirt as saying. According to Kennedy's telling of it, Wirt blamed himself for not recognizing the good qualities of these northerners earlier: "What a fool I have been to join in these vulgar prejudices against the Yankees! We judged them by their peddlers. It would be just as if they were to judge us by our black-legs."[67]

Whether Wirt actually experienced such an epiphany regarding northern character does not really matter. After all, Kennedy had described a similar conversion in *Swallow Barn,* in which the Yankee traveler, Mark Littleton, sheds his sectional prejudice after getting to know his Virginia relatives. In both his novel and the biography, Kennedy minimized the cultural divergence that secessionists were beginning to exploit. He himself had formed numerous friendships across sectional boundaries and saw such social interplay as natural and necessary. One of his southern correspondents was William Gilmore Simms, who reviewed the Wirt biography in the April 1850 issue of the *Southern Quarterly Review.*[68]

In his lengthy, multilayered review, Simms probes the character and accomplishments of Wirt, his biographical subject Patrick Henry, and Wirt's biographer Kennedy. Knowing Wirt as he had, Kennedy's portrait of him was too "warm." While accomplished, Wirt was before all else a self-promoter, and vanity was his greatest fault. Unlike Henry, Wirt lacked daring and spontaneity in the courtroom. "Wirt never seemed entirely to forget that it is Wirt who is speaking," Simms recalls. Nor did his literary productions merit the praise they had received. Whereas Wirt's writing is "excessively florid and elaborately finished," Kennedy's is "stern, direct, forcible" and careful to avoid "excess and ornament." Wirt and Kennedy were different as practicing lawyers, too. "Wirt strove to rise in argument into eloquence, while the care of Kennedy was to absorb his eloquence in his argument."[69]

Nonetheless, Wirt had risen from nothing and addressed many of his personal failings over his lifetime. He had been a great southern statesman who deserved the tribute of biography, an honor seldom bestowed on southerners by northern intellectuals, Simms noted resentfully: "Our histories are slurred over by Yankee historians . . . our heroes receive but cold applause." Such neglect was purposeful, he insisted. It was one more example of "northern aggression," this time on an intellectual front, which was "destined irrecoverably to rend all our ties asunder."[70]

When compared to Poe's calm critique of *Horse-Shoe Robinson* fifteen years earlier, Simms's recurring invectives against the North show how much sectional relations had deteriorated. Naturally, Kennedy's description of Wirt's epiphany regarding northern character provoked a strong reaction. "Does Mr. Kennedy mean to convey the idea that the Union is paramount to all other considerations?" Simms asks. "When government of the country becomes a tyranny, the citizen is absolved from his allegiance," he declares. The North was attempting "to pluck from us all the securities we have enjoyed, to fill our land with strife and insurrection, and to make fatal overthrow of the domestic institution upon which all our interests depend."

Near the end, Simms presents a challenge to pro-Union conservatives like Kennedy. If you care so much about the Union, then do something about its treatment of the South: "Let those who preach the blessings of the Union, only labor as industriously to bring back the government to justice, and to proper recognition of the constitution, and then the chances are that the Union would need no hosannas." It was a challenge that Kennedy and men like him would place at the top of their political agendas but, after a decade of trying, would fail to deliver on.[71]

As the 1840s drew to a close, sectional politics became more troubling. The fierce debate over the disposition of the "Mexican Cession" (the territory ceded by Mexico after the war), and the question of whether that territory should enter the Union as free or slave, dominated public attention and the affairs of state. To make matters worse, the two major parties seemed less equipped than ever to mollify these tensions. Many northern Democrats followed Van Buren into the Free-Soil Party, and, in other parts of the North, Democrat–Free-Soil coalitions were struck. Large numbers of antislavery Whigs also hived off to join the Free-Soilers. In the South, Calhoun tried to separate Whigs from their party with his "Southern Address" in late 1849. Before long, Alexander Stephens, Robert Toombs, and several other southern Whigs bolted from the party. Toombs declared on the House floor, "I am for disunion."[72]

What is more, the rift created within the Whig Party by the nominating process worsened after Taylor's inauguration. The party found itself divided between its orthodox wing, which looked forward to Henry Clay's return to the Senate and a restoration of Whig principles, and its moderate wing, whose members called themselves "Taylor Republicans" and sought to broaden the party's appeal to new voters. By denying orthodox Whigs their share of political appointments, the Taylor administration irreparably damaged the party's cohesiveness. Political patronage was the sinew that held antebellum parties together, and the Whigs would never recover from Taylor's mismanagement of it.[73]

Kennedy tried to rise above the internecine struggle that divided his party. Even though he believed that Reverdy Johnson's "clique influence" had badly damaged the party in Maryland, Kennedy endeavored to build a working relationship with Johnson once the latter became Taylor's attorney general. Even though he was identified as a Clay supporter, Kennedy did better than most orthodox Whigs procuring federal appointments for his home state. The same genial personality and literary reputation that had opened doors for Kennedy as a lobbyist years before now empowered him as an elder statesman, navigating between the Clay and Taylor factions of his party.[74]

During the fall of 1849, Kennedy learned that Taylor wanted to visit a cattle show in Baltimore and arranged to meet him. Arriving unannounced with a single servant, Taylor had trouble getting a room at Barnum's Hotel because the clerk did not recognize him. The next day Kennedy accompanied Taylor to the cattle show. In his journal, Kennedy commented positively on Taylor's "plainness." It was not until they had visited most of the cattle stalls that someone identified the president and a crowd formed around the two men. During their time together, they discussed internal improvements, a protective tariff, and livestock breeding.[75]

Not long after Taylor's visit, Henry Clay had occasion to visit Baltimore. Clay had recently returned to the Senate at the age of seventy-one. While his supporters applauded his return, it struck terror into Taylor men. Many remembered how Clay had read President Tyler out of the party with the "Whig Manifesto" less than a decade before. When he arrived in Baltimore, Reverdy Johnson's Taylorite clique publicly snubbed Clay. However, Kennedy spent a morning in the privacy of his library with Clay, gave a large dinner party for him, and accompanied him to the theater. Clay was less than two months away from introducing legislation to bring the Mexican Cession into the Union, and, while Kennedy did not record much about their conversations, it is very possible that they discussed Clay's ideas.[76]

One reason to suspect that they discussed the subject is that Kennedy became an ardent supporter of Clay's proposals once they were presented to the Senate in late January 1850. President Taylor's plan for the Mexican Cession came first, however. It simply called for the admission of California as a free state and the organization of the remaining lands as territories. These territories would have the option of choosing whether to be free or slave at a later date. Included in Taylor's message to the Senate was his commitment to defend the Union at all costs. "Whatever dangers may threaten it I shall stand by it and maintain its integrity," he declared ominously.[77]

Clay's plan was much more comprehensive than Taylor's and included the admission of California as a free state, organization of the remaining lands acquired from Mexico as territories, definition of the Texas boundary as well as disposition of the state's debt, elimination of the slave market in the District of Columbia, maintenance of interstate slave trade, and, most controversial of all, enactment of a more rigorous fugitive slave law. Although it would be subjected to nine months of volatile debate and wrenching negotiation and would be modified in many of its details, Clay's plan would eventually become the celebrated "Compromise of 1850."[78]

A critical juncture in Senate proceedings was the decision whether or not to create a "committee of thirteen" to draft the compromise bill in its many details. Clay was to head the committee, which, once approved by the Senate, would deal a death blow to the Taylor plan. Kennedy worked behind the scenes to ensure support for the committee by Maryland's two rival senators, Thomas

Pratt and James Pearce. Securing this support was no small feat because Pratt was an ally of Reverdy Johnson and a staunch Taylor man. Furthermore, Taylor tenaciously defended his plan and made support for it a test of loyalty. As leader of the anti-Johnson faction in Maryland, Pearce hated Pratt and Johnson. In spite of these obstacles, Kennedy appears to have been instrumental in bringing both senators into line behind Clay's committee. As it turned out, the votes of the Maryland senators were pivotal in its passage.[79]

The Compromise of 1850 did not become law until September of that year. It probably would not have succeeded at all had President Taylor not died in July and Millard Fillmore, who favored the compromise, succeeded him. The death of John C. Calhoun at the end of March 1850 also facilitated passage of the bill. Even though it included the controversial fugitive slave law and would not resolve sectional tensions with the "finality" its supporters promised, the Compromise of 1850 was landmark legislation. The admission of California as a free state and the establishment of Texas boundaries alone made it that. Furthermore, the early debates over the compromise were the last time that the "Great Triumvirate " of Clay, Webster, and Calhoun debated together in the Senate.

Congressional voting patterns for and against the various parts of the compromise legislation showed that the Whig and Democratic Parties were badly divided by the time the compromise had been hammered out. Among the Whigs, southerners generally supported the compromise and northerners opposed it. Many northern Whigs objected to any compromise with the South and were especially offended by the tougher fugitive slave law. Among the Democrats, the reverse pattern was true. Most southern Democrats strongly opposed the admission of California as a free state. Northern Democrats, for their part, had few problems with the fugitive slave legislation and felt the overall compromise was a good one.[80]

However, the Whig Party probably emerged from 1850 more battered than its opposition. After all, the highest concentration of Whigs lived in the North, and many members there felt deeply betrayed by their party. Furthermore, the fact that many southern Whigs had voted with northern Democrats for the compromise was an ominous sign for the party. Robust interparty rivalry had been the lifeblood of Whig success. Finally, another change in Whig administration added more confusion to an already fractured and dispirited party. While he tried to correct the patronage mistakes of his predecessor, Fillmore was too late and was himself forced to purge many Taylorites and anticompromise party members. During the balance of his administration, Fillmore failed to reunite the Whig Party and would preside over its demise.[81]

While he continued to follow politics closely during the rest of 1850, Kennedy was already engaged in a new literary project. For several years, he had thought about revising and republishing *Swallow Barn* and his other novels. During a visit to Philadelphia in the fall of 1849, Rufus Griswold, the editor of the Whig literary magazine, *American Review,* had urged Kennedy to undertake the project. Probably with the help of James Fenimore Cooper, Kennedy arranged to have a revised edition of *Swallow Barn* published by the New York firm of George P. Putnam. The new edition would be part of an American authors series that included writers such as Cooper and Washington Irving. Kennedy was delighted to learn that he would be remunerated the same as these authors. Since the books in the series were to be illustrated, he arranged to have his cousin and noted illustrator David Strother create the necessary artwork.[82]

Kennedy had reasons other than pride and money for revising and republishing *Swallow Barn.* Like many Whigs, he had always believed that literature contributed to preserving national character. In the preface to the new *Swallow Barn,* Kennedy expressed his desire to recover from the past "what belonged to us as characteristically American." More important, however, he was anxious to explain his support for the recent compromise legislation to both his northern and southern friends. Perhaps naively, he saw a new edition of *Swallow Barn* as the right vehicle to do this. As a Border Whig, Kennedy saw the need for compromise in times of crisis as obvious. He would deploy the power of literature to help ensure that others in both sections of the country saw things as he did. Much as the Nat Turner uprising had influenced the original version of *Swallow Barn,* the Compromise of 1850 would cast its shadow over the revised edition.

Kennedy made more revisions to *Swallow Barn* than to his other two novels, also republished over the next several years by Putman. To start with, Kennedy jettisoned the long history of Captain John Smith, which was irrelevant to the novel's development. While some minor changes modernized the vocabulary or improved the phrasing of the 1832 version, others took the edge off Kennedy's descriptions of the Swallow Barn plantation and its master, Frank Meriwether. For example, the mansion is no longer described as an "irregular pile" architecturally, nor is it compared to an "unlucky bark" washed ashore on the banks of the James River. Similarly, Meriwether is no longer simply "kind" to his slaves but is now both "kind and considerate." Whereas they had regarded their master with "profound reverence" before, Meriwether's bondsmen now hold him in "affectionate reverence." Swallow Barn, which had been an "agreeable" place for slaves to labor before, now becomes a "happy" place for them. Other textural changes made during the revision of the novel help accomplish this subtle shift in tone.[83]

Although he treats the conditions in which slaves live and work more favorably, Kennedy makes no attempt to soften his disparaging description of the slaves themselves. He continues to describe them as "untamed monkeys" and "careless animals," just he did in the novel's original edition. Furthermore, David Strother's illustrations in the revised edition tend to reinforce these negative images. This was how Kennedy had always beheld blacks, and he felt no compulsion to describe them differently.[84]

In addition to his ingrained prejudices, Kennedy had every reason to portray the slaves in his revised novel as ill equipped and unprepared for emancipation. After all, the Compromise of 1850 was intended to protect the institution of slavery where it existed and, by doing so, insulate the Union from sectional strife for as long as possible. In keeping with these objectives, Kennedy used his revised text to elaborate on those aspects of black character he believed justified the black race's continuing servitude. Kennedy goes about this in the chapter entitled "The Quarter," in which Frank Meriwether and Mark Littleton tour the plantation's slave quarter. Behind the thin mask of Littleton's northern objectivity, Kennedy elaborates on what he sees as the problematic nature of black character. "I came here as a stranger, in great degree, to the negro character," Littleton explains. Nonetheless, after a short stay in the Old Dominion, Littleton seems remarkably articulate on the subject. He is fully convinced of the helplessness and dependency of the black man. "In the present stage of his existence," Littleton observes,

> he presents himself to my mind as essentially parasitical in nature. I mean that he is, in his moral constitution, a dependent upon the white race; dependent for guidance and direction even to the procurement of his most indispensable necessities. Apart from this protection he has the helplessness of a child,—without foresight, without faculty of contrivance, without

> thrift of any kind. We have instances, in the neighborhood of this estate, of individuals of the tribe falling into the most deplorable destitution from want of that constant supervision which the race seems to require. This helplessness may be the due and natural impression which two centuries of servitude have stamped upon the tribe. But it is not the less a present and insurmountable impediment to that most cruel of all projects—the direct, broad emancipation of these people."[85]

Littleton goes on to disparage blacks for their obsequiousness and imitative behavior, especially the older ones for their "profuse bows and compliments" and the younger ones for their "aping of style" and "dandyism in dress." Blacks seem to him like frail vines clinging to the sturdy trunks of their white masters for support. It never occurs to Littleton (or Kennedy) that such behavior is crucial for survival in a condition of complete servitude.

And yet, Littleton realizes that there is something oddly appealing about these people. "Their fondness for music and dancing is a predominant passion," he observes in the revised text. Music seems to accompany them wherever they go. The men whistle on their way to the fields, and the women sing as they lay wash out to dry. Nor can the hardest day's work deter them from dancing. They celebrate with a gaiety that is remarkable. What is more, blacks love the outdoors and are consummate sportsmen. They are, Littleton concludes, "the most good-natured, careless, and happily constructed human beings I have ever seen."[86]

While intended to show that slaves were happy with their lot, Littleton's shift in attitude is nonetheless startling for readers. It shows that the instability of the original novel continues to disrupt the revised text. More broadly, the revised *Swallow Barn* mirrors the increasing confusion of white Americans about who black people were, what they signified about human nature, and what role they should have in national life. At midcentury, both scientific and popular opinion seemed more confounded by the issues of race and slavery than ever before. During the 1840s and 1850s, some natural philosophers argued for the theory of polygenesis—the notion that blacks were a separate species from whites—against those who continued to support the unity of mankind. These decades also witnessed the peak popularity of minstrelsy, with its ambivalence of mockery and envy toward black language, musical forms, and social behavior. Most important of all, white Americans debated what the destiny of blacks living among them should be. During this time, advocates for the immediate abolition of slavery contended with those who supported African colonization or defended slavery as a positive good.[87]

Kennedy was also perplexed by these issues. Throughout his novel, black characters whistle, sing, and play the banjo much as they had during his visits to western Virginia. Through his character Ned Hazard, he recalls his fondness for black childhood companions and yet describes their race in the most disparaging terms. While in Congress, Kennedy had reported out a bill in support of African colonization. While beginning to revise his novel, he exchanged letters with Jacob Prout, a black man from Baltimore who had gone to Liberia on a colonization ship. Prout appealed to him as "a friend of colonization" and asked for some books on law and medicine. Kennedy noted that Prout's letters were "well written" and later received some African coffee from him.[88]

Kennedy had already hinted at colonization in the story of Abe and the recalcitrant slave's banishment from Swallow Barn by ship. In his revision, Kennedy is more explicit about colonization. "Perhaps they are destined, ultimately, to that national existence in the clime from which they derived their origin," Littleton wonders as he observes Meriwether's slaves. At another point in the revised text, Meriwether expresses the hope that a state-funded enterprise would someday relocate his slaves to a "proper asylum."

While more explicit about colonization in the revised text, Kennedy imposes strict conditions on such a project. Littleton describes Swallow Barn's slaves as somewhere in the "middle stage of progress" toward eventual nationhood and refers to their present servitude as a "beneficial guardianship." Such language calls to mind Thomas Dew's view of slavery as a justifiable means to advance primitive people to higher levels of civilization. More worrisome still, Meriwether indicates that his slaves would only be dispatched to a new homeland when "the roots of slavery begin to lose their hold on our soil." In other words, Meriwether and his fellow slaveholders might not surrender their slaves until they no longer need them. In the end, Kennedy's treatment of colonization in the revised text is so tentative and conditional that it seems less a solution to the problem of slavery than an excuse to leave it undisturbed until it disappears naturally. While many placed their full faith in colonization, Kennedy was not one of them.[89]

In the revised edition of *Swallow Barn,* Kennedy assigns Frank Meriwether two tasks. One is to suggest ways to protect the integrity of the slave family, and the other is to warn northern antislavery men against interfering in the South's domestic affairs. Most Whigs believed the family was the basic building block of society, and antislavery Whigs had singled out the breakup of slave families as the institution's most egregious aspect. The practice had even caused some southern clergymen to endorse reforms. Northern abolitionists had become fanatical over the issue.[90]

"We have no right to put man and wife asunder," Meriwether confesses to Littleton. Meriwether suggests that the separation of slave couples should be forbidden by law. Such laws should also prohibit "the separation of children from the mother—at least during that period when one requires the care of the other," Meriwether adds. He believes that past disregard for such attachments has been responsible for the odium attached to slavery by the North. The implementation of new laws to protect the integrity of the slave family would effectively "disarm" all but the most unreasonable critics of slavery, he predicts.[91]

Meriwether's second task, and by far the more important one, is to signal the danger of continued northern agitation against southern slavery. Such agitation has its origins in the "impulsive prejudice" and "imperfect knowledge" of northerners, he insists. Southerners alone are equipped to deal with the question of slavery. For now, the South's sentiments are "temperate and wise," but continuing assaults on her institutions could easily lead to "ultraisms" and the adoption of "bold dogmas tending to these extreme views." Meriwether sees the situation as extremely volatile and a threat to sectional relations.[92]

Kennedy expunges some of Meriwether's earlier ideas from the revised text. Although he should have removed it entirely, he curtails Meriwether's ridiculous plan for a slave "feudatory" in the revised text and eliminates some of the medieval terms used to describe it. Similarly, he eliminates the reference to whipping slaves in Virginia and the ludicrous comparison between that punishment and those administered to criminals in New York City.[93]

Finally, Kennedy goes about qualifying his overall verdict on slavery. Where he had earlier condemned slavery as "indefensible," he now suggests that it is only so "as an original question." This appears to exonerate the post-Colonial South for slavery's origination, much as Thomas Dew and others had done, and implies that slavery might be defensible in the national era. Kennedy had made a similar argument in the Maryland legislature years before. As a tired and spurious notion, it brings little persuasive power to the revised text.

Kennedy adds a second temporal consideration to his discussion of slavery. In the 1832 version of his novel, he states that slavery was "theoretically and morally wrong" but goes on to say, somewhat convolutedly, that it has been "made to appear wrong in all its modifications" by its northern critics. In the revised text, Kennedy adds that these critics of slavery have made "its continuance, even for one day" appear wrong. While subtle, this language implies that southern slavery is justifiable because it is a temporary institution. Nor does Meriwether bring a great deal of clarity when he summarizes the situation in the revised text. "We neither regard slavery as a good, nor account it, except in some favorable conditions, as profitable," he tells Littleton. "The most we can say is that, as matters stand, it is the best auxiliary within our reach."[94]

So, what is the reader to conclude from the revised edition of *Swallow Barn*? On its surface, it seems to make little sense. Viewed in the context of when the two editions were written, however, Kennedy's revisions reveal his intentions. Superimposed on a text written two decades earlier, he scatters vague palliatives and half-hopes to calm the passions of antislavery forces in the North, while defending the prerogatives of slave owners in the South. In the wake of the crisis of 1850, Kennedy's overall objective is to preserve the national status quo. This means warning the North not to intercede in southern affairs and advising patience regarding the eventual disposition of slavery. The depiction of benevolent slave masters and contented slaves, embedded in the narrative of *Swallow Barn,* aims to reduce the urgency of emancipation and lower the temperature of the slavery debate. Still, Kennedy means his warnings about the dangers of precipitous intervention in the slave system to be taken seriously. For him and other socially conservative Whigs, the preservation of the Union outweighed all other considerations. The revised edition of *Swallow Barn,* then, can be seen as the literary complement to the Compromise of 1850 and the novel's defense of southern slavery its main message.

These factors did not seem to negatively affect the reception of *Swallow Barn* when it reached booksellers during the fall of 1851. George Putnam told Kennedy that the book had been "remarkably well received" and that most reviews were excellent. After all, *Swallow Barn* had been out of print for over two decades, and the reading public was interested in its subject matter. With few exceptions, most northern reviewers ignored the novel's views on slavery and focused on its picturesque depiction of the Old Dominion and the cast of colorful characters.

Southern reviewers were more interested in Kennedy's stance on slavery and his opinion of blacks. The *Southern Quarterly Review* summarized the novel as dealing with "the country gentleman of Virginia in his most important relationship—that of a master." The review noted that the slave never appears in the novel except "in his natural, always amicable, and always happy character." The review quoted Littleton's analysis of black character in its entirety. Several southern newspapers did the same.[95]

After reading the revised *Swallow Barn,* William Gilmore Simms wrote Kennedy that the book was "a genial & natural picture of Virginia life." More important, it was the plea for understanding of southern issues Simms had asked for in his review of the Wirt biography. It was, Simms wrote, "the most conclusive answer to the abolitionists (if they *would* be answered) that could be made." However, it was too late, Simms told his friend. Secession was "inevitable" and only a matter of time.[96]

Though he was correct in believing that literature could influence national destiny, Kennedy's revised *Swallow Barn* would not be the book to do it. As his novel was being shipped to bookstores, Harriet Beecher Stowe's *Uncle Tom's Cabin* was running as a serial in the abolitionist newspaper *National Era.* It would be published in book form during the spring of 1852. In a letter to Simms, Kennedy dismissed such abolitionist writing as "mawkish sentimentality" and boasted that his own novel would provide the "antidote to this abolitionist mischief."[97]

Uncle Tom's Cabin sold over 300,000 copies during its first year. Kennedy correctly observed that the heavy-handed sentimentality of writers like Stowe helped sell their novels. But Stowe did more than romanticize the gentleness of her black main character. She looked slavery in the eye and described its terrible reality, while Kennedy ignored it. Whereas he attempted to calm the national conscience, she strove to awaken it. One need only compare the frightful condition of Simon Legree's plantation in *Uncle Tom's Cabin* with Meriwether's benevolent sanctuary in *Swallow Barn*—or Legree's vicious treatment of his slaves with Meriwether's enlightened paternalism—to understand the different perspectives of the two authors.[98]

Eighteen fifty-two was an important year for Kennedy and his party. The Whig national convention was held in Baltimore's Maryland Institute during June. It was attended by over 3,000 delegates and lasted six days. However, sweltering heat and bitter contention ruined the gathering. Many northern

Whigs recoiled when the party approved a pro-compromise platform. "We deify it, execrate it, spit upon it," Horace Greeley wrote. Similarly, southern Whigs were uneasy with the nomination, after an exhausting fifty-three ballots, of Winfield Scott. Scott's last-minute endorsement of the compromise seemed tentative, and his relationship with William Seward, hated by many southerners, did not make the candidate seem "safe" regarding the section's particular interests. The convention selected William Graham of North Carolina as Scott's running mate. In a coincidence tinged with foreboding, their acceptance speeches appeared in the same June 30 newspapers that announced the death of Henry Clay.[99]

When William Graham became the Whig vice-presidential nominee, he resigned as President Fillmore's secretary of the navy. Fillmore offered the job to Kennedy, a friend from their Third Street days as congressmen and a trusted supporter during the difficult months after Taylor's death. Kennedy had advised the new president on patronage issues and defended his pro-compromise position, especially his enforcement of the Fugitive Slave Law. During the spring of 1851, the arrest of fugitive slave Thomas Sims in Boston had sparked widespread rioting and a bitter legal battle before he was extradited to Georgia. Fillmore supported the return of Sims, and Kennedy praised his friend's courage as "a good and true Whig."[100]

Although he only served nine months, Kennedy loved the job of secretary of the navy. During his first month, he was confronted with a crisis between Britain and the United States over fishing rights in the Bay of Fundy, known as the "Codfish War." "Up at dawn and at Codfish again!" he wrote in his journal. He presided over the Perry expedition to Japan, Elisha Kane's second expedition to Greenland, and various other naval surveys and explorations. Kennedy also recommended exploring the coast of Liberia and its inland territory as possible sites for the further colonization of American blacks.[101]

Kennedy was too busy with navy matters to actively participate in the election of 1852. The Democrats chose Franklin Pierce of New Hampshire and William King of Alabama as their presidential and vice-presidential candidates, respectively. Both parties endorsed the compromise and a "revenue only" tariff in their platforms. The Democrats jeered at the Whigs for abandoning the protective tariff, one of their last remaining principles. With little difference in their platforms and a booming economy, the parties depended on the appeal of their candidates. Whereas Scott was suspect in the South, Pierce was known as a "doughface," or northerner with southern sympathies. Nathaniel Hawthorne wrote Pierce's campaign biography, which, given the candidate's lackluster background, emphasized his recent "growth" toward presidential capability. For their part, the Whigs worried about Scott's propensity for foolishness, and Benjamin Wade warned that he could not win unless he "kept his mouth shut." During the campaign, however, Scott ham-handedly tried to curry favor with Irish Catholics, declaring, "I love to hear the Irish brogue!" As if on cue, large numbers of Protestant Whigs headed for the doors.[102]

Kennedy, Crittenden, Scott, and several other Whig leaders waited in a Washington telegraph office for the results on election night. "Bad accounts of defections by our friends," Kennedy wrote early in the evening. He was right. Many northern Whigs had gone over to Pierce, and many southern Whigs had simply stayed home. Scott won only four out of thirty-one states, gaining only forty-two electoral votes versus 254 for Pierce. The Democrats swept governorships, state legislatures, and reduced the Whigs to only a third of the House seats. The Senate results promised to be equally dire when the new state legislatures met to choose their senators. "Scott bears it well," Kennedy observed as the evening came to a sad end. The Whig Party had run its course.[103]

CHAPTER 6

The Quarter Revisited

American history has its comeback stories, but the Whig Party is not one of them. The party's feebleness after the Scott debacle made it vulnerable to the seismic events of the mid-1850s. The Kansas-Nebraska Act of 1854 effectively repealed the long-standing Missouri Compromise and divided the two national parties along sectional lines as never before. In the South, a new brand of political orthodoxy favored "popular sovereignty" for the Nebraska territories and brooked no dissent from local Whigs. In the North, the so-called Whig heartland, the rise of political nativism swept away the remnants of the party. In urban areas from Boston to Baltimore, where anti-Catholic and anti-immigrant sentiment was most intense, the American Party, or "Know-Nothings" as they were called, scored stunning victories at Whig and Democratic expense. Given their Protestant base, the Whigs suffered most from these incursions. By the beginning of 1855, Whig newspapers were declaring the party defunct.[1]

Kennedy's political life should logically have ended with the Whig demise. Instead, like a number of his colleagues wandering in the wilderness, he endeavored to transfer the principles of his former party to a new, more viable political movement, first to the Know-Nothings and later to the Constitutional Union Party. Although minor episodes in the country's political evolution, these interstitial movements were important ideological stepping stones for men like Kennedy en route to becoming Republicans. Given his devotion to the Union and social conservatism, he could not have embraced Republicanism with its sectional character and abolitionist taint in 1856 or 1860. Only after accepting the party of Lincoln as the sole means of restoring the Union—and recognizing that no compromise on southern slavery was possible—would Kennedy end his political wandering.[2]

Shortly after the Whig collapse, Kennedy and Fillmore had discussed the need for a new, conservative "Union party" to make a fresh start against the badly divided Democrats. Given their meteoric rise in the mid-1850s, the Know-Nothings seemed like a promising vehicle for the formation of such a party. Working with Fillmore and a handful of other Whigs, Kennedy played a major role in trying to bring the remnants of the party together with the nativists. Writing to a former Whig colleague, he predicted that the two parties would inevitably combine forces to "crush all the mischievous *sectionalism* which is now struggling for ascendency in American politics." Kennedy was also instrumental in maneuvering Fillmore into position as the Know-Nothing's presidential candidate in 1856. With that objective in mind, Fillmore took the secret Know-Nothing oath in his Albany home during January 1855. Kennedy, however, hung back from taking this critical step.[3]

There were various reasons for Kennedy's interest in the Know-Nothing Party and for his promotion of Fillmore as its presidential candidate. Kennedy's friendship with Fillmore and gratitude for having been invited into his cabinet certainly played a role. More important, Kennedy, Fillmore, and the other Whigs involved in this venture were under the mistaken impression that they could usurp control of the Know-Nothing leadership and steer the party toward their own purposes. In addition, there were certain aspects of Know-Nothingism that appealed to Kennedy and other former Whigs. Among these were the new party's emphasis on national unity, the moral certitude of its rhetoric, and its no-party pretentions.[4]

At least one scholar has accused Kennedy of being a nativist at heart. However, such a judgment does not stand up to scrutiny. Granted, Kennedy railed against the Democratic Party's manipulation of immigrant voters and called for more rigorous naturalization and voter registration laws on several occasions. Furthermore, he tended to see the world in Manichaean terms and, as he grew older, became more elitist in his social views. He likely saw many recently arrived immigrants fitting comfortably among the ignorant and indolent character types he had satirized in *Quodlibet*.[5]

And yet, Kennedy's father had emigrated from Northern Ireland, and he himself was a lifelong member of Baltimore's Hibernian Society. Even though he had been baptized a Presbyterian, he did not share that denomination's animosity toward Catholics. Anyone reading *Rob of The Bowl* could imagine Kennedy belonging to the Church of Rome. Furthermore, Kennedy never singled out the Irish for ridicule in his novels. Someone like Teague O'Regan, the ignorant "bog trotter" of Hugh Henry Brackenridge's *Modern Chivalry*, has no equivalent in Kennedy's novels. While he objected to their political manipulation by the Democratic Party, Kennedy was sympathetic to the economic plight of the Irish in their homeland and in America. In a long journal entry from 1848, he recounted the sad story of Mary White, who worked for a neighbor of the Kennedys and was the sole survivor of a family that had perished in the Irish potato famine. That same year, Kennedy attended a meeting of the Friends of Ireland in Baltimore, at which he was elected a vice president. In describing the meeting to a friend, he referred to Ireland as "that unhappy land of *our* fathers" and went on to say that he "should be glad to see her sons in the United States."[6]

Nor did Kennedy express any real animosity toward newly arrived Germans, the other pariah group of the nativists. Even though he was not fond of the Germans who had moved into Berkeley County, Virginia, Kennedy's fictional portraits of Germanic types such as Hafen Bok, Arnold de la Grange, and Claus Debor (the "Dutch Doctor") were relatively benign. Moreover, in his biography of William Wirt, Kennedy described how his mentor's features "suggested his connection with the German race." He went on to compare Wirt's handsome countenance with a "portrait of Goethe." In a journal entry from 1850, Kennedy recalled helping a group of German immigrants find their way in the streets of Baltimore. He expressed embarrassment at his poor command of their language and resolved to study it more diligently.[7]

Most important, certain aspects of Know-Nothing culture were anathema to Kennedy's character and temperament. To begin with, the Know-Nothings had more than their share of crackpots. The leader of the Baltimore party, Henry Winters Davis, was a case in point. In his 1852 book, *The War of Ormuzd and Ahriman in the Nineteenth Century,* Davis advocated American intervention in European affairs in the defense of democracy against monarchies. Other nativists spoke and wrote wildly about "Popish plots" to subvert the Republic and about sordid goings-on behind the walls of Catholic convents and monasteries. Furthermore, the Know-Nothing Party in Maryland and elsewhere tended to favor "new men" over established political leaders. These political neophytes carried no political baggage but had little else to recommend them. Much to Kennedy's dismay, his youngest brother Anthony, whom he described as amiable but without much of a brain, was elected on the nativist ticket to the U.S. Senate in 1856. Kennedy himself had dreamed of this honor. However, because he had been part of the prior political establishment and refused to take the Know-Nothing oath, Kennedy did not qualify under the rules of nativist politics.

Even more disturbing than the quality of its leadership was the level of violence that the Know-Nothings brought to the conduct of politics. Kennedy remarked despairingly about the large, unruly mob that took over Monument Square and burned an effigy of Monseigneur Bedini, the alleged "butcher of Bologna." Worse still, Know-Nothing street gangs like the "Rip Raps" and "Pug Uglies" regularly disrupted opposition political gatherings, intimidated voters at polling places, and terrorized Catholic neighborhoods. Kennedy deplored this kind of social disorder and could never condone it as political strategy.[8]

In the end, the fusion of pro-Union Whigs and Know-Nothings fell victim to the same kind of sectional discord that had wrecked the Whigs and Democrats. At their February 1856 convention, the Know-Nothings split over the issue of slavery and, after narrowly selecting Fillmore as their presidential candidate, ceased to function as a national party. Fillmore's support would come from the "rump" of southern nativists who had nominated him. During this same time, the fledgling Republican Party in the North drew political energy from what amounted to guerrilla warfare between pro- and antislavery forces in "Bleeding Kansas." The brutal assault on Massachusetts senator Charles Sumner by a South Carolinian on the Senate floor added to northern outrage and drove more northern Whigs, antislavery Democrats, and disaffected Know-Nothings into the Republican ranks. In their first presidential election, the Republicans chose the handsome but politically inept John C. Fremont to head their ticket.[9]

In the three-cornered presidential election of 1856, the Democratic candidate, James Buchanan of Pennsylvania, faced Fremont in the North and Fillmore in the South. Having been out of the country as minister to Great Britain during the passage of the controversial Kansas-Nebraska Act, Buchanan was able to heal some of the divisions within the Democratic Party. Furthermore, Buchanan pledged "non-interference" with slavery in the states, territories, and nation's capital. When the election was over, 112 of Buchanan's 178 electoral votes had come from the South. Nonetheless, this was well ahead of Fremont's 114 electoral votes and Fillmore's 8. Only Maryland had gone for Fillmore.

For Kennedy and the fusion Whigs, these results were disheartening. Clearly, their attempt to harness nativism to revitalize the Whig Party had backfired. Rather than helping to mend the tattered remains of the Whig

Party, the Know-Nothings purged the combined party of its more established figures and forced any suitable recruits to take the secret oath. In the North, the Know-Nothings ended up serving as a crossover movement from the Whigs to the Republican Party. In the South, where Fillmore and the southern Know-Nothings failed to gain meaningful traction, many Whigs simply went over to the Democrats. As a result, most former Whigs were lodged in opposing political and sectional camps. With the Republicans representing northern antislavery interests and the Democrats fast becoming a de facto southern party, American politics were well on their way to becoming fully sectionalized.[10]

In the face of these developments, Kennedy did more than just step away from politics. He fled abroad. He and his wife Elizabeth had already taken a short trip to England in the spring of 1856, just after Edward Gray's death and before the Fillmore campaign had gotten under way. Now, during the summer of 1857, the Kennedys embarked on a European sojourn of nearly fifteen months. It was during this second trip that Kennedy renewed his friendship with the British author William Makepeace Thackeray.

The authors had met several times during Thackeray's two lecture tours of the United States a few years before. Both were bright, genial personalities and became fast friends. During a stay at the Kennedys' townhouse in Baltimore, Thackeray mentioned his plan for a novel to be called *The Virginians,* set during the American Revolution. Drawing from his extensive library, Kennedy lent Thackeray several books as source material. When the two met again in Paris during September 1858, Thackeray was sick in bed but hard at work on the novel. He was having trouble describing the countryside between Fort Duquesne in western Pennsylvania and the headwaters of the Potomac. Kennedy knew the area and offered to help. During October, he prepared some notes for his friend.

This collaboration gave rise to the story that Kennedy had written the fourth chapter of the second volume of *The Virginians.* The story probably had its origins in a biographical sketch on Kennedy written by his friend John H. B. Latrobe. However, Thackeray's daughter denied it. Reading the novel today, one can detect a hint of Kennedy. As the hero and his party from Fort Duquesne make their way east, crossing the Laurel Hills and Alleghenies, poplars and oaks give way to maples, and the forest becomes redder. Entering the pass at Will's Creek, the travelers are surrounded by high, white cliffs with eagles wheeling overhead. The style is Thackeray's with a few rustic touches from his friend.[11]

By the time the Kennedys returned, Baltimore was experiencing its worst political turmoil ever. In an effort to retain political power in the city, the Know-Nothings were using the muscle of their street gangs to intimidate voters and drive their Democratic rivals from the field. At polling places, they placed tubs of bloody water in which to plunge immigrants trying to vote, and brawling mobs of nativist thugs were invading Irish neighborhoods. After a dozen citizens were killed and hundreds wounded, the Democratic governor threatened to call up the militia to restore order.[12]

Politics at the national level had deteriorated as well, largely due to President Buchanan's actions. Both his alleged influence in the Supreme Court's *Dred Scott* decision, which essentially opened up the territories for the expansion of slavery, and his support for the proslavery "Lecompton constitution" in Kansas, subsequently rejected as fraudulent by Congress, enraged antislavery elements in the North. Influential Republicans such as Horace Greeley, William Seward, and Abraham Lincoln claimed that the president, the nation's highest court, and southern plantation owners were involved in a "slave-power conspiracy."[13]

As Baltimore's urban violence escalated and Kennedy's health declined, he spent more time at the nearby Patapsco estate that, along with the adjacent spinning mill, his wife and sister-in-law had inherited from their father. The main house sat on a bluff overlooking the Patapsco River and was a mile from the village of Ellicott's Mills. Surrounded by his expanding library and enjoying the pleasures of rural life, Kennedy entertained a steady stream of distinguished visitors and maintained a lively correspondence with his many literary and political contacts. Delighted with Kennedy's withdrawal from active politics, a local Democratic newspaper described him as an old rheumatoid who directed his Baltimore ward chiefs from a luxurious country estate. In fact, Kennedy's Patapsco retreat was unpretentious and his involvement in city politics marginal.[14]

As he watched the political system collapsing and the country edging toward sectional crisis, Kennedy lost all regard for political leadership in Maryland and the nation. He wrote to his uncle Philip Pendleton, "how lamentably destitute [we are] of men in public station of whom we can speak with pride." In another letter to his uncle, he declared that those in political office were no better than "a miserable array of charlatans and make believe statesmen, little clap-trap demagogues and mock statesmen, manufactured out of blackguards."[15]

Kennedy's despair was shared by many Americans, especially as the 1850s came to a jarring end. During October 1859, the fanatical abolitionist John Brown, along with some two dozen of his followers, attacked the federal armory at Harpers Ferry, Virginia. Kennedy watched trainloads of troops pass by his Patapsco house on the way to get control of the situation. "He thought he would be joined by thousands of negroes," Kennedy commented, "and fought with much heroic courage until overwhelmed."[16]

Though put down quickly, Brown's raid had tremendous repercussions. Northern newspapers, according to Kennedy, were filled with "the mad outrage of the abolitionists." Respected writers and opinion leaders in the North eulogized Brown as a fallen hero of the abolitionist movement. In the South, the public was seized by a hysteria not seen since the Turner uprising. In the weeks that followed, the public learned that Brown had received financial support from a circle of prominent northern intellectuals. Based on his southern contacts, Kennedy became increasingly worried about "the perpetuity of the Union" after the Harpers Ferry incident. Heretofore cautious southerners, Kennedy told his friend Henry Tuckerman, were "calculating the advantages that would accrue to their section by a separation from the North."[17]

Still, the presidential election ritual commenced in the face of these rising passions. In keeping with tradition, the Democratic convention met first during April. The party's choice of Charleston, South Carolina, as its venue proved a mistake. Kennedy's friend George Bryan invited him to attend as an observer, but he declined because of ill health. Had he gone, he would have seen the great party tear itself apart. Led by secessionist "fire-eaters," the implacable southern wing of the party bolted the convention before a platform could be agreed on or a candidate chosen. The Democrats would reconvene in June to try again.[18]

Far more harmonious was the Baltimore gathering of the Constitutional Union Party in early May. For months leading up to it, Kennedy, John Crittenden, and other ex-Whigs had been hard at work organizing a conservative alternative to the Republicans. "There is much work to be done," Kennedy wrote in his journal, "and I am dragged into the hottest of it." Kennedy saw the new party as an antidote to the "sectional fanaticism" threatening to divide the country. Crittenden, seen by many as the heir to Henry Clay as "Union-saver," met with Kennedy several times to prepare an address outlining the party's objectives and calling for a national convention. A dozen or so conservative Whigs and several "Fillmore Know-Nothings" signed the address. Given its preponderance of ex-Whigs, however, many saw the Constitutional Union as a "ghost" of that party.[19]

Much of Kennedy's time was spent bringing as many Know-Nothings as possible into the new party. Still, the Know-Nothings regarded the Whigs as a "broken down" party and resented any attempt to rejuvenate it. Kennedy became "disgusted with the intrigue" of the Know-Nothings and was forced to call on his brother Anthony, still serving as the nativist senator from Maryland, for help. The night before the Constitutional Union convention, the two brothers, Crittenden, and an assortment of former Whigs and Know-Nothings dined together at the Kennedy townhouse.[20]

The Constitutional Union Party's platform was simple: "to recognize no political principles other than *the Constitution of the Country, the Union of the States and Enforcement of the Laws.*" The party took no position on extension of slavery in the territories. In fact, no mention of slavery was allowed during the convention. Since Crittenden refused to run and most other potential nominees were in their seventies, the younger but lackluster Tennessean John Bell was chosen to head the party's ticket. While he and his wife owned 160 slaves between them, Bell had voted against both the Kansas-Nebraska Act and the Lecompton Constitution while in the Senate. Edward Everett, ex-governor of Massachusetts, former Whig congressman, and fellow Fillmore cabinet member with Kennedy, was chosen as Bell's running mate. Initially, Everett refused the nomination. Only after Kennedy appealed to his friend did Everett agree to join the ticket.[21]

The strategy of the Constitutional Union Party was not to win the 1860 election outright but to position its candidate for a runoff election in the House of Representatives (if no candidate achieved a majority in the electoral college, as had happened in 1824). This plan assumed that the Republicans would nominate William Seward, ex-governor of New York and its long-serving senator, and that his antislavery reputation would deny him an electoral majority. Few expected the Republicans to nominate the more moderate Abraham Lincoln instead.

Although he worked closely with Crittenden in organizing the new party, Kennedy was never one to mince words in a political fight and thought the

Constitutional Union's platform too vague and its rhetoric too soft. The competitive stance of the Constitutional Union was "very tame," he warned Crittenden, and unlikely to dislodge many voters from its rivals. Even though he put Crittenden up at his townhouse during the convention, Kennedy was unable to convince his colleague to strengthen the party's appeal to voters. Always a team player, however, Kennedy sponsored a large rally in Baltimore's Monument Square after the convention adjourned. One speaker after another praised the Union and fed the patriotic spirit of the crowd. At the height of the excitement, organizers wheeled a wagon holding a huge bell into the square and led the crowd in chanting "Our Bell rings to the sound of the Union. Try it!" In the end, the party's symbolism was as weak as its platform and its candidate. It would pale against the image of Abe Lincoln, the "Rail-Splitter."[22]

In June, Democrats reconvened in Baltimore but were unable to mend their intraparty differences. Kennedy watched the proceedings in disbelief: "They formed each fragment into a convention—the one nominating Douglas and Fitzpatrick and the other Breckenridge and Lane—and having done all they could to make their discord incurable, adjourned on Saturday night." The Democrats would go into the election of 1860 divided, insuring a Republican victory and the likelihood of secession. The fire-eaters had done their job well.[23]

In Chicago that same month, at the largest convention the country had ever seen, the Republican Party endeavored to moderate its image by passing over the front-runner William Seward and nominating the more moderate Abraham Lincoln. The party wooed ex-Whigs with promises of a higher tariff, a Pacific railroad, and homestead legislation. Many former Know-Nothings, who despised Seward for his Catholic sympathies, also joined the party. Most important, the Republicans reiterated their opposition to the expansion of slavery in the territories.[24]

The four-way presidential race of 1860 pitted Lincoln against Stephen Douglas in the North and Bell against John Breckenridge in the South. Even though it had nominated a moderate antislavery candidate, the Republican Party positioned itself as the defender of the Union against the threat of slave power. Lincoln won every northern state except New Jersey and Missouri, giving him a majority of electoral votes and avoiding a runoff in the House of Representatives. Although he retained the support of many Catholics and immigrants, Douglas could not overcome his party's association with the expansion of slavery. In the South, Breckenridge campaigned on an aggressive proslavery platform and captured most of the region. Kennedy, of course, voted for Bell and Everett. However, the party Kennedy had worked hard to establish carried only Virginia, Kentucky, and Tennessee. To his disappointment, Maryland went for Breckenridge.[25]

The fallout from the election of 1860 was immediate. "The papers bring us a perfect tempest of wrath," Kennedy recorded in his journal, "against Lincoln's election in the South. South Carolina, Georgia, Alabama, and Mississippi are full of threats of secession." Because it had gone for Breckenridge, Kennedy also worried about Maryland. Over the next several weeks, he met with members of the state legislature and urged Governor Thomas Hicks not to call a special session until things cooled off.[26]

Although politics dominated the news in 1860, everyday life in the Republic carried on. Given his commitment to community and his multiplicity of interests, Kennedy had many nonpolitical responsibilities at this time. He continued as a trustee and provost of the University of Maryland and occasionally lectured there. In April 1860, he was elected president of the Peabody Institute, a liberal-arts educational foundation endowed by his wealthy merchant friend George Peabody as a gift to Baltimore. Kennedy supervised the construction of the institute's buildings on Monument Square and helped assemble its magnificent library. Representing his wife and sister-in-law's interests, he oversaw the Gray Manufacturing Company in Patapsco. Working with Lippincott, his Philadelphia publisher, Kennedy brought out a new edition of *Quodlibet.*[27]

Still, these activities supplied only temporary distractions from the unsettling events between Lincoln's election and the attack on Fort Sumter. Rumors, speculation, and hard news generated optimism one day and despair the next. "There are many indications of alarm in the public mind," Kennedy wrote at the time of Lincoln's election. One was a collapsing stock market, which forced brokers and investors into bankruptcy and caused companies to shed workers. Another was the formation of armed volunteer groups, some for and some against the Union. In early December, President-Elect Lincoln's message to the nation appeared in newspapers. It was "moderate and sensible," Kennedy commented in his journal, "which perhaps is wise just now." When South Carolina seceded two weeks later, Kennedy became irate. "It is mock-heroic of men who do not comprehend their own incapacity, who mistake secession for a just sentiment of honor," he wrote. "They will live to repent the wickedness of this act," he predicted, "which is destined to be visited upon them in the ruin of their country and the detestable fame it is to confer upon them."[28]

While historians have described the clash between the sections as a "political war," they have often underemphasized the role of political writers like Kennedy in forming public opinion and influencing events. Although Kennedy had always played this role, his physical condition now forced him to make it his primary political undertaking. He had turned sixty-five before Lincoln's victory and was in poor health. Lame from horse falls and plagued with rheumatism and skin disorders, he was no longer fit for public office. Nor would there be a uniform and military rank for him. Yet, Kennedy was never one to sit idly by. After all, he commanded a national reputation, had powerful friends, and could write. In the struggle for the Union, his weapons would be letters, articles, and pamphlets.[29]

During December 1860, the lame-duck Thirty-sixth Congress formed a special committee to address the sectional crisis. It produced the so-called Crittenden Plan, proposing a constitutional amendment to restore the Missouri Compromise line and extend it to the Pacific. Anthony Kennedy was doubtful the plan would be passed into legislation and suggested to his brother that Congress was not the place to achieve such a settlement. This suggestion may have encouraged John Kennedy in his campaign for a settlement outside of Congress. Immediately after Lincoln's election, he began writing "a tract on disunion." By mid-December, he had given it a name—"The Border States, their power and duty in the current disordered condition of the country"—and sent a manuscript to his publisher. After South Carolina seceded, Kennedy started mailing his "Border States" pamphlet to newspaper editors, state governors, and influential politicians. By Christmas, he had mailed some fifty copies to the nation's capital and probably twice that number to other localities. Visitors to his Baltimore and Patapsco residences—among them Edward Everett, Robert Winthrop, and William Appleton—could not leave without copies of "The Border States" in their luggage.[30]

Kennedy's pamphlet called for a "border confederation," both as a buffer between the North and South and as a way of mediating between them. The Border States, he argued, were "the most authentic representation of conservative power in the Union." They understood the South's position on slavery and shared nothing of the North's reforming zeal, especially its infatuation with abolitionism. Kennedy's pamphlet and his accompanying letters to various politicians called for a peace conference to develop a compromise agreeable to both sections. Over Christmas, for example, he wrote Governor Beriah Magoffin of Kentucky, soliciting his help in "some scheme for joint deliberations and action by the Border States in accordance with the views presented in my pamphlet." Two weeks later, Magoffin responded with a promise of support. However, the real impetus for what became known as the Washington Peace Conference came from Virginia, where one of the state's sitting congressman, Alexander Boteler, and a former one, William C. Rives, pushed hard for it. Both had been involved in the Constitutional Union Party and were doubtlessly targeted by Kennedy's mailings. It was Virginia governor John Letcher who set the time and place for the conference.[31]

The Washington Peace Conference met in the new annex of Willard's Hotel between February 4 and 26, 1861. At its peak, 133 "peace commissioners" attended the conference, representing twenty-one of the thirty-three states. The Deep South did not attend. The conference declared itself dedicated to "the great work of reconciliation and adjustment" and took Congress's Crittenden Plan, recommended five days earlier but not yet approved, as its starting point. Kennedy could not attend because of poor health, but he would have found the gathering awkward. Former president John Tyler, whom Kennedy had vilified in his "Whig Manifesto" years before, chaired the conference, and former Maryland congressman and Democratic rival Benjamin Howard, whom Kennedy had satirized as Middleton Flam in *Quodlibet,* served as its secretary.[32]

The country had mixed views of the peace conference. Horace Greeley's *New York Tribune* dubbed it "The Old Gentlemen's Conference" because of the advanced age of its participants, but the *Albany Evening Journal* saw it as the nation's last hope for peace. In the end, the conference had no official status and was too late. Nor was it properly constituted without the Deep South. Furthermore, Republican attendees could not agree to concessions regarding slavery in the territories without going back on their most important campaign pledge. However, the Republicans did want to prolong the conference until Lincoln was safely inaugurated. Lincoln's arrival at Willard's Hotel in the last week of the conference only complicated its work. After three weeks of speeches and debate, the conference approved a nearly identical version of the Crittenden Plan and forwarded it to Congress. Kennedy was delighted to learn the conference had arrived at a settlement. "So here is the day of sunshine on our troubles!" he wrote.[33]

In the final days of the Thirty-sixth Congress, the conference's peace plan went down to defeat, mainly due to Republican opposition. More disappointments followed. Before Lincoln could be sworn in, seven southern states had seceded and chosen their own president. On April 12, 1861, the Confederate nation attacked Fort Sumter. "Yesterday was the birthday of Henry Clay," Kennedy noted sadly. "It was signalized by a most memorable and melancholy act, the opening of the Civil War by the assault of the Carolina batteries upon Fort Sumter . . . The South is wild with joy in the secession states."[34]

So, why had it finally come to this? Even though he had written it several months before the attack on Fort Sumter, Kennedy devoted much of "The Border States" to exploring the roots of the sectional crisis. After a lengthy refutation of the South's constitutional arguments for secession, he set about apportioning blame across both sections. In the South, he singled out the "contrivers of disunion" in South Carolina and Tidewater Virginia. In particular, the plotters in South Carolina were motivated by selfish and delusionary dreams. "They behold their Arcadia," he wrote, "with its phantoms of untold wealth, its free ports, its illimitable cotton fields, its flattering alliances, [and] its swarms of reinforcements from the shores of Africa." Kennedy believed South Carolina and Tidewater Virginia were pockets of treason in a South otherwise supportive of peace and the Union.[35]

However, Kennedy laid most of the blame for the national crisis at the doorstep of New England. He condemned the "sanctimonious vanity" of the region's moral reformers and the hypocrisy of its cotton magnates who, he pointed out, had "shared in the profits of slavery" for decades. Recently, New England had been driven to distraction by its "pedagogues," "shining light preachers," and "strong minded women." Everything would have been fine had they kept their "pious politics and cheap philanthropies" to themselves. Instead, they had embarked on a "system of assault" and "treasonable disturbances" against the peaceful communities of the South. Not satisfied with mere agitation, New Englanders had engaged in "stealthy abduction of slaves" and "provoked servile insurrections." They were responsible, Kennedy asserted, for "opening a Pandora's box of murder, rapine, implacable hatred and revenge."[36]

Kennedy was clearly reacting to disclosures of northern support for the Harpers Ferry raid, continuing circumvention of the Fugitive Slave Law by northern legislatures, and rising levels of abolitionist activity during the late 1850s. But what made his diatribe so startling was its sweeping condemnation of reform movements in general. In spite of their efforts, temperance advocates had gotten nowhere, and "alcohol [had] gained the day." Similarly, abolitionists had proven "utterly impotent to arrest the steady increase in slave labor." Kennedy implied that the institutions that had championed these ineffective and socially disruptive causes should be held accountable for the current crisis. Many of these disruptive notions had begun as "discourses from the pulpit" but had quickly spread to "the kitchens and primary schools and factories of New England."[37]

"Slavery would have slept under the quiet surface of society," Kennedy insisted, had New England's zealots just left it alone. Instead, the region's thoughtless assaults on slavery threatened to obliterate half the nation's wealth and turn the South "back into a jungle for wild beasts." Furthermore, he argued, slavery was "a very appropriate and necessary agent of civilization." Slavery had been "a clear gain to the savage it has civilized." Slavery, he declared, "has been a *blessing* to him" (italics added).[38]

Written on the brink of national crisis, Kennedy's "The Border States" was as emotionally charged as his Texas letter had been fifteen years earlier. However, whereas Kennedy had mocked the idea that slavery was a "blessing" then, he now called it that himself. He had signaled his shift to a more conservative stance regarding slavery a decade before in the revised edition of *Swallow Barn.* In that text, he had included a damning assessment of black character and questioned the readiness of enslaved blacks for new freedoms and privileges. He had staunchly defended the right of the South to deal with slavery at its own pace and warned the North against intervening in southern affairs. In "The Border States," he went further. He granted the South moral justification for its peculiar institution.

A much more conservative Kennedy had written "The Border States," one who dismissed moral reform in general as a danger to the country's social and economic well-being. Although never a reforming zealot, he had frequently given voice to his didactic nature and encouraged moral intervention by a variety of institutions. What is more, his novels had been replete with moralizing views on temperance, personal industry, family values, and religious observation. Kennedy had lauded institutions such as the home, the work place, schools, and churches as vital sources of social cohesion and moral advancement. Now, he rejected these institutions as destabilizing influences on the nation's social and economic order. Just as surprising, Kennedy singled out "strong minded women" in his rant against northern reform movements. Here, he probably had Harriet Beecher Stowe in mind. Still, Kennedy had always admired strong women like his mother and early schoolteachers and honored them with featured roles in his novels. Now, such women were being blamed for leading the nation to war.

For Kennedy and many former Whigs, the tension between their reforming impulse and social conservatism had always been a problem. While their belief system called for moral and economic progress, such progress needed to be gradual and never disruptive to the social and economic order. As they approached elderhood, Kennedy and men like him naturally tilted toward conservatism. They valued a society with its decorous finish untarnished, its bourgeois niceties undisturbed, and its social hierarchies unthreatened. More than ever, constitutional guarantees, the rule of law, and the protection of property dominated their thinking.[39]

In "The Border States," this long-standing tension between reform and restraint finally snapped. In assigning blame for the national crisis, Kennedy was willing to forsake those institutions for social uplift he had once venerated. Furthermore, he was prepared to concede to the South both its economic and moral arguments for slavery, all in the interest of preserving peace and the Union. In the end, Kennedy's pamphlet was less a thoughtful analysis of unfolding events and more a cry of despair at what was happening to his beloved Union.

After Fort Sumter, events moved quickly. "Civil War is taking over the country," Kennedy wrote, "[with] reports of troops being raised in many quarters. The flag of the Southern Confederacy is hoisted in many places." Rumors spread that the new president of the Confederacy, Jefferson Davis, had ordered an attack on Washington. Throughout Maryland, former Breckenridge and Lane clubs were said to be arming for that purpose. After Lincoln's call up of seventy-five thousand troops to suppress the rebellion, Kennedy met with Governor Hicks and urged him to provide troops from Maryland only to protect the nation's capital, not to invade the South.[40]

A week after the shelling of Fort Sumter, the situation in Baltimore exploded. A pro-Confederate mob attacked soldiers of the Massachusetts Sixth Regiment attempting to pass through the city en route to Washington. Four soldiers and a dozen citizens were killed. Many more were wounded. For several weeks, pandemonium reigned in the city. Militia groups and partisan newspapers sparred for the loyalty of a divided citizenry. Order was only restored when federal troops under General Benjamin Butler occupied the city in mid-May. Lincoln suspended habeas corpus throughout the state, and federal authorities began arresting suspected secessionists (including Baltimore's mayor and police commissioners) and closed down prosouthern newspapers.[41]

During this turmoil, Kennedy again took up his pen. He wrote Salmon Chase, Lincoln's secretary of treasury and a former Washington Peace Conference attendee, suggesting that a reshuffling of the president's cabinet might create better sectional representation and be seen by the South as a peace overture. He also asked that a new peace conference be convened. In early May, Kennedy published an article entitled "The Great Drama" in the *Baltimore American* and the *National Intelligencer.* The article argued passionately that Maryland stay in the Union. He urged Marylanders to ignore the "wretched slanders of fanatics" who would brand them as "submissionists" for their loyalty to country. He asked citizens of the state to remember their "brave ancestors" who had fought and died for the nation's independence. "Stand by your ancient flag," Kennedy pleaded, and "keep her [Maryland] where your fathers placed her."[42]

"The Great Drama" became a rallying cry for the formation of a state-level Union Party. Many Unionists urged Kennedy to be the party's nominee for the upcoming congressional election. He declined due to ill health and the view that he could serve the party more effectively in Baltimore. Working behind the scenes, Kennedy drew on his knowledge of ward and county politics to ensure the party's success in the November gubernatorial elections. He contributed several more articles to local newspapers promoting the Union cause.[43]

Given the divided state of politics in Maryland, Kennedy's fervent Unionism was destined to create problems and cost him friendships. He was snubbed in the streets of Baltimore and excluded from many social events. At the University of Maryland, where as provost he handed out diplomas in June, those graduates known to sympathize with the South were applauded, and bouquets tied with red and white ribbons, the colors of the Confederacy, were thrown on stage. Kennedy and those graduates with Union sympathies were hissed and booed. During a church service Kennedy attended, certain members of the congregation rose to their feet when a prayer for President Lincoln was read. Kennedy was alternately amused and disgusted by these examples of disloyalty and disrespect.[44]

Although he had not voted for him in 1860, Kennedy believed President Lincoln was a reasonable man. In "The Border States," he described Lincoln as representing "the moderate, conservative division of the Republican party." On July 4, 1861, Kennedy had the opportunity to meet the president for the first time at the White House. Kennedy and Reverdy Johnson had an appointment to discuss the release of the Baltimore police commissioners from the custody in which they had been placed several weeks earlier. Secretary of the Navy Gideon Welles and Secretary of State William Seward were also at the meeting. At first somewhat brusque with his visitors, Lincoln soon relaxed and spoke "cordially" with them and listened with "good will" to their request. He promised to raise the issue of the police commissioners at the next cabinet meeting. Kennedy was impressed with Lincoln, mentioning in a journal entry that the president's portraits had misrepresented him in stature and appearance. Kennedy's admiration for Lincoln would grow over time.[45]

Although the country was literally falling apart, most perceptions of what sort of conflict lay ahead remained remarkably naive. Shortly before his meeting with Lincoln, Kennedy called on Winfield Scott at the War Department, where the aging Mexican War hero and former Whig presidential candidate was serving as general-in-chief of Union forces. The conversation soon turned to military strategy. According to Kennedy's account of their discussion, Scott was "mathematically certain" of a quick Union victory. Given the North's vast superiority in men and money, as well as Scott's plan to isolate the South with a naval blockade and control of its rivers, victory would take a year at the most and require "no great amount of bloodshed." Scott's assessment was only slightly less optimistic than Kennedy's view that the North and the South were "playing a game of bravado" and would soon agree to peace terms.[46]

The Battle of Bull Run on July 21, 1861, proved both men wrong and dashed hopes of an early peace. Kennedy calculated that his extended family in Virginia furnished at least forty combatants on the Confederate side. The rout of federal forces on the battlefield stunned the Lincoln administration and the northern public. "The news casts a melancholy over every friend of the Union," Kennedy wrote. Its defeat at Bull Run also damaged the image of the Union internationally. While Great Britain had declared itself neutral in the American conflict, the danger of British material aid to the Confederacy and, worst of all, diplomatic recognition of the rebel state worried the Lincoln government. Whatever England did, France was likely to follow suit. With these problems in mind, Secretary of State Seward invited Kennedy to Washington to discuss "a matter of public concern."[47]

During late October and early November 1861, Kennedy met several times with Seward and President Lincoln regarding a "secret mission" to repair relations with Great Britain. The mission would consist of Kennedy, Edward Everett, and Charles McIlvaine, the Episcopal bishop of Ohio. Everett had formerly served as minister to Britain, and McIlvaine had close ties to the Church of England. As an internationally published author, Kennedy was known to the British reading public and its literary community. Kennedy was a friend of Thackeray, for example, who was a prominent voice in England and favored letting the South go its own way. Adding to the urgency of the mission was the knowledge that the Confederacy was about to dispatch James Mason and John Slidell, former U.S. congressmen turned Confederate diplomats, to Europe to plead the southern cause.[48]

Fortunately for Kennedy, relations with Great Britain improved just as the northern mission was about to depart. During a November 7 meeting at the White House, Seward and Lincoln shared a diplomatic dispatch from a reliable source in England saying that there had been "a signal change," as Kennedy described it, "against any intention to recognize the Southern Confederation or violate the blockade." Seizing the opportunity, Kennedy argued that the mission should be postponed but that he would be available if needed in the future. Because his oldest son had just died, Everett also wanted to delay the mission. Lincoln and Seward concurred.[49]

In the end, a mission was sent to England without Kennedy and Everett. By the time of the "*Trent* affair," provoked by the interdiction of a British steamer and the capture of Confederate emissaries Mason and Slidell by a Union warship, the new mission was on its way to deal with the diplomatic crisis that followed. Still, Kennedy had made important contacts in the Lincoln government and, as he had in earlier days promoting the tariff, took full advantage of his access to high office.[50]

In recent local elections, Maryland's Union Party had soundly defeated the so-called States' Rights Party. During a meeting with Seward, Kennedy told him that "the Government might now deal with Maryland as a loyal state." Kennedy suggested throwing as much business as possible into Baltimore. In conversations with various members of Lincoln's cabinet and officials in the war and navy departments, Kennedy lobbied on behalf of the "Union Mechanics of Baltimore" and several manufacturing firms in the city. Assigning armament contracts to Maryland companies would "encourage Union feeling in the State."[51]

Because Kennedy's stature and experience were useful to the Lincoln administration, their relationship was reciprocal. In addition to promoting the Union cause in Baltimore, Kennedy helped ensure that important foreign visitors came away sympathetic to the North. In this capacity, he squired Anthony Trollope, the popular British novelist, around Baltimore and its nearby military camps. Trollope was a personal friend of Thackeray but more pro-Union. Since Trollope was certain to write about his American visit when he returned home, the Lincoln administration wanted to keep him that way. Although Trollope and his wife had spent months traveling around the North, Baltimore was their first trip to the South. Enlisting the help of General John A. Dix, the city's occupying commander and a charmer compared to the obtuse Butler before him, Kennedy introduced the visitors to Union troops by day and feted the pair with dinner parties at night. Kennedy showed Trollope the Peabody Institute, still under construction, as an example of the city's cultural strides. By the time Trollope departed, Kennedy described him as "a very decided friend of the Union and hopeful of our success in restoring the order and harmony of the government."[52]

As anticipated, Trollope's travelogue *North America* appeared in late 1862. The author explained that the United States had been "torn to pieces by the weight of its discordant parts." Nonetheless, he branded southern secession a "revolutionary" act. "Nobody, no single Southerner can really believe that the Constitution of the United States as framed in 1787, or altered since, intended to give the separate States the power of seceding as they pleased," he argued in language similar to Kennedy's. Trollope went on to sanctify the Union cause. In the North, Trollope pointed out, labor was considered "honorable," but in the South it was "servile" and "dishonorable." Trollope knew where he stood on honest work and did not anticipate "any change in the Creator's fiat on this matter." Such sentiments played well with British workers, starved though they were for American cotton.[53]

Traveling frequently to Washington, Kennedy got to know Lord Lyons, the head of the British legation there. Lyons was painfully shy but interested in literature. The two men got along well. After several discussions with Lyons, Kennedy was convinced that he was sympathetic to the Union and against

British intervention in the war. "Lord Lyons is manifestly for peace and well disposed in favor of the Union," Kennedy wrote in his journal. However, winning over certain of Lyons's countrymen proved more challenging. Kennedy was less sure where Lord Hartington and his traveling companion Colonel Leslie, who visited Baltimore during December 1862, stood regarding the Union and Confederate sides. Hartington was especially hard to read. At one point, he confided to Kennedy that Confederate emissary James Mason had impressed London society as a "coarse man." At a dinner party in London, he explained, Mason had corrected his host Lord Ashley on the pronunciation of the word "chew." It was "chaw," Mason had insisted, and to demonstrate he had pulled a large plug of chewing tobacco from his pocket. In spite of stories like this, Kennedy thought Hartington was "decidedly inclined to side with the south in our quarrel." A few days later, Hartington and Leslie crossed over the front lines into the Confederacy under cover of darkness. In Richmond, they were hosted by President Davis and General Robert E. Lee. They later bivouacked with General J. E. B. Stuart. Against the patrician Lee and debonair Stuart, Kennedy's charm and arguments had their limits.[54]

Kennedy advised the Lincoln administration on a number of other matters, including the treatment of Union prisoners in the Mid-Atlantic theatre and the hospital capacity in and around Baltimore. The latter became an urgent concern when the Confederacy invaded Maryland during the first week of September 1862.[55]

The strategy behind the invasion of Maryland was based on faulty intelligence regarding civilian sentiment in the state. In thinking they could "liberate" Maryland from the Union, the Confederacy underestimated efforts by Kennedy and others like him in converting public opinion to the Union cause as well as the Lincoln administration's suppression of secessionist influence. As General Lee entered Frederick, Maryland, with the Army of Northern Virginia, few locals rallied to the Confederate banner. "The rebels are greatly disappointed at their reception in the state," Kennedy wrote. "They expected to see a rising of fifty thousand men to join their standards. They have not got five hundred, whilst they are losing greatly by desertion."[56]

Since no one knew in which direction Lee would march after seizing Frederick, Baltimore was in full alarm and expected an attack. Union mortar boats stood ready in the harbor to bombard the city if taken. Secessionists were rumored to be writing to Lee to avoid the city since it would be "shelled out" and destroyed. Guessing the Confederates might move north, Kennedy took a carriage to his country retreat at Patapsco. En route he encountered forces belonging to General George McClellan's Army of the Potomac attempting to intercept Lee. After removing some valuables from his country house and closing down the nearby factory, Kennedy hurried back to Baltimore. He caught sight of several Confederate scouts on the way.[57]

On September 17, 1862, the two armies engaged in a vicious twelve-hour battle just east of Sharpsburg, Maryland, at Antietam Creek. With total casualties of twenty-six thousand, it was the bloodiest day of the war. "News this morning of a splendid victory," Kennedy wrote the next day. Though not an especially religious man, he attended church twice that day.[58]

In early October, he had the chance to discuss the results of the battle and Lincoln's Preliminary Emancipation Proclamation that followed it with Secretary of State Seward at Patapsco. The secretary had taken the opportunity to visit Kennedy for a few days, while Lincoln was conferring with General McClellan at the Antietam battlefield. Seward thought the Union victory had marked a turning point in the war and, according to Kennedy, was "cheerful and sanguine of a new train of successes." Kennedy did not record much of their conversation about Lincoln's proclamation. Since Kennedy was peripherally involved with the American Colonization Society, he may have believed, as Lincoln still did, that some policy of removal would address the problem of freed slaves after the war. What is more, the proclamation did not apply to slaves in either Maryland or the newly created state of West Virginia, where many of Kennedy's relatives lived. The two did discuss the future of Texas, a portion of which was occupied by Union troops. Kennedy recommended that Texas be divided into several states after the war and opened to German immigrants. Many of these immigrants had successfully cultivated cotton without slaves. Such experience would be important for the future, Kennedy believed. "It would dispel the common view that cotton cannot be provided but by slave labor," he told Seward.[59]

Following the Battle of Antietam, elements of Lee's army sought refuge and recuperation in the Blue Ridge Mountains. General Stuart's cavalry headed for Martinsburg and, at the end of September, set up camp at the estate of Adam Stephen Dandridge II, known locally as "The Bower." There, on the serenely beautiful site that had served as the setting for *Swallow Barn,* Stuart's entourage established their tent headquarters on the mansion's front lawn and in the adjacent oak grove for several weeks. Dandridge was a southern sympathizer and proved an exemplary host. His slaves served elaborate banquets in the mansion's dining room and on tables set up on the lawn. Half of Stuart's officers were said to be in love with one or more of Dandridge's six daughters. During late September, Stuart and nearly two thousand of his men made a lightning raid on Chambersburg, Pennsylvania. While Stuart's raid was a major news story, it is unclear whether Kennedy knew anything about events at The Bower.[60]

When Lincoln's final Emancipation Proclamation was published in the first days of 1863, Kennedy's reaction was lukewarm. He saw it neither as a military necessity for the Union nor as a moral milestone for the nation but rather as something forced on Lincoln by the radical wing of his party. "A great stroke of statesmanship as the Radicals think it!" Kennedy wrote. "It is likely to prove like everything else for their gratification to be only a new element of division without practical advantage to anybody but the enemy." Nonetheless, Kennedy believed slavery's days were numbered in Maryland. "Slavery is in a course of rapid decrease in the State," he declared, and, if slaveholders wanted anything for their property, they had best act quickly. In the end, Marylanders would vote to abolish slavery without compensation as part of a new state constitution. By fall 1864, Maryland's eighty thousand slaves would be free.[61]

Like many hopeful predictions about the war, those Seward expressed to Kennedy at Patapsco proved too optimistic. The Union victory at Antietam was followed by crushing defeats at Fredericksburg and Chancellorsville. Even after Lee's second invasion of the North was thwarted at Gettysburg with astonishing losses on both sides, the war continued. Like many observers, Kennedy's opinions regarding the causes and the desired outcome of the war changed over its long duration. He set them down in a series of eleven articles appearing in the *National Intelligencer* from January 1863 through March 1864. Entitled "Mr. Ambrose's Letters on the Rebellion," these articles took the form of a correspondence between a pro-Union southerner named Ambrose and the newspaper's editor. In them, Ambrose traced the origins of the war and speculated about the peace that would follow it.[62]

Kennedy proved a poor poseur behind the thinly developed character of Ambrose. Regarding the act of secession, Kennedy ploughed much of the same legal ground he had in "The Border States." But, now, three years into the war, he was more vehement in his condemnation of the South. He called its act of secession "a dreadful catastrophe" that had led the country through "an ocean of blood and many years of sorrow." What is more, the precipitous behavior of the South in leaving the Union caused Kennedy to think again about the causes of the war. "The inadequacy of reasons given for this momentous struggle would compel us to believe," he wrote, "that the ostensible causes are not the real ones, and that we must seek elsewhere for the true exposition of the [secession] movement."[63]

"Slavery, of itself and for itself, is not the cause of the rebellion," Kennedy declared. Granted, slavery had helped shape the indolent habits and imperious behavior of the plantation class. So, too, the "phantom of negro equality" had haunted non-slave-owning whites and had been shamelessly exploited by the South's ruling elite. But, Kennedy reasoned, slavery had never really been in danger of extinction before the war. "I do not believe that there was one intelligent, leading and thinking man in the South," he ventured, "who imagined that slavery was in any kind of danger from the National Government or the State Governments." Rather, he concluded, the conspirators who were behind the scheme of secession "had a much deeper purpose than the removal of any imagined danger to the security of their institution."[64]

That deeper purpose, Kennedy argued, was nothing short of empire building. For decades, southerners had cast envious eyes toward the tropical domains below them, where warm climates, political instability, and what most of them considered degraded cultures invited the expansion of southern slavery. Southern adventure seekers had already carried out a number of "filibustering" expeditions in these tropical lands. "The Cuban expeditions miscarried; the Sonora failed; [and] the Nicaraguan forays were defeated," he reminded his readers. The object of secession, then, had been to establish a "Great Southern Confederation," which would encompass the southern states, the Caribbean, and much of Latin America. "This large domain would be organized under one Confederate Government and provided with the cheapest and most docile and subservient of all labor," Kennedy explained. "[I]ts lands were to be parceled out into principalities, and its land lords were to revel in the riches of Aladdin's lamp."[65]

The scheme to build a tropical empire involved, Kennedy averred, the so-called Knights of the Golden Circle, a secret society founded by a Virginia physician, journalist, and promoter named George Washington Lafayette Bickley. The "golden circle" was an imagined empire in a sixteen-degree radius from Havana. Bickley established a filibustering newspaper, the *American*

Cavalier, in Baltimore in 1859 and held a large meeting of the society in White Sulfur Springs, Virginia, near where Kennedy sometimes vacationed, the same year. Kennedy had heard enough about the Knights of the Golden Circle to connect them to the southern scheme of empire building. However, most historians believe that Bickley exaggerated his membership and that it consisted mostly of lower-class whites attracted to the society's secret oaths, elaborate robes, and other arcane claptrap. One of its few notable members was William Lowndes Yancey.[66]

So, who were the conspirators behind this empire-building scheme? Kennedy believed they numbered no more than "one hundred men." They belonged to two different but related groups, one composed of southern fire-eaters within the Democratic Party and the other drawn from the uppermost echelon of planter society. Members of the former group had helped lay the psychological groundwork for secession by railing against the "consolidating despotism" of the federal government and repeating the Democratic mantra of "Let us alone!" In the end, these men had split the Democratic Party and hijacked its southern wing for their secessionist aims.[67]

The latter group was made up of the most powerful members of the planter class and accounted for the majority of Kennedy's secessionist cabal. These men belonged to that "worshipful order, jocund and complacent in the patriarchal dignity conferred by hereditary bondsmen and acres." Still, these gentlemen were not what they seemed. Behind their genteel manners and cool demeanor, these elites were deadly serious about their own economic interests and stood to gain the most from political independence. They resented the North's growing dominance in national affairs and felt constrained in the expansion of their own peculiar institution. By spreading the "pestilent fallacy of sovereignty of the State" in their communities, these elite planters had persuaded their poorer white neighbors that the federal government was "a monster of such horrid proportions and propensities as to be no longer endured by free people." Once safely out of the Union, these ambitious planters, Kennedy predicted, would waste no time pursuing their "dazed visions of Empire."[68]

The last installment of "Mr. Ambrose's Letters" dealt with the anticipated demise of slavery and the disposition of freed slaves in the South. Contrary to what he had said in "The Border States," Kennedy no longer claimed that slavery was a "blessing." Now, the prospect of its termination was all that mattered to him. Slavery was a "spent force," he declared. He would leave it to future generations to deliver a verdict on the institution: "It [slavery] is about to pass with all its imputed merits and demerits, its wrongs and crimes, its false pretenses, its transient service and whatever modicum of good which it is capable, into the store house of things finished upon the earth, and to be henceforth committed to the accusing record of history." Kennedy's farewell to this most troublesome of American institutions was punctuated by a sigh of relief.

Looking beyond the war and a Union victory, Kennedy was optimistic about the future of the South's freed slaves. He urged white southerners to embrace their former bondsmen with "kind and friendly treatment." The South knew its former slaves better than anyone else, he observed, and was in the best position to manage their tutelage toward full citizenship. For this reason, the program for the advancement of the freed slaves, he insisted, should be left to the state governments. Within a decade or so, the former slave would rise "from debasement up to the enjoyment of every faculty and every right he may prove himself able to exercise." For those who could fulfill certain residency and literacy requirements, these rights would even include suffrage.[69]

By the time he sat down to write "Mr. Ambrose's Letters," Kennedy had taken a tougher stance toward the South and its peculiar institution. Even if his publishers had asked him to, Kennedy could not have reworked *Swallow Barn* a second time. The course of events had left the novel beyond the reach of literary revision. It would have been impossible to treat Frank Meriwether's expositions on states' rights doctrine, his manipulation of community opinion, or his ruminations on the future of slavery the same way he had in an earlier time. Now, Kennedy was accusing Tidewater planters like Meriwether of having masterminded secession. By 1863, Kennedy had shed much of his ambivalence about the South.

Certain aspects of "Mr. Ambrose's Letters," however, were naggingly inconsistent and at times illogical, especially its odd characterization of the secession movement and its overly optimistic outlook regarding emancipation. To begin with, Kennedy's emphasis on empire building as the primary reason for secession seemed exaggerated and farfetched. While some southerners may have dreamed about a Caribbean or Latin American empire, such expansionist schemes were never central to the secession movement and were never seriously pursued by the Confederacy after its founding. Very likely, Kennedy thought that such an exotic notion would bolster his argument that secession had been a narrowly managed conspiracy and lacked support by rank-and-file southerners. Still, the idea that most southerners had not endorsed secession needed a more credible theory of why the South had seceded than Kennedy could provide. How, after all, were the tremendous sacrifices made by southern soldiers on the fields of Antietam and Gettysburg to be explained? Perhaps, if Kennedy had been young enough to face these men across the battle lines at these engagements, he would have understood that something deeper and more fundamental lay at the heart of southern nationalism.[70]

And why, after having condemned states' rights doctrine in such unequivocal terms, would Kennedy recommend that a project as critical as the economic and social advancement of freed slaves be entrusted to the state governments of the former Confederacy? Was Kennedy so naïve as to think that southern whites, following the dual humiliation of military defeat and black emancipation, would treat their former bondsmen with friendliness and kindness, let alone expend meager postwar resources on them?

Unfortunately, the language in "Mr. Ambrose's Letters" betrayed the weakness of its author's professed commitment to this important project. Looking forward to a South without slavery, Kennedy referred to those to be freed there as "the debris which the demolition of that institution has left on the field." What is more, in explaining why he believed that freed slaves would advance so rapidly in free society, Kennedy gave the same reasons that he had previously used to rationalize their servitude—"namely, that the negro is by nature the most amicable, imitative, and pliable of all human beings." Just how this combination of alleged submissiveness and likely white resistance to emancipation would end happily for the freed slave remained unexplained. Tellingly, Kennedy described the postbellum social order he envisioned in the South as a "Restoration."[71]

Even if white southerners had been willing to accept freed slaves into their society with some measure of equality, Kennedy understood from his own experience just how daunting the economic and social advancement of the former slaves would be. In 1858, he had manumitted a black family that had somehow come into his possession in the neighborhood of Martinsburg, Virginia, and made plans to move the family to Pennsylvania. Having lived their entire lives near Martinsburg and lacking any useful skills other than farming, the family refused to leave Virginia and had fallen badly into debt during the nine months after obtaining freedom. "These poor blacks I fear will never be able to support themselves," Kennedy confided to his journal. For all that had been said about the civilizing benefits of slavery, the institution had left former slaves desperately unprepared for their new freedoms.[72]

In the end, Kennedy's strong sense of nationalism and deeply ingrained social conservatism dictated much of what went into "Mr. Ambrose's Letters." So overwhelming was his own nationalism that Kennedy was unable to conceptualize the notion of a rival nationalism in the South. As a result, he was forced to invent an outlandish explanation for secession. But Kennedy's self-deception would not end there. At the end of the war, he would interpret the South's surrender as an act of repentance rather than military exhaustion. "So sudden . . . too general," he would write in the 1865 book version of *Mr. Ambrose's Letters*, "to allow anyone to doubt its sincerity."[73]

Nor could Kennedy envision life in the postwar South except through the lens of a social conservative. Of course, he wanted to see slavery abolished forever at the end of the war. After all, its survival threatened that of his beloved Union. Nonetheless, like most of his countrymen at the time, he distinguished between emancipation and racial equality. As a conservative ex-Whig, Kennedy believed in historical gradualism, and, his optimistic rhetoric about black uplift notwithstanding, he was reluctant to disrupt the organic makeup of southern society any more than it had been. Furthermore, as a resident of the borderland, he understood better than most northerners that sectional reconciliation would depend heavily on whether the South would be allowed to control its own domestic policies. Viewed cynically, Kennedy was ahead of his time in this realization.

"Mr. Ambrose's Letters" would influence how many northerners came to view the causes of the war. Over the years, slavery would fade as the major cause of the conflict. So, too, the fate of freed slaves would become less important than the reunion of North and South. Kennedy's experience in government, reputation as an author, and what one publication would call his "intimate connection with Southerners" gave him special credibility after the war. His essays would be republished several times.[74]

By the time the last installment of "Mr. Ambrose's Letters" appeared in March 1864, the end of the war was still more than a year away. During the spring and summer, ghastly battlefield reports and burgeoning casualty lists emanating from the Wilderness Campaign, Cold Harbor, and the Siege of Petersburg seemed to sap the spirit of the northern public once again. Even though Lincoln's newly appointed general in chief, Ulysses S. Grant, was closing in on the Confederate capital at Richmond, the slow and bloody course of the war seemed to foreshadow defeat for President Lincoln in the November election. Then, as the election drew closer, the fall of Atlanta, the clearing of the Shenandoah Valley, and the capture of Mobile Bay began to turn the tide of northern opinion in the president's favor. Even so, the election appeared to hang in the balance. Visiting his friend Robert Winthrop in Boston, Kennedy declined an invitation to attend that city's prestigious Saturday Club and hurried back to Baltimore, where he cast his vote for Lincoln. Kennedy's efforts were hardly necessary. When the votes were counted, Lincoln had won a 55 percent majority of the popular vote, the largest since Andrew Jackson in 1828.[75]

Within five weeks of Lincoln's second inauguration, Lee's surrender to Grant at Appomattox signaled the end of the war. Amid the flag waving and street celebrations, Kennedy recorded in his journal, "SO ENDS THIS STUPENDOUS, WICKED AND FUTILE REBELLION. Our duty is gratitude to God, amnesty and forgiveness to the weak and foolish who have erred, charity for their faults, and brotherly assistance to all who repent." Lee had capitulated to Grant within a hundred miles of where Cornwallis had surrendered to Washington. Never again, Kennedy predicted, would the South attempt to "sever the territory bequeathed to us from our fathers." Already, he had heard rumors that "a strong Union feeling [was] manifesting itself in Richmond." Such feelings would only intensify over time, Kennedy believed, now that "the pressure of Davis's despotism was taken off the Southern people."[76]

These celebrations came to an abrupt end a week later, when the well-known Maryland actor and Confederate sympathizer John Wilkes Booth took the president's life. Seward was badly wounded in the assassination plot. "Never has a blacker crime been committed with so little object," Kennedy declared in his journal. As the full extent of Booth's conspiracy became known and suspicions of southern sponsorship began to circulate, Kennedy became furious and lashed out at the South. "How ignominiously have the *chivalry* of the rebellion displayed themselves to the world as their fortunes began to wane!" The retreating armies of the Confederacy had stopped civilian trains, abusing passengers and robbing women of their jewelry. Rebel forces had looted Richmond and set half the city ablaze. Perhaps worst of all, Kennedy added, they had "hanged and roasted negroes [and] massacred them when made prisoners." The news of Lincoln's murder seemed to shock Kennedy, at least temporarily, out of his complacency regarding the embittered mentality of the defeated South and its implications for postwar reconciliation and race relations.[77]

After almost a week of mourning ceremonies in the nation's capital, Lincoln's body began its long, winding trip back to Springfield, Illinois. The nine-car funeral train stopped in major cities along the way. The first of these was Baltimore, where the president's remains were carried from the Camden Street Station to the Merchant Exchange Building for public viewing. At the head of the cortege was the hearse, shrouded in black and drawn by four black horses. Several regiments of cavalry, artillery, and infantry followed it. Bands played melancholy tunes along the length of the procession. In spite of an intermittent rain, the sidewalks were crowded with mourners, including many blacks convulsed with grief. Kennedy went down to Baltimore Street to pay his respects to the former president. "I could not restrain my tears," he confided to his journal.[78]

For Kennedy and many Americans, the memory of the deceased president became freighted with a profound sense of veneration and loss. For many, Lincoln became the martyred hero of the nation's mending psyche. In a letter to a British friend, Goldwin Smith, Kennedy wrote, "The life of Lincoln seems like a heavenly mission." In just four years, he explained, this extraordinary man of humble origins but shrewd intelligence had "saved the Republic" and "secured the complete and perfect liberation of four million slaves." Lincoln had lifted the "curse" of slavery not only from America but from the world. "The extinction of slavery here makes it impossible anywhere," he predicted. Kennedy was clearly caught up in the hyperbole of the moment and seemed compelled to exaggerate the war's outcome to his foreign friend. He would soon learn how imperfectly the liberation from slavery was proceeding in his own country and how entrenched the institution remained elsewhere.[79]

With the war finally over and his seventieth birthday behind him, Kennedy had intended to take his wife and sister-in-law to Europe in the fall of 1865. However, a bout of poor health and the press of business matters delayed the trip so long that they decided to visit Cuba instead. The party would travel by rail to St. Louis, by steamboat down the Mississippi to New Orleans, and by ship across the Gulf of Mexico to Havana. As was his habit, Kennedy recorded his impressions along the way, including those of the South nine months after its defeat and of life on the exotic island of Cuba.[80]

The Kennedys began their journey down the Mississippi in the second week of December. The weather was cold and the river muddy brown. Along the shoreline the trees were bare, and there was little sign of human activity. Fortunately, the *Ida Handy* was a large and comfortable side-wheeler, and its fifty or so passengers converged daily on the saloon level for cards, liquor, and conversation. It was a diverse group, made up of tourists like the Kennedys, northern business men, displaced planters, Confederate veterans, and several Europeans traveling in various capacities. As talk aboard intensified, it became clear to Kennedy just how embittered many southerners were about the outcome of the war and how rabid their hatred was for blacks freed by it. As the burned wreck of the *Niagara* came into view one day, an inebriated southerner recalled that all the white passengers on the vessel's upper levels had been rescued, but the black troops below deck had perished almost to a man. Regarding the fate of the "nigger troops," the wag said that had been "a pretty good way to get rid of them."[81]

On another occasion, a former Confederate captain en route to Arkansas described his scheme to "fix the niggers" there. "Hire 'em by the year," the ex-captain explained, "and charge them with everything, and deduct the amount of their wages at the end of the year." Once in debt, black workers would be unable to leave their employers. Neighboring planters would help see to it that the indebted blacks could not get away, and no steamer would take them. Such a scheme would "make them better for us than they were before," the ex-captain predicted.[82]

At this point in the conversation, Kennedy suggested to the former rebel that the state might also help by passing a law "that no negro have the right to bring a suit in court, or give testimony in any case." It is impossible to know what motivated Kennedy to make such a cynical suggestion. Was he simply being facetious, or was he serious? And why would he record such a suggestion in his journal? One can only hope that Kennedy was trying to draw his conversation partner out, in order to learn as much as possible from him. At least, Kennedy concluded his account with what appeared to be an expression of concern: "I have reason to believe that this man was disclosing to me a scheme and a purpose which was conceived by men of more power and influence than himself."[83]

Along its cheerless course, the *Ida Handy* put in at several ruined river towns. At Vicksburg, a number of passengers disembarked to see the crude caves where the town's inhabitants had sought shelter during the Union siege. The caves were becoming a popular tourist attraction. Natchez and Baton Rouge were also impoverished, depopulated vestiges of once-thriving commercial centers. "Private fortunes have been stricken down and strangers from the North are gradually filling the places which the disasters of the war have left behind," Kennedy observed. "Never did such retribution fall upon such a people."[84]

New Orleans, where the Kennedys arrived the week before Christmas, seemed "very badly shaken by the war." The town was suffering from food shortages, and many domestic slaves had left their former masters. Commercial activity was struggling to recover, and real estate prices remained depressed. Union soldiers were everywhere. Christmas was devoid of much pleasantry, Kennedy noted in his journal, as people made the best of "the terrible affliction which has visited the country." He spent hours talking to residents of the town about the war. Not surprisingly, he categorized those with whom he spoke by their former politics. Old Whigs, he concluded naively, were repentant about the rebellion and had never really supported it. Former Democrats, on the other hand, were "not as well advanced in their loyalty as this." However, it was the women of the town who were the most intransigent. "They muttered their hatred for the Yankees on the streets and in the theater," he observed, "with little caution against being overheard."[85]

The condition of the freed slaves was another topic of conversation. One former Marylander told Kennedy that planters along the river were paying freed slaves as high as thirty dollars a month but were withholding wages until the end of the year. In the meantime, these planters were charging the freed slaves exorbitant rates for everything—"pork at 40 cents a pound, and whiskey (which was supplied bountifully) at $2.50 a bottle!" As a consequence, freed blacks across the region were being reenslaved through their accumulation of debt. This time, Kennedy seemed more concerned about the problem and wrote a letter of introduction for the former Marylander to General Absalom Baird. An acquaintance of Kennedy from Baltimore, Baird had recently been appointed head of the local Freedman's Bureau, an organization established by Congress to manage, among its other duties, the transition of blacks from slavery to free labor in the postwar South. According to Kennedy, the former Marylander had a "very satisfactory interview" with Baird.[86]

On January 2, 1866, the Kennedys left New Orleans for Havana aboard the steamer *Morning Star*. The ship was badly overloaded and soon ran aground on a sand bar at the mouth of the Mississippi. In addition to the fifty white passengers on board, an equal number of wounded black troops en route to New York were quartered below deck. Many were quite sick and living on meager rations provided by the army. Kennedy arranged with the boat's steward to get the sickest of these black troops additional provisions, presumably at his own expense. After a week stuck on the sand bar, the ship finally floated free and continued on to Cuba.[87]

Kennedy's first impressions of Cuba, as the *Morning Star* entered the harbor of Havana on January 11, never really changed during his two-month stay on the island. Even from a distance, Morro Castle looked cold and forbidding. Although brightly painted, the buildings along the harbor were squat, blocky structures, their crude stucco walls perforated by small barred windows. The dockside was a chaotic tangle of mule carts and swarthy stevedores. Kennedy thought that he might as well have landed in Morocco or Algiers. It all looked "entirely *un-American*" to him.[88]

It also f*elt* un-American to him. He found Havana's commercial life stunted and its infrastructure backward. There was little manufacturing other than cigar making, and the lack of a local currency hampered the exchange of goods. Public transportation was almost nonexistent, and most streets were so narrow as to be nearly impassable. "Cubans were a people who had grown old under the influence of centuries of mutual suspicion and distrust," Kennedy theorized, "and too inveterate in custom to attempt any step in the pathway to modern progress."[89]

In spite of its deficiencies, Cuba attracted a variety of American visitors after the Civil War who had different reasons for being there. Robert Toombs, an old Georgia Whig from Kennedy's past and one of the first U.S. senators to declare himself a secessionist, headed a group of Confederate exiles who refused to make peace with the Union. They talked wildly of stealing ex-slaves from the South and establishing plantations in Mexico. Secretary of State Seward was also on the island, on a Caribbean tour in search of fueling stations for the navy. He was still suffering from stab wounds received the night of Lincoln's assassination. Seward and Kennedy made speeches during a large dinner at the governor general's palace where, because hardly anybody understood English, the group was "deaf and dumb to every word." The two enjoyed a good laugh afterward.[90]

Kennedy thought Cuban culture was vapid. The local brand of Spanish was grating to his ear, and the elite class, he discovered, spoke little else. Kennedy had trouble locating a bookstore and, when he did, found nothing worth reading. The amusements of the town's best families were few and simple, consisting of riding up and down the main avenue, the so-called Paseo, in their carriages and attending the theater. Both activities allowed the town's wealthiest women to show off their jewelry and elegant dresses. Their husbands favored plain black suits and spent most of their leisure gambling.[91]

Most disturbing of all for Kennedy was the pall of cruelty that hung over the island. Kennedy attended a bullfight and a cockfight, both of which he thought barbaric. He also commented on the brutality with which Cubans treated their domestic animals. Mules and horses were cruelly overburdened and beaten mercilessly by their drivers. All of this, Kennedy wrote, "gives the stranger an unpleasant conviction of the habitual and unconscious cruelty of the people."[92]

Tiring of life in the center of Havana, Kennedy and his party occasionally rode out to the environs. No matter which direction they traveled, they encountered gangs of blacks and "coolies" in chains and under heavy guard along the road. These unfortunates, a guide explained, were "robbers and brigands" who had been arrested for some alleged infraction and sold by the authorities to local employers for varying lengths of service. These employers had complete discretion over the treatment of their captive laborers, some of whom, it was rumored, were being punished for their political beliefs. "This odious spectacle is strange," Kennedy observed, "by contrast to the gay and thronging crowds that we meet every day in their eager pursuit of pleasure of that drive upon the Paseo."[93]

Kennedy may have wondered whether he had wandered into a real-world version of Vandalia, the fictional kingdom that he and Peter Hoffman Cruse had concocted years before in the *Red Book*. After all, here was the intellectually vacuous elite, not so different from the "Tawney-Traders" of that satirical piece, indulging in their luxurious pursuits on the backs of a ruthlessly degraded and mercilessly exploited lower order of society. There seemed to be few limits to the inhumanity that such extreme social stratification and endemic cruelty could produce. Still, Kennedy had not yet witnessed the full effect of this dynamic.

In mid-February, Kennedy had the opportunity to visit a sugar plantation. Located east of Havana in the area of Matanzas, it was one of the most beautiful settings he had ever seen. The plantation dominated a lush river valley with distant views of the sea. The main house was palatial in its massive proportions and architectural refinement. It belonged to one of the island's most powerful planters, Don Cosme de Torriente.[94]

After lunch with their host, Kennedy and his party were given a tour of the plantation. Their first stop was the grinding mill. There, slaves and mules were harnessed together to an enormous beam that turned the millstone. A sullen overseer walked behind this line of men and beasts as they marched in circles. He wore a sword at his side and brandished a whip to keep the group in motion. Feeding the hopper above the millstones was an old black woman on a ladder. Kennedy estimated that she was about fifty years old. She dragged a set of heavy chains attached to an iron ring around her waist and a smaller one around her ankle. The old woman gathered the sugar cane from the ground and carried it on her shoulder up the ladder to the hopper. "It was a heavy weight which exacted a painful stooping to the ground and toilsome ascent of the steps," Kennedy observed. He guessed the old woman was being punished for some offense. It could have been for almost anything, he speculated, from working too slowly to attempting an escape from the plantation. "The poor woman's countenance expressed her anguish," he wrote, "but expressed it in vain and to a task master whose heart was stone."[95]

When they could endure this pitiful scene no longer, Kennedy and his party moved on to the slave quarter. It consisted of a square acre of pounded earth, without a shrub or blade of grass on it, surrounded by a ten-foot-high stone wall. This enclosure was empty by day, and the visitors entered it through an iron gate. In the middle of the open space stood a broken-down stone furnace, with a large caldron for boiling corn or whatever provisions the slaves were allowed. At the end of every day, Kennedy learned, the plantation's slaves were herded into the enclosure like cattle and ate out of the caldron with their hands. Along the inside of the wall, crude sheds had been erected for sleeping. Kennedy inspected several of them. They were dark and filthy, their floors covered with tattered blankets and soiled coverlets. "Such wretchedness, I have never seen, such parsimony and such cruel neglect," he recorded in disgust.[96]

The depth of human degradation to which slavery had descended on the Matanzas sugar plantation shocked Kennedy. In his research for *Swallow Barn,* he and Peter Hoffman Cruse had toured the Tidewater area of Virginia, where the demands of tobacco growing on field slaves had little in common with the deadly rigors of sugar cultivation. Similarly, the smaller farms and mixed agriculture around Martinsburg, where Kennedy had experienced his most intimate connection to slavery, had encouraged a less brutal rendition of the institution. It is not known whether Kennedy ever visited a sugar plantation in the Deep South, though he knew that being consigned to such a place was the Virginia slave's worst nightmare. Regardless of his previous exposure to variations of the system in his own country, nothing had prepared him for the dehumanizing spectacle of slavery in Cuba. "I thank my God," he wrote as he prepared to leave the island, "that, at last, the day has dawned, which having driven the abomination of slavery from our land, is soon to witness its extirpation in this, its most painful and wretched abode."[97]

The Kennedys arrived back in New Orleans in mid-March 1866 and, two weeks later, began their trip back to Baltimore by way of Montgomery, Atlanta, and Charleston. Much of this route retraced the destructive path of General William Tecumseh Sherman across the former heartland of the Confederacy. The terrible condition of the railroads and the ruined condition of towns along the way made travel difficult. There were few hotels in operation and little food for guests. As a signature on his grim work, Sherman had left iron rails from torn up railroad tracks twisted around tree trunks along the way. In abandoned fields across the region, charred chimneys marked where plantation houses had stood. The acrid scent of destruction lingered in the air.

Charleston seemed to Kennedy "a shattered and suffering city." As the cradle of the rebellion, it had been subjected to hard treatment by Union forces. A large portion of the city was blackened rubble from bombardment and fire. Still sadder were the people, among them Kennedy's friends William Gilmore Simms and George Bryan. Simms, author of over sixty novels and a defiant secessionist before the war, was a broken man. Kennedy spent considerable time with his old friend, in an effort at reconciliation.[98]

Even though he had read numerous descriptions of the postwar South, Kennedy was taken aback by "the overwhelming loss and privation [that] had been brought upon this community." The wasted landscape his party saw everywhere they went was the consequence of "a war of unexampled passion and ferocity . . . waged with such cruelty and persistence as never equaled for years." Once again, Kennedy asked himself, "—to do what?" What had this terrible war been about? What could account for such destruction of property and loss of life? Perhaps because of what he had witnessed in the sugar fields of Matanzas and was now seeing in the ruined countryside left by Sherman's army, Kennedy finally acknowledged the real cause of the war: "Yes, this wretched rebellion which we have just vanquished originated in no better aspiration than the permanent defense of the great crime of slavery."[99]

The Kennedys arrived back in Baltimore in April 1866. However, within ninety days they were off again, this time on a European tour that would last nearly two and a half years. Although his journal of the trip contained its share of interesting highlights, Kennedy allowed his boredom and weariness to depress its overall tone. He believed that he and his party were traveling too fast through too many countries to appreciate what they were seeing. "Rome is as wearisome as an Old Curiosity Shop," he complained, "where I am constantly oppressed with the feeling that I have no time to see anything with that tranquil delay which is essential to a fair appreciation or satisfactory enjoyment." Like his fictional observer-narrator in *Swallow Barn,* Mark Littleton, Kennedy would have preferred a more lingering, ruminative approach to sightseeing. Furthermore, Kennedy was too much of an American to write enthusiastically about Europe. Unlike Irving and Cooper, he had never spent much time in Europe and did not seem comfortable describing places with which he had little in common. He was homesick most of the time.[100]

Shortly after returning from Europe in October 1868, Kennedy made his last public appearance. The event was a large gathering of the Maryland Republican Committee at Baltimore's Front Street Theater. It was the last canvas before the presidential election that would send General Ulysses S. Grant to the White House. Kennedy was the keynote speaker and relished the occasion. He began by dismissing the Democrats as far too "varied and changeful" to have ever attracted his political allegiance. Those attendees who remembered *Quodlibet* may have hoped that Kennedy would develop the point at the expense of their opponents. Instead, he chose to talk about the "constancy" of the Republican Party, which, he declared, espoused "the principles in which I was educated." These included devotion to the Union, support for the national prosperity, and a commitment to popular freedom. In closing, he referred to his recent travels abroad. Following its great internal struggle, America was now regarded by the European powers as something it had not been before—"a *real* government, permanent, indissoluble, invincible, and fully adapted to all the exigencies of national life." Looking to the future, Kennedy predicted that America's mission in the world would be "to make popular freedom the final heritage of all nations."[101]

When not traveling abroad, Kennedy occupied himself by writing newspaper articles and corresponding with his political and literary acquaintances. He also devoted himself to supervising the final phase of construction at the Peabody Institute. However, his health was failing, forcing him to curtail his exertions to a few hours a day. In 1869, he was diagnosed with an abdominal tumor that frequently disabled him with severe pain. Socially, he limited himself to visits from Josias Pennington and a few other old friends.[102]

In the summer of 1870, Kennedy appeared to rally and traveled to Newport, Rhode Island, where he stayed in a cottage belonging to his sister-in-law Martha. There too, old friends came by to see him. Oliver Wendell Holmes called on him twice during early August and found him cheerful and full of talk on a range of subjects. On Sunday, August 14, Kennedy felt good enough to take a walk along the town's spectacular seaside cliffs. The next day, however, pain and exhaustion kept him bedridden. He died on Thursday, August 18, 1870, and was buried at Baltimore's Green Mount Cemetery the following Sunday.[103]

Conclusion

Kennedy died just two months after his friend and fellow novelist William Gilmore Simms. He had first met the South Carolinian in 1840, and though their friendship was interrupted by the Civil War, they renewed it afterward. Since they had carried on an active correspondence and were both considered "romantic regionalists" of the antebellum period, some literary historians have lumped Kennedy and Simms together.

Yet, the two were very different. A provincial southerner alienated from his own society, Simms was convinced by the early 1850s that the Union would be broken up. As a resident of the borderland with literary and political connections across the nation, Kennedy loathed the idea of disunion and never wavered in his loyalty to country. Furthermore, while Simms eschewed political involvement of any kind, Kennedy was addicted to politics and devoted his life to it. As a consequence, his novels were saturated with his political views and resonated with the issues of his day. Simms recognized this tendency in his friend and criticized him for it: "I have foreborne as much as possible the points of collision between us—your Whiggism . . . and your estimate of parties."[1]

Kennedy and Simms also differed on the subject of slavery. Simms was a slave owner and defiantly proslavery. Kennedy, on the other hand, struggled with race and slavery all his life. His ambivalence toward these issues destabilized his best-known novel *Swallow Barn,* and he oscillated between calling slavery a "crime" and a "blessing" in his essays before and after the Civil War. Although he resided in a slave state, Kennedy refused to own slaves and either sold or manumitted those that came into his possession.

While Kennedy's infatuation with politics irked Simms, it is a boon to historians attempting to identify the divergent cultural formations that led to the great Whig-Democratic rivalry of the antebellum period. As a novelist and politician, Kennedy mixed his passions freely, and his writing reveals the lineaments of Whig culture before the party called itself into existence and chose a name. In other words, the oppositional mentality and political-economic imperatives that became Whig culture were well established in Kennedy's mind before the party challenged the Democrats at the polls. It took the leadership of Henry Clay, a developing grasp of party organization, and the unfolding events of the period to transform this cultural formation into political partisanship.[2]

Kennedy's value to historians is that his development as a nationalistic, economically progressive, and morally didactic Whig can be traced over the course of his political and writing life. Unlike Simms, he saw party politics and didactic literature as complementary vehicles for advancing his vision of America's future. Kennedy's nationalism had its origins in the War of 1812 and found its earliest expression in his "Swiss Traveller" essays. That same nationalism later fueled his opposition to the nullification movement, President John Tyler's states' rights aberrations, and, after the Whigs' demise, southern secession. Similarly, Kennedy's early economic agenda in the Maryland legislature anticipated his later embrace of Clay's American System, with its emphasis on a protective tariff, internal improvements, and a central bank. Finally, Kennedy's moral didacticism, a product of his early campaign of self-improvement, became conjoined with his nationalism and economic progressivism. Notions of homespun republicanism, self-cultivation, and social uplift imbued his writing with a sense of moral certitude. This moral certitude pervades Kennedy's novels *Horse-Shoe Robinson* and *Rob of The Bowl,* his speeches on the protection of industry, and his political pamphlets "The Whig Manifesto" and "Defense of the Whigs." Countering Democratic pleas for individual freedom and a laissez-faire state, Kennedy's moral didacticism lent both passion and justification to his arguments for activist governance and social intervention.

However, Whig activism and intervention had its limits. The Whig's reforming zeal was tempered by conservative restraint. Economic progress and social change needed to be gradual and never disruptive. Kennedy's own conservatism increased with age. By the time of the Mexican War, he had lost his youthful jingoism and opposed the annexation of Texas. So, too, he supported Clay's Compromise of 1850 and defended President Millard Fillmore's enforcement of its controversial Fugitive Slave Law. Like many Whigs, Kennedy espoused the principle of compromise as a means of avoiding confrontation and conflict. He celebrated the power of compromise in the Apple-pie Branch episode of *Swallow Barn* and, on the eve of the Civil War, sought an eleventh-hour compromise that would hold the Union together.

In the end, compromises in the face of an intractable South delayed resolution of the slavery problem and tore apart the Whig Party. Kennedy's ambivalence toward race and slavery in *Swallow Barn* reflected the debilitating indecisiveness that made the party irrelevant by the 1850s. The novel's race-based rationale for the continuation of slavery, its flirtation with African colonization, and its vague notions for reforming the slave system typified the conflicted attitudes and moral confusion of many antebellum Americans. It took the emergence of the Republican Party to deal boldly with slavery and the Civil War to end it permanently.

Near the end of his life, Kennedy acknowledged that slavery was a "crime" and had caused the war. This view separated him from Simms and other southerners who admitted neither. What is more, Kennedy saw the Republicans take up the legacy of Whig programs. With the South neutralized and Democrats weakened, the Republicans forged ahead with railroad building, a protective tariff, homestead legislation, and the founding of land-grant colleges. At his last public appearance, Kennedy could say that the Republican Party represented the principles for which he stood.[3]

But had Kennedy's views on race changed? Would he have described blacks in 1870 in the demeaning way he had in the pages of *Swallow Barn?* It is possible that some shift in his views had occurred. What he had seen in Cuba had exposed him to real horrors of slavery and elicited his sympathy for those who still suffered under its burdens. He also appears to have been concerned about the poor treatment of former slaves in the postwar South. And, yet, in "Mr. Ambrose's Letters," Kennedy suggested leaving the fate of freed slaves to state governments. Furthermore, in his last public appearance, he praised the "magnanimity and clemency" Republicans had shown the defeated South. It is possible that, had he lived, Kennedy might have supported the Republican "compromise of 1877" with the Democrats, which removed the last federal troops from the South and ended the protection of southern blacks under Reconstruction. After all, the principle of compromise was also part of the Republicans' Whig legacy.[4]

Although he has faded from popular memory, John Pendleton Kennedy is still there for those who know where to look. At Green Mount Cemetery in Baltimore, Kennedy is surrounded by family and friends, among them his wife

Elizabeth (who joined him there in 1889), father-in-law Edward Gray, sister-in-law Martha, and best friend Josias Pennington. At the city's prestigious Peabody Institute, Kennedy's portrait greets visitors entering the main library. His best-known novel, *Swallow Barn,* remains in print and is occasionally taught in university classrooms. The Bower, the model for the novel's fictional plantation, survived the Civil War intact and still belongs to the Dandridge family. High above the Arctic Circle, on the western side of Greenland, the Kennedy Channel, honoring the former secretary of the navy, flows peacefully past Cape Andrew Jackson. However, few visit the region to appreciate the irony. So, too, the old rivalry has grown cold.[5]

NOTES

Abbreviations Used in Notes

KP	John Pendleton Kennedy Papers. The original Kennedy papers consist of 130 volumes and are in the possession of the Peabody Institute in Baltimore, Maryland. A microfilm edition of the papers also exists at various universities and research institutions.
HSR	John Pendleton Kennedy. *Horse-Shoe Robinson.* 1835. Reprint, with an intro. by Ernest E. Leisy. New York: Hafner, 1962.
ROTB	John Pendleton Kennedy. *Rob of the Bowl: A Legend of St. Inigoe's.* 1838. Reprint, Whitefish, MT: Kessinger, 2007.
SB (1832)	John Pendleton Kennedy. *Swallow Barn; or, A Sojourn in the Old Dominion.* Philadelphia: Carey and Lea, 1832.
SB (1851)	John Pendleton Kennedy. *Swallow Barn; or, A Sojourn in the Old Dominion.* 1851. Reprint, with an intro. by Lucinda H. MacKethan, Baton Rouge: Louisiana State, 1986.

Introduction

1. This is a rough quotation from William Shakespeare's *Richard III,* Act 4, scene iv. See "Speech on Bill making appropriations for Civil and Diplomatic Services for the year 1939," in John Pendleton Kennedy, *Political and Official Papers* (New York, 1872), 228–266.

2. The Panic of 1837 ushered in an economic depression that lasted until 1843. See Samuel Rezneck, *Business Depressions and Financial Panics* (Westport, CT, 1971), 75–89; Douglass C. North, *Economic Growth of the United States, 1790–1860* (New York, 1966), 200–203; and Michael Holt, *The Rise and Fall of the American Whig Party: Jacksonian Politics and the Onset of the Civil War* (New York, 1999), 64–76.

3. Robert V. Remini, *Andrew Jackson and the Bank War: A Study in the Growth of Presidential Power* (New York, 1967), 111–115; Donald B. Cole, *A Jackson Man: Amos Kendall and the Rise of American Democracy* (Baton Rouge, 2004), 177–192; John F. Marszalek, *The Petticoat Affair: Manners, Mutiny, and Sex in Andrew Jackson's White House* (New York, 1997), 162–182; and Andrew Burstein, *The Passions of Andrew Jackson* (New York, 2004), 167–169.

4. John E. Semmes, *John H. B. Latrobe and His Times, 1803–1891* (Baltimore, 1917), 225; and KP, "Ego" scrapbook of clippings, *New York Times* (undated).

5. John Pendleton Kennedy [Mark Littleton, pseud.], *Swallow Barn; or, A Sojourn in the Old Dominion* (Philadelphia, 1832); Kennedy [Littleton, pseud.], *Horse-Shoe Robinson: A Tale of the Tory Ascendency* (Philadelphia, 1835); and Kennedy, *Rob of The Bowl: A Legend of St. Inigoe's* (Philadelphia, 1838). Henceforth, all citations for Kennedy's second and third novels are taken from available reprints. Unlike with *Swallow Barn,* Kennedy made very few changes from the original editions.

6. *Swallow Barn* has been subjected to a wide range of interpretations speculating on Kennedy's motives in writing it as well as its overall meaning. See John Pendleton Kennedy, *Swallow Barn, or A Sojourn in the Old Dominion,* with Introduction by Lucinda H. MacKethan (1851; reprint, Baton Rouge, 1986), xi, xiii, xxii–xxvi; Lewis P. Simpson, *The Dispossessed Garden: Pastoral and History in Southern Literature* (Athens, GA, 1975), 45, 48–52; Susan J. Tracy, *In the Master's Eye: Representations of Women, Blacks, and Poor Whites in Antebellum Southern Literature* (Amherst, 1995), 156, 213; Scott Romine, *Narrative Forms of Southern Community* (Baton Rouge, 1999), 78–79; J. V. Ridgely, *John Pendleton Kennedy* (New York, 1966), 29, 53; Charles H. Bohner, *John Pendleton Kennedy: Gentleman from Baltimore* (Baltimore, 1961), 63–64, 88; Louis D. Rubin Jr., *The Edge of the Swamp: A Study in the Literature and Society of the Old South* (Baton Rouge, 1989), 50; John L. Hare, *Will the Circle Be Unbroken? Family and Sectionalism in the Virginia Novels of Kennedy, Caruthers, and Tucker, 1830–1845* (New York, 2002), x, 16–17, 23; and Paul C. Jones, *Unwelcome Voices: Subversive Fiction in the Antebellum South* (Knoxville, 2005), 123–124, 130–132, 153.

7. KP, "A Fragment of Autobiography written around 1825." The Kennedy Papers contain three such autobiographical fragments written between 1825 and 1847, which Kennedy never succeeded in consolidating. Since they contain much of the same material, they are referred to collectively as "KP, autobiographical fragments." Daniel Walker Howe, *The Political Culture of the American Whigs* (Chicago, 1979); Lawrence Frederick Kohl, *The Politics of Individualism: Parties and the American Character in the Jacksonian Era* (New York, 1989); and Susan Dunn, *Dominion of Memories: Jefferson, Madison and the Decline of Virginia* (New York, 2007).

8. KP, journal entries, Sept. 21, 1830, July 28, Sept. 1, 1831; Daniel Walker Howe, *What Hath God Wrought: The Transformation of America, 1815–1848* (New York, 2007), 357–360; Richard Walsh and William Lloyd Fox, eds., *Maryland: A History, 1632–1974* (Baltimore, 1974), 269–270; William W. Freehling, *Prelude to Civil War: The Nullification Controversy in South Carolina, 1816–1836* (New York, 1965), 144–147; Richard E. Ellis, *The Union at Risk: Jacksonian Democracy and the Nullification Crisis* (New York, 1987), 64–68; and Stephen B. Oates, *The Fires of Jubilee: Nat Turner's Fierce Rebellion* (New York, 2004), 69–88.

9. Holt, *Whig Party;* Albert D. Kirwan, *John J. Crittenden: The Struggle for the Union* (Lexington, KY, 1962); Robert V. Remini, *Henry Clay: Statesman for the Union* (New York, 1991); John H. B. Latrobe, *The History of the Mason-Dixon Line* (Philadelphia, 1855), 5–6; and Russ Castronovo, "Compromised Narratives along the Border: Mason-Dixon Line, Resistance, and Hegemony," in David E. Johnson and Scott Michaelson, eds., *Border Theory: The Limits of Cultural Politics* (Minneapolis, 1997), 30–32.

10. Kennedy represented Maryland's 4th congressional district from April 1838 until March 1839 and then again from March 1841 until March 1845. See http://bioguide.congree.gov; *Niles' National Register,* Sept. 18, 1841; Kennedy, *Political and Official Papers,* 319–351; and Kennedy, *Quodlibet* (1840; reprint, Upper Saddle River, NJ, 1970).

11. KP, journal entries, July 5, 1847, July 28, 30, Sept. 14, 1852; Bohner, *Kennedy,* 158–161; Henry T.

Tuckerman, *The Life of John Pendleton Kennedy* (New York, 1871), 178–180, 217–233; Michael Holt, *The Political Crisis of the 1850s* (New York, 1978), 87–89; and William E. Gienapp, "The Whig Party, Compromise of 1850, and Nomination of Winfield Scott," *Presidential Studies Quarterly* 14, no. 3 (Summer 1984): 399–415.

12. Andrew Burstein, *America's Jubilee: A Generation Remembers the Revolution after Fifty Years of Independence* (New York, 2001), 34–58; and John Pendleton Kennedy, *Memoirs of the Life of William Wirt,* 2 vols. (Philadelphia, 1849).

13. Kennedy's southern friend was William Gilmore Simms, a prolific novelist and editor of the *Southern Quarterly Review.* Harriet Beecher Stowe's *Uncle Tom's Cabin* first appeared as a newspaper serial in June 1861. See Holt, *Political Crisis,* 87–89; William Gilmore Simms, *The Letters of William Gilmore Simms* (Columbia, SC, 1953), 122–123; Kennedy, *Swallow Barn* (1851 ed.) with MacKethan intro., 455–458; KP, journal entries, Sept. 18, Oct. 11, 1851, and "Ego" scrapbook; and Claire Parfait, *The Publishing History of* Uncle Tom's Cabin (Abingdon, UK, 2008), 14–17, 69.

14. Howe, *Political Culture,* 81–82, 124–125, 150, 299.

15. For the connection between cultural formation and party politics, see Joanne B. Freeman, *Affairs of Honor: National Politics in the New Republic* (New Haven, 2002), 289–293; Joel H. Silbey, "To One Another or Another of These Parties Every Man Belongs," in Byron E. Shafer and Anthony J. Badger, eds., *Contesting Democracy: Substance and Structure in American Political History, 1775–2000* (Lawrence, KS, 2001), 69–72; and Meg Jacobs and Julian E. Zelizer, "The Democratic Experiment: New Directions in American Political History," in Meg Jacobs, William J. Novak, and Julian E. Zelizer, eds., *The Democratic Experiment: New Directions in American Political History* (Princeton, 2003), 6–8.

16. John Pendleton Kennedy, "The Swiss Traveller," in *The Portico: A Repository for Science and Literature* (Baltimore, 1816); John Pendleton Kennedy and Peter Hoffman Cruse, *Red Book,* 2nd ed., 2 vols. (Baltimore, 1820–1821); "The Border States: Their Power and Duty in the Present Disordered Condition" in Kennedy, *Political and Official Papers,* 543–586; and John P. Kennedy, *Mr. Ambrose's Letters on the Rebellion* (New York, 1865).

17. Existing biographies of Kennedy vary in both quality and emphasis. J. V. Ridgely is brief and at times oddly negative regarding Kennedy's literary production. Charles Bohner's work, while well researched, is unfocused and devotes too much time to the "social" Kennedy. Edward Gwathmey is guilty of numerous factual errors. Henry Tuckerman, Kennedy's friend and executer of his estate, compiled a loose collection of letters and documents connected by a thin narrative, typical of biographies at the time. See Ridgely, *Kennedy;* Bohner, *Kennedy;* Tuckerman, *Kennedy;* and Edward M. Gwathmey, *John Pendleton Kennedy* (New York, 1931). Michael Holt has called the demise of the Whig Party "the most critical event" in the breakdown of the political party system before the Civil War. See Holt, *Political Crisis,* 10–11.

1. The Early Years

1. KP, "A Fragment of Biography written about 1825." See also Steven Mintz, *Huck's Raft: A History of American Childhood* (Cambridge, MA, 2004), 81–82; and Bertram Wyatt-Brown, *Southern Honor: Ethics and Behavior in the Old South* (New York, 1982), 140.

2. KP, autobiographical fragments.

3. Ibid.

4. Jan Lewis, *The Pursuit of Happiness: Family and Values in Jefferson's Virginia* (New York 1983), 21–23; T. H. Breen, "Looking Out for Number One: Conflicting Cultural Values in Early Seventeenth-Century Virginia," in *South Atlantic Quarterly* 37 (1979): 341–360; KP, autobiographical fragments; and the *Potomac Guardian and Berkeley Advertiser,* Oct. 2, 1794.

5. KP, autobiographical fragments.

6. John Pendleton Kennedy, "Baltimore Long Ago," in *At Home and Abroad* (New York, 1872), 86–92; Semmes, *Latrobe,* 181; and Gary Lawson Browne, *Baltimore in the Nation, 1789–1861* (Chapel Hill, 1980), 49–50.

7. Donald R. Hickey, *The War of 1812: A Forgotten Conflict* (Urbana, 1989), 56, 68–70; Browne, *Baltimore in the Nation,* 43–44; Joyce Appleby, *Inheriting the Revolution: The First Generation of Americans* (Cambridge, MA, 2000), 28, 34–35; and Alexander Keyssar, *The Right to Vote: The Contested History of Democracy in the United States* (New York, 2009), 29, 342–343.

8. Some scholars have overemphasized Kennedy's connection to his mother's home place. William R. Taylor, on the other hand, has argued that Kennedy's visits there were no more than "summer excursions." See KP, autobiographical fragments; and William R. Taylor, *Cavalier and Yankee: The Old South and the American National Character* (New York, 1979), 188.

9. Berkeley County, where Martinsburg is located, contained 22,006 inhabitants in 1800. Of these, only 3,971 were slaves and 203 free blacks. See KP, autobiographical fragments; and mapserver.lib.virginia.edu.

10. Kennedy, "Baltimore Long Ago," 87–89; Walsh and Fox, *Maryland,* 171–175; and mapserver.lib.virginia.edu.

11. Van Wyck Brooks described Baltimore as an urban expression of the South. However, Barbara Fields has argued that Baltimore was connected to the South but never economically or culturally subservient to it. See Van Wyck Brooks, *The World of Washington Irving* (New York, 1944), 271; and Barbara Jeanne Fields, *Slavery and Freedom on the Middle Ground: Maryland During the Nineteenth Century* (New Haven, 1985), 7, 51–52.

12. KP, autobiographical fragments.

13. Joyce Appleby has described how this urban, commercial culture became different from that of rural areas at this time. Sociologist David Riesman has defined "chimney-corner" society as one dependent on family and communal socialization. Riesman has argued that exposure to new institutions and new flows of printed content "increased each child's power to select." See Appleby, *Inheriting the Revolution,* 3, 63, 75, 89, 99–102; and David Riesman, Nathan Glazer, and Reuel Denney, *The Lonely Crowd: A Study of the Changing American Character* (New York, 1953), 107–112.

14. Lawrence Frederick Kohl has argued that certain members of the generation emerging between the American Revolution and 1830 became more independent as they extricated themselves from the "thick web" of traditional society. Both Daniel Walker Howe and Steven Mintz have stressed the importance of education and volunteer associations in the development of this group's increased sense of autonomy. See Kohl, *Politics of Individualism,* 5–7; Mintz, *Huck's Raft,* 83, 87–93; and Daniel Walker Howe, *Making the American Self: Jonathan Edwards to Abraham Lincoln* (Cambridge, MA, 1997), 107–111.

15. David Riesman coined the terms "inner-directed" and "tradition-directed" for these two social typologies. The applicability of Riesman's typologies to the Early Republic has been suggested by several historians of the period. See Riesman, *Lonely Crowd,* 40–41, 44, 56–58, 60–63; Kohl, *Politics of Individualism,* 7, 15–17; and Daniel Walker Howe, *Reviews in American History* 66 (1981): 461.

16. KP, autobiographical fragments.

17. Walsh and Fox, *Maryland,* 175–178; Hickey, *War of 1812,* 56–59; North, *Economic Growth,* 53–54; and J. C. A. Stagg, *The War of 1812: Conflict for a Continent* (New York, 2012), 33–35.

18. Kennedy estimated that his father's brothers covered between $20,000 and $40,000 of his father's debt, extraordinary sums for the time. See KP, autobiographical fragments; and Walsh and Fox, *Maryland,* 176–178.

19. KP, autobiographical fragments.

20. Ibid.

21. Ibid.

22. Ibid.; Howe, *Making the American Self,* 107; Richard L. Bushman, *The Refinement of America: Persons, Houses, Cities* (New York, 1993), 35–36, 96–98; and Jean V. Matthews, *Toward a New Society: American Thought and Culture, 1800–1830* (Boston, 1991), 52–54, 72–75.

23. Howe, *Making the American Self,* 16, 50–57, 107; Bushman, *Refinement of America,* 35–36, 96–98; Margaret Drabble, ed., *The Oxford Companion to English Literature* (New York, 1985), 5–7, 487–488, 579, 690–692; and Harry Hayden Clark, *Transitions in American Literary History* (New York, 1975), 94, 116–117.

24. Lawrence Klein and Anthony Pollock have debated the nature and extent of Joseph Addison's influence. See Lawrence E. Klein, "Addison Afterlives: Joseph Addison in Eighteenth-Century Culture" in *Journal of Eighteenth-Century Studies* 35, no. 1 (Mar. 2012): 102–118; and Anthony Pollock, "Neutering Addison and Steele: Aesthetic Failure and the Spectatorial Public Sphere," in *Early American Literature* 74, no. 3 (Fall 2007): 707–734.

25. Jonathan Swift's work fell into the hard-edged Juvenalian genre of British satire as opposed to the milder Horatian style favored by Addison, Steele, and Pope. Swift's satirical essay "A Modest Proposal," for example, suggested cannibalism to reduce the number of poor children in Ireland. See Howe, *Making the American Self,* 50–57, 107; Jonathan Swift, *Gulliver's Travels,* with intro. by Michael Seidel (1726; reprint, New York, 2003), xix–xxii; and Leo Damrosch, *Jonathan Swift: His Life and His World* (New Haven, 2013), 416–420.

26. Given their high cost, the ability to borrow books was critical for poorer youths like Kennedy. See William Charvat, *The Profession of Authorship in America, 1800–1870* (Columbus, OH, 1968), 30–33.

27. KP, autobiographical fragments; and Howe, *Making the American Self,* 22, 55, 63, 118–129, 129–132.

28. KP, autobiographical fragments.

29. David Riesman has argued that inner-directed individuals "find both the definition and the evaluation of [themselves] depending on the company [they] keep . . . schoolmates, teachers, peers, and superiors." This typology, per Riesman, projects its own standards onto others. See Riesman, *Lonely Crowd,* 66, 86–87, 103, 200–201; Howe, *Making the American Self,* 54–56; and KP, autobiographical fragments.

30. Although it is contained in an autobiographical fragment from 1825, Kennedy indicated that the story of Cud was set down fifteen years earlier. Kennedy burned many of his early papers in what he described as a "great auto-de-fe," much to his later regret. See KP, autobiographical fragments.

31. Ibid.

32. Riesman, *Lonely Crowd,* 107–108; and Appleby, *Inheriting the Revolution,* 3–5.

33. KP, autobiographical fragments.

34. Five installments of "The Swiss Traveller" appeared in the *Portico* between February and August 1816. The older friend who encouraged Kennedy to write them was probably Hugh Young, someone Kennedy admired and a member of Baltimore's Delphian Society, the sponsor of the *Portico.* Kennedy was not identified as the author of "The Swiss Traveller" until the 1950s. See KP, autobiographical fragments; Kennedy, "The Swiss Traveller" in the *Portico;* Bohner, *Kennedy,* 28–29; and William S. Osborne, "'The Swiss Traveller' Essays: Earliest Literary Writing of John Pendleton Kennedy," in *American Literature* 30 (May 1958): 228–233.

35. Jasper M. Trautsch, "'Mr. Madison's War' or the Dynamic of Early American Nationalism?," in *Early American Studies* 10, no. 3 (Fall 2012): 644–645; John C. McCloskey, "The Campaign of Periodicals after the War of 1812 for National American Literature," in *Proceedings of the Modern Language Association* 50, no. 1 (Mar. 1935): 264–266; and Andrew Burstein, *The Original Knickerbocker: The Life of Washington Irving* (New York, 2007), 97–99.

36. Ridgely, *Kennedy,* 22.

37. Kennedy's "Mr. Sidney" may have been modeled on Algernon Sidney (1623–1683), who fought against the Crown in the English Civil War, wrote the popular *Discourses Concerning Government,* and, like Kennedy's Mr. Sidney, spent many years in exile. Algernon Sidney was one of the most popular writers on civil liberty and freedom for America's revolutionary generation. The myth of Switzerland as a mountainous utopia of virtue and liberty probably began with Albrecht von Haller's 1732 poem, *Die Alpen.* Kennedy may have gotten his inspiration from Joseph Addison's essay on Switzerland as a political Shangri-la, published in an early issue of *The Tatler.* See "The Swiss Traveller," *Portico* 1, no. 2 (Feb. 1816): 145; Bernard Bailyn, *The Ideological Origins of the American Revolution* (Cambridge, MA, 1967), 34–35; and Simon Schama, *Landscape and Memory* (New York, 1996), 478–479.

38. It is not clear who the model for Manly was. Possibly, it was Colonel Manly of Royall Tyler's 1787 comedy of errors, *The Contrast.* Tyler's Manly was a simply dressed, thoroughly masculine embodiment of pure republican sentiments. Or, possibly, he was Basil Manly, a Marylander who served in the Revolution as a captain and moved to Chatham County, North Carolina. A devout Catholic who married a Baptist, he died in 1824. See Andrew Burstein, *Sentimental Democracy: The Evolution of America's Romantic Self-Image* (New York, 1999), 289–290; Scott E. Casper, *Constructing American Lives: Biography and Culture in Nineteenth-Century America* (Chapel Hill, 1999), 32, 36, 56; and www.docsouth.unc.edu.

39. *Portico* 1, no. 2 (Mar. 1816): 242, 244; *Portico* 1, no. 4 (Apr. 1816): 316, 318, 320.

40. Stagg, *War of 1812,* 118–125, 161, 132; and Hickey, *War of 1812,* 58–60, 73–74, 117–118.

41. *Portico* 1, no. 3 (Mar. 1816): 241–242; 1, no. 2 (Feb. 1816): 145; 1, no. 6 (June 1816): 501; and 1, no. 8 (Aug. 1816): 143.

42. *Portico* 1, no. 6 (June 1816): 497–499. Kennedy may have gotten some of his misogynistic inspiration from British poet Thomas Otway's *The Orphan* (1680): "Who was the Cause of a long

ten year war, / And laid at least old Troy in Ashes? Woman. / Destructive, damnable, deceitful Woman!"

43. One cause of the war was the very jingoism expressed by Kennedy. Many newspapers clamored for war, and the "War Hawks" in Congress more-or-less forced President Madison to declare war. See *Portico* 1, no. 2 (Feb. 1816): 241; 1, no. 6 (June 1816): 495, 500–501; and 1, no. 8 (Aug. 1816): 146–147; Burstein, *Sentimental Democracy,* 237–240; and Trautsch, "Mr. Madison's War," 631, 643–650.

44. *Portico* 1, no. 3 (Mar. 1816): 241.

45. Stagg, *War of 1812,* 129, 133–135; Trautsch, "Mr. Madison's War," 643–644; Walsh and Fox, *Maryland,* 177–178; and Paul A. Gilje, *Free Trade and Sailors' Rights in the War of 1812* (New York, 2013), 11–16, 24–28.

46. KP, autobiographical fragments; and *Portico* 1, no. 6 (June 1816): 499.

47. Fought on August 24, 1814, the Battle of Bladensburg pitted around 6,000 Americans against some 4,500 British. British losses were heavy, with 180 killed and 300 wounded, compared to American losses of only a dozen killed and 30 wounded. The comrade Kennedy carried from the field was James McCulloch, who later figured prominently in the Supreme Court case *McCulloch v. Maryland.* See KP, autobiographical fragments; Stagg, *War of 1812,* 129–133; Hickey, *War of 1812,* 195–198; and Anthony S. Pitch, *The Burning of Washington: The British Invasion of 1814* (Annapolis, 1998), 79–85.

48. KP, Kennedy to Philip Pendleton, Aug. 29, 1814; Stagg, *War of 1812,* 129, 133–135; and William M. Marine, *The British Invasion of Maryland, 1812–1815* (Baltimore, 1913), 172. General Ross landed some 4,600 troops fourteen miles from Baltimore on September 11, 1814. American forces numbered about 3,200. British casualties the next day were 384 versus 213 for the Americans. The unsuccessful naval bombardment of Fort McHenry took place on the night of September 13, inspiring Francis Scott Key to write a poem that was later set to music as the "Star-Spangled Banner." See Pitch, *Burning of Washington,* 94–199; Stagg, *War of 1812,* 133–134; and Joseph W. A. Whitehorne, *The Battle for Baltimore, 1814* (Baltimore, 1997), 177–183.

49. The Battle of New Orleans culminated on January 8, 1815. On that day, the British suffered almost 2,000 casualties versus only 70 American. Many believed the lopsided outcome was divinely ordained. See *Portico* 1, no. 8 (Aug. 1816): 146; Hickey, *War of 1812,* 211–212, 296–298; Burstein, *Sentimental Democracy,* 240–242; John William Ward, *Andrew Jackson: Symbol of an Age* (New York, 1962), 111–113, 141; and Robert V. Remini, *The Battle of New Orleans: Andrew Jackson and America's First Military Victory* (New York, 1999), 191–198.

50. Jasper Trautsch has suggested that the American Revolution was incomplete because it never became a "mass phenomenon" and that it took the War of 1812 to accomplish this important step in nation building. See Trautsch, "Mr. Madison's War," 632–633; Douglas T. Miller, *The Birth of Modern America, 1820–1850* (New York, 1970), 19–29; Edward Halsey Foster, *Civilized Wilderness: Backgrounds to American Romantic Literature, 1817–1860* (New York, 1975), 10, 15; and Alan Taylor, "Dual Nationalisms: Legacies of the War of 1812," in Pietro S. Nivola and Peter J. Kastor, eds., *What So Proudly We Hailed: Essays on the Contemporary Meaning of the War of 1812* (Washington, DC, 2012): 82–86.

51. North, *Economic Growth,* 102–103; Miller, *Birth of Modern America,* 29–31; and George Dangerfield, *The Awakening of American Nationalism, 1815–1828* (New York, 1965), viii, 8, 32.

2. Entering Public Life

1. Kennedy, *William Wirt,* 2:203.

2. Thomas Jefferson to John Cartwright, June 5, 1824, in Merrill D. Peterson, ed., *The Portable Jefferson* (New York, 1975), 580–581.

3. North, *Economic Growth,* 186, 193; Dangerfield, *American Nationalism,* 17–19; Jack Larkin, *The Reshaping of Everyday Life, 1790–1840* (New York, 1988), 8–9, 55; and Sean Wilentz, *The Rise of American Democracy: Jefferson to Lincoln* (New York, 2005), 244–245.

4. The collapse of cotton prices in 1819 heightened southern concerns about their economy. The northern-sponsored Tallmadge Amendment, calling for the exclusion of slavery in Missouri, was seen by southern congressmen as a direct attack on their section. David Brion Davis has argued that "the Union would never be the same" after the Missouri Crisis. See Wilentz, *American Democracy,* 223–231; C. Edward Skeen, *1816: America Rising* (Lexington, KY, 2003), 63–64; and David Brion Davis, *Inhuman Bondage: The Rise and Fall of Slavery in the New World* (New York, 2006), 276–279.

5. William Taylor has characterized this period as one of "introspection and self-criticism." See Taylor, *Cavalier and Yankee,* 18; and Appleby, *Inheriting the Revolution,* 52.

6. Browne, *Baltimore in the Nation,* 59–60.

7. William Wirt is quoted from John M. Grammer, *Pastoral and Politics in the Old South* (Baton Rouge, 1996), 133. See also Robert A. Ferguson, *Law and Letters in American Culture* (Cambridge, MA, 1984), 11–12; Perry Miller, *The Life of the Mind in America from the Revolution to the Civil War* (New York, 1965), 109–116; and Alexis de Tocqueville, *Democracy in America* (1835; reprint, New York, 1945), 1:286, 288.

8. Semmes, *Latrobe,* 201–203; Walsh and Fox, *Maryland,* 256, 265–268; and Bohner, *Kennedy,* 25–26.

9. KP, autobiographical fragments.

10. The doctrine of judicial review was first cited by the U.S. Supreme Court in the 1803 *Marbury v. Madison* decision. By Justice John Marshall's retirement in 1835, it was well established. Edmund Burke believed that institutions such as the legal system and established religion made society cohere. See Grammer, *Pastoral and Politics,* 133; Ferguson, *Law and Letters,* 20, 23; Howe, *Political Culture,* 51, 236–237; and KP, autobiographical fragments.

11. Bohner, *Kennedy,* 27; Ferguson, *Law and Letters,* 26, 66; Semmes, *Latrobe,* 101; and KP, autobiographical fragments.

12. Tuckerman, *Kennedy,* 107; and KP, autobiographical fragments.

13. North, *Economic Growth,* 180–181; Browne, *Baltimore in the Nation,* 70–74; and Semmes, *Latrobe,* 100–101.

14. Tuckerman, *Kennedy,* 108–109; and Semmes, *Latrobe,* 222.

15. Jay B. Hubbell, *The South in American Literature, 1607–1900* (Durham, 1954), 237–239.

16. Ferguson, *Law and Letters,* 17, 78, 87, 99.

17. David Tomlinson, "A Publisher's Advice to Young Authors: John P. Kennedy and Peter H. Cruse Serve a Literary Apprenticeship," *Southern Literary Journal* 14, no. 1 (Fall 1981): 56–58. The idea that the *Red Book* authors would mingle with Baltimoreans but remain detached observers recalls Joseph Addison in an early issue of the *Spectator:* "whenever I see a cluster of people, I al-

ways mix with them, though I never open my lips . . . I live in the world rather as a Spectator of mankind, [rather] than as one of the species." See Kennedy, *Red Book,* 1:ix, 77; and Joseph Addison, *The Works of Joseph Addison* (New York, 1864), 18.

18. Kennedy, *Red Book,* 1:62, 88, 135.

19. Joseph Robinson kept his shop open until 9 p.m. on days when new installments of the *Red Book* appeared. See advertisement in the *Baltimore Patriot,* Dec. 21, 1819. Edward Everett was editor of the *North American Review* and Andrews Norton a noted professor at Harvard Divinity School. Their letters are reprinted in Tuckerman, *Kennedy,* 111.

20. Browne, *Baltimore in the Nation,* 36, 55–56, 64, 74; Walsh and Fox, *Maryland,* 169–170, 188–189; and Tuckerman, *Kennedy,* 108–109.

21. Walsh and Fox, *Maryland,* 191; North, *Economic Growth,* 184–185; Dangerfield, *American Nationalism,* 87; and Rezneck, *Business Depressions,* 56–57.

22. North, *Economic Growth,* 182–188; and Rezneck, *Business Depressions,* 53–55.

23. McCulloch helped arrange the unsecured stock purchases for Smith and Buchanan at the Second Bank of the United States. Had the ensuing scandal been exposed while the U.S. House of Representatives was in session during January 1819, the Second Bank might have been dismantled then and there. It is also surprising that the Supreme Court's landmark decision, *McCulloch v. Maryland,* took place against this sordid background. See North, *Economic Growth,* 181, 184; Dangerfield, *American Nationalism,* 80–81; Browne, *Baltimore in the Nation,* 74–76; and Howe, *What Hath God Wrought,* 144–145.

24. Browne, *Baltimore in the Nation,* 77, 91; Maryland State Archives, *House of Delegates Votes and Proceedings,* Feb. 2, 1820; and www.msa.md.gov. *Niles' Register* is quoted in Rezneck, *Business Depressions,* 60–61, 65. See also Tuckerman, *Kennedy,* 110.

25. There are echoes of Joseph Addison's *Spectator* throughout the *Red Book.* For example, Addison also took aim at exclusive men's clubs and the dullness of their members: "The Hum-Drum club . . . was made up of very honest gentlemen, of peaceable dispositions, that used to sit together, smoke their pipes, and say nothing, til midnight. The Mum club is an institution of the same nature and as great an enemy of noise." See Addison, *Works of Addison,* 29; and Kennedy, *Red Book,* 1:13–15.

26. Kennedy, *Red Book,* 1:156, 174; and Tomlinson, "Publisher's Advice," 65–66.

27. Wirt's letter is quoted from Ridgely, *Kennedy,* 26. See also Kennedy, *Red Book,* 1:49, 83, 143.

28. Kennedy, *Red Book,* 1:178–182.

29. Browne, *Baltimore in the Nation,* 94–95.

30. Kennedy, *Red Book,* 1:26.

31. Ibid., 1:108.

32. Ibid., 1:80–83.

33. Ibid., 1:62, 72.

34. Alan Trachtenberg has called this type of observed, urban narrative "processional" and has traced it back to Addison and Steele's *Spectator.* It later became a favorite device of Walt Whitman. See Alan Trachtenberg, *Lincoln's Smile and Other Enigmas* (New York, 2008), 135–136; and Kennedy, *Red Book,* 1:73.

35. Barbara Fields has suggested that slavery was still an integral part of Baltimore's urban life in 1820, after which it began to fade. See Fields, *Slavery and Freedom,* 7, 17, 49, 57, 62; Browne, *Bal-*

timore in the Nation, 99–100; Richard C. Wade, *Slavery in the City: The South in 1820–1860* (New York, 1964), 53, 77, 202, 325–329; and *Baltimore Patriot,* Jan. 22, 1821, Dec. 19, 1822, Jan. 2, 1823.

36. Captain Clive Symmes published his "No. 1 Circular" in 1818, locating the polar holes between 12 and 16 degrees latitude North, in Siberia. See *Symmes' Theory of Concentric Spheres* (Cincinnati, 1826) and www.olivercrowlery.com/text/1818symm.

37. It is very likely that either Symmes or one of his followers wrote *Symzonia.* See Captain Adam Seaborne [pseud.], *Symzonia: A Voyage of Discovery* (New York, 1820); review article in *Literary Gazette, or Journal of Criticism, Science, and the Arts* 1, no. 1 (1821); and Jared Gardner, *Master Plots: Race and the Founding of American Literature, 1787–1845* (Baltimore, 1998), 116–117.

38. Dressing boxes were used by ladies in eighteenth-century France and England, and possibly by Virginia plantation mistresses, to store cosmetics, jewelry, and small items of apparel. See Antique Boxes at "The Sign of the Hygra," London, www.hygra.com; and Richard Beale Davis, *Literature and Society in Early Virginia, 1608–1840* (Baton Rouge, 1973), 69.

39. Kennedy, *Red Book,* 2:13–15, 92–99.

40. It is the calm, cool manner used to describe the fate of the Tawnies that invites comparison to Swift's "A Modest Proposal." See Swift, *Gulliver's Travels,* 225, 262–268, 302; and Damrosch, *Jonathan Swift,* 374–376, 416–420.

41. While one Poe scholar has examined *Symzonia* as a source of Poe's novel, none has investigated the *Red Book.* See Harry Levin, *The Power of Blackness: Hawthorne, Poe, Melville* (Athens, OH, 1958), 118–121; Swift, *Gulliver's Travels,* 262–268, 302; and Edgar Allan Poe, *The Narrative of Arthur Gordon Pym of Nantucket* (1838; reprint, New York, 2002), 135–138, 143, 178.

42. The decline of tobacco growing in Maryland contributed to the excess of slaves available for shipment to the Gulf Coast. Austin Woolfolk is mentioned in Alexis de Tocqueville's *Journey to America* and Gustave de Beaumont's *Marie, or Slavery in the United States,* as well as Frederick Douglass's autobiography. See Seth Rockman, *Scraping By: Wage Labor, Slavery, and Survival in Early Baltimore* (Baltimore, 2009), 235–237, 342; Walter Johnson, *Soul by Soul: Life Inside the Antebellum Slave Market* (Cambridge, MA, 1999), 7, 139, 215; Steven Deyle, *Carry Me Back: The Domestic Slave Trade in American Life* (New York, 2005), 98–99; Leo Damrosch, *Tocqueville's Discovery of America* (New York, 2010), 170–172; and Frederick Douglass, *Narrative of the Life of Frederick Douglass, An American Slave* (1845; reprint, New York, 1985), 54.

43. Barbara Fields has estimated that some 12% of Maryland's slave population went on the block between 1830 and 1840. See Fields, *Slavery and Freedom,* 24; and Wade, *Slavery in the City,* 77.

44. Larry Tise has argued that proslavery arguments were well developed by 1820. See Larry E. Tise, *Proslavery: A History of the Defense of Slavery in America, 1701–1840* (Athens, GA, 1987), 8–15; Davis, *Inhuman Bondage,* 186–192; and Kennedy, *Red Book,* 2:13.

45. Thomas Jefferson wrote that the slave owner exercises the "the most boisterous passion, the most unremitting despotism . . . Our children see this and learn to imitate it." Alexis de Tocqueville claimed that "the influence of slavery . . . affects the character of the master . . . his tastes are those of an idle man." See Thomas Jefferson, *Notes on the State of Virginia,* with intro. by William Peden (1787; reprint, Chapel Hill, 1996), 162–163; and Tocqueville, *Democracy in America,* 1:378–379.

46. The final installment of the *Red Book* appeared on Mar. 16, 1821. See KP, Cruse to Kennedy, Jan. 9, 24, 1821; and Tomlinson, "Publisher's Advice," 67.

47. Bohner, *Kennedy,* 37–37, 53–55, 69, 72; and Tuckerman, *Kennedy,* 112–113.

48. Tuckerman, *Kennedy,* 106–116; and Bohner, *Kennedy,* 26–27.

49. Browne, *Baltimore in the Nation,* 105–107; and Walsh and Fox, *Maryland,* 256–257, 267.

50. *Baltimore Patriot,* Dec. 13, 21, 1819, Jan. 10, Feb. 3, 1820; and Maryland State Archives, *House of Delegates Votes and Proceedings,* Dec. 13, 16, 21, 1819, Jan. 3, 20, Feb. 15, 1820, Jan. 29, 1821, Jan. 7, 1823, www.msa.gov.

51. Fields, *Slavery and Freedom,* 17–22; Walsh and Fox, *Maryland,* 256–257; and Browne, *Baltimore in the Nation,* 4–5, 37, 64–65, 84–85.

52. Walsh and Fox, *Maryland,* 258–259; *Baltimore Patriot,* Feb. 17, 1820; and *Votes and Proceedings,* Jan. 21, 29, 31, Feb. 15, 1820.

53. *Votes and Proceedings,* Dec. 7, 19, 1820, Jan. 24, 29, Feb. 16, 1821; and *Maryland House of Delegates Session Laws, 1820,* 625:159.

54. *Votes and Proceedings,* Jan. 31, Feb. 6, 12, 1820; *Baltimore Patriot,* Jan. 23, 30, Feb. 1, 1821; Bohner, *Kennedy,* 49–50; and Tuckerman, *Kennedy,* 114.

55. *Votes and Proceedings,* Jan. 3, 7, 10, 12, Feb. 5, 1820, Feb. 7, 1821, Dec. 17, 1822; and *Baltimore Patriot,* Jan. 10, 12, 1820, Dec. 4, 17, 1822.

56. Jeffrey R. Brackett, *The Negro in Maryland: A Study of the Institution of Slavery* (1889; reprint, Freeport, NY, 1969), 47–50.

57. It is unclear why petitions to bring slaves into Maryland were increasing at this time. It is possible that some southern planters were returning unneeded, "rented" slaves to Maryland in the wake of declining cotton prices after 1819. See North, *Economic Growth,* 124, 144; Walsh and Fox, *Maryland,* 189, 205; Brackett, *Negro in Maryland,* 64–65; and *Easton (MD) Republican Star,* Feb. 13, 1821.

58. KP, "Newspaper clippings: political affairs . . . misc. articles by and about Kennedy."

59. Kennedy was on solid footing here. Working in wheat and tobacco in the Chesapeake was less harsh than in rice, cotton, and sugar in the Deep South. See Ira Berlin, *Many Thousands Gone: The First Two Centuries of Slavery in North America* (Cambridge, MA, 1998), 146–148, 266, 345–347.

60. KP, "Newspaper clippings."

61. The "Denmark Vesey conspiracy" was uncovered in May 1822. Because Vesey never confessed and the extent of the conspiracy was never known, some historians have questioned the existence of the conspiracy. However, scholarship by Douglas Egerton has shown that it was real and extensive. See *Votes and Proceedings,* Dec. 10, 1821; Davis, *Inhuman Bondage,* 222–226; Robert L. Paquette and Douglas R. Egerton, "Of Facts and Fables: New Light on the Denmark Vesey Affair," *South Carolina Historical Magazine* 105, no. 1 (Jan. 2004): 8–48; and Douglas R. Egerton, *He Shall Go Out Free: The Lives of Denmark Vesey* (Lanham, MD, 1999), 120, 132–136, 142–144, 152–153, 200.

62. *Votes and Proceedings,* Dec. 17, 18, 1822.

63. I have analyzed the 37 to 34 vote to reject the Dalrymple report according to the three regions of Maryland: northern counties with relatively few slaves, Eastern Shore counties with some slaves, and southern counties with large numbers of slaves. Barbara Fields has used this division of the state. A vote to reject the Dalrymple report represented a vote against the status quo of slavery in Maryland. Conversely, a vote to accept the report supported slavery as it existed in the state. The percentage of slave populations has been taken from the 1820 U.S. Census. (See table below.)

Regional Analysis of 1822 Maryland House of Delegates Vote on Dalrymple Report Regarding Slave Importation Law

MARYLAND REGION	SLAVES AS % OF TOTAL POPULATION	# DELEGATES VOTING TO ACCEPT/ REJECT REPORT	% DELEGATES VOTING TO REJECT REPORT
Northern	13	8/14	64
Eastern	28	11/16	60
Southern	46	15/7	32

See *Baltimore American,* Dec. 22, 1822; and *Baltimore Patriot,* Dec. 24, 1822; *Votes and Proceedings,* Dec. 18, 20, 1822; Fields, *Slavery and Freedom,* 12–15; and mapserver.lib.virginia.edu.

64. Large numbers of slaves continued to enter Maryland after the 1822 debate on the slave importation law. See *Session Laws, 1822,* 627:18; *Frederick-town (MD) Republican Gazette and Advertiser* and *Easton Gazette,* Jan. 4, 1823; *Session Laws, 1823,* 628:3; and Brackett, *Negro in Maryland,* 66.

65. David J. Rothman, *The Discovery of the Asylum: Social Order and Discord in the New Republic* (1971; reprint, New York, 2002), 69–73; and Howe, *Political Culture,* 74–86.

66. Walsh and Fox, *Maryland,* 201–202; *Proceedings and Votes,* Dec. 10, 1821; and *Baltimore Patriot,* Dec. 18, 1821.

67. Walsh and Fox, *Maryland,* 123–124; *Proceedings and Votes,* Jan. 22, Feb. 1, 1821, Jan. 9, 17, 19, 23, 25, 1822.

68. *Baltimore Patriot,* Dec. 12, 1822; *Proceedings and Votes,* Feb. 2, 1821; Rothman, *Asylum,* xxiii–xxiv, 71, 84; Rockman, *Scraping By,* 226–227; and Jeffrey A. Mullins, "'The Sweat of Thy Brow': Education, Manual Labor and the Market Revolution," in Scott C. Martin, ed., *Cultural Change and the Market Revolution in America, 1789–1860* (Lanham, MD, 2005), 160–163.

69. *Proceedings and Votes,* Jan. 1, 1822.

70. Browne, *Baltimore in the Nation,* 86–87; *Proceedings and Votes,* Dec. 11, 1821, Dec. 17, 1822, Feb. 11, 13, 1823; and the *Baltimore Patriot,* Dec. 18, 1821.

71. The so-called Bonus Bill would have spent the dividends from the Second Bank of the United States on internal improvements. Financed by private investors and the State of New York, work on the Erie Canal began in mid-July 1817 and was completed in early 1825. See Dangerfield, *American Nationalism,* 19–20; Skeen, *1816,* 98–100, 113–115; Peter L. Bernstein, *Wedding of the Waters: The Erie Canal and the Making of a Great Nation* (New York, 2005), 180–186, 196; and John F. Stover, "Canals and Turnpikes: America's Early-Nineteenth-Century Transportation Network," in Joseph R. Frese and Jacob Judd, eds., *An Emerging Independent American Economy, 1815–1875* (Tarrytown, NY, 1980), 81–85.

72. George Washington had solicited $150,000 each from Maryland and Virginia for the Potomac Canal. However, the War of 1812 and engineering hurdles soon drove the project into bankruptcy. The history of the Chesapeake-Delaware Canal dated back to 1764 but never got off the ground. First chartered in 1793, the Susquehanna Canal was deemed a financial failure by 1812. See George Rogers Taylor, *The Transportation Revolution, 1815–1860* (New York, 1951), 34, 41–44; and Walsh and Fox, *Maryland,* 172–173.

73. Whereas Baltimore's southern location had been an advantage for its prewar Caribbean trade, it was too far from Europe relative to other eastern ports after the war. Furthermore, Baltimore had failed to secure a regular packet line to Liverpool, as New York and Philadelphia had. Finally, the Erie Canal threatened to route the bulk of western commerce through New York City. See Browne, *Baltimore in the Nation,* 82–84; and North, *Economic Growth,* 176, 184–188. See also *Proceedings and Votes,* Jan. 4, Feb. 9, 1822; and *Baltimore Patriot,* Jan. 7, Feb. 19, 1822.

74. *Proceedings and Votes,* Feb. 9, 1833.

75. Browne, *Baltimore in the Nation,* 107–111; and Walsh and Fox, *Maryland,* 172–175, 191–193.

76. *Proceedings and Votes,* Dec. 10, 1822, Jan. 7, Feb. 18, 1823; *Baltimore Patriot,* Feb. 13, 20, 1823; *Baltimore American,* Feb. 17, 18, 1823; and KP, "Letters from schoolfellows, fellow students and early friends, 1812–32," specifically, V. Pennington to Kennedy, 1823 (incomplete date); W. Howard to Kennedy, Feb. 12, 1823; and J. L. Cook to Kennedy, Feb. 14, 1823.

77. The "American Farmer" articles were authored by William Kenworthy, a writer employed by Kennedy's political opponents. See *Baltimore Patriot,* Aug. 11, 12, 15, 1823; and Tuckerman, *Kennedy,* 115.

78. *Baltimore Patriot,* Sept. 17, 1823.

79. Browne, *Baltimore in the Nation,* 164–166; Walsh and Fox, *Maryland,* 195–196; and Stover, "Canals and Turnpikes," 86–88.

80. Bohner, *Kennedy,* 53; and Tuckerman, *Kennedy,* 115–116.

81. Kennedy described his meeting with Adams some years later in a letter to Robert Winthrop. See KP, "Letters of John Pendleton Kennedy," Kennedy to R. C. Winthrop (undated); Tuckerman, *Kennedy,* 118–119; and Bohner, *Kennedy,* 53.

82. Tuckerman, *Kennedy,* 119–120; and Bohner, *Kennedy,* 54.

83. KP, journal entry, May 31, 1852.

84. Kennedy wrote his friend Virgil Maxcy in late 1823 asking, "What do you think of the people of Baltimore being all alive for Jackson?" See October 11, 1823, letter quoted in Mark H. Haller, "The Rise of the Jackson Party in Maryland, 1820–1829," *Journal of Southern History* 28, no. 3 (Aug. 1962): 311.

85. In the election of 1824, Jackson received 99 electoral votes, Adams 84, Crawford 41, and Clay 37. If there was a "corrupt bargain," it was probably struck between Adams and Clay at a meeting on Jan. 9, 1825. See Burstein, *Passions of Andrew Jackson,* 149–158; Remini, *Henry Clay,* 249, 258–266, 273; and Wilentz, *American Democracy,* 243–251, 253, 255–256.

86. Rhys Isaac has called attention to the systematically balanced and proportioned architecture and landscaping of the Virginia estate, intended to communicate natural harmony as well as the social control of its aristocratic master. Lucinda MacKethan has called this "the symmetry of plantation life." See Jack McLaughlin, *Jefferson and Monticello: Biography of a Builder* (New York, 1988), 339–340; Rhys Isaac, *The Transformation of Virginia, 1740–1790* (Chapel Hill, 1982), 19, 35, 38; and Lucinda Hardwick MacKethan, *The Dream of Arcady: Place and Time in Southern Literature* (Baton Rouge, 1980), 47.

87. Kennedy, *William Wirt,* 2:193.

88. Ibid., 194.

3. The Whig in *Swallow Barn*

1. Most of the citations in this chapter have been taken from the original 1832 version of *Swallow Barn.* Because Kennedy made numerous revisions to the 1851 version of the novel, the 1832 *Swallow Barn* is the more spontaneous literary production and more accurately reflects the author's attitudes during the late 1820s and early 1830s. See Kennedy, *Swallow Barn* (1832), 1:19; Kennedy, *Swallow Barn* (1851), with MacKethan intro., xxii–xxiii; and Taylor, *Cavalier and Yankee,* 187, 361.

2. Kennedy removed the "dormant windows . . . face without eyebrows" line from the 1851 version of *Swallow Barn.* Likewise, he eliminated the "irregular pile" and "unlucky bark" references. These revisions created a more positive image of the plantation. See Kennedy, *SB* (1832), 1:20.

3. Ibid. The description of the old barn was removed from the 1851 version.

4. Lewis Simpson has examined the symbolic importance of Monticello with respect to the Old Dominion's Enlightenment pretensions, as well as their collapse in the face of the slavery controversy. See Simpson, *Dispossessed Garden,* 25–27, 34; MacKethan, *Dream of Arcady,* 42–47; and Davis, *Literature and Society in Early Virginia,* 248–249, 252–253.

5. J. V. Ridgely has characterized Kennedy's ambivalent perspective as a kind of "dual vision" and *Swallow Barn* as "free fantasy." Lewis Simpson has accused Kennedy of being a proslavery intellectual and portraying plantation life as a pastoral Utopia. Other scholars, Charles Bohner and William Osborne among them, have deemed Kennedy's representation of the Old Dominion as true and accurate. William Taylor has called Kennedy an "Indian giver" and suggested that the author was working through his own conflicted feelings about the Old Dominion. For these and other interpretations, see Ridgely, *Kennedy,* 3, 27, 54; Bohner, *Kennedy,* 63; Simpson, *Dispossessed Garden,* 47–51; Taylor, *Cavalier and Yankee,* 151, 185; J. P. Kennedy, *Swallow Barn; Or, A Sojourn in the Old Dominion* (1851; reprint, New York, 1962), with intro. by William Osborne, xviii–xix; and Jan Bakker and Benjamin H. Newcomb, *Pastoral in Antebellum Southern Romance* (Baton Rouge, 1989), 42.

6. *Baltimore Patriot,* Feb. 14, July 15, 20, Sept. 21, 25, 29, Oct. 10, 1826; Walsh and Fox, *Maryland,* 263–266; and Haller, "Rise of the Jacksonian Party in Maryland," 316.

7. KP, autobiographical fragments, and Kennedy to Elizabeth Gray, Aug. 16, 1828.

8. Dangerfield, *American Nationalism,* 284; Dunn, *Dominion of Memories,* 24–27; and Davis, *Literature and Society in Early Virginia,* 307–322.

9. KP, "Misc. notes and early drafts on *Swallow Barn*"; and Kennedy, *Swallow Barn* (1832), 1:6–7, 184–189.

10. The Old Republicans, or "Quids," as they were called (from *tertium quid,* or third force), continued to reiterate Jefferson's objections to the intrusions of central government in states' rights and to complain about the corrupting influence of "consolidation." See *SB* (1832), 1:26–27, 77, 185–188; KP, journal entry, Jan. 19, 1830; Dunn, *Dominion of Memories,* 100–101, 108–109; Wilentz, *American Democracy,* 287–288; and Howe, *What Hath God Wrought,* 82–83.

11. At the Jacksonians' first Maryland convention on May 21, 1827, Virgil Maxcy, who gave the main address, reassured attendees that Jackson supported internal improvements. See Walsh and Fox, *Maryland,* 266–277; Haller, "Rise of Jacksonian Party in Maryland," 318; and *Baltimore Patriot,* June 10, 27, 1828.

12. *Baltimore Republican,* June 6, July 15, 1826, July 11, 28, 1828, Oct. 8, 1830; and Semmes, *Latrobe,* 202–203.

13. For examples of Kennedy's working man's rhetoric and background on the working man's cause, see his "No Piles of Hoarded Wealth" (1833), in George E. Probst, ed., *Happy Republic: A Reader in Tocqueville's America* (New York, 1962), 9–12; *Baltimore Patriot,* Feb. 5, Mar. 10, 1829; Mullins, "Sweat of Thy Brow," 160–162; and John F. Kasson, *Civilizing the Machine: Technology and Republican Values in America, 1776–1900* (New York, 1976), 46–47.

14. The Maysville Road veto message encouraged self-funded, state-level programs for internal improvement and endeavored to restrict federal funding to interstate projects only. See Howe, *What Hath God Wrought,* 357–362; Wilentz, *American Democracy,* 328, 379; Walsh and Fox, *Maryland,* 269–270; and Haller, "Rise of Jacksonian Party in Maryland," 324–325.

15. KP, journal entry, Sept. 21, 1830.

16. John Kennedy Sr. had moved his family from Baltimore to Berkeley County, Virginia, in 1820, leaving his oldest son behind. At first the family lived at "Clayton," a plantation inherited by Nancy Kennedy from her father. In 1825, for reasons that are unclear, the family moved to "The Bower." See Bohner, *Kennedy,* 72; *SB* (1851), xx; Ridgely, *Kennedy,* 36; and KP, Kennedy to Elizabeth Gray, Aug. 11, 1828, and misc. drafts and notes on *Swallow Barn.*

17. Bohner, *Kennedy,* 77; Semmes, *Latrobe,* 430–431; and KP, journal entries, Oct. 19, 1829, May 11, 15, 16, 19, Sept. 28, 1830.

18. Bohner, *Kennedy,* 34, 90; and KP, journal entry, Feb. 4, 1830.

19. The *Portico,* the same literary magazine that had published "The Swiss Traveller," tenaciously held to the neoclassical style and fought a rear guard action against romanticism. The magazine criticized Walter Scott's work as "contemptible production." See Clark, *Transitions in American Literary History,* 111–113; and Michael O'Brien, *Rethinking the South: Essays in Intellectual History* (Athens, GA, 1993), 74–75.

20. Kennedy and Cruse had drawn on Washington Irving and James Kirk Paulding's *Salmagundi* for the *Red Book.* However, it was *Knickerbocker's History of New York* that established Irving as America's ranking author, at least until the ascendency of James Fenimore Cooper during the mid-1820s. See Burstein, *Original Knickerbocker,* 70–90; and Washington Irving, *Sketch Book of Geoffrey Crayon, Gent,* with an afterword by Perry Miller (1819–1820; reprint, New York, 1961), 372–373.

21. Both Andrew Burstein and Perry Miller have described Irving's depressed mental state following these events. See Burstein, *Original Knickerbocker,* 117–119, 139, 158, 161, 174–175; and Irving, *Sketch Book,* 375–378.

22. While Irving's *Sketch Book* included "Rip Van Winkle" and "The Legend of Sleepy Hollow," it also introduced Bracebridge Hall and its master, Simon Bracebridge, to American readers. Irving's *Bracebridge Hall* focused more single-mindedly on the British squirearchy and the nation's village life. See Burstein, *Original Knickerbocker,* 141, 162–163; Clark, *Transitions in American Literary History,* 134–136; Irving, *Sketch Book;* and Irving, *Bracebridge Hall* (1822; reprint, London, 1882).

23. Because it was a complex movement across many art forms, a comprehensive definition of Romanticism is hard to come by. The overall movement began in eighteenth-century Germany and France with the rejection of Enlightenment rationalism and what one historian has called the "mimetic view" of creativity, especially the imitation of classical aesthetics. Romanticism stressed

the primacy of the individual and the "soul within" as the only genuine source of creative inspiration. As a literary movement, it tended toward the imaginary as opposed to the purely rational, emphasized the individual over society, and often sought source material in the historical past, sometimes focused on national or regional peculiarities. Romantic writers were deeply interested in external nature and, most important, individual perceptions of it. See Irving, *Bracebridge Hall,* 27–28, 67–73, 89, 115–116; Clark, *Transitions in American Literary History,* 166–168, 204–212; Michael O'Brien, *Conjectures of Order: Intellectual Life and the American South, 1810–1860* (Chapel Hill, 2004), 2:691–696; Peter Gay, *Naked Heart: The Bourgeois Experience: Victoria to Freud,* vol. 4 (New York, 1995), 40–45; and Tim Blanning, *The Romantic Revolution: A History* (New York, 2011), x, xiv–xv, 11–36, 128–129, 135.

24. Irving, *Sketch Book,* 70–71; and Drabble, *Oxford Companion to English Literature,* 401–402, 743.

25. The rambling narrator had been used by William Wirt in his 1803 *The Letters of the British Spy* and James Kirke Paulding in his 1817 *Letters from the South.* See Irving, *Sketch Book,* 13–15; Irving, *Bracebridge Hall,* 13; Taylor, *Cavalier and Yankee,* 73, 179, 182, 237; and *SB* (1851), xix.

26. Michael O'Brien has described *Swallow Barn* as "something of a tour of eighteenth and early nineteenth-century literature, where one bumps into a little Fielding here, some Irving there, a dash of Scott." See O'Brien, *Conjectures of Order,* 2:762; Ridgely, *Kennedy,* 39, 47, 50–51; *SB* (1851), xiii–xiv, xvii, xix, xxiii; Bohner, *Kennedy,* 78; Hubbell, *South in American Literature,* 447–448; and Taylor, *Cavalier and Yankee,* 180–181.

27. Harry Hayden Clark has described Irving in England as a disengaged wanderer, observing a society with which he "had nothing to do." See Clark, *Transitions in American Literary History,* 135.

28. KP, Misc. notes and early drafts of *Swallow Barn.*

29. In his early notes on *Swallow Barn,* Kennedy wrote that "Mark Littleton is entirely ignorant of the manners and customs of Virginia and is imbibed with the common feelings of the North in regard to [what] Southern institutions are." See *SB* (1832), 1:4; and KP, notes and early drafts of *Swallow Barn.*

30. More than a million votes were cast in the presidential election of 1828, nearly four times the number in 1824. Jackson won 68 percent of the electoral votes and 56 percent of the popular votes. During the 1820s and 1830s, Baltimore manufacturers routinized their production processes and shed workers. The massive influx of immigrants increased the pressure on wages. See KP, journal entries, Feb. 4, Sept. 21, 1830; Wilentz, *American Democracy,* 210, 282, 308–309; Browne, *Baltimore in the Nation,* 135–136; Charles Sellers, *The Market Revolution: Jacksonian America, 1815–1846* (New York, 1991), 281–289; and Glenn C. Altschuler and Stuart M. Blumin, *Rude Republic: Americans and Their Politics in the Nineteenth Century* (Princeton, 2000), 16–17.

31. While the tariff of 1824 increased the price of many manufactured goods, the tariff of 1828 went even further. For example, it raised the duty on cotton cloth, the material used to clothe slaves, to nearly fifty percent. See KP, journal entry, Sept. 21, 1830; Remini, *Henry Clay,* 330–331; Louis P. Masur, *1831: The Year of Eclipse* (New York, 2001), 146–147; and Merrill D. Peterson, *The Great Triumvirate: Webster, Clay and Calhoun* (New York, 1987), 169–170.

32. Vernon Parrington was the first to claim that Gray's influence converted Kennedy from a southern agrarian to a northern industrialist. Most critics have deemed this notion exaggerated. See Vernon L. Parrington, *The Romantic Revolution in America,* vol. 2 of *Main Currents of American*

Thought (New York, 1927), 2:48–50; Bohner, *Kennedy,* 63–66; Ridgely, *Kennedy,* 29; and Kennedy, *Horse-Shoe Robinson* (1835; reprint with an intro. by Ernest E. Leisy, New York, 1962), xii.

33. Southern congressmen were able to defeat tariff legislation prior to the 1820s but, partially as a result of reapportionment, were unsuccessful against the tariffs of 1824 and 1828. See Howe, *What Hath God Wrought,* 271–275; F. W. Taussig, *Tariff History of the United States* (New York, 1892), 22–23, 73–75, 83; and Carl William Kaiser Jr., *History of the Academic Protectionist–Free Trade Controversy in America* (Philadelphia, 1939), 22–23, 41–42, 133.

34. "A Review of Mr. Cambreleng's Report from the Committee of Commerce, in the House of Representatives, at the First Session of the Twenty-first Congress," in Kennedy, *Political and Official Papers,* 9–86; KP, journal entries, Apr. 12, 26, 1830; and Dangerfield, *American Nationalism,* 277–278.

35. Kennedy, *Political and Official Papers,* 35–38.

36. At one point in his papers, Kennedy refers to his father's old coachman during the Shrub Hill days as "Sam." We do not know if this was the same slave. See KP, journal entry, Dec. 16, 1830, and autobiographical fragments.

37. Slavery historian Eugene Genovese called this phenomenon a "catastrophic misunderstanding." Slave owners often took a paternalistic approach to their slaves, and slaves feigned reciprocal behavior to perpetuate better treatment. Peter Kolchin has characterized slaveholder paternalism as "fragile and elastic." See Eugene D. Genovese, *Roll, Jordan, Roll: The World the Slaves Made* (New York, 1972), 142–144; and Peter Kolchin, *American Slavery, 1619–1877* (New York, 1993), 126–127.

38. Wirt's comments on *Swallow Barn* were part of a May 22, 1832, letter to Dabney Carr, as quoted in Bohner, *Kennedy,* 84.

39. *SB* (1832), 1:51–52, 125–127; and KP, Misc. early notes and drafts of *Swallow Barn.*

40. *SB* (1832), 1:20, 51- 63, 125–126; Tuckerman, *Kennedy,* 122–123, 128–130; and KP, Misc. notes and early drafts of *Swallow Barn* and autobiographical fragments.

41. According to Daniel Howe, "Presbyterian Princeton had an academic empire in the South comparable to Yale's in the North." See Howe, *What Hath God Wrought,* 459; Taylor, *Cavalier and Yankee,* 41; O'Brien, *Conjectures of Order,* 29; and Browne, *Baltimore in the Nation,* 41.

42. *SB* (1832), 1:52, 62–65.

43. Kennedy had three younger brothers living in Virginia at this time—Andrew, Philip, and Anthony. See KP, autobiographical fragments.

44. *SB* (1832), 2:100–101.

45. Irving, *Bracebridge Hall,* 5, 9, 81; and KP, Misc. notes and early drafts of *Swallow Barn.*

46. KP, Kennedy to Philip Pendleton, Aug. 29, 1814; journal entries, Jan. 19, Sept. 21, 1830; and Kennedy to his wife Elizabeth, Aug. 2, 1850.

47. Kennedy described Meriwether in the 1832 version of *Swallow Barn* as a "thorough-bred Virginian" with a "substantial planter look" but removed both descriptors from the 1851 version of the novel. See *SB* (1832), 1:25, 28.

48. Simon Bracebridge holds forth at one point on how turnpikes and carriages contribute to the "effeminacy" of the younger men, since they are less often on horseback and therefore less manly than their predecessors. See *SB* (1832), 1:77–78; and Irving, *Bracebridge Hall,* 60.

49. William Taylor has pointed out that many educated southerners became anxious during this time over what they perceived as "the disappearance of rational appeal as an instrument of persuasion." See Taylor, *Cavalier and Yankee,* 63; and *SB* (1832), 1:27, 2:168, 286.

50. *SB* (1832), 1:205.

51. Philip Barbour represented Virginia in the U.S. House of Representatives for fifteen years before Jackson appointed him to the Supreme Court. Barbour was among the most radical group of Old Republicans, called "Quids." See Dunn, *Dominion of Memories,* 100; and www.michaelariens.com/ConLaw/Justices/Barbour.

52. *SB* (1832), 1:79–81.

53. Kennedy was also inspired in this episode by *Bracebridge Hall,* wherein Squire Bracebridge's statements on a particular subject "have been carried from the parlour to the kitchen by listening domestics, and being apparently sanctioned by such high authority, the whole house became infected with them." See *SB* (1832), 1:79–81; and Irving, *Bracebridge Hall,* 81.

54. Irving, *Bracebridge Hall,* 94; and *SB* (1832), 1:75.

55. *SB* (1832), 1:180–182; and T. H. Breen, *Tobacco Culture: The Mentality of the Great Tidewater Planters on the Eve of Revolution* (Princeton, 1987), 41–43, 160–162, 175–177.

56. Beginning in the 1830s, domestic travel literature came into vogue, much of it about the South. See Matthews, *Toward a New Society,* 107; and Lewis Perry, *Boats Against the Current: American Culture between Revolution and Modernity, 1820–1860* (Lanham, MD, 1993), 129–131.

57. Lewis Simpson has maintained that Kennedy employed large tranches of pastoralism in order to effect a "transformation of the Southern plantation into Arcadia." However, William Taylor has interpreted Kennedy's pastoralism as guardedly critical of its subject matter. Jan Bakker has suggested that there was "something wrong" with the pastoralism in *Swallow Barn* and that the description of the James River is meant as "a stultifying emblem of rural stasis and isolation." See Simpson, *Dispossessed Garden,* 44; Taylor, *Cavalier and Yankee,* 151, 185; and Bakker and Newcomb, *Pastoral in Antebellum Southern Romance,* 47–48.

58. Historians have trouble getting a clear picture of poor whites due to widespread stigmatizing of them by better-off antebellum southerners. Depending on the locality, they were called "crackers," "sandhillers," "rednecks," or "po' white trash." See Jeff Forret, *Race Relations at the Margins: Slaves and Poor Whites in the Antebellum Southern Countryside* (Baton Rouge, 2006), 2–11; and *SB* (1832), 1:182–188.

59. Howe, *What Hath God Wrought,* 396–404; Wilentz, *American Democracy,* 319–321; and KP, journal entry, Dec. 31, 1831.

60. Among the moral reformers supporting the Cherokee and other tribes were Theodore Frelinghuysen and Catherine Beecher. Frelinghuysen was a U.S. senator from New Jersey and hugely active in the temperance movement and Christian missionary work. Beecher was a pioneer in women's education and the "mother" of home economics. Both would become dedicated Whigs. See Howe, *What Hath God Wrought,* 74–75, 347–355; Masur, *1831,* 119–128; and David S. Reynolds, *Waking Giant: America in the Age of Jackson* (New York, 2008), 92–95.

61. KP, Misc. notes and early drafts of *Swallow Barn;* and James L. Machor, *Reading Fiction in Antebellum America: Informed Response and Reception Histories, 1820–1865* (Baltimore, 2011), 317–319.

62. R. V. Ridgely has called Kennedy's poor whites "men in decline." See J. V. Ridgely, *Nineteenth-Century Southern Literature* (Lexington, 1980), 56; Irving, *Bracebridge Hall,* 55, 94; Richard

Chase, *The American Novel and Its Tradition* (Baltimore, 1957), 60–63; and Henry Nash Smith, *Virgin Land: The American West as Symbol and Myth* (Cambridge, MA, 1950), 59–70.

63. KP, autobiographical fragments; and *SB* (1832), 1:119–122.

64. *SB* (1832), 119–122.

65. William Tynes Cowan, "The Slave in the Swamp: Disrupting the Plantation Narrative" (Ph.D. diss., William and Mary, 2001), 105, 109.

66. Reynolds, *Waking Giant,* 175–176.

67. Brenda Stevenson has observed that alcoholism ran across class lines in antebellum Virginia, and the state abounded in "tippling" houses, "grog" shops, and private stills. See *SB* (1832), 1:196–198, 2:80–81; and Brenda E. Stevenson, *Life in Black and White: Family and Community in the Slave South* (New York, 1996), 32–33.

68. Sensationalist novels about the evils of drink began appearing in the 1830s and culminated in the 1854 best seller of all, *Ten Nights in a Bar-Room.* See Joseph R. Gusfield, *Symbolic Crusade: Status Politics and the American Temperance Movement* (Champaign, IL, 1963), 36–57; Howe, *Political Culture,* 170, 184–185; and David S. Reynolds, *Beneath the American Renaissance: The Subversive Imagination in the Age of Emerson and Melville* (Cambridge, MA, 1988), 61, 65–73.

69. Frederick Law Olmsted would later call poor, non-slaveholding whites in the South a "dead peasantry." Other visitors observed that this low class of men had been crowded out of the economy by the slave-owning elite. See Dunn, *Dominion of Memories,* 37–41; Kolchin, *American Slavery,* 179–181; Perry, *Boats Against the Current,* 39–43; and Sellers, *Market Revolution,* 16, 408–409.

70. The sentence, "They were scattered about like chiefs. . . . baronial independence," was removed from the 1851 version of the novel.

71. At the time of *Swallow Barn*'s writing, two-thirds of white males in the Old Dominion could not vote, and the state's antiquated constitution grossly favored the Tidewater aristocracy in the House of Burgesses. See *SB* (1832), 1:74–76; Kolchin, *American Slavery,* 178–179; Dunn, *Dominion of Memories,* 151–154; and Leonard L. Richards, *Slave Power: The Free North and Southern Domination, 1780–1860* (Baton Rouge, 2000), 58–60.

72. Kennedy's use of feudal references and chivalric language has been interpreted in a variety of ways. Michael O'Brien has argued that southern readers could tell when Kennedy was being serious or indulging in a playful "burlesque" of southern manners. On the other hand, Susan Page Ward has suggested that Kennedy employed these devices to show his "affectionate approval" of life in the Old Dominion. Taking a more extreme position, Lewis Simpson has accused Kennedy of using chivalric language to achieve "a ratification of slavery." See O'Brien, *Rethinking the South,* 53–56; Simpson, *Dispossessed Garden,* 44–48; Romine, *Narrative Forms,* 78–79; and Susan Page Ward, "Development of the Theme of Chivalry in Nineteenth-Century Southern Literature" (PhD diss., Duke University, 1980), 49–52.

73. Irving, *Bracebridge Hall,* 19, 22, 27–30, 71–75, 115–122; and *SB* (1832), 1:45–49, 269–275.

74. These romantic allusions are too numerous to cite here. For a small sampling, see *SB* (1832), 1:10–13, 15, 59, 108, 129, 149, 187. The interpolated tale, "The Chronicle of John Smith," occupies thirty-four pages in the 1832 version of *Swallow Barn* and was probably necessary to fill out the two-volume format that was standard at the time. It was almost entirely eliminated from the one-volume 1851 version. See *SB* (1832), 2:281–315; KP, journal entry, Dec. 10, 1829; and Parrington, *Romantic Revolution,* 50–51.

75. Mark Twain's comment that Sir Walter Scott caused the Civil War was never meant to be taken seriously. Yet, historian Rollin Osterweis lent credence to this view in the late 1960s. He argued that southern romanticism was the antebellum South's "third leg," along with slavery and the plantation system. See Rollin G. Osterweis, *Romanticism and Nationalism in the Old South* (Baton Rouge, 1968), 14, 62–63.

76. Jan Lewis has focused on the shift from Enlightenment rationalism to a more emotional mindset in post-Revolutionary Virginia. Harry Hayden Clark and Michael O'Brien have explored the belated transition in southern letters from the neoclassical to romantic style. See Lewis, *Pursuit of Happiness,* 38–39, 68, 115, 191; Simpson, *Dispossessed Garden,* 38–39, 55, 65; Clark, *Transitions in American Literary History,* 110–112, 116, 132; and O'Brien, *Rethinking the South,* 43, 45–47, 53, 74–75.

77. At least three so-called Virginia novels predated *Swallow Barn*—the anonymous *Tales of an American Landlord* (1824), George Tucker's *The Valley of Shenandoah* (1824), and James Ewell Heath's *Edge Hill* (1828). Of these, we know Kennedy read *Edge Hill,* which he described in a letter to his friend Thomas White. However, *Edge-Hill* and *Swallow Barn* have little in common. Slavery as an institution is practically invisible in Heath's novel, and, when slaves do appear, they are treated with utmost respect by the author. Furthermore, Heath's love match between Charles Fitzroyal and Ruth Elmore is poorly developed compared to Kennedy's between Ned Hazard and Bel Tracy. Other Virginia novel conventions–such as the plantation master, the southern belle, and slave dialect—are less well drawn in Heath's novel. More interesting are the similarities between *Edge-Hill* and Kennedy's second novel, *Horse-Shoe Robinson.* See KP, Misc. drafts and notes on *Swallow Barn; SB* (1851), xviii–xix; Taylor, *Cavalier and Yankee,* 148–149, 153; Richard Beale Davis, "Virginia Novels before 'Swallow Barn,'" in *Virginia Magazine of History and Biography* 71, no. 3 (July 1963): 279–289; Boston Public Library, Ms. Gris. 626, Kennedy to Thomas White, Mar. 3, 1834; and James Ewell Heath ["A Virginian," pseud.], *Edge-Hill, or, The Family of the Fitzroyals* (Richmond, 1828), 1:10, 42, 47, 101–102, 186–187, 2:8, 216, 223–224.

78. Michael O'Brien has pointed out that the romanticism of Virginia, especially in the state's Tidewater area, was "lusher, more fanciful" than in the rest of the South. See O'Brien, *Rethinking the South,* 47; and Dunn, *Dominion of Memories,* 24–27, 100–101, 108–109.

79. James McPherson and Paul Quigley have described how the construction of "ethnic nationalism" became codified in the South by 1860. Regional journals and newspapers throughout the region maintained that southerners were descended from different Old World stock than northerners and were ethnically superior to them. See James McPherson, "The Historian Who Saw Through America," *New York Review of Books* 55, no. 19 (Dec. 4, 2008): 45–47; and Paul Quigley, *Shifting Grounds: Nationalism and the American South, 1848–1865* (New York, 2012), 139–144.

80. Rollin Osterweis mistakenly argued that *Swallow Barn* was modeled on the novels of Walter Scott. His suggestion that the character of Miles Rutherford was based on *Ivanhoe*'s swineherd Gurth, for example, is simply wrong. Gurth has too many good qualities, such as bravery and sense of duty, to make such a comparison credible. See Osterweis, *Romanticism and Nationalism,* 62–64; Walter Scott, *Ivanhoe* (1819, reprint, New York, 2001), 33–34, 124, 322; Tracy, *In the Master's Eye,* 53, 57, 68; Romine, *Narrative Forms,* 67–70; Simpson, *Dispossessed Garden,* 44–51; and Davis, "Virginia Novels Before *Swallow Barn,*" 287–293.

81. *SB* (1832), 1:257, 167, 288.

82. Ibid., 1:48, 84, 94, 120.

83. Ibid., 1:168–169, 191.

84. Ibid., 1:279–280, 137–143

85. Ibid., 1:45–46, 176.

86. Catherine Clinton has argued that around 1830 conceptions of womanhood separated, the North celebrating the "frugal housewife" and the South the "cult of chastity." She has also observed that coquetry became "a stable of the southern social scene." See Catherine Clinton, *The Plantation Mistress: Women's World in the Old South* (New York, 1982), 63–64, 93, 97, 137, 173–174.

87. Michael O'Brien has made the point that both southern and northern readers understood and enjoyed the courtship parody in Kennedy's novel. See O'Brien, *Rethinking the South,* 54. For an analysis of female novel reading in the Early Republic, see Cathy N. Davidson, *Revolution and the Word: The Rise of the Novel in America* (New York, 2004), 201–207.

88. Some privileged southern women engaged in charitable work but less so than northern women at this time. The isolation of plantation life and the tendency of southern women to stick to their class inhibited such activity. See Clinton, *Plantation Mistress,* 11–12; Elizabeth Fox-Genovese, *Within the Plantation Household: Black and White Women of the Old South* (Chapel Hill, 1988), 22–23; and Elizabeth R. Varon, *We Mean to Be Counted: White Women and Politics in Antebellum Virginia* (Chapel Hill, 1998), 1–9.

89. Lucinda MacKethan has suggested that Bel Tracy may have been modeled after one of Kennedy's "Dandridge cousins" or after such romantically inclined heroines as Richard Brinsley Sheridan's Lydia Languish and Walter Scott's Di Vernon. See *SB* (1851), xx, xxxiii; and KP, Kennedy to Elizabeth Gray, Aug. 28, 1828.

90. *SB* (1832), 1:42–43.

91. Susan Tracy has argued that Bel Tracy is no more than a "girl-child playing at being a woman." Kathryn Lee Seidel, on the other hand, has written that Bel is an "athletic, talented horsewoman" with an "inner vivacity and passion" that make her memorable. Seidel has suggested that Margaret Mitchell reached back to Bel Tracy to create Scarlett O'Hara. See Tracy, *In the Master's Eye,* 75–76, 87; Kathryn Lee Seidel, *The Southern Belle in the American Novel* (Tampa, 1985), 53, 130; and *SB* (1832), 1:95, 221, 269, 2:138–139.

92. Jacksonian Democracy was a largely male affair and paid far less attention than its Whig opposition to moral issues important to women. Women such as Sara Josepha Hale and Catherine Beecher became extremely active as publicists for the Whig cause. See Howe, *What Hath God Wrought,* 4, 342; Howe, *Political Culture,* 4, 342; and Wilentz, *American Democracy,* 505, 902.

93. KP, Kennedy to Elizabeth Gray, Aug. 11, 1828.

94. Plantation mistresses were expected to maintain their social refinement, regardless of the burden of their plantation duties. See Clinton, *Plantation Mistress,* 20–29, 197–198.

95. *SB* (1832), 1:33–36.

96. Ashland was a six-hundred-acre showplace that boasted a wide variety of crops and livestock, much of it devoted to the improvement of agriculture. Lucretia Clay maintained a spacious greenhouse, a four-acre fruit and vegetable garden, and a large dairy. See Remini, *Henry Clay,* 204–205; Howe, *Political Culture,* 130–131; and David S. Heidler and Jeanne T. Heidler, *Henry Clay: The Essential American* (New York, 2011), 396–398.

97. Scottish moral philosopher Adam Ferguson saw man's progress as necessarily gradual and

evolutionary. Per Ferguson, occasional compromises insured stability. For Clay and other Whigs, compromise and principle were *not* opposites. The preservation of the Union, for example, depended upon continual adjustments of rival interests. Furthermore, as the Whig Party attempted to join together its disparate parts, compromise became increasingly important. Between 1830 and 1835, Clay increased the number of slaves at Ashland from about fifteen to around fifty. See Kohl, *Politics of Individualism,* 24–27, 63–65, 84–85; Howe, *Political Culture,* 15–17, 73–74, 124–125, 139; Thomas Brown, *Politics and Statesmanship: Essays on the American Whig Party* (New York, 1985), 117–118, Marvin Meyers, *The Jacksonian Persuasion: Politics and Belief* (Stanford, 1957), 11–15; and Joel H. Silbey, *The American Political Nation, 1838–1893* (Stanford, 1991), 115–118.

98. Clay had called slavery "an evil" in the Apr. 25, 1798, *Lexington Gazette,* during his first run for Congress. In the Distribution Bill of 1833, Clay proposed that government surpluses from the tariff and federal land sales be given to the states for internal improvements, education, and African colonization. See Remini, *Henry Clay,* 26, 182, 205; Howe, *What Hath God Wrought,* 409; and Freehling, *Prelude to Civil War,* 122.

99. *SB* (1832), 1:101, 232–233, 262.

100. Freehling, *Prelude to Civil War,* 50–51, 110–122, 133; and Dunn, *Dominion of Memories,* 97–99, 103–106, 111.

101. *SB* (1832), 1:215.

102. In his earliest manuscripts, Kennedy called his character "Billy Wart." While Kennedy's portrayal of Wart was humorous but affectionate, there is some evidence that William Wirt did not appreciate being made fun of. See KP, Misc. notes and drafts of *Swallow Barn,* and Wirt to Dabney Carr, May 23, 1832, as quoted in Bohner, *Kennedy,* 84.

103. Nationalistic jurists, whether early Federalists or later Whigs, showed little interest in John Locke's idea of "contractualism" but praised the authority of the law to hold a nation together. See Howe, *Political Culture,* 227–231; and Matthews, *Toward A New Society,* 23–25.

104. *SB* (1832), 1:210, 282, 312.

105. Scott Romine has argued that Kennedy made this episode purposely trivial in order to create an "absence of conflict" in *Swallow Barn.* However, several other scholars have suggested that the Apple-pie episode is about sectional tensions in the Union and their possible resolution. See *SB* (1832), 1:230, 291; Romine, *Narrative Forms,* 81–82; *SB* (1851), xxxiii; and Hare, *Will the Circle Be Unbroken,* 13–14.

106. KP, Misc. notes and drafts of *Swallow Barn.*

107. *SB* (1832), 1:151–152; and KP, Manuscript of *Swallow Barn.*

108. *SB* (1832), 1:57; Kolchin, *American Slavery,* 125–127; Stevenson, *Life in Black and White,* 177–178, 181, 204–205; Walter Johnson, *Soul by Soul: Life Inside the Antebellum Slave Market* (Cambridge, MA, 1999), 214–215; and James Oakes, *The Ruling Race: A History of American Slaveholders* (New York, 1982), 26, 172–173, 277.

109. *SB* (1832), 1:33–34, 75–76, 111, 2:61, 78, 92; Genovese, *Roll, Jordan, Roll,* 145–149; Davis, *Inhuman Bondage,* 228–229; and Kolchin, *American Slavery,* 118–121.

110. *SB* (1832), 1:270–275.

111. Ibid., 1:22–23.

112. Ibid., 1:8.

113. Rockman, *Scraping By,* 231–234; Fields, *Slavery and Freedom,* 62–63; Wade, *Slavery in the Cities,* 328–329; and *Baltimore Patriot,* Jan. 13, May 7, 1830, Mar. 25, 31, 1831, May 27, 1834.

114. While Kennedy revised his 1851 version of *Swallow Barn* to soften the image of the planter class, he actually made some of his descriptions of blacks more disparaging. Sadly, Kennedy's racial views may have hardened over the intervening decades, or, sadder still, he may have thought his revised descriptions were more amusing. See *SB* (1832), 1:11–12.

115. Historians have disagreed on whether antebellum racial prejudice against blacks owed more to historical perceptions or to more recent aspects of American culture. David Brion Davis and Winthrop Jordan have emphasized older influences, while George Fredrickson has favored more recent developments. See Davis, *Inhuman Bondage,* 57, 59, 74–75; George M. Fredrickson, *The Black Image in the White Mind: The Debate on Afro-American Character and Destiny, 1817–1914* (New York, 1971), 35, 37, 41, 48, 50, 74; and Winthrop D. Jordan, *White over Black: American Attitudes Toward the Negro, 1550–1812* (Chapel Hill, 1968), 216–265, 491–511.

116. Philip Morgan has commented on slaves' love of colorful clothes and headgear, often cast-offs from their masters. House slaves especially constructed their own outfits as one way of expressing their individuality and status. See Philip D. Morgan, *Slave Counterpoint: Black Culture in the Eighteenth-Century Chesapeake and Low Country* (Chapel Hill, 1998), 130–132, 599–601, 608–609.

117. David Brion Davis has described Greco-Roman slavery as "proto-racist." Sub-Saharan enslavement by medieval Arabs associated social degradation with dark-skinned races. Winthrop Jordan has pointed out that the English discovery of the chimpanzee (then called orangutan) coincided with northern Europe's earliest involvement with the West African slave trade. See Davis, *Inhuman Bondage,* 57, 59, 73–75; and Jordan, *White Over Black,* 216–265; Jefferson, *Notes on the State of Virginia,* 138–139; and *SB* (1832), 1:116, 155, 2:57, 78, 219.

118. George Fredrickson has suggested that the increase in racial prejudice during the 1830s was related to the rise of egalitarianism and competitive individualism during this period. Baltimore was especially prone to racial conflicts in the 1830s, due to its large number of immigrants and blacks. The autobiography of Frederick Douglass provides a rare description of these tensions from a black perspective. David Roediger and Jean Baker have examined the use of anti-black rhetoric to enlist the Irish as well as other poorer voting groups into the Democratic Party. See Fredrickson, *Black Image,* 41–43; Fields, *Slavery and Freedom,* 33, 47–48; Rockman, *Scraping By,* 255–258; and Douglass, *Narrative of the Life of Frederick Douglass,* 130–133; David R. Roediger, *The Wages of Whiteness: Race and the Making of the American Working Class,* rev. ed. (London, 1991), 140–141, 147–148; and Jean H. Baker, *Affairs of Party: The Political Culture of Northern Democrats in the Mid-Nineteenth Century* (Ithaca, 1983), 77, 86, 221. Minstrelsy became popular in the late 1820s. David Reynolds has called phrenology the "pop psychology of its day." See Reynolds, *Waking Giant,* 232–235, 299–300; Matthews, *Toward A New Society,* 83; and Robert C. Toll, *Blacking Up: The Minstrel Show in Nineteenth-Century America* (New York, 1976), 30, 34, 38–40.

119. The two German pioneers in phrenology were Franz Joseph Gall and Johann Gaspar Spurzheim. In the United States, Bowdoin College, Washington Medical College, and the University of Maryland were early adopters of phrenology in their curricula. Edgar Allan Poe declared that phrenology had "assumed the majesty of science" in the March 1835 issue of the *Southern Lit-*

erary Messenger. See Reynolds, *Waking Giant,* 232–235; Andrew Delbanco, *Melville: His World and Work* (New York, 2005), 200–201; Peter Gay, *Tender Passions: The Bourgeois Experience: Victoria to Freud,* vol. 2 (New York, 2001), 216–117; and www.eapoe.org/works/criticism.

120. *Baltimore Patriot,* Oct. 16, 1830; Reynolds, *Waking Giant,* 233–234; Matthews, *Toward A New Society,* 73–74; and KP, journal entries, Feb. 15, Sept. 28, Dec. 16, 1830.

121. *SB* (1832), 1:116–117, 2:246, 1:11, 2:79.

122. Ibid., 2:78–79.

123. David Reynolds has noted that the "core of minstrelsy humor was the supposedly absurd efforts of blacks to copy the dress and deportment of whites." See Reynolds, *Waking Giant,* 300.

124. Thomas Rice usually sang his signature song at the start of each performance:

"Weel about and turn about
And do jis so,
E'bry time I weel about
I jump Jim Crow."

See Toll, *Blacking Up,* 30–34; David Ewen, *Songs of America* (Westport, 1978), 21–22; and www.streetswing.com/hist.

125. KP, journal entry, Apr. 25, 1831, and autobiographical fragments; *SB* (1832), 1:112; Semmes, *Latrobe,* 187; and *Baltimore Patriot,* Feb. 2, 1834.

126. Irving, *Bracebridge Hall,* 11, 59.

127. *SB* (1832), 2:215–216, 222; 1:31–32; 1:112–113, 32–33; 2:216.

128. The idea of the "trickster" slave seems to have had some African origins. It has been seen as a subtle form of rebellion that allowed the slave some autonomy while keeping his master off balance. See *SB* (1832), 1:31–32, 111–113, 190, 253–254; 2:92; Genovese, *Roll, Jordan, Roll,* 582–583; and Romine, *Narrative Forms,* 75–77.

129. *SB* (1832) 2:92.

130. *SB* (1832), 1:61–62, 52–53, 132, 2:57–58, 62.

131. Irving, *Bracebridge Hall,* 77–79, 91–92; *SB* (1832), 2:225–227.

132. Swift, *Gulliver's Travels,* 225, 262–268, 302.

133. *SB* (1832), 2:215–218.

134. Susan Tracy has identified Kennedy's *Swallow Barn* and William Gilmore Simms's *The Foragers* as the only two southern novels that actually show how slaves lived. See Tracy, *In the Master's Eye,* 143; and *SB* (1832), 2:233–234.

135. Oates, *Fires of Jubilee,* 69–88.

136. The Kennedys left for Virginia from Washington on July 28, 1831, and, according to Kennedy's journal, "spent two weeks at Bath, visiting Cumberland, Winchester, Martinsburg, Charlestown, etc," prior to returning to the Baltimore area on September 1, 1831. See KP, journal entries, July 28, Sept. 1, 1831.

137. *Richmond Compiler,* Aug. 24, 1831; *Richmond Enquirer,* Aug. 26, 1831; *Norfolk Herald,* Aug. 26, 1831.

138. Oates, *Fires of Jubilee,* 96–104.

139. Ibid., 106–108; and KP, journal entries, Sept. 1, Nov. 19, Dec. 31, 1831.

140. Andrew Kennedy delivered a manuscript to the publishers Carey and Lea on Feb. 2, 1832. After negotiating with the firm on Kennedy's behalf, Peter Cruse left the same or another form of the manuscript at the publishers on May 1, 1832. According to Kennedy's journal, *Swallow Barn* became available at Baltimore booksellers on May 18, 1832. See KP, journal entries, Feb. 1, Mar. 1, May 18, 1832.

141. Thomas Gray interviewed Turner on November 1, 1831. Turner was tried two days later and hanged on November 11. Even though so-called trial pamphlets had become hugely popular by the 1830s, Gray's *Confessions* was a standout in terms of sales. See Scot French, *The Rebellious Slave: Nat Turner in American Memory* (Boston, 2004), 47–51; and Kenneth S. Greenberg, *The Confessions of Nat Turner and Related Documents* (Boston, 1996), 8–11.

142. Thomas Ritchie's review of Gray's pamphlet in the *Richmond Enquirer* pointed out that some of the facts in *Confessions* were wrong and that the language Turner used was too sophisticated. Most historians, however, believe that Gray stuck relatively close to the facts as they were known at the time. See Thomas C. Gray, *The Confessions of Nat Turner, Leader of the Late Insurrection in Southampton, Va.* (1831; reprint, Miami, FL, 1969), 4, 6–7, 10; Mary Kemp Davis, *Nat Turner before the Bar of Judgement: Fictional Treatments of the Southampton Slave Insurrection* (Baton Rouge, 1999), 62; Greenberg, *Confessions and Related Documents,* 10–11; and Oates, *Fires of Jubilee,* 175–176.

143. *Richmond Enquirer,* Aug. 30, 1831, Jan. 5, 19, 1832.

144. *Richmond Constitutional Whig,* Sept. 3, 1831; and *Richmond Enquirer,* Jan. 21, 1832.

145. Dunn, *Dominion of Memories,* 49–56; Oates, *Fires of Jubilee,* 37; and Joseph Clarke Robert, *The Road from Monticello: A Study of the Virginia Slavery Debate of 1832* (1941, reprint, New York, 1970), 13.

146. Of the 134 members of the House of Delegates, 60 favored some form of emancipation and a similar number were against it. About a dozen "compromisers" held the balance of power. The voting for and against emancipation divided geographically, with the Blue Ridge Mountains being the divider. Calhoun visited Governor Floyd on December 3, 1831. See Robert, *Road from Monticello,* 20–21, 29–30, 33–38; Dunn, *Dominion of Memories,* 52–56; Howe, *What Hath God Wrought,* 325–326, 401, 407; Oates, *Fires of Jubilee,* 137–139; and the *Richmond Enquirer,* Jan. 19, 24, 26, 1832.

147. Published in Richmond during the fall of 1832, Dew's *Review of the Debate in the Virginia Legislature of 1831 and 1832* was not entirely original in its ideas. The idea that slavery advanced a "primitive" people had been offered up in 1826 by Edward Brown. Nonetheless, historians have come to regard Dew's *Review* as the foundational text for the important shift from the "necessary evil" to "positive good" view of slavery. See Fredrickson, *Black Image,* 44–46; Kolchin, *American Slavery,* 191; Dunn, *Dominion of Memories,* 57–60; Robert, *Road from Monticello,* 52–53; and O'Brien, *Conjectures of Order,* 2:940–941, 944–968.

148. Overseers were generally drawn from the poor white class and were looked down upon by plantation masters. See Forret, *Race Relations at the Margins,* 116–118.

149. *SB* (1832), 2:225–227. Thomas Jefferson had included a passage about slavery being forced on the American colonies in his first draft of the Declaration of Independence. Thomas Dew used the same argument in his *Review.* See Pauline Maier, *American Scripture: Making the Declaration of Independence* (New York, 1998), 113, 121–122, 146–147.

150. *SB* (1832), 2:227–228.

151. James Oakes has stated that whipping was "the disciplinary centerpiece of plantation slavery" and that it became more prevalent during the 1840s and 1850s. Philip Morgan has called the whip slavery's "indispensable and ubiquitous instrument." Kennedy removed this "mode of punishment" argument from the 1851 version of his novel. See *SB* (1832), 2:228-229; Oakes, *Ruling Race,* 159–160, 163, 166–167; and Morgan, *Slave Counterpoint,* 266–267.

152. *SB* (1832), 2:228–229.

153. Kennedy treated Meriwether's "feudatory" scheme even less seriously in the 1851 version of his novel. See *SB* (1832), 2:230–231; and *SB* (1851), 459–460.

154. Richmond *Constitutional Whig,* Sept. 3, 1831; and *Niles' Weekly Review,* Nov. 18, 1831.

155. *SB* (1832), 2:244.

156. Brenda Stevenson has noted the influence of the "elderly slave women" in the slave quarter. Presumably, Meriwether dealt with Lucy in this way before she went mad. See Stevenson, *Life in Black and White,* 227–228; and *SB* (1832), 2:242–244.

157. William Taylor has suggested that Kennedy's sentimental portraits of Abe and his mother, Lucy, "unknowingly prepared the way for writers like Mrs. Stowe." Kennedy used the story of Luke and Walter Hazard to claim that, even when slaves had the opportunity to escape from their masters during the Revolutionary War, they remained loyal. In fact, many slaves used the war to either escape from their masters or join the British forces in the South. Interestingly, this is one element Kennedy may have borrowed from James Ewell Heath's *Edge-Hill,* in which a loyal slave serves beside his master during the war and is rewarded for it. Brenda Stevenson has explained how slaves became a commodity in Virginia, with slave owners showing little respect for the integrity of the slave family. Not only were children increasingly sold to the Deep South without a parent, but the age of slave children sold dropped as low as eight. See *SB* (1832), 2:233–235, 240; Taylor, *Cavalier and Yankee,* 305; Heath, *Edge-Hill,* 2:213–219, 311; Stevenson, *Life in Black and White,* 181, 204–205; Davis, *Inhuman Bondage,* 200–201; Sylvia R. Frey, *Water from the Rock: Black Resistance in a Revolutionary Age* (Princeton, 1991), 224.

158. Lucinda MacKethan has argued that Kennedy became so entangled in the issue of slavery by the end of his novel that he was forced to abandon satire completely and retreat into the romantic form. Richard Chase has suggested that romanticism frees the author from verisimilitude. See MacKethan's introduction to *SB* (1851), xxvi–xxviii; and Chase, *American Novel,* ix, 18–19.

159. Interestingly, this mention of "monotonous avocations" was Kennedy's only allusion to the real drudgery of slave life anywhere in his novel. See *SB* (1832), 2:249, 239–241.

160. Ibid., 2:253. Both Lucinda MacKethan and William Taylor have connected Abe to Nat Turner. See Taylor, *Cavalier and Yankee,* 301–302; and *SB* (1851), xxvi.

161. *SB* (1832), 2:250, 255, 257.

162. Ibid., 2:258.

163. *Swallow Barn* reached booksellers during May 1832. Two thousand copies were printed and were wholesale priced at $1.50 for both volumes (retail pricing was probably in a range of $1.75 to $2.50). After costs, the publishers Carey and Lea made about $1,500 profit. Kennedy received $782 for his efforts. Although the novel sold well, there were no further domestic printings until the 1851 edition appeared. Carey and Lea arranged a copyrighted English edition with Murray, and the novel was published in England in August 1832. See David Kasur, ed., *Cost Book of Carey*

and Lea (Philadelphia, 1963), 114; *The National Union Catalog: Pre-1956 Imprints* (London, 1968), 293:34; and KP, journal entries, Oct. 9, 1832, Apr. 17, 1851.

164. Evidently, Alexander H. Everett was familiar with the *Red Book* and Kennedy's tariff pamphlets. Everett urged Kennedy to devote himself more fully to literature. See "Swallow Barn," review, *North American Review* 36 (1833), 519.

165. *New York Review* and *Baltimore American* (both undated reviews) in KP, "Book reviews and other scraps."

166. The original letter from Kennedy to Carey has been lost. Fortunately, we have Carey's extensive and reiterative reply. See KP, "Letters, correspondence with publishers, 1832–51."

167. *New England Magazine,* July 1832, 77.

168. Taylor, *Cavalier and Yankee,* 71–74, 178–179; and Casper, *Constructing American Lives,* 19–20, 48–50.

169. *SB* (1832), 2:318–320.

4. Tippecanoe and *Horse-Shoe* Too

1. *Baltimore Sun,* July 6, 1840.

2. KP, Kennedy to his wife Elizabeth, July 7, 10, 1840.

3. Even though they did not adopt a formal "platform" at their December 1839 convention in Harrisburg, the Whigs identified what they saw as the worst abuses of the Democratic administration and then defined their issues relative to them. See Holt, *Whig Party,* 104–105; Howe, *What Hath God Wrought,* 574–576; and Altschuler and Blumin, *Rude Republic,* 17–18, 36–46, 79–82.

4. Whig depictions of William Henry Harrison showed the candidate, plow firmly in hand, standing before a small, humble log cabin. In fact, Harrison lived in a palatial dwelling, did little farming himself, and was descended from a line of wealthy Virginia planters. See Robert Gray Gunderson, *The Log-Cabin Campaign* (Lexington, Kentucky, 1957), 4, 169, 74–77.

5. KP, journal entries, Feb. 18, June 18, 1832, Kennedy to wife Elizabeth on Christmas 1832, and scrapbook of newspaper clippings and reviews entitled "Ego"; and Semmes, *Latrobe,* 243–244.

6. Edward Stanwood, *American Tariff Controversies in the Nineteenth Century* (New York, 1903), 1:301; Rezneck, *Business Depressions,* 39; KP, journal entry, Oct. 24, 1831; and *Baltimore Patriot,* Oct. 28, 1831.

7. Freehling, *Prelude to Civil War,* 144–147, 150–153, 204–227; Ellis, *Union at Risk,* 64–68; and Stephanie McCurry, *Masters of Small Worlds: Yeoman Households, Gender Relations, and the Political Culture of the Antebellum South Carolina Low Country* (New York, 1995), 10–18, 64–67, 113–129.

8. "Address to the Friends of Domestic Industry Assembled in Convention, at New York, October 26, 1831, to the People of the United States," in Kennedy, *Political and Official Papers,* 87–89, 109, 120, 133, 137.

9. Ibid., 109–111. Kennedy was influenced by two prominent Baltimore protectionists. One was Daniel Raymond, later known as the founder of American political economy, and the other was Hezekiah Niles, editor of *Niles' Weekly Register.* See Matthews, *Toward A New Society,* 140–141; Rockman, *Scraping By,* 241–242; Howe, *Political Culture,* 110–111; Sellers, *Market Revolution,* 289; and Malcolm Rogers Eiselen, *The Rise of Pennsylvania Protectionism* (Philadelphia, 1974), 49–51.

10. Howe, *Political Culture,* 45, 122, 126–129, 133, 137; Kohl, *Politics of Individualism,* 147–148; and Kennedy, *Political and Official Papers,* 110–111.

11. KP, Kennedy to Elizabeth, Aug. 20, 1840; and Tuckerman, *Kennedy,* 246–252.

12. Reynolds, *Waking Giant,* 64–67; Rockman, *Scraping By,* 148–149; and Sean Wilentz, *Chants Democratic: New York City and the American Working Class, 1788–1850* (New York, 1984), 192, 199–200, 215.

13. North, *Economic Growth,* 69–70; Jefferson, *Notes on the State of Virginia,* 165; Appleby, *Inheriting the Revolution,* 156–57; and Lewis, *Pursuit of Happiness,* 160–164.

14. Daniel Feller, *The Jacksonian Promise: America, 1815–1840* (Baltimore, 1995), 134–136; and Kasson, *Civilizing the Machine,* 41, 81–82.

15. Kennedy, *Political and Official Papers,* 110.

16. Ibid., 134.

17. Ibid., 135–136.

18. Clay first used the term "American System" in an 1820 congressional speech about U.S.–Latin American relations. In March 1824, however, he employed the term in support of the tariff increase of that year. Henceforth, the term became widely recognized as a rubric for nationalistic economic programs such as the tariff, the national bank, and internal improvements. See Heidler and Heidler, *Henry Clay,* 78, 167, 179; Kennedy, *Political and Official Papers,* 109; KP, journal entry, Feb. 2, 1832; and Tuckerman, *Kennedy,* 172–173.

19. The differences between Jackson and Calhoun had a long history, dating back to Jackson's unauthorized military actions in Florida during 1818 and Calhoun's criticism of them (unknown to Jackson at the time but later revealed to him). Divergent views between Jackson and Calhoun over states' rights and the Union came to a head during the April 1830 Jefferson Day dinner. Calhoun's main rival, Martin Van Buren, did his best to undercut Calhoun's standing with Jackson during the Peggy Eaton Affair and at every other opportunity. See Marszalek, *Petticoat Affair,* 54, 79–80, 106, 124–126, 159.

20. Howe, *What Hath God Wrought,* 353–355; Wilentz, *American Democracy,* 361–362; Freehling, *Prelude to Civil War,* 235–244, 251–252; and Remini, *Henry Clay,* 384–389.

21. KP, journal entry, Feb. 18, 1832; Kennedy to his wife, Feb. 10, 14, 1832; Tuckerman, *Kennedy,* 173; Bohner, *Kennedy,* 118; and Gunderson, *Log-Cabin Campaign,* 22–23.

22. Remini, *Henry Clay,* 395–396; Howe, *What Hath God Wrought,* 400–401; and Stanwood, *American Tariff Controversies,* 306–311.

23. The charter of the Second Bank of the United States was not due to expire until 1836. The decision to introduce legislation to recharter the bank during the Twenty-Second Congress turned out to be a fatal miscalculation. See Holt, *Whig Party,* 15–18; Howe, *What Hath God Wrought,* 378–379; and Remini, *Henry Clay,* 388–398.

24. In the presidential election of 1832, Jackson won 55 percent of the popular vote versus 37 percent for Clay and 8 percent for Wirt. Jackson won 219 electoral votes versus 49 for Clay and 7 for Wirt. See Holt, *Whig Party,* 16–17; Wilentz, *American Democracy,* 373–374; and Howe, *What Hath God Wrought,* 383–385.

25. Holt, *Whig Party,* 28–29; Howe, *Political Culture,* 77–78; and E. Malcolm Carroll, *Origins of the Whig Party* (Durham, 1925), 119, 123–125.

26. The kidnapping and suspected murder of stonecutter William Morgan, who planned to publish an exposé of the Masonic Order in 1826, ignited a massive protest movement against Masons in New York State. Partly because of lower-class paranoia over a perceived conspiracy by the power elite, and in part because of grassroots organizing by shrewd anti–Van Buren politicians such as newspaperman Thurlow Weed, the Antimason Party was winning elections handily throughout the North by the late 1820s. See Wilentz, *American Democracy,* 275–279; Holt, *Whig Party,* 12–15; Howe, *What Hath God Wrought,* 266–270; Feller, *Jacksonian Promise,* 102–103; and Ronald P. Formisano, *The Transformation of Political Culture: Massachusetts Parties, 1790s–1840s* (New York, 1983), 197–201.

27. Feller, *Jacksonian Promise,* 66–69; Holt, *Whig Party,* 27; Howe, *Political Culture,* 50–55; Richard Hofstadter, *The Idea of a Party System: The Rise of Legitimate Opposition in the United States, 1780–1840* (Berkeley, 1969), 240–244.

28. Peter Hoffman Cruse died on September 7, 1832. See KP, journal entries, Feb. 16, Oct. 3, Nov. 11, Dec. 3, 1832; Wilentz, *American Democracy,* 373–374; Holt, *Whig Party,* 17–18; and Remini, *Henry Clay,* 409–410.

29. The South Carolina Nullification Convention passed its ordinance declaring both the tariffs of 1824 and 1828 unlawful on November 24, 1832. The state would cease to collect duties after February 1, 1833. See KP, journal entries, Nov. 11, Dec. 3, 1832; and Freehling, *Prelude to Civil War,* 262–264.

30. Kennedy began writing *Horse-Shoe Robinson* on October 11, 1832. While he may have dashed off the first few chapters, Kennedy spent considerable time reworking his second novel, according to his friend John Latrobe. See KP, H. C. Carey to Kennedy, Feb. 29, 1832; journal entry, Oct. 11, 1832; and "Manuscript Notes, Sketches and Drafts for *Horse-Shoe Robinson.*" See, also, Semmes, *Latrobe,* 431–432.

31. With the partial exception of Washington Irving, most American authors had indulged in a kind of postcolonial mimicry of British letters. Cooper's first novel, *Precaution,* was very much in that mode. With *The Spy,* however, Cooper had brought a uniquely American approach to Sir Walter Scott's model for historical romances. Within the next two decades, historical romances became America's favorite form of fiction. In addition to Kennedy's *Horse-Shoe Robinson* (1835), these works would include Catherine Maria Sedgwick's *Hope Leslie* (1827), William A. Caruther's *The Cavaliers of Virginia* (1832), William Gilmore Simms's *Yamassee* (1835), Robert Montgomery Bird's *Nick of the Woods* (1837), D. P. Thompson's *The Green Mountain Boys* (1839), and Charles Fenno Hoffman's *Greyslaer* (1840). Cooper himself added *The Red Rover* (1827), *The Pioneers* (1823), *The Last of the Mohicans* (1826), and *The Deerslayer* (1841) to this stable. See Chase, *American Novel,* 52–54; Wayne Franklin, *James Fenimore Cooper: The Early Years* (New Haven, 2007), 278, 357; and Richard Ruland and Malcolm Bradbury, *From Puritanism to Postmodernism: A History of American Literature* (New York, 1992), 101–102.

32. Unlike with *Swallow Barn,* Kennedy made very few changes between the 1835 edition and later versions of the novel. All *Horse-Shoe Robinson* citations are taken from the 1962 Hafner reprint, with an intro. by Ernest E. Leisy.

33. Kennedy's choice of words in the 1835 preface is interesting. At one point, he argues that the view that the Revolutionary War happened too recently to write about historically has been

"*nullified* by common consent" (emphasis added). Curiously, none of the scholars who have examined *Horse-Shoe Robinson* have connected it to the nullification crisis. However, one need only compare *Horse-Shoe Robinson* with William Gilmore Simms's *The Partisan,* written at the same time and about the same events, to detect Kennedy's underlying agenda in the novel. See *HSR,* ix–xxvi; Ridgely, *Kennedy,* 65–91; Bohner, *Kennedy,* 87–100; Taylor, *Cavalier and Yankee,* 318–319; and Charles H. Brichford, "That National Story: Conflicting Visions of the Revolution in Kennedy's *Horse-Shoe Robinson* and Simms's *The Partisans,*" *Southern Literary Journal* 21 (Fall 1988): 64–85.

34. Before Cooper, historians and novelists had portrayed the American Revolution as a spontaneous, nearly universal uprising against a foreign oppressor, not as a kind of civil war that often divided families and communities. See *HSR,* xx; Parrington, *Romantic Revolution,* 51; and Chase, *American Novel,* 22–23.

35. Natty Bumppo figured prominently in Cooper's *The Pioneers* (1823) and *The Prairie* (1827). Other rough-hewn backwoods types included Nimrod Wildfire in James Kirk Paulding's *The Lion of the West* (1830) and Bron Bones in Washington Irving's "The Legend of Sleepy Hollow" (1820), not to mention the countless frontier humorists and storytellers who worked the lecture circuit or wrote for the penny press during the 1820s and 1830s. J. V. Ridgely has described Robinson as a "shape-shifter and trickster." Ridgely has also argued that Kennedy never really met the real-life Robinson. However, Charles Bohner and Rhoda Coleman Ellison have identified enough about the real "Robinson" (actually named James Robertson) to put the issue of historical origin to rest. Evidently, a newspaperman named Alexander Meeks located an old Revolutionary veteran believed to have been the model for Kennedy's hero in Alabama in 1837 and interviewed him there. "Robinson" (or Robertson) died the following year and was buried in Romulus, Alabama. See *HSR,* 16–18, 54, 309, 539, 541, 546–550; Smith, *Virgin Land,* 60–68, 87; Reynolds, *Beneath the American Renaissance,* 457–458; Ridgely, *Kennedy,* 68, 81; Bohner, *Kennedy,* 98–100; Rhoda Coleman Ellison, "An Interview with Horse-Shoe Robinson," *American Literature* 31 (1959): 329–332; and R. W. B. Lewis, *The American Adam: Innocence, Tragedy, and Tradition in the Nineteenth Century* (Chicago, 1955), 91, 100.

36. Kennedy wrote Thomas White, editor of the *Southern Literary Messenger,* during March 1834 about Heath's *Edge-Hill.* Kennedy said he had read the novel when it first appeared in 1828, owned a copy, and thought it "one of the best romances of our country." See Boston Public Library, Ms. Gris., Kennedy to Thomas White, Mar. 3, 1834; and Heath, *Edge-Hill,* 1:10, 42–47, 104, 183, 2:142–154.

37. Heath's novel has not held up well over time. Richard Beale Davis attributes this to *Edge-Hill*'s plot weaknesses and overly sentimental characterizations. See Davis, *Literature and Society,* 250–254.

38. The character of Mildred Lindsay became so dominant during the writing of Kennedy's novel that he seriously considered naming it after her. At one point, he stated that he was working on his novel "Mildred Lindsay" and, another time, wrote "Horse-Shoe Robinson—or Mildred Lindsay (I don't [know] which I will call it)." See KP, journal entries, Dec. 18, 1832, June 12, 1833.

39. *HSR,* 127–128.

40. *HSR,* 137.

41. John Majewski has noted that writers critical of the slave system often called attention to the desultory, ramshackle appearance of slave-based agriculture in the South in order to illustrate

the system's inferiority to free labor. See John Majewski, *Modernizing a Slave Economy: The Economic Vision of the Confederate Nation* (Chapel Hill, 2009), 46–47; "Swiss Traveller," *Portico* 1, no. 4 (Apr. 1816), 319; and *HSR*, 96.

42. *HSR*, 137–138, 147, 150, 159.

43. According to his notes, Kennedy intended such scenes as Wat Adair's skinning of the live wolf and, later in the novel, Tarleton's trampling of a patriot's grave to shock the sensibilities of his readers and characterize the enemies of the Revolution as immoral and uncivilized. See *HSR*, 171–174, 469, 547; KP, "Manuscript Notes, Drafts and Sketches for *Horse-Shoe Robinson*"; and Daniel Wickberg, "What is the History of Sensibilities? On Cultural Histories, Old and New," *American Historical Review* 112, no. 3 (June 2007): 679–680.

44. *HSR*, 160, 221–223, 230, 432, 496.

45. Ibid., 59.

46. "Swiss Traveller," *Portico* 2, no. 8 (Aug. 1816), 146–147; and *Red Book*, 1:13–15.

47. *HSR*, 63, 151, 87, 119, 372.

48. Ibid., 16–18.

49. Ibid., 17–18, 309. Robinson's character has intrigued both literary critics and intellectual historians, though few have agreed on exactly how to describe it. Charles Brichford has argued that Robinson was "likeable in a way that [Cooper's] Leather-Stocking never is." Ernest Leisy has suggested that Robinson was less "poetical" than Leather-Stocking but much more "social and joyous." William Taylor has detected a trace of the cavalier in Robinson. Whatever their assessments, most scholars have credited Kennedy with developing in Robinson a character of depth and originality. See Brichford, "That National Story," 68–69; Taylor, *Cavalier and Yankee*, 195–196; *HSR* with Leisy intro., xxi–xxii; Ridgely, *Kennedy*, 79, 81; and Ward, "Development of the Theme of Chivalry," 73.

50. *HSR*, 68–75.

51. Ibid., 16, 20–21, 30, 241, 450, 541.

52. William J. Cooper Jr., *The South and the Politics of Slavery, 1828–1856* (Baton Rouge, 1978), 30–32; Holt, *Whig Party*, 28–30, 107; and Gunderson, *Log-Cabin Campaign*, 117, 208, 216.

53. Georgia Spelman has suggested that Robinson may embody Kennedy's vision of the "American industrial worker." In fact, Kennedy's second novel is replete with industrial references. Kennedy opens the novel with mentioning "the spirit of improvement" sweeping across the land. He calls attention to the "hum of industry" and the "clatter of the mill." At one point, Major Butler compares the nation's patriotism to iron mining. "We have not yet exhausted our mines of strength," he tells Mildred Lindsay, "but that much rough ore still lies unturned to the sun." See Georgia Peterman Spelman, "The Whig Rhetoric of John Pendleton Kennedy, Spokesman for Industry" (PhD diss., Indiana University, 1974), 77; and *HSR*, 15,18, 47, 229.

54. *HSR*, 54, 541, 546–550; Howe, *Political Culture*, 21, 29, 131; and Kohl, *Politics of Individualism*, 147–149.

55. Ridgely, *Kennedy*, 80–83; Chase, *American Novel*, 60–63; and Lewis, *American Adam*, 98–100.

56. "Swiss Traveller," *Portico* 1, no. 6 (June 1816), 497–499; *Red Book*, 1:26, 80–83; and *SB* (1832), 1:48, 84, 94, 120, 47.

57. *HSR*, 162–163, 277–284, 377–541; and Machor, *Reading Fiction in Antebellum America*, 76–77.

58. *HSR*, 62, 47, 233, 113.

59. For overall background on women in benevolent societies, see Nancy F. Cott, *The Bonds of Womanhood: "Women's Sphere" in New England, 1780–1835* (New Haven, 1977); Christine Stansell, *City of Women: Sex and Class in New York, 1789–1860* (New York, 1986); and Mary P. Ryan, *Cradle of the Middle Class: The Family in Oneida County, New York, 1790–1865* (New York, 1986). For the role of women in the South, specifically in the Virginia Colonization Society, see Varon, *We Mean to Be Counted*, 42–53. Women were very active in the Maryland chapter of the Colonization Society. Kennedy gave a lecture there in January 1833. See Semmes, *Latrobe*, 145–146; *Baltimore Patriot*, May 7, 1830, Mar. 25, 31, 1831, May 27, 1834; and KP, journal entry, Dec. 12, 1832, and autobiographical fragments.

60. Sara Josepha Hale glorified the American home and became the arbiter of female taste and deportment, first with her *Ladies' Magazine* and later with her *Godey's Lady's Book.* Catherine Beecher, daughter of Henry Ward Beecher and sister of Harriet Beecher Stowe, became a pioneer in women's education and employment. See Howe, *What Hath God Wrought*, 605; Reynolds, *Waking Giant*, 112; Kohl, *Politics of Individualism*, 72–73; Gunderson, *Log-Cabin Campaign*, 4, 8, 121, 131–139; Howe, *Political Culture*, 4, 222; and Taylor, *Cavalier and Yankee*, 115–126. The newspaper quote appeared in the Sept. 3, 1840, *Cleveland Axe*, and has been taken from Gunderson's *Log-Cabin Campaign*, 138.

61. *HSR*, 340. 119, 340, 372, 377, 388, 392, 520. J. V. Ridgely has called the character of Mildred Lindsay a "wax doll." However, Ernest Leisy has suggested that Mildred's resolution is remarkable for the heroine of a historical romance. See Ridgely, *Kennedy*, 77; *HSR* with Leisy intro., xx; and KP, "Notes on *Horse-Shoe Robinson.*"

62. *HSR*, 340.

63. Ibid., 106, 341, 344–345.

64. KP, autobiographical fragments.

65. *HSR*, 82–83, 90–96.

66. Ibid., 90–96, 124, 351–354.

67. The British gothic style was probably a reaction to neoclassical decorum and sentimental novels. Its founding text was Horace Walpole's *The Castle of Otranto* (1764). Charles Brockden Brown pioneered the American gothic style with his novels *Wieland* (1798), *Ormond* (1799), and *Arthur Mervyn* (1800). Brown used his novels to explore psychological instability and madness, themes Edgar Allan Poe would probe more fully in the 1830s. Susan Zieger has called attention to the literary trope of the addicted scholar, one with an "indiscriminate appetite" for knowledge and "dangerous habits of intense study." See Charles Brockden Brown, *Wieland and the Memoirs of Carwin the Biloquist*, with an intro. by Jay Fliegelman (1798; reprint, New York, 1991), xiii, xix; Levin, *Power of Blackness*, xii, 21–22; Susan Zieger, *Inventing the Addict: Drugs, Race, and Sexuality in Nineteenth-Century British and American Literature* (Amherst, 2008), 39–45; and Teresa A. Goddu, *Gothic America: Narrative, History, and Nation* (New York, 2011), 7, 10, 55.

68. Mesmerism spawned professional mesmeric healers, nearly as popular as phrenologists. Originating in Germany, various water treatments were thought to have healing benefits. The Swedish thinker Emmanuel Swedenborg only added to the mass phenomenon of spiritualism. See Reynolds, *Waking Giant*, 226–228, 234–235, 373; O'Brien, *Conjectures of Order*, 426, 435–436,

1068–1069; Matthews, *Toward A New Society,* 72–74, 125–127; and Philip F. Gura, *American Transcendentalism: A History* (New York, 2007), 59–64, 163.

69. KP, autobiographical fragments.

70. *HSR,* 83, 90, 113, 124, 351–352.

71. Ibid., 545, 530.

72. Ibid., 479, 514, 180, 490, 188, 202–205.

73. Ibid., 433–442. In chapter 46, entitled "Rustic Funeral," Kennedy celebrated at length what Victorian culture considered a "good death." John Ramsay died bravely in battle and was afforded a decent burial by his family and friends. See Drew Gilpin Faust, *This Republic of Suffering: Death and the American Civil War* (New York, 2008), 6–17.

74. Brichford, "That National Story," 67; Spelman, "Whig Rhetoric of John Pendleton Kennedy," 77; and Taylor, *Cavalier and Yankee,* 200–201.

75. *HSR,* 536–539, 542–548.

76. The author of the original edition of *Horse-Shoe Robinson* was identified as "Mark Littleton, author of *Swallow Barn,*" and the book was dedicated to Washington Irving. *Horse-Shoe Robinson* was by far Kennedy's most popular novel and was reprinted twenty-two times. In 1836, the novel was dramatized for the New York stage by Clarence Dane. A second stage version was produced in 1856 by C. W. Tayleure. In 1897, the novel was condensed for school children. See *National Union Catalog,* 293:34; KP, journal entry, Apr. 17, 1851; Ridgely, *Kennedy,* 84–85; and Bohner, *Kennedy,* 97–98.

77. The letter from Irving to Kennedy is quoted in Tuckerman, *Kennedy,* 166–171.

78. Slavery and slaves are treated very marginally in *Horse-Shoe Robinson.* On one occasion, Widow Dimrock's slave Tony talks back to his owner, as Carey does in *Swallow Barn.* Neither Mildred's young slave Endymion nor her older slave Isaac make more than momentary appearances. See *HSR,* 58, 374, 388, 401; and KP, "Book Reviews and other scraps, 1832–51," and "Ego."

79. Edgar Allan Poe worked at the *Southern Literary Messenger* from December 1835 until January 1837. The magazine had a variety of sponsors and contributors, among them Thomas Dew and James Heath, reflecting a wide range of views on slavery. See Robert D. Jacobs, "Poe in Richmond: The Double Image," in R. C. Simonini Jr., *Southern Writers: Appraisals in Our Time* (Freemont, NY, 1961), 39–47; and Terence Whalen, "Average Racism: Poe, Slavery, and the Wages of Literary Nationalism," in J. Gerald Kennedy and Liliane Weissberg, *Romancing the Shadow: Poe and Race* (New York, 2001), 9–19.

80. Poe harbored a distrust of what he called "omni-prevalent Democracy," which, he believed, could lead to social and racial instability. Poe also cultivated, according to Betsey Erkkila, "a kind of aristocracy of the mind," seeing intellectuals like himself above the masses. See Levin, *Power of Blackness,* 257; Betsey Erkkila, "Poetics of Whiteness: Poe and the Racial Imaginary," in Kennedy and Weissberg, *Romancing the Shadow: Poe and Race,* 49–50, 55–56; and *Southern Literary Messenger* 1, no. 9 (May 1835): 522–524, available at http://quod.lib.umich.edu.

81. Latrobe debunked as "sheer fabrication" the commonly told story that Kennedy bought Poe a suit of clothes and sent him off to take a bath. Nonetheless, Poe was poverty stricken and living with an old aunt in Baltimore at the time of the contest. See Semmes, *Latrobe,* 559; KP, journal entry, Nov. 11, 1833; Ridgely, *Kennedy,* 66, 86; and Machor, *Reading Fiction in Antebellum America,* 90.

82. Robert Jacobs has observed that Poe was given to "self-dramatization." See Jacobs, "Poe in Richmond," 21; and Boston Public Library, Ms. Gris., Kennedy to Poe, Mar. 3, 1834, Sept. 19, 1835; and Poe to Kennedy, Sept. 11, 1835, Jan. 22, 1836, Oct. 25, 1845.

83. Poe was found delirious in the streets of Baltimore. He died at a local hospital on October 7, 1849. In his journal, Kennedy said that Poe had stopped in Baltimore en route from Richmond to New York, where he was living, and "fell in with some companion here who seduced him to the bottle." See KP, journal entry, Oct. 10, 1840.

84. Philadelphia had its "Wistar Club," Charleston its "Conversation Club," and the Boston area its "Transcendentalist Club." The Monday Club lasted from 1831 until 1840 or 1841. See O'Brien, *Conjectures of Order,* 426–427; and KP, "Monday Club. Private journal of certain events. March 18, 1835–October 26, 1840."

85. KP, journal entry, June 12, 1833; and Tuckerman, *Kennedy,* 363–364.

86. President Jackson's "Proclamation" was issued on December 10, 1832. The details of what became the "Force Bill" were debated in Congress until the bill's passage on February 20, 1833. The bill was probably misnamed, since only a small section of it authorized use of military force to suppress the nullifiers if necessary. The Verplanck Bill was brought forward by Julian G. Verplanck, House member from New York and a free trader. See Charles M. Wiltse, *John C. Calhoun: Nullifier, 1829–1839* (New York, 1949), 171–187; Freehling, *Prelude to Civil War,* 286–292; Remini, *Henry Clay,* 421–422; and Heidler and Heidler, *Henry Clay,* 251–256.

87. The idea for a Clay-sponsored tariff bill probably originated with his brother-in-law and ex-Louisiana senator James Brown. Among the northern industrialists who encouraged Clay was E. I. DuPont. See Remini, *Henry Clay,* 224–225; Peterson, *Great Triumvirate,* 218–219; Howe, *What Hath God Wrought,* 406–408; and Heidler and Heidler, *Henry Clay,* 252–253.

88. KP, journal entry, July 13, 1833.

89. Ibid.

90. Peterson, *Great Triumvirate,* 230–231; Freehling, *Prelude to Civil War,* 292–293; Wiltse, *Calhoun,* 185–186; and Remini, *Henry Clay,* 427–428.

91. Howe, *What Hath God Wrought,* 408; Peterson, *Great Triumvirate,* 218–219; and Heidler and Heidler, *Henry Clay,* 253–254.

92. Jackson went along with the Clay-Calhoun tariff because his advisers warned him that his confrontation with states' rights men was tearing the party apart. Still, when the Senate reconvened in late 1833, six southern members declared themselves anti-Jackson men. For the most part, South Carolina settled down politically after the crisis. A lot of this had to do with the sharp rise in cotton prices. See Freehling, *Prelude to Civil War,* 287; Howe, *What Hath God Wrought,* 408–409; Holt, *Whig Party,* 39–40, 46; and Cooper, *South and the Politics of Slavery,* 47–49.

93. Rezneck, *Business Depressions,* 82–83; and *New York Spectator,* Oct. 17, 1833.

94. Kennedy addressed the American Institute on October 17, 1833. The address was published in the December 1833 *Mechanics Magazine.* See Probst, *Happy Republic,* 10–12.

95. George Leggett was a radical Jacksonian "Loco-Foco" who believed that government should not tamper with the social order or private industry. Leggett was so laissez faire that he even opposed the post office. See Meyers, *Jacksonian Persuasion,* 30–31, 191–195, 202.

96. Marvin Meyers has suggested that Jacksonian reform, whether directed at the Second

Bank of the United States or federally funded internal improvements, was essentially a "dismantling operation." See Meyers, *Jacksonian Persuasion,* 25; and Probst, *Happy Republic,* 12–13.

97. *New-York American,* Oct. 23, 1833; *New York Spectator,* Oct. 17, 1833; and KP, journal entry, Nov. 7, 1833.

98. Several historians, Michael Holt and Daniel Howe among them, have argued that Jackson's "removal" program was the galvanizing event that brought the anti-Jackson opposition together. See Holt, *Whig Party,* 23–24, 28–30; Howe, *What Hath God Wrought,* 386–393, 402; Meyers, *Jacksonian Persuasion,* 195–198; and Wilentz, *American Democracy,* 392–401.

99. Semmes, *Latrobe,* 401; Walsh and Fox, *Maryland,* 200–201, 271–273; Browne, *Baltimore in the Nation,* 122–125; Bohner, *Kennedy,* 119–120; Howe, *What Hath God Wrought,* 343, 393; *Proceedings and Votes,* Jan. 1, 1823; and KP, journal entry, Dec. 10, 1833.

100. By 1836, twenty-eight Democratic congressmen who had voted against rechartering the bank had switched parties over the issue of removal. See Howe, *What Hath God Wrought,* 386–390, 402; Wilentz, *American Democracy,* 397; Holt, *Whig Party,* 26; and Carroll, *Origins of the Whig Party,* 117, 119, 123–124.

101. Because the Whigs used Jackson's alleged executive tyranny to rally their disparate forces, some historians have suggested that the Whig Party was about personal politics and lacked substance. However, Michael Holt and Daniel Howe have argued that the enlargement of presidential power was itself a real issue. Even historian Sean Wilentz, no admirer of the Whigs, has concurred with this view. See Holt, *Whig Party,* 27–30; Howe, *What Hath God Wrought,* 390–392; Remini, *Henry Clay,* 456–459, 463–464; Heidler and Heidler, *Henry Clay,* 266–267; Wilentz, *American Democracy,* 402; and Richard P. McCormick, *The Second American Party System: Party Formation in the Jacksonian Era* (Chapel Hill, 1966), 163–165.

102. James Harrington (1611–1677) wrote his great republican work, *The Commonwealth of Oceana,* in 1656. See Howe, *Political Culture,* 77–79, 216–217; and Bailyn, *Ideological Origins,* 8–9, 71, 77.

103. Jackson's response to the Senate's motion of censure, better known as his "Protest," was published on April 18, 1834. Jackson maintained that, if such a measure became necessary, impeachment by the House of Representatives was the only recourse for Congress. Jackson also defended a president's right to organize his cabinet as needed and to deposit federal funds where he thought best. See Holt, *Whig Party,* 24–25; and Howe, *What Hath God Wrought,* 391–392.

104. *Baltimore Patriot,* Apr. 24, 1834.

105. *Baltimore Patriot,* Apr. 24, 1834; Walsh and Fox, *Maryland,* 273; and KP, "Ego."

106. Walsh and Fox, *Maryland,* 274–274; and Holt, *Whig Party,* 34–37.

107. Cotton played the leading role in the economic boom of the 1830s. The value of cotton exports increased from $25 million in 1831 to $71 million in 1836. Federal land sales during the same period rose from $4 million to $16 million. See North, *Economic Development,* 194–197; Rezneck, *Business Depressions,* 75; and Peter Termin, *Jacksonian Economy* (New York, 1969), 124.

108. Historians have argued about the causes of the 1837 Panic. Blame has been assigned to the Jackson administration, eastern bankers, land speculators, and British merchants and bankers. Most historians have characterized Jackson's hard-money policy as naïve and his Specie Circular as ill timed. See Termin, *Jacksonian Economy,* 13–17, 124; North, *Economic Development,* 194–199,

202–203; Wilentz, *American Democracy,* 349, 437; Howe, *What Hath God Wrought,* 395; Holt, *Whig Party,* 37; and Jessica M. Lepler, *The Many Panics of 1837: People, Politics, and the Creation of a Transatlantic Financial Crisis* (New York, 2013), 47, 53, 107–108, 178, 189.

109. Holt, *Whig Party,* 41–49; Remini, *Henry Clay,* 479–481; and Heidler and Heidler, *Henry Clay,* 272–275.

110. Holt, *Whig Party,* 61; and Lepler, *Many Panics of 1837,* 108, 150–151.

111. Walsh and Fox, *Maryland,* 201; Rockman, *Scraping By,* 154–155; and KP, "Ego," and journal entry, Aug. 16, 1836.

112. Wilentz, *American Democracy,* 402–403, 436; Howe, *What Hath God Wrought,* 430–434; and Harriet Martineau, *Society in America* (1837; reprint, New York, 1962), 108–109.

113. Reznick, *Business Depressions,* 77–78; and Sellers, *Market Revolution,* 354–356.

114. Resnick, *Business Depressions,* 81–85; and Lepler, *Many Panics of 1837,* 107–108, 150–155, 184–187.

115. Regarding the Whig view of history, William Taylor has written that "Beneath a surface of seemingly imperturbable optimism . . . ran a strong undercurrent of fear and uneasiness." Similarly, Lawrence Kohl has observed that, "If Whig hopes were utopian, their fears were apocalyptic." See Taylor, *Cavalier and Yankee,* 127–128; Kohl, *Politics of Individualism,* 68; Reynolds, *Waking Giant,* 281–284; and Howe, *Political Culture,* 49, 73–75.

116. Kennedy, *Rob of The Bowl,* 7. Kennedy's third novel is the most difficult of the author's works to find today. I have used the 2007 reprint from Kessinger Publishing's Rare Imprints series. As with *Horse-Shoe Robinson,* Kennedy made few changes between the original and later editions.

117. Charles Bohner has gone to some lengths to verify the historical basis of Kennedy's novel. See Bohner, *Kennedy,* 102–109.

118. For Kennedy's thoughts on historical fiction, see Kennedy, *At Home and Abroad,* 37. For the acceptability of fictional embellishments of historical novels among nineteenth-century readers, see Lionel Gossman, *Between History and Literature* (Cambridge, MA, 1990), 94–96; and Avrom Fleishman, *The English Historical Novel: Walter Scott to Virginia Woolf* (Baltimore, 1971), 23–26. Sir John Falstaff appeared in Shakespeare's *Henry IV* and *The Merry Wives of Windsor.* Mistress Quickly, the hostess of the Boar's Head Tavern, also appears in several of Shakespeare's plays. See Bohner, *Kennedy,* 100–112; Ridgely, *Kennedy,* 92–110; and Taylor, *Cavalier and Yankee,* 200–201.

119. William Taylor has suggested that Kennedy's Old Catholic Maryland was a somewhat desperate attempt to develop a "Cavalier myth" to counter the "Puritan myth" of the North. More plausibly, J. V. Ridgely has argued that *Rob of The Bowl* "is not the image of seventeenth-century Maryland but a projected view of nineteenth-century America." See Taylor, *Cavalier and Yankee,* 200–201; and Ridgely, *Kennedy,* 102–105.

120. *ROTB,* 4–5, and 9.

121. Ibid., 49, 55–56.

122. Ibid., 9–10, 26, 51.

123. Ibid., 46–50, 162–163.

124. Ibid., 3, 48, 158–160, 170–171.

125. Ibid., 51, 53–54, 111, 115, 218, 222, 224–230, 287.

126. Ibid., 49.

127. The 1820s and 1830s saw numerous offshoots from mainstream Protestantism. While some were "evangelicalized" denominations, a number were distinctly new sects and cults. See Whitney R. Cross, *The Burned-Over District: The Social and Intellectual History of Enthusiastic Religion in Western New York, 1800–1850* (New York, 1950); William G. McLoughlin, *Revivals, Awakenings, and Reform* (Chicago, 1978); *Baltimore Patriot,* Sept. 29, 1826; Tuckerman, *Kennedy,* 229; and Remini, *Henry Clay,* 654.

128. Holt, *Whig Party,* 30–32, 270–272, 674, 729; Howe, *Political Culture,* 50–51, 138, 244; and Hofstadter, *Idea of a Party System,* 22–23, 32–33, 223–226.

129. *ROTB,* 10, 17, 26, 35–36, 230–233.

130. Ibid., 61, 96–97, 207–210, 258–263.

131. Ibid., 18, 31–33, 93–94, 96–97, 207–210, 258–263.

132. Ibid., 18, 118, 124, 162.

133. Ibid., 132–143. Van Buren had a serious image problem, according to his biographer Ted Widmer. Short and a particularly neat dresser with large whiskers, Van Buren lent himself to lampooning. Since he had neither military experience nor much education, he was suspected of using trickery to achieve his political success. See Cooper, *South and the Politics of Slavery,* 144; and Ted Widmer, *Martin Van Buren* (New York, 2005), 132–133.

134. *ROTB,* 267, 277–278, 316–320.

135. The *Gentleman's Magazine* was edited by William Evans Burton and Edgar Allan Poe. Poe had moved there after leaving the *Southern Literary Messenger.* The review was probably written by Burton. See *Gentleman's Magazine* 4 (May 1839): 65; Bohner, *Kennedy,* 111; Ridgely, *Kennedy,* 112–113; and *National Union Catalog,* 293:34.

136. Semmes, *Latrobe,* 431; Bohner, *Kennedy,* 123–124; and KP, "Manuscript Notes on *Rob of The Bowl.*"

137. *Baltimore Patriot,* July 8, 27, 1837, Apr. 14, 26, 27, 1838; KP, Kennedy to Philip Pendleton, July 22, 1838; and Bohner, *Kennedy,* 123–125.

138. William M. Gouge had proposed the independent treasury in his 1833 *History of Banking and Paper Money,* which soon became the Bible of hard-money Democrats. See Remini, *Henry Clay,* 501–506; Wilentz, *American Democracy,* 460–463; and Heidler and Heidler, *Henry Clay,* 291, 318–319.

139. "The Sub-Treasury Speech, Delivered in the House of Representatives, on the 22nd and 23rd June, 1838," in Kennedy, *Political and Official Papers,* 187–191.

140. Ibid., 201–204.

141. Remini, *Henry Clay,* 558, 586; Heidler and Heidler, *Henry Clay,* 319, 323, 359; and Howe, *What Hath God Wrought,* 507, 591, 815.

142. "Speech on the Bill Making Appropriations for Civil and Diplomatic Services for the Year 1839," in Kennedy, *Political and Official Papers,* 190–192, 207–210, 228–266.

143. Ibid., 214, 219, 240–241, 250- 252. The *Globe* was founded by Francis P. Blair and began publishing in December 1830. It replaced Duff Green's *Telegraph* as the Democratic Party organ. Martin Van Buren felt the *Telegraph* was too supportive of Calhoun. See W. Stephen Belko, *The Invincible Duff Green: Whig of the West* (Columbia, MO, 2006), 188–190.

144. Bohner, *Kennedy*, 128.

145. KP, journal entry, Dec. 15, 1839.

146. The word "quodlibet" means a question posed as a philosophical exercise. In *Rob of The Bowl*, Jasper Dauntrees used the word in this way: "There was a thesis debated, a quodlibet wrangle concerning some knot in the cobweb of theology." See KP, journal entry, Dec. 24, 1839; *ROTB*, 187; and *Quodlibet*, 3, 47, 155, 186.

147. Kennedy, *Quodlibet*, 2–3, 29–30.

148. Historian Donald Cole has suggested that the character of Eliphalet Fox was based on Amos Kendall, the editor of the Jacksonian newspaper *Globe*. Possibly, Fox was a composite of Amos Kendall and James Cox. See Kennedy, *Quodlibet*, xviii, 2–3, 29–30, 47–49, 82–84, 113, 154; Walsh and Fox, *Maryland*, 266, 282; Browne, *Baltimore in the Nation*, 95; Bohner, *Kennedy*, 132, 136–137; and Cole, *A Jackson Man: Amos Kendall*, 226–227.

149. Vernon Parrington has described *Quodlibet* as "the most vivacious criticism of Jacksonianism in our library [and] one of our few distinguished political satires." See Parrington, *Romantic Revolution*, 55.

150. Kennedy, *Quodlibet*, 139, 144, 149–153, 156, 132–133.

151. Ibid., 145–146.

152. Ibid., 107–108.

153. Ibid., 65.

154. Ibid., 127–129.

155. This passage is reminiscent of Swift's *Gulliver's Travels*, where the learned men at the Academy of Lagado carry sacks of *things* around for non-verbal discourse. "[S]ince words are only *things*, it would be a convenience . . . to carry such *things* as were necessary to explain [a] particular business." See Swift, *Gulliver's Travels*, 188–189; Kennedy, *Quodlibet*, 58–59, 118; and Kennedy, *Political and Official Papers*, 250.

156. Kennedy, *Quodlibet*, 56, 155, 158.

157. Ibid., 169–170.

158. Ibid., 199–200, 208–209.

159. The first-ever Whig national convention met in Harrisburg, Pennsylvania, on December 4, 1839. Reverdy Johnson, head of the Maryland Whig Party, attended, but evidently Kennedy did not. Regarding William Henry Harrison, the *Baltimore Republican* wrote on December 11, 1839, "Give him a barrel of hard liquor, and settle a pension of two thousand dollars a year on him, and, my word for it, he will sit out the remainder of his days in his log cabin." The *Albany Evening Post* quotation has been taken from Michael Holt. See Holt, *Whig Party*, 101, 104, 106–107; Widmer, *Martin Van Buren*, 133–135; and Gunderson, *Log-Cabin Campaign*, 75–77.

160. Kennedy, *Quodlibet*, 112–114, 142–143, 237; and KP, Kennedy to his wife, Oct. 21, 1840.

161. *Quodlibet* was reprinted in 1843, 1860, and, most recently, 1970. Although never a popular work, *Quodlibet* was praised by John Quincy Adams, William Gilmore Simms, and other prominent figures when it first came out. See Ridgely, *Kennedy*, 116–117; Bohner, *Kennedy*, 134–138; and KP, journal entry, Dec. 6, 1840.

162. KP, journal entry, Dec. 6, 1840.

163. Holt, *Whig Party*, 112–113.

5. Return to *Swallow Barn*

1. KP, journal entry, Feb. 8, 1841.

2. Clay's comment regarding Harrison's health was included in a Dec. 8, 1840, letter to Peter Porter and is quoted in Remini, *Henry Clay,* 576. See also, Holt, *Whig Party,* 122–123; and KP, journal entry, Feb. 22, 1841.

3. Holt, *Whig Party,* 110, 124–125; Remini, *Henry Clay,* 568–570; and KP, journal entries, Jan. 26, Feb. 22, 1841.

4. KP, journal entry, Mar. 7, 1841; Howe, *What Hath God Wrought,* 569; and Widmer, *Martin Van Buren,* 142.

5. KP, journal entry, Mar. 22, 1841.

6. Holt, *Whig Party,* 104; and *Niles' National Register,* Nov. 28, 1840.

7. KP, journal entries, Mar. 22, 31, Apr. 3, 1841; and Kennedy, *Political and Official Papers,* 220.

8. KP, journal entries, Apr. 4, 7, 17, 20, May 17, 29, 1841; Bohner, *Kennedy,* 143–145; and Holt, *Whig Party,* 122–123.

9. Holt, *Whig Party,* 129–136; Howe, *What Hath God Wrought,* 591–594; Wilentz, *American Democracy,* 524–525; and Remini, *Henry Clay,* 581–599.

10. Webster remained in Tyler's cabinet allegedly to complete negotiations with the British on the Webster-Ashburton Treaty. After concluding the treaty in November 1842, however, Webster stayed in the Tyler cabinet until May 1843. See Holt, *Whig Party,* 133–135; Cooper, *South and the Politics of Slavery,* 178–180; and Peterson, *Great Triumvirate,* 329–334.

11. KP, Kennedy to Philip Pendleton, July 13, 1841, and journal entries, Sept. 17, 19, 1841.

12. Ibid., journal entries, Sept. 19, 1841, July 5, 1842; *Niles' National Register,* Sept. 18, 1841; Holt, *Whig Party,* 137–138; and Bohner, *Kennedy,* 149.

13. Holt, *Whig Party,* 139, 148, 150–151, 154; Remini, *Henry Clay,* 606–610, 658; and Peterson, *Great Triumvirate,* 357.

14. Bohner, *Kennedy,* 158–61; Tuckerman, *Kennedy,* 178–180; and KP, journal entry, July 5, 1842.

15. This passage was part of a letter from Kennedy to his friend Josias Pennington and is quoted from Tuckerman, *Kennedy,* 185.

16. The Cape Palmas settlement was never successful economically and was under constant pressure from surrounding tribes. It would eventually be merged with Liberia to the North. See P. J. Staudenraus, *The African Colonization Movement, 1816–1865* (New York, 1961), 176, 190, 308; and John Pendleton Kennedy, *Report of Mr. Kennedy, of Maryland, from the Committee on Commerce of the House of Representatives of the United States on the African Slave Trade* (1843; reprint, Freeport, New York, 1971), 7, 68, 84.

17. Howe, *What Hath God Wrought,* 593, 765; and Stanwood, *American Tariff Controversies,* 1:326–327.

18. Cave Johnson of Tennessee was responsible for turning Kennedy's first attempt to pass the telegraph bill into a joke. The bill passed the House by a vote of 89 to 83 with numerous abstentions on Feb. 25, 1843. See Bohner, *Kennedy,* 145–157; Howe, *What Hath God Wrought,* 1–3, 670–698; and Carleton Mabee, *The American Leonardo: A Life of Samuel F. B. Morse* (New York, 1943), 258–259.

19. "A Defense of the Whigs," in Kennedy, *Political and Official Papers,* 317, 388, 440, 356; and KP, journal entry, Mar. 27, 1843, and Henry Clay to Kennedy, Dec. 3, 1843.

20. Kennedy, *Political Papers,* 319–325.

21. New England Federalists met from Dec. 15, 1814, to Jan. 5, 1816, to discuss their grievances with the War of 1812, geographic enlargement of the country, and southern political power. Some radicals at the meeting recommended succession. The term "Hartford Convention Federalist" became synonymous with subversion and treason. See James M. Banner, *To the Hartford Convention: The Federalists and the Origins of Party Politics in New England* (New York, 1970), 109–112; and Kennedy, *Political and Official Papers,* 319–325, 328–329, 323.

22. Kennedy, *Political and Official Papers,* 323, 325, 329, 330–331.

23. Ibid., 343, 341, 338, 351.

24. Maryland Federalists held on to power much longer than they did in other states. They lived on as "Blue Lights" and "Coodies" well into the 1820s. William Cooper has pointed out that southern Whigs "made Jackson into a Federalist, who maligned the Constitution in the spirit of the Adamses and Alexander Hamilton." See Walsh and Fox, *Maryland,* 163, 242–244, 256–257; Haller, "Rise of the Jacksonian Party in Maryland," 307–308; and Cooper, *South and the Politics of Slavery,* 54–55.

25. Kennedy, *Political and Official Papers,* 345–346, 349–350.

26. Ibid., 393–396, 417, 420, 443–444.

27. Remini, *Henry Clay,* 658; Peterson, *Great Triumvirate,* 357; Holt, *Whig Party,* 160–166; and KP, Kennedy to his wife, Sept. 1, 1844.

28. President Tyler had urged Congress to approve an annexation treaty as early as 1842. John C. Calhoun took over the job of secretary of state in April 1844, after Abel Upshur was killed in an explosion at a naval review. In July 1845, John O'Sullivan, editor of the magazine *Democratic Review,* coined the term "Manifest Destiny." See Holt, *Whig Party,* 170–173; Wilentz, *American Democracy,* 562–564; and Edward L. Widmer, *Young America: The Flowering of Democracy in New York City* (New York, 1999), 50–51.

29. Howe, *Political Culture,* 101, 140–141, 187.

30. Dangerfield, *American Nationalism,* 65–69; Remini, *Henry Clay,* 639–641; Holt, *Whig Party,* 172–177; and Heidler and Heidler, *Henry Clay,* 386–387.

31. The Pakenham Letter was used by Calhoun to fan fears that Britain intended to sign its own treaty with Texas and abolish slavery there. Evidently, Calhoun intended his letter to split the two national parties along sectional lines and place him in the leadership of the southern factions. Why Tyler went along with Calhoun's letter remains a mystery. See Holt, *Whig Party,* 171–172; Peterson, *Great Triumvirate,* 346–347; Wilentz, *American Democracy,* 566–567; and Cooper, *South and the Politics of Slavery,* 191–204.

32. Kennedy dated his Texas letter May 17, 1844. The letter appeared in the *Baltimore Patriot* on May 19, the *Baltimore American* on May 22, and the *National Intelligencer* on May 21, 1844. See "Letter on the Annexation of Texas," in Kennedy, *Political and Official Papers,* 604–614; and KP, journal entry, Oct. 13, 1844.

33. Kennedy, *Political and Official Papers,* 607–609.

34. While treaty agreements required a two-thirds vote in the Senate, new states could be admitted to the Union with a majority vote and a joint resolution. See Holt, *Whig Party,* 173; Howe,

What Hath God Wrought, 680; and KP, journal entry, Oct. 13, 1844.

35. Holt, *Whig Party,* 180–181; Peterson, *Great Triumvirate,* 363–365, 381; Remini, *Henry Clay,* 660–661; and Heidler and Heidler, *Henry Clay,* 390–391.

36. Holt, *Whig Party,* 156–157, 184, 187–195, 200, 203–205; Peterson, *Great Triumvirate,* 363, 365; Heidler and Heidler, *Henry Clay,* 390–392; and Tyler Anbinder, *Nativism and Slavery: The Northern Know Nothings and the Politics of the 1850s* (New York, 1997).

37. Clay's Nov. 20, 1844, letter to Seward is quoted from Remini, *Henry Clay,* 664. Greeley's Nov. 13, 1844, editorial is from Holt, *Whig Party,* 199. Kennedy's letter appeared in the *New York Tribune* on Nov. 29, 1844, and is from Bohner, *Kennedy,* 165. See, also, Heidler and Heidler, *Henry Clay,* 392.

38. Michael Holt has traced the unsigned *American Review* article to Kennedy through a letter from the magazine's owner, George H. Colton, to Kennedy. See Holt, *Whig Party,* 206–207, 212–213.

39. Ibid., 233–237, 246–247. Much of the credit for building up the Whigs' national organization went to Connecticut congressman Truman Smith, who, according to Michael Holt, was "the closest equivalent to a modern national party chairman."

40. Ibid., 251–255; Howe, *What Hath God Wrought,* 828–829; and Robert W. Merry, *A Country of Vast Designs: James K. Polk, the Mexican War, and the Conquest of the American Continent* (New York, 2009), 285–289.

41. Howe, *What Hath God Wrought,* 826–827; Anbinder, *Nativism and Slavery,* 11, 27, 30; and Reynolds, *Beneath the American Renaissance,* 64–66.

42. Jean H. Baker, *Ambivalent Americans: The Know-Nothing Party in Maryland* (Baltimore, 1977), 4–7; and KP, journal entry, July 12, 1845.

43. Holt, *Whig Party,* 229; and KP, journal entry, Jan. 2, 1846.

44. KP, journal entries, June 9, 1845, Apr. 11, 18, 25, May 2, 1847.

45. Ibid., journal entries, Dec. 24, 1843, Mar. 18, 1846.

46. Ibid., July 12, 1845, Mar. 18, Nov. 28, 1846.

47. Ibid., Jan. 30, 1841, Sept. 30, 1842, July 12, 1845.

48. The major problem was that Maryland had insisted on continuing both the Chesapeake and Ohio Canal and the Baltimore and Ohio Railroad, when it was clear that only the latter project was viable. See Walsh and Fox, *Maryland,* 290–297; and KP, journal entry, Mar. 11, 1847.

49. Clay's quote is from Remini, *Henry Clay,* 684–785. See, also, Heidler and Heidler, *Henry Clay,* 413–417; Howe, *What Hath God Wrought,* 776–778; and KP, journal entries, Apr. 16, 21, 24, 1847.

50. KP, journal entry, Sept. 13, 1847; and Bohner, *Kennedy,* 176–177.

51. Holt, *Whig Party,* 244–246; Walsh and Fox, *Maryland,* 292–293; and KP, journal entries, Oct. 7, 11, 1847.

52. Holt, *Whig Party,* 292.

53. KP, journal entries, Apr. 11, 17, 1847.

54. Ibid., journal entries, Jan. 8, 12, Feb. 28, Mar. 4, 18, Sept. 26, Oct. 26, 1848; and Holt, *Whig Party,* 269–272.

55. It would be a mistake to say that Kennedy and Crittenden viewed the Taylor boom in the same way. Kennedy was far more interested in preserving the integrity of the Whig Party, whereas

Crittenden fully supported the idea of transforming the party into what became known as "Taylor Republicanism." See KP, journal entries, Nov. 30, Dec. 5, 1847, Jan. 6, 7, 8, Mar. 16, Apr. 14, 15, 25, 27, June 9, 1849; and Holt, *Whig Party,* 397, 405–409, 427.

56. The radical Philadelphia newspaper editor and author of the popular novel *Quaker City,* George Lippard, had met with Taylor to sound out his alleged nonpartisanship. Taylor's letter back to Lippard was widely published and helped bring disaffected Democrats into the Taylor camp. See Holt, *Whig Party,* 360–361.

57. Ibid., 368–381. Taylor captured 1,361,000 votes versus 1,222,000 for the Democratic candidate Lewis Cass. Taylor's electoral margin was 163 to 127. Voter turnout declined from 79 percent in 1844 to 73 percent in 1848.

58. KP, journal entries, Jan. 1, Mar. 4, 5, 6, 1848.

59. Ibid., journal entries, Mar. 5, Apr. 18, May 5, 1849, May 5, 1850; and Ridgely, *Kennedy,* 122–123.

60. Casper, *Constructing American Lives,* 4–5, 34–35, 39–40, 52–61; Widmer, *Young America,* 108–112; Bohner, *Kennedy,* 112, 180–183; Hubbell, *South in American Literature,* 238–239, 490–491; and Machor, *Reading Fiction in Antebellum America,* 31, 48, 76, 81.

61. KP, journal entry, Jan. 27, 1848.

62. Scott Casper has pointed out that many nineteenth-century biographies had clear didactic aims. They provided models for emulators who read and learned from them. See Casper, *Constructing American Lives,* 54; and Kennedy, *William Wirt,* 1:23, 43–44, 48.

63. Kennedy, *William Wirt,* 2:210–213.

64. Ibid., 2:233–234.

65. Ibid., 2:58, 104, 161, 166–167, 169.

66. Ibid., 2:170, 194, 297.

67. Ibid., 2:273–274.

68. William Gilmore Simms, "Kennedy's Life of Wirt," in *Southern Quarterly Review* 17 (Apr. 1850): 192–236.

69. Ibid., 193, 198–199, 201, 204, 206. Simms argued that Kennedy *had* described the full personality of Wirt, to include his joyous and often playful nature. Most critics disagree with this view of Kennedy's biography.

70. Ibid., 197–198, 206, 214–215. Simms believed Wirt's acceptance of the Antimason Party's nomination for president was completely foolish and an example of his vanity. However, Simms believed Wirt had been a hard-working and wise attorney general.

71. Ibid., 228–229.

72. The Treaty of Guadalupe Hidalgo, ratified by the Senate on March 10, 1848, added a huge land mass called the "Mexican Cession" to the United States. It included land in the current states of California, New Mexico, and parts of Arizona, Colorado, Utah, and Oklahoma. The Free-Soil and abolitionist movements were different. The Free-Soil Party was concerned with the livelihood of free white laborers in the North and not at all with enslaved blacks in the South. See KP, journal entry, Mar. 6, 1849; Howe, *What Hath God Wrought,* 809–810; Holt, *Whig Party,* 387–388, 467, 484; and David M. Potter, *The Impending Crisis, 1848–1861* (New York, 1976), 36–37, 72, 80.

73. After the election of 1848, John Crittenden, the original architect of "Taylor Republicanism," chose to remain governor of Kentucky. John Clayton of Delaware became secretary of state and took the creation of a new Taylor party to its limits. Clayton denied patronage to orthodox

Whigs and wanted to eliminate the name "Whig" altogether. See Holt, *Whig Party,* 406–409, 414–418, 435; and William F. Hartford, *Money, Morals, and Politics: Massachusetts in the Age of the Boston Associates* (Boston, 2001), 119–120.

74. KP, journal entries, Mar. 20, Apr. 7, May 10, 11, June 4, Sept. 28, Oct. 4, 12, 1849, Jan. 10, 24, 1850.

75. Ibid., journal entry, Oct. 12, 1849.

76. Remini, *Henry Clay,* 716; and KP, journal entry, Nov. 29, 1849.

77. Remini, *Henry Clay,* 728, 732–733.

78. Entire books have been written about the Compromise of 1850. Clay began to campaign for his compromise in the Senate on January 29, 1850, and continued until August 1, when the so-called Omnibus Bill (a bundled version of his legislation, which Clay had unwisely agreed to) came unraveled and Clay departed Washington in frustration. During his absence, however, Congress passed the various parts of Clay's bill into law with some modifications. In the end, Clay received credit for the compromise and was widely lauded for saving the Union. Taylor's words are quoted from David Potter, *Impending Crisis,* 91. See also Holt, *Whig Party,* 478–480; Remini, *Henry Clay,* 732–734; and Heidler and Heidler, *Henry Clay,* 462–468.

79. Holt, *Whig Party,* 497; and KP, Kennedy to Rufus Griswold, Mar. 9, 1850, and Joseph Gale to Kennedy, Mar. 3, 1850.

80. Holt, *Political Crisis,* 87–89; and Heidler and Heidler, *Henry Clay,* 468–475.

81. Holt, *Whig Party,* 231, 460- 461, 543, 551.

82. Rufus Griswold's *American Review* competed with John O'Sullivan's *Democratic Review* to set the standards of American literary taste. George Putnam was a Whig but associated with the Democratic "Young America" literary circle that included Cooper and Nathaniel Hawthorne. After the Civil War, David Hunter Strother would become an even more successful illustrator using the pseudonym of "Porte Crayon." See Widmer, *Young America,* 38, 102, 104, 108, 120; Bohner, *Kennedy,* 186, 193; and KP, journal entries, July 12, 1845, Dec. 14, 1847, Oct. 10, Nov. 18, 1849.

83. Putnam reprinted *Horse-Shoe Robinson* in 1852 and *Rob of The Bowl* in 1854. See *SB* (1832), 1:20, 28, 116–117, 2:32, 56–58, 231–315, 258; *SB* (1851), 27–28, 34, 37, 107, 308, 310, 495–500; and *National Union Catalog,* 293:34.

84. *SB* (1832), 1:116–117, 2:56–58; and *SB* (1851), 107, 308, 310.

85. *SB* (1851), 453–454.

86. Ibid., 454–455.

87. Men like Samuel George Morton and Josiah Nott argued for the theory of polygenesis, while J. L. Cabell of the University of Virginia held to the unity of mankind idea. Eric Lott has persuasively argued that white audiences at minstrel shows both envied and despised the carefree attitudes and spontaneous musical expressions of blacks. See Fredrickson, *Black Image,* 25–27, 52–59, 74, 83, 87; and Eric Lott, *Love and Theft: Blackface and the American Working Class* (New York, 1993), 8–9, 40, 49–50.

88. KP, journal entries, Oct. 21, 1848, July 19, 1849.

89. *SB* (1851), 453, 456, 474–475; and Fredrickson, *Black Image,* 44–45.

90. Howe, *Political Culture,* 46, 168; Kolchin, *American Slavery,* 125–127, 174–175; Reynolds, *Waking Giant,* 186–193; and Davis, *Inhuman Bondage,* 202–203.

91. *SB* (1851), 459.

92. Ibid., 558.

93. *SB* (1832), 2:229–231; and *SB* (1851), 457, 459–460.

94. *SB* (1832), 2:227; and *SB* (1851), 455, 458.

95. "Kennedy's Swallow Barn, or a Sojourn in the Old Dominion," *Southern Quarterly Review* 5, no. 9 (Jan. 1852): 82–86 (Review signed "J. G. B."). See also *Southern Literary Messenger* 17, no. 11 (Dec. 1851): 764.

96. Simms wrote to Kennedy on May 12, 1852. See Simms, *Letters of William Gilmore Simms,* 122–123, and KP, journal entries, Sept. 18, Oct. 11, 1851, and "Ego" scrapbook.

97. *Uncle Tom's Cabin* ran in the *National Era* from May 1851 to April 1852 and was published in book form by J. P. Jewitt of Boston in March 1852. See KP, Kennedy to William Gilmore Simms, Mar. 8, 1851; Parfait, *Publishing History of* Uncle Tom's Cabin, 14, 17, 69–70; and David S. Reynolds, *Mightier than the Sword:* Uncle Tom's Cabin *and the Battle for America* (New York, 2011), 121–129.

98. Stowe indulged in what some critics have called "romantic racism" or the idea that blacks were more gentle and spiritual than whites. Susan Zieger has observed that Simon Legree, as a cruel, drunken slave owner, performs "specific cultural work" in Stowe's novel. See Harriet Beecher Stowe, *Uncle Tom's Cabin* (Boston, 1852; reprint, with an intro. by Darryl Pinkney, New York, 1998), ix, xix–xx, 376–377; Reynolds, *Waking Giant,* 370–371; and Ziegler, *Inventing the Addict,* 81–85.

99. Winfield Scott and Millard Fillmore were deadlocked for most of the balloting. Daniel Webster, who commanded enough votes to give Fillmore the nomination, refused to withdraw from the contest. Scott was initially an anti-Compromise Whig but switched positions at the convention. Henry Clay died on June 29, 1852. The Greeley quote appears in both Holt and Gienapp. See Holt, *Whig Party,* 712–724; and Gienapp, "Whig Party," 399–415.

100. The Kennedy quote about Fillmore is from Michael Holt, *Whig Party,* 605–606. See also Wilentz, *American Democracy,* 651–652; and KP, journal entry, July 12, 1852.

101. The "Codfish War" traced its origins back to the Treaty of Ghent in 1818. In 1852, the British navy began seizing American fishing vessels in areas where the British insisted that they had exclusive fishing rights. While Perry's expedition has been substantially written about, Kane's has not. Elisha Kent Kane made two voyages to Greenland in search of the lost British explorer Sir John Franklin during 1851 and 1852. See KP, journal entries, July 28, 30, Sept. 14, 1852; Kennedy, *Political and Official Papers,* 505; Tuckerman, *Kennedy,* 222–223, 217–233; and Bohner, *Kennedy,* 206–207.

102. The 1852 Democratic convention in Chicago was also a troubled event. Lewis Cass and Stephen Douglas were deadlocked for the presidential nomination until the party turned to dark horse Franklin Pierce on the forty-eighth ballot. See Casper, *Constructing American Lives,* 195–201; Holt, *Whig Party,* 712, 717, 737, 754; and Richards, *Slave Power,* 183–184.

103. Holt, *Whig Party,* 737, 754, 761; and KP, journal entry, Nov. 2, 1852.

6. The Quarter Revisited

1. The Kansas-Nebraska Act began as an attempt by Illinois senator Stephen A. Douglas to organize the Nebraska Territories for transcontinental railroad building. Once set in motion, how-

ever, neither Douglas nor President Franklin Pierce could resist southern pressure to repeal the Missouri Compromise and replace it with "popular sovereignty," or the right of new states formed north of the old compromise line to be free or slave. The so-called Know-Nothings burst onto the scene in the fall 1854 elections. Horace Greeley gave the party its name because of its penchant for secrecy. In January 1855, the *Albany State Register* declared the Whig Party defunct. See Holt, *Whig Party,* 803, 839–840, 911; Potter, *Impending Crisis,* 146–176, 237–239; Wilentz, *American Democracy,* 671–677; and Anbinder, *Nativism and Slavery,* 52–60, 100–102.

2. Eric Foner, *Free Soil, Free Labor, Free Men: The Ideology of the Republican Party Before the Civil War* (New York, 1970), 243, 247–256; Holt, *Political Crisis,* 176–177; William E. Gienapp, *The Origins of the Republican Party, 1852–1856* (New York, 1987), 419–420; and Douglas R. Egerton, *Year of Meteors: Stephen Douglas, Abraham Lincoln, and the Election that Brought on the Civil War* (New York, 2010), 102, 113.

3. Kennedy's colleague was John N. Reynolds. See Kennedy to Reynolds, Nov. 18, 1854, and Feb. 27, 1855, KP, "Letters from May 1853 to November 1855." For cooperation between Kennedy and Fillmore in forming the Know-Nothing alliance, see Holt, *Whig Party,* 801–802, 857, 907–909, and 929.

4. Baker, *Ambivalent Americans,* 35, 41; and Holt, *Whig Party,* 912–913.

5. Charles Bohner has accused Kennedy of being a nativist. See Bohner, *Kennedy,* 165–167; and KP, journal entries, Dec. 15, 1839, Oct. 7, 11, 1847.

6. Tuckerman, *Kennedy,* 33, 95, 409–411; Hugh Henry Brackenridge, *Modern Chivalry* (1815; reprint, New Haven, 1965), 219–226, 242–245; *ROTB,* 49, 56–58; and KP, journal entry, Mar. 12, 1848, and Kennedy to James J. Ryan, May 9, 1848.

7. *SB* (1832), 2:376–384; *ROTB,* 14, 20–24, 132–145; *William Wirt,* 1:15; Tuckerman, *Kennedy,* 362; and KP, journal entry, Aug. 13, 1855.

8. Baker, *Ambivalent Americans,* 29, 34–35, 40–41, 96–97; Brown, *Baltimore in the Nation,* 196–210; Walsh and Fox, *Maryland,* 304–306, 310; Holt, *Whig Party,* 934–935; and KP, Kennedy to R. C. Winthrop, Feb. 21, 1856.

9. The Know-Nothing convention divided over the controversial "Section Twelve" of the party's platform, endorsing the finality of the Kansas-Nebraska Act. Armed conflict between pro- and antislavery settlers in Kansas quickly exposed the dangers of "popular sovereignty." Among the worst events of this guerilla war were the "sack of Lawrence" and the "Pottawatomie massacre," both in May 1856. The brutal caning of Senator Charles Sumner by House representative Preston Brooks occurred on May 21, 1856, after Sumner's highly provocative speech against Andrew Butler of South Carolina. See Anbinder, *Nativism and Slavery,* 206–211; Cooper, *South and the Politics of Slavery,* 366–369; Potter, *Impending Crisis,* 207–214; and Wilentz, *American Democracy,* 677–693.

10. Potter, *Impending Crisis,* 209–211, 254–255, 261–265; and Holt, *Whig Party,* 966–981.

11. Thackeray's *The Virginian* was serialized in the British periodical *Punch* from 1857 through 1859. See Tuckerman, *Kennedy,* 296, 364; Bohner, *Kennedy,* 218–220; KP, "Journal of a Tour in Europe beginning August 1857 ending October 1858," and journal entries, Sept. 26, 30, Oct. 4, 1858, Jan. 17, 1864; and W. M. Thackeray, *The Virginians* (Philadelphia, 1868), vol. 2, chap. 4, 38–40.

12. Baker, *Ambivalent Americans,* 4–10; and Walsh and Fox, *Maryland,* 314–330.

13. Dred Scott claimed he had become free by residing in the Wisconsin Territory, north of the Missouri Compromise line. However, the Supreme Court under Roger B. Taney ruled

that Congress had exceeded its powers with its 1820 Compromise legislation. The accusations of collusion between Buchanan and the Supreme Court arose from a letter from Buchanan to a member of the court about the case, as well as an alleged conversation about it between Taney and Buchanan at his inauguration. Kansans were divided between the free-state Topeka and the proslavery Lecompton governments. See Potter, *Impending Crisis,* 267–327; Holt, *Political Crisis,* 201–206; Richards, *Slave Power,* 200–206; and James M. McPherson, *Battle Cry of Freedom: The Civil War Era* (New York, 1988), 178–179.

14. The newspaper was the April 14, 1860, *Cecil Democrat* (Elton, Maryland). The reference is from Jean H. Baker, *The Politics of Continuity: Maryland Political Parties from 1858 to 1870* (Baltimore, 1973), 40–41. See also Tuckerman, *Kennedy,* 140–142, 264–265.

15. KP, Kennedy to Philip Pendleton, May 11, Sept. 29, 1859.

16. KP, journal entry, Oct. 17, 1859.

17. The raid on Harper's Ferry took place on Oct. 18, and Brown was hung on Dec. 2, 1859. Brown had received encouragement and financial support from the "Secret Six," a group of Unitarian, antislavery intellectuals in Boston. See KP, journal entries, Oct. 17, 18, 19, 1859, Jan. 8, 1860; Tuckerman, *Kennedy,* 308–309; McPherson, *Battle Cry of Freedom,* 210–211; Tony Horwitz, *Midnight Rising: John Brown and the Raid that Sparked the Civil War* (New York, 2011), 210, 214–215; William L. Barney, *The Road to Secession: A New Perspective on the Old South* (New York, 1972), 146–154; and W. Caleb McDaniel, *The Problem of Democracy in the Age of Slavery: Garrisonian Abolitionists and Transatlantic Reform* (Baton Rouge, 2013), 226.

18. The Democratic convention met in Charleston on April 23, 1860. After ten days, the southern Democrats, led by "fire-eater" William Lowndes Yancey, bolted the gathering. See KP, journal entry, Apr. 20, 1860; Wilentz, *American Democracy,* 755–757; and Egerton, *Year of Meteors,* 65–82.

19. KP, journal entries, Jan. 25, Feb. 3, 9, 13, 20, 1860; Potter, *Impending Crisis,* 416–417; and Egerton, *Year of Meteors,* 87–88.

20. KP, journal entries, Apr. 1, 18, May 8, 9, 1860.

21. The Constitutional Union convention met on May 9, 1860. Twenty-three states attended, but the Upper South dominated the gathering. Most historians agree that John Bell was probably a poor choice as a presidential candidate. At sixty-three, he looked older than his years and was a dull, uninspiring speaker. See KP, journal entries, May 10, 23, 1860; Potter, *Impending Crisis,* 416–417; Hartford, *Money, Morals, and Politics,* 80, 98, 100, 198; Egerton, *Year of Meteors,* 82–97; and Don Green, "Constitutional Unionists: The Party that Tried to Stop Lincoln and Save the Union," *Historian* 69, no. 2 (Summer 2001): 231–235.

22. Mark Neely has compared 1860 campaign lithographs by William H. Rease to point out the rich imagery of the Republicans versus the blandness of the Constitutional Union Party. See KP, Kennedy to Crittenden, Feb. 20, 1860, and journal entries, Feb. 20, Apr. 19, May 10, June 18, 1860; Green, "Constitutional Unionists," 234–235, 252; Egerton, *Year of Meteors,* 91–97, 97–98, 113; Mark E. Neely Jr., *The Boundaries of American Political Culture in the Civil War Era* (Chapel Hill, 2005), 31–35; and Baker, *Politics of Continuity,* 41.

23. The northern Democrats nominated Illinois senator Stephen A. Douglas as their presidential candidate and the southern Democrats John C. Breckenridge, a Kentuckian and the sitting vice president. The southerners chose Joseph Lane of Oregon as their vice-presidential candidate. Douglas selected Alabama senator and slave owner Benjamin Fitzpatrick as his running mate.

When Fitzpatrick came under heavy pressure not to run, the northern Democrats substituted Herschel V. Johnson, the moderate governor of Georgia. See KP, journal entry, June 25, 1860; Holt, *Political Crisis,* 205–208; Wilentz, *American Democracy,* 755–758; and Egerton, *Year of Meteors,* 8–13, 154–170.

24. The Republican strategy in 1860 was to add the "lower North" to Fremont's 1856 win. The tariff would play a significant role in winning Pennsylvania. See Potter, *Impending Crisis,* 215, 422–429, 245; Holt, *Political Crisis,* 214–217; Foner, *Free Soil,* 191, 202–203, 214–216, 234; and Egerton, *Year of Meteors,* 131–143.

25. In the election of 1860, Lincoln won 1,865,908 popular votes versus Douglas's 1,380,202, Breckenridge's 848,019, and Bell's 590,901 (electoral votes were 180, 12, 72, and 39, respectively). See Holt, *Political Crisis,* 215–220, 226–232; Wilentz, *American Democracy,* 764–767; McPherson, *Battle Cry of Freedom,* 221–225; Adam Goodheart, *1861: The Civil War Awakening* (New York, 2011), 40, 47–48, 51–52; and Stephanie McCurry, *Confederate Reckoning: Power and Politics in the Civil War South* (Cambridge, MA, 2010), 39–49.

26. KP, journal entries, Nov. 9, 20, 26, 28, 1860.

27. George Peabody contributed $1,400,000 to establish the Peabody Institute in Baltimore. While its original charter called for a broad range of cultural activities, the Peabody today focuses on music education. See KP, journal entries, Apr. 1, 21, May 1, 6, June 19, 22, July 1, 14, 1860, Feb. 4, 1861; Tuckerman, *Kennedy,* 199, 390–399; and Ray Edwin Robinson, "The History of the Peabody Conservatory of Music" (PhD diss., Indiana University, 1969), 42, 51, 59, 75.

28. Lincoln's message appeared in newspapers on Dec. 4, 1860. The South Carolina convention passed its ordinance of secession on Dec. 20, 1860. See Wilentz, *American Democracy,* 769; and KP, journal entries, Dec. 4, 17, 21, 1860.

29. Tuckerman, *Kennedy,* 264–265.

30. Egerton, *Year of Meteors,* 303–308; and KP, journal entries, Nov. 9, Dec. 16, 17, 19, 20, 22, 1860, Feb. 4, 1861.

31. KP, journal entries, Dec. 25, 1860, Jan. 7, 1861; Egerton, *Year of Meteors,* 307–308; and Robert Gray Gunderson, *The Old Gentlemen's Convention: The Washington Peace Conference of 1861* (Madison, 1961), 25, 43–44.

32. Egerton, *Year of Meteors,* 309–310; and Bohner, *Kennedy,* 136–137.

33. Gunderson, *Old Gentlemen's Convention,* 47, 53, 84–85; and KP, journal entries, Feb. 15, 22, 1861.

34. The seven seceding states in the Deep South adopted the provisional constitution of the Confederate States of America in Montgomery, Alabama, on February 7, 1861. The peace conference proposal went down to defeat in the Senate on March 4, 1861, Inauguration Day. See Potter, *Impending Crisis,* 498–499; Egerton, *Year of Meteors,* 314–315; and KP, journal entries, Apr. 13, 14, 1861.

35. Egerton, *Year of Meteors,* 73–75; and "The Border States," in Kennedy, *Political and Official Papers,* 514–586.

36. Kennedy, *Political and Official Papers,* 578–579.

37. Ibid., 579–580.

38. The view that northern reform movements had helped bring on the Civil War persisted long after Kennedy's time. Writing in the early part of the nineteenth century, revisionist his-

torians such as Ulrich Phillips and William Dunning portrayed northern reformers as reckless, misguided fools. See Kennedy, *Political and Official Papers,* 557–583; James McPherson, "What Drove the Terrible War?" in *New York Review of Books* 58, no. 12 (July 12, 2011): 34–35; and Andrew Delbanco, *The Abolitionist Imagination* (Cambridge, MA, 2013), 17–21, 84–85.

39. Examples of Kennedy's growing conservatism include his support for the Fugitive Slave Law and his praise for President Fillmore's enforcement of it, as well as his advocacy of flogging while secretary of the navy. He believed its abolishment in 1850 had undermined shipboard discipline. See Holt, *Whig Party,* 605–606; KP, Robert Winthrop to Kennedy, Dec. 23, 1852; and Allan Nevins, *Ordeal of the Union* (New York, 1947), 1:121.

40. KP, journal entries, Apr. 16, 18, 1861.

41. The mob attacked the Massachusetts Sixth on April 19, 1861. General Benjamin Butler occupied Baltimore on May 14. See KP, journal entries, Apr. 19, 20, 23, 1861; Walsh and Fox, *Maryland,* 336–351; and James M. McPherson, *Tried by War: Abraham Lincoln as Commander in Chief* (New York, 2009), 26–30, 49.

42. The "Great Drama" appeared in the *Baltimore American* on May 11 and the *National Intelligencer* on May 14, 1861. Kennedy signed it "E. Pluribus Unum," but he was soon identified as the author. See KP, journal entries, Apr. 20, 25, May 1, 9, 11, 15, 1861; and the *National Intelligencer,* May 14, 1861.

43. KP, journal entries, May 16, 18, 21, 30, June 1, 1861.

44. Ibid., journal entries, Apr. 25, Dec. 25, 1861, Mar. 1, 1862, and Kennedy to Robert C. Winthrop, Jan. 21, 1862; and Tuckerman, *Kennedy,* 314–315.

45. KP, journal entry, July 4, 1861.

46. Ibid., journal entries, Jan. 4, May 30, 1861.

47. Ibid., July 22, Nov. 20, 1861. Britain declared its neutrality in the American conflict on May 14, 1861. Still, the Union defeat at Bull Run and the passage of the highly protective Morrill Tariff earlier in the year soured relations between the two countries. See KP, journal entry, Oct. 20, 1861; and Amanda Foreman, *A World on Fire: Britain's Crucial Role in the American Civil War* (New York, 2010), 86, 92–94, 139–141.

48. Kennedy was guarded about his White House meetings. Only when they were concluded did he add a "footnote" explaining the secret mission in the margins of his journal. See KP, journal entries, Oct. 20, 21, 22, 26, Nov. 4, 8, 1861; and Foreman, *A World on Fire,* 87, 164–165.

49. According to Kennedy's account of the meeting, the diplomatic dispatch was from John Motley, an American historian living in England and someone Seward trusted. An example of the favorable turn in British attitude is a comment by George Campbell, Duke of Argyll and member of Lord Palmerston's ministry, reported in the *Illustrated London News*: "Gentlemen, I think we ought to admit, in fairness to the Americans, that there are some things worth fighting for, and that national existence is one of these." See KP, journal entries, Nov. 7, 8, 1861; and Foreman, *A World on Fire,* 34–35, 92–93, 95, 163–164.

50. The mission that eventually went to Europe consisted of Charles McIlvaine; John Hughes, Catholic archbishop of New York; General Winfield Scott, now retired from his army command; and Thurlow Weed, Seward's close friend and former political manager. The *Trent* affair commenced on November 8, 1861, when Union navy captain Charles Wilkes forcefully boarded the British mail ship *Trent* and took Confederate emissaries James Mason and John Slidell prisoner.

See Foreman, *A World on Fire,* 164, 175–177, 189–190, 196; Walter Stahr, *Seward: Lincoln's Indispensable Man* (New York, 2012), 307–323; and Alexander DeConde, *A History of American Foreign Policy,* 2nd ed. (New York, 1971), 245–248.

51. In the fall 1861 elections for the Maryland governorship and state legislature, the Union Party defeated the States' Rights Party, 57,502 votes to 26,070. See KP, journal entries, Nov. 7, 8, 9, 11, 18, 1861; and Walsh and Fox, *Maryland,* 352–355.

52. KP, journal entries, Dec. 4, 11, 13, 1861.

53. Anthony Trollope, *North America,* (Leipzig, 1862), 1:8, 13–14, 18–19.

54. KP, journal entries, Nov. 8, 9, Dec. 10, 1862; and Foreman, *A World on Fire,* 5, 62, 80–81, 354–355, 388, 453–454.

55. KP, journal entries, Oct. 21, 23, Nov. 2, 11, Dec. 17, 20, 28, 1861, June 18, Sept. 22, 1862.

56. James M. McPherson, *Crossroads of Freedom: Antietam* (New York, 2002), 91–92; Richard Slotkin, *The Long Road to Antietam: How the Civil War Became a Revolution* (New York, 2012), 151, 154-159; and KP, journal entry, Sept. 12, 1862.

57. KP, journal entry, Sept. 7, 1861.

58. Ibid., journal entry, Sept. 18, 1861; and McPherson, *Crossroads of Freedom,* 129–131.

59. Lincoln's Preliminary Emancipation Proclamation was issued on September 22, 1862. It threatened to free all slaves in the seceding states if they did not return to the Union by the end of the year. Slaves would not be affected in the Border States, including West Virginia, which had been created by Congress in June. Lincoln was actively exploring colonization schemes at the time of his preliminary proclamation. However, he made no further mention of colonization and shut down all projects associated with it after issuing his final proclamation on January 1, 1863. See KP, journal entries, Jan. 5, Sept. 30, Oct. 4, 5, 1862; Stahr, *Seward,* 343, 347; and Eric Foner, *The Fiery Trial: Abraham Lincoln and American Slavery* (New York, 2010), 219, 230–237, 239, 258–259.

60. Stuart stayed at The Bower from September 28 to October 26, 1862, except for two days when he and 1,800 of his men made their raid on Chambersburg, Pennsylvania. Kennedy's parents lived at The Bower after leaving Baltimore, and his father died there in 1836. See Bohner, *Kennedy,* 223–224; Burke Davis, *Jeb Stuart: The Last Cavalier* (New York, 1957), 209–214, 236–240; and Henry Kyd Douglas, *I Rode With Stonewall* (Chapel Hill, 1940), 188–189.

61. Marylanders approved a new constitution on October 13, 1864, by the narrowest of margins. Slaves freed by the new constitution were denied the vote and public schooling for their children. See KP, journal entries, Jan. 1, 2, 1863; Walsh and Fox, *Maryland,* 370–377; and Foner, *Fiery Trial,* 274–277.

62. The Battle of Gettysburg lasted from July 1 through July 3, 1863. It was the bloodiest battle of the war and, according to Allen Guelzo, its pivotal engagement. Kennedy was probably inspired to write "Mr. Ambrose's Letters" by Sidney G. Fisher's essay "The Trial of the Constitution" at the end of 1862. After reading it, Kennedy wrote in his journal, "I wish I could write something of this kind that would be useful in the present difficulties." See KP, journal entry, Dec. 26, 1862; and Allen C. Guelzo, *Gettysburg: The Last Invasion* (New York, 2014), 413–421, 462–465.

63. All citations are from the 1865 book version of "Mr. Ambrose Letters." See John P. Kennedy, *Mr. Ambrose's Letters on the Rebellion* (New York, 1865), iii, vii, 6, 20, 46.

64. Ibid., 90–95.

65. Ibid., 103–105. The most famous filibusterer was William Walker, who temporarily gained

control of Nicaragua and briefly became its president. Walker had earlier led a small army into the State of Sonora, Mexico. Another southern radical, John Quitman, helped fund several abortive expeditions to Cuba. Narciso Lopez, led a large expedition of mostly Americans to the island in 1851. His force was wiped out, and Lopez was garroted at Morro Castle. See Barney, *Road to Secession,* 74–76; Robert E. May, *Southern Dreams of a Caribbean Empire, 1854–1861* (Baton Rouge, 1973), 25–28, 47, 88–113, 129–131; Tom Chaffin, "'Sons of Washington': Narciso Lopez, Filibustering, and U. S. Nationalism, 1848–1851," *Journal of the Early Republic* 15, no. 1 (Spring, 1995): 79–108; Matthew Pratt Guterl, *American Mediterranean: Southern Slaveholders in the Age of Emancipation* (Cambridge, MA, 2006), 22–27, 94–103; and Walter Johnson, *River of Dark Dreams: Slavery and Empire in the Cotton Kingdom* (Cambridge, MA, 2013), 328–351, 363–364, 369–371.

66. George Bickley had earlier founded a chapter of George Lippard's secret labor organization, the "Brotherhood of the Union," in Wayne, Virginia, and borrowed most of his organizational structure, secret ritual, and costumes from Lippard. David Keehn has exhaustively researched the Knights but ignores their roots in Lippard's organization. See David C. Keehn, *Knights of the Golden Circle: Secret Empire, Southern Secession, Civil War* (Baton Rouge, 2013), 106–108, 131–132, 140–142, 187–189; John Hope Franklin, *The Militant South, 1800–1861* (1956; reprint, Urbana, 2002), 124–128; and Roger Butterfield, "George Lippard and His Secret Brotherhood," *Pennsylvania Magazine of History and Biography* 79, no. 3 (July 1955): 300–305.

67. No serious historians have suggested that the secessionist movement was as narrowly based as Kennedy described it. That said, Stephanie McCurry has argued that the southern public was badly manipulated by self-interested planters and radical secessionists. So, too, Pat Quigley has observed that the radicals' activism and potent propaganda was necessary to turn vague notions of southern "victimhood" and being "hemmed in" into actual motives for secession. Nor have more than a handful of historians argued that the desire for Caribbean or Latin American empire building was a reason for secession. Granted, the South had always harbored designs on Cuba. Both Democratic platforms in 1860 advocated acquisition of the island. This does not mean that some northerners didn't *think* the South was interested in Caribbean and Latin American expansion. In 1854, the abolitionist Wendell Phillips wrote, "We shall have Cuba in a year, Mexico in five . . . The future seems to unfold a vast Slave Empire united with Brazil & darkening the whole West." See Barney, *Road to Secession,* 16–21, 65–78; Egerton, *Year of Meteors,* 190, 220, 292–293; May, *Southern Dreams,* 218, 236, 242; Guterl, *American Mediterranean,* 1–27; Majewski, *Modernizing a Slave Economy*; McCurry, *Confederate Reckoning,* 42–43, 77–84; McDaniel, *Problem of Democracy,* 203; and Paul Quigley, *Shifting Grounds: Nationalism and the American South, 1848–1865* (New York, 2012), 13–17, 76–77, 85, 105, 113.

68. KP, Kennedy to Philip Pendleton, Mar. 30, 1863; and Kennedy, *Mr. Ambrose's Letters,* 118–120, 143, 167, 182.

69. Kennedy, *Mr. Ambrose's Letters,* 239–244.

70. Most recent historians of the Civil War agree that the preservation of slavery was central to southern nationalism and the founding of the Confederacy. Most quote Confederate Vice President Alexander Stephens's "cornerstone speech" as the starting point of their arguments. Regarding the new nation, Stephens said, "its cornerstone rests, upon the great truth that the negro is not equal to the white man; that slavery, subordination to the superior race, is his natural and moral condition." Stephanie McCurry has argued that nonslaveholding men were heavily propa-

gandized by fears that emancipation would endanger their women. Coleman Hutchison has called the Confederacy a "response nation," a reactive entity that dwelt on anti-Lincoln sentiment, hatred of abolitionism, and the alleged moral corruption of northern life. Paul Quigley and Chandra Manning have emphasized the importance of the war as the unifying force in southern nationalism. See McCurry, *Confederate Reckoning,* 12–13, 21, 29, 36, 94, 347; Quigley, *Shifting Grounds,* 6, 9–12, 15, 32–34, 52–53, 170–171, 183; Coleman Hutchison, *Apples and Ashes: Literature, Nationalism, and the Confederate States of America* (Athens, GA, 2012), 11, 70, 110–111, 121–123; Gary W. Gallagher, *Becoming Confederates: Paths to a New National Loyalty* (Athens, GA, 2013), 25–26, 45–46, 70–71; and Chandra Manning, *What This Cruel War Was Over: Soldiers, Slavery, and the Civil War* (New York, 2007), 11–12, 29–39, 61–63, 138–141, 217–218.

71. Kennedy, *Mr. Ambrose's Letters,* 240–244.

72. The black family that Kennedy had somehow acquired consisted of an older couple named Thomas and Matilda and several of their children. Kennedy arranged for someone in Harrisburg, Pennsylvania, to help the family when they arrived there. However, by the end of December 1858, the family was still in Virginia and had run up a considerable amount of debt. It is unclear what happened to the family after that. See KP, journal entries, July 27, 28, 1857, Dec. 22, 1858; and Tuckerman, *Kennedy,* 348–349.

73. Kennedy concluded the 1865 book version of *Mr. Ambrose's Letters* with these words. See Kennedy, *Mr. Ambrose's Letters,* 244.

74. "Mr. Ambrose's Letters" was reprinted first by Hurd and Houghton in 1865 and by G. P. Putnam in 1872. The *Nation* described Kennedy as having "an intimate connection to Southerners." The quotation appeared in a Putnam advertisement. See John P. Kennedy, *Occasional Addresses and Letters of Mr. Ambrose on the Rebellion* (New York, 1872).

75. McPherson, *Tried by War,* 218–219, 221, 246–247; Foner, *Fiery Trial,* 308–310; and Bohner, *Kennedy,* 231.

76. KP, journal entries, Apr. 10, 11, 1865.

77. Lincoln was assassinated on April 14, 1865, and died the following morning. Secretary of State Seward was badly wounded by one of Booth's accomplices. The one assigned to kill Vice President Johnson got cold feet. See KP, journal entry, Apr. 15, 1865; and Jay Winik, *April 1865: The Month That Saved America* (New York, 2006), 222–229.

78. KP, journal entry, Apr. 21, 1865; and Winik, *April 1865,* 356–359.

79. KP, journal entry, June 8, 1865, and Kennedy to Goldwin Smith, June 8, 1865.

80. KP, "Journal of a Visit to Cuba, November 28, 1865–April 8, 1866."

81. Ibid., journal entries, Dec. 11, 12, 1865.

82. Ibid., journal entry, Dec. 12, 1865.

83. Ibid.

84. Ibid., journal entries, Dec. 15, 16, 17, 1865.

85. Ibid., Dec. 25, 31, 1865.

86. The Freedman's Bureau was established by Congress in March 1865. A part of the Department of War, it was responsible for the resettlement, education, and general protection of freed slaves. It functioned with mixed results until 1871, when it was discontinued by President Grant. See Eric Foner, *Reconstruction: America's Unfinished Revolution, 1863–1877* (New York, 1988), 69–70, 142–144, 170; and KP, "Visit to Cuba," journal entry, Dec. 31, 1865.

87. KP, "Visit to Cuba," journal entry, Jan. 9, 1866.

88. Ibid., journal entries, Jan. 11, 12, 1866.

89. Ibid., Jan. 12, 20, 1866.

90. Ibid.

91. Ibid., journal entry, Feb. 4, 1866.

92. Ibid., journal entries, Feb. 4, 8, 1866.

93. Other visitors to Cuba around this time shared these negative impressions. Richard Henry Dana Jr., for example, commented on the limited pastimes of Havana's elite, as well as the number of "chain gangs" on the roads. Anthony Trollope thought Havana was an ugly town and characterized Cuba as "a slave country." John Muir noted the cruel treatment of animals on the island. See Alan Ryan, ed., *The Reader's Companion to Cuba* (New York, 1997), 11–14, 31–37, 42–43, 46, 55; and KP, "Visit to Cuba," journal entry, Feb. 15, 1866.

94. KP, "Visit to Cuba," journal entry, Feb. 23, 1866.

95. Ibid.

96. Several historians of slavery, Stanley Elkins among them, have argued that slavery in Cuba was less harsh than in the United States. However, John Blassingame has shown that Elkins and others based their analysis on a comparison of slave codes, not the actual treatment of slaves reported by visitors to the island. These visitors described filthy lodgings surrounded by high stone walls and iron gates. Slaves suffered from poor food, lack of sleep, and overwork. Adult slaves usually lived no more than eight to ten years after being enslaved. They were punished with stocks, iron collars, and whipping. Those attempting to escape were subjected to the *novena,* twenty-five lashes a day for nine consecutive days. One experienced traveler thought Cuba's slaves the worst treated in the world. See John W. Blassingame, "Bibliographical Essay: Foreign Writers View Cuban Slavery," *Journal of Negro History* 57, no. 4 (Oct. 1972): 415–419; and KP, "Visit to Cuba," journal entry, Feb. 23, 1866.

97. At the time of Kennedy's visit to Cuba, over a quarter of the island's population was enslaved. Most of the more than 350,000 slaves on the island worked on sugar plantations. While gradual emancipation would begin in 1868, Cuba would not achieve complete emancipation until 1884. See Davis, *Inhuman Bondage,* 324–325; and KP, "Visit to Cuba," journal entry, Feb. 23, 1866.

98. KP, journal entry, Apr. 5, 1866.

99. Ibid.

100. KP, "Journal of trip to Europe, June 27, 1866–Oct. 17, 1868," 160.

101. Kennedy gave his last public address on October 31, 1868. See Tuckerman, *Kennedy,* 460–463.

102. Ibid., 463–465.

103. In his will, Kennedy asked that all his journals, letters, manuscripts, and other private papers be locked in "a strong walnut box" at Baltimore's Peabody Institute and not opened until 1900. Only Kennedy's executor and biographer, Henry Tuckerman, had the chance to go through these papers before they were secured. This unusual request delayed scholarly research on Kennedy until the early twentieth century, at which time Vernon Parrington "rediscovered" him. See Tuckerman, *Kennedy,* 464–465, 484; and Parrington, *Romantic Revolution,* 56.

Conclusion

1. Drew Gilpin Faust, *A Sacred Circle: The Dilemma of the Intellectual in the Old South, 1840–1860* (Philadelphia, 1977), 18–19, 28–30, 133; and KP, William Gilmore Simms to Kennedy, May 1, 1850.

2. The connection between culture formation and the rise of political movements is discussed in Freeman, *Affairs of Honor,* 289–293; Silbey, "To One or Another of These Parties Every Man Belongs," 69–72, 78; and Jacobs and Zelizer, "Democratic Experiment," 6–8.

3. For the influence of Whig programs on the Republican Party, see Foner, *Free Soil,* 19–20, 168–175; Marc Egnal, *Clash of Extremes: The Economic Origins of the Civil War* (New York, 2009), 320–325; and Charles W. Calhoun, *From Bloody Shirt to Full Dinner Pail: The Transformation of Politics and Governance in the Gilded Age* (New York, 2011), 5–6, 22–24, 51.

4. Historians have debated the details of the "compromise of 1877," which settled the disputed presidential election the previous year and ended Reconstruction. The Democratic presidential candidate Samuel Tilden had won the popular vote, but several electoral votes were in dispute in the South. An electoral commission awarded the election to Republican candidate Rutherford B. Hayes after assurances were allegedly given regarding his future policies toward the South. After taking office, Hayes removed federal troops from South Carolina and Louisiana. See Calhoun, *Bloody Shirt,* 56–59; Foner, *Reconstruction,* 577–581, 588, 598; William H. Rehnquist, *Centennial Crisis: The Disputed Election of 1876* (New York, 2004), 177–179, 203; and C. Vann Woodward, *Reunion and Reaction: The Compromise of 1877 and the End of Reconstruction* (New York, 1951), 117–120, 125, 167–169.

5. The painting of Kennedy is by Mathew Wilson. Originally built in the Federal style, The Bower was "Gothicized" in 1881. Fire gutted the house in 1892, but it was faithfully restored afterward. See the National Register of Historic Places, www.wvculture.org/shpo/nr/pdf/jefferson/82004321.pdf. Arctic explorer Elisha Kane, whose second voyage to Greenland had been commissioned by Kennedy while secretary of the navy, honored his benefactor by naming the 110-mile passage between Ellesmere Island, Canada, and the northwestern coast of Greenland after him. Cape Andrew Jackson forms the southern mouth of the Kennedy Channel on its Greenland side. See Bohner, *Kennedy,* 207; and *Encyclopedia of World Explorers* (Lisse, Netherlands, 2004), 205. *Swallow Barn* remains in print, thanks to the Louisiana State University Press.

BIBLIOGRAPHY

KENNEDY PAPERS AND EARLY WORKS

The John Pendleton Kennedy Papers, consisting of 130 volumes of his journals, manuscripts, letters, scrapbooks, and other material, are in the possession of the Peabody Institute in Baltimore, Maryland. They are described in Lloyd W. Griffin, "The John Pendleton Kennedy Papers," *Maryland Historical Magazine* 48 (Dec. 1953), 326–336. A microfilm edition was produced by the National Historical Publications Commission in the 1970s and is available at some universities and research institutions. John B. Boles, then of Towson State College, wrote a helpful guide to the microfilm edition.

Kennedy's early literary endeavors such as "The Swiss Traveller," *Red Book,* and the 1832 edition of *Swallow Barn* are among the holdings of the American Antiquarian Society in Worchester, Massachusetts.

BOOKS AND ARTICLES

Addison, Joseph. *The Works of Joseph Addison.* New York: Harper, 1864.

Altschuler, Glenn C., and Stuart M. Blumin. *Rude Republic: Americans and Their Politics in the Nineteenth Century.* Princeton: Princeton UP, 2000.

Anbinder, Tyler. *Nativism and Slavery: The Northern Know-Nothings and the Politics of the 1850s.* New York: Oxford UP, 1992.

Appleby, Joyce. *Inheriting the Revolution: The First Generation of Americans.* Cambridge, MA: Belknap, 2000.

Bailyn, Bernard. *The Ideological Origins of the American Revolution.* Cambridge, MA: Harvard UP, 1967.

Baker, Jean H. *Affairs of Party: The Political Culture of Northern Democrats in the Mid-Nineteenth Century.* Ithaca: Cornell UP, 1983.

———. *Ambivalent Americans: The Know-Nothing Party in Maryland.* Baltimore: Johns Hopkins UP, 1977.

———. *The Politics of Continuity: Maryland Political Parties from 1858 to 1870*. Baltimore: Johns Hopkins UP, 1973.

Bakker, Jan, and Benjamin H. Newcomb. *Pastoral in Antebellum Southern Romance.* Baton Rouge: Louisiana State UP, 1989.

Banner, James M. *To the Hartford Convention: The Federalists and the Origins of Party Politics in New England.* New York: Knopf, 1970.

Barney, William L. *The Road to Secession: A New Perspective on the Old South.* New York: Praeger, 1972.

Belko, W. Stephen. *The Invincible Duff Green: Whig of the West.* Columbia: U of Missouri P, 2006.

Berlin, Ira. *Many Thousands Gone: The First Two Centuries of Slavery in North America.* Cambridge, MA: Harvard UP, 1998.

Bernstein, Peter L. *Wedding of the Waters: The Erie Canal and the Making of a Great Nation.* New York: Norton, 2005.

Blanning, Tim. *The Romantic Revolution: A History.* New York: Modern Library, 2011.

Blassingame, John W. "Bibliographical Essay: Foreign Writers View Cuban Slavery." *Journal of Negro History* 57, no. 4 (October 1972): 415-419.

Bohner, Charles H. *John Pendleton Kennedy: Gentleman from Baltimore.* Baltimore: Johns Hopkins UP, 1961.

Brackenridge, Hugh Henry. *Modern Chivalry.* 1815. Reprint, New Haven: College and University Press, 1965.

Brackett, Jeffrey R. *The Negro in Maryland: A Study of the Institution of Slavery.* 1889. Reprint. Freeport, NY: Books for Libraries, 1969.

Breen, T. H. "Looking Out for Number One: Conflicting Cultural Values in Early Seventeenth Century Virginia." *South Atlantic Quarterly* 37 (1979): 341–360.

———. *Tobacco Culture: The Mentality of the Great Tidewater Planters on the Eve of Revolution.* Princeton UP: Princeton, 1987.

Brichford, Charles H. "That National Story: Conflicting Visions of the Revolution in Kennedy's *Horse-Shoe Robinson* and Simms's *The Partisans.*" *Southern Literary Journal* 21 (Fall 1988): 64–85.

Brooks, Van Wyck. *The World of Washington Irving.* New York: Dutton, 1944.

Brown, Charles Brockden. *Wieland and the Memoirs of Carwin the Biloquist.* 1798. Reprint, with an intro. by Jay Fliegelman. New York: Penguin, 1991.

Brown, Thomas. *Politics and Statesmanship: Essays on the American Whig Party.* New York: Columbia UP, 1985.

Browne, Gary Lawson. *Baltimore in the Nation, 1789–1861.* Chapel Hill: U of North Carolina P, 1980.

Burstein, Andrew. *America's Jubilee: A Generation Remembers the Revolution after Fifty Years of Independence.* New York: Vintage, 2001.

———. *The Original Knickerbocker: The Life of Washington Irving.* New York: Basic, 2007.

———. *The Passions of Andrew Jackson.* New York: Vintage, 2004.

. *Sentimental Democracy: The Evolution of American's Romantic Self Image.* New York: Hill and Wang, 1999.

Bushman, Richard L. *The Refinement of America: Persons, Houses, Cities.* New York: Oxford UP, 1993.

Butterfield, Roger. "George Lippard and His Secret Brotherhood." *Pennsylvania Magazine of History and Biography* 79, no. 3 (July 1955): 300–305.

Calhoun, Charles W. *From Bloody Shirt to Full Dinner Pail: The Transformation of Politics and Governance in the Gilded Age.* New York: Hill and Wang, 2010.

Carroll, E. Malcolm. *Origins of the Whig Party.* Durham: Duke UP, 1925.

Casper, Scott E. *Constructing American Lives: Biography and Culture in Nineteenth-Century America.* Chapel Hill: U of North Carolina P, 1999.

Castronovo, Russ. "Compromised Narratives along the Border: The Mason-Dixon Line, Resistance, and Hegemony." In Scott Michaelson and David E. Johnson, eds., *Border Theory: The Limits of Cultural Politics.* Minneapolis: U of Minnesota P, 1997.

Chaffin, Tom. "'Sons of Washington': Narciso Lopez, Filibustering, and U.S. Nationalism, 1848–1851." *Journal of the Early Republic* 15, no. 1 (Spring 1995): 90–98.

Charvat, William. *The Profession of Authorship in America, 1800–1870.* Columbus: Ohio State UP, 1968.

Chase, Richard. *The American Novel and Its Tradition.* Baltimore: Johns Hopkins UP, 1957.

Clark, Harry Hayden. *Transitions in American Literary History.* New York: Octagon, 1975.

Clinton, Catherine. *The Plantation Mistress: Women's World in the Old South.* New York: Pantheon, 1982.

Cole, Donald B. *A Jackson Man: Amos Kendall and the Rise of American Democracy.* Baton Rouge: Louisiana State UP, 2004.

Cooper, William J., Jr. *The South and the Politics of Slavery, 1828–1856.* Baton Rouge: Louisiana State, 1978.

Cott, Nancy F. *The Bonds of Womanhood: "Women's Sphere" in New England, 1780–1835.* New Haven: Yale UP, 1977.

Cowan, William Tynes. "Slave in the Swamp: Disrupting the Plantation Narrative." Ph.D. diss., William and Mary, 2001.

Cross, Whitney R. *The Burned-Over District: The Social and Intellectual History of Enthusiastic Religion in Western New York, 1800–1850.* New York: Oxford UP, 1950.

Damrosch, Leo. *Tocqueville's Discovery of America.* New York: Farrar, Straus and Giroux, 2010.

———. *Jonathan Swift: His Life and His World.* New Haven: Yale UP, 2013.

Dangerfield, George. *The Awakening of American Nationalism, 1815–1828.* New York: Harper, 1965.

Davidson, Cathy N. *Revolution and the Word: The Rise of the Novel in America.* New York: Oxford UP, 2004.

Davis, Burke. *Jeb Stuart: The Last Cavalier.* New York: Rinehart, 1957.

Davis, David Brion. *Inhuman Bondage. The Rise and Fall of Slavery in the New World.* New York: Oxford UP, 2006.

Davis, Mary Kemp. *Nat Turner before the Bar of Judgement: Fictional Treatments of the Southampton Slave Insurrection.* Baton Rouge: Louisiana State UP, 1999.

Davis, Richard Beale. *Literature and Society in Early Virginia, 1608–1840.* Baton Rouge: Louisiana State, 1973.

———. "Virginia Novels before 'Swallow Barn.'" *Virginia Magazine of History and Biography* 71, no. 3 (July 1963): 279–289.

DeConde, Alexander. *History of American Foreign Policy,* 2nd ed. New York: Scribner's, 1971.

Delbanco, Andrew. *The Abolitionist Imagination.* Cambridge, MA: Harvard UP, 2013.

———. *Melville: His World and Work.* New York: Vintage, 2005.

Deyle, Steven. *Carry Me Back: The Domestic Slave Trade in American Life.* New York: Oxford, 2005.

Douglas, Henry Kyd. *I Rode with Stonewall.* Chapel Hill: U of North Carolina P, 1940.

Douglass, Frederick. *Narrative of the Life Frederick Douglass, An American Slave.* 1845. Reprint, New York: Penguin, 1985.

Drabble, Margaret, ed. *The Oxford Companion to English Literature.* New York: Oxford, 1985.

Dunn, Susan. *Dominion of Memories: Jefferson, Madison, and the Decline of Virginia.* New York: Basic, 2007.

Egerton, Douglas R. *He Shall Go Out Free: The Lives of Denmark Vesey.* Lanham, MD: Rowman and Littlefield, 2004.

———. *Year of Meteors: Stephen Douglas, Abraham Lincoln, and the Election that Brought on the Civil War.* New York: Bloomsbury, 2010.

Egnal, Marc. *Clash of Extremes: The Economic Origins of the Civil War.* New York: Hill and Wang, 2009.

Eiselen, Malcolm Rogers. *The Rise of Pennsylvania Protectionism.* Philadelphia: U of Pennsylvania P, 1974.

Ellis, Richard E. *The Union at Risk: Jacksonian Democracy and the Nullification Crisis.* New York: Oxford UP, 1987.

Ellison, Rhoda Colman. "An Interview with Horse-Shoe Robinson." *American Literature* 31 (1959): 329–332.

Erkkila, Betsey. "Poetics of Whiteness: Poe and the Racial Imaginary." In Gerald J. Kennedy and Liliane Weissberg, *Romancing the Shadow: Poe and Race.* New York: Oxford UP, 2001.

Ewen, David. *Songs of America.* Westport: Greenwood, 1978.

Faust, Drew Gilpin. *A Sacred Circle: The Dilemma of the Intellectual in the Old South, 1840–1860.* Philadelphia: U of Pennsylvania P, 1977.

———. *This Republic of Suffering: Death and the American Civil War.* New York: Vintage, 2008.

Feller, Daniel. *The Jacksonian Promise: America, 1815–1840.* Baltimore: Johns Hopkins UP, 1995.

Ferguson, Robert A. *Law and Letters in American Culture.* Cambridge, MA: Harvard UP, 1984.

Fields, Barbara Jeanne. *Slavery and Freedom on the Middle Ground: Maryland During the Nineteenth Century.* New Haven: Yale UP, 1985.

Foner, Eric. *The Fiery Trial: Abraham Lincoln and American Slavery.* New York: Norton, 2010.

———. *Free Soil, Free Labor, Free Men: The Ideology of the Republican Party Before the Civil War.* 1970. Reprint, New York: Oxford UP, 1995.

———. *Reconstruction: America's Unfinished Business, 1863–1877.* New York: Harper, 1988.

Foreman, Amanda. *A World on Fire: Britain's Crucial Role in the American Civil War.* New York: Random House, 2010.

Formisano, Ronald P. *The Transformation of Political Culture: Massachusetts Parties, 1790–1840s.* New York: Oxford UP, 1983.

Forret, Jeff. *Race Relations at the Margin: Slaves and Poor Whites in the Antebellum Southern Countryside.* Baton Rouge: Louisiana State UP, 2006.

Foster, Edward Halsey. *Civilized Wilderness: Backgrounds to American Romantic Literature, 1817–1860.* New York: Free Press, 1975.

Foucault, Michel. *Madness and Civilization.* 1966. Reprint, New York: Pantheon, 2007.

Fox-Genovese, Elizabeth. *Within the Plantation Household: Black and White Women of the Old South.* Chapel Hill: U of North Carolina P, 1988.

Fleishman, Avrom. *The English Historical Novel: Walter Scott to Virginia Woolf.* Baltimore: Johns Hopkins UP, 1971.

Franklin, John Hope. *The Militant South, 1800–1861.* 1956. Reprint, Urbana: U of Illinois P, 2002.

Franklin, Wayne. *James Fenimore Cooper: The Early Years.* New Haven: Yale UP, 2007.

Fredrickson, George M. *The Black Image in the White Mind: The Debate on Afro-American Character and Destiny, 1817–1914.* New York: Harper, 1971.

Freehling, William W. *Prelude to Civil War: The Nullification Controversy in South Carolina, 1816–1836.* New York: Oxford UP, 1965.

———. *The Road to Disunion: Secessionists at Bay 1776–1854*. New York: Oxford UP, 1990.

———. *South Vs. South: How Anti-Confederate Southerners Shaped the Course of the Civil War*. New York: Oxford UP, 2001.

Freeman, Joanne B. *Affairs of Honor: National Politics in the New Republic*. New Haven: Yale UP, 2002.

French, Scot. *The Rebellious Slave: Nat Turner in American Memory*. Boston: Houghton Mifflin, 2004.

Frey, Sylvia R. *Water from the Rock: Black Resistance in a Revolutionary Age*. Princeton: Princeton UP, 1991.

Gallagher, Gary W. *Becoming Confederates: Paths to a New National Loyalty*. Athens: U of Georgia P, 2013.

Gardner, Jared. *Master Plots: Race and the Founding of American Literature, 1787–1845*. Baltimore: Johns Hopkins UP, 1998.

Gay, Peter. *Tender Passions: The Bourgeois Experience: Victoria to Freud*. Vol. 2. New York: Oxford UP, 2001.

———. *The Naked Heart: The Bourgeois Experience: Victoria to Freud*. Vol. 4 New York: Norton, 1995.

Genovese, Eugene D. *Roll, Jordan, Roll: The World the Slaves Made*. New York: Vintage, 1972.

Gienapp, William E. *The Origins of the Republican Party, 1852–1856*. New York: Oxford UP, 1987.

———. "The Whig Party, Compromise of 1850, and Nomination of Winfield Scott." *Presidential Studies Quarterly* 14, no. 3 (Summer 1984): 399–415.

Gilje, Paul A. *Free Trade and Sailors' Rights in the War of 1812*. New York: Cambridge UP, 2013.

Goddu, Teresa A. *Gothic America: Narrative, History, and the Nation*. New York: Columbia UP, 2011.

Goodheart, Adam. *1861: The Civil War Awakening*. New York: Vintage, 2011.

Gossman, Lionel. *Between History and Literature*. Cambridge, MA: Harvard UP, 1990.

Grammer, John M. *Pastoral and Politics in the Old South*. Baton Rouge: Louisiana State UP, 1996.

[Gray, Thomas]. *The Confessions of Nat Turner, Leader of the Late Insurrection in Southampton, Va*. 1831. Reprint, Miami, FL: Mnemosyne, 1969.

Green, Don. "Constitutional Unionists: The Party that Tried to Stop Lincoln and Save the Union." *Historian* 69, no. 2 (Summer 2001): 231-235.

Greenberg, Kenneth S. *The Confessions of Nat Turner and Related Documents*. Boston: Bedford/St. Martin's, 1996.

Guelzo, Allen C. *Gettysburg: The Last Invasion*. New York: Vintage, 2014.

Gunderson, Robert Gray. *The Log-Cabin Campaign.* Lexington: UP of Kentucky, 1957.

———. *The Old Gentlemen's Convention: The Washington Peace Conference of 1861.* Madison: U of Wisconsin P, 1961.

Gura, Philip. *American Transcendentalism: A History.* New York: Oxford UP, 2007.

Gusfield, Joseph R. *Symbolic Crusade: Status Politics and the American Temperance Movement.* Urbana: U of Illinois P, 1963.

Guterl, Matthew Pratt. *American Mediterranean: Southern Slaveholders in the Age of Emancipation.* Cambridge, MA: Harvard UP, 2006.

Gwathmey, Edward M. *John Pendleton Kennedy.* New York: Thomas Nelson, 1931.

Haller, Mark H. "The Rise of the Jackson Party in Maryland, 1820–1829." *Journal of Southern History* 28, no. 3 (Aug. 1962): 307–326.

Hare, John L. *Will the Circle Be Unbroken? Family and Sectionalism in the Virginia Novels of Kennedy, Caruthers, and Tucker, 1830–1845.* New York: Rutledge, 2002.

Hartford, William F. *Money, Morals, and Politics: Massachusetts in the Age of the Boston Associates.* Boston: Northeastern UP, 2001.

Heath, James Ewell [pseud. "A Virginian"]. *Edge-Hill, or, the Family of the Fitzroyals.* 2 vols. Richmond: T. W. White, 1828.

Heidler, David S., and Jeanne T. Heidler. *Henry Clay: The Essential American.* New York: Random House, 2011.

Hickey, Donald R. *The War of 1812: A Forgotten Conflict.* Urbana: U of Illinois P, 1989.

Hofstadter, Richard. *The Idea of a Party System: The Rise of Legitimate Opposition in the United States.* Berkeley: U of California P, 1969.

Holt, Michael F. *The Political Crisis of the 1850s.* New York: Norton, 1978.

———. *The Rise and Fall of the American Whig Party: Jacksonian Politics and the Onset of the Civil War.* New York: Oxford UP, 1999.

Horwitz, Tony. *Midnight Rising: John Brown and the Civil War.* New York: Holt, 2011.

Howe, Daniel Walker. *Making the American Self: Jonathan Edwards to Abraham Lincoln.* Cambridge, MA: Harvard UP, 1997.

——— *The Political Culture of the American Whigs.* Chicago: U of Chicago P, 1979.

______ *Reviews in American History* 66 (1981): 461-462.

———. *What Hath God Wrought: The Transformation of America, 1815–1848.* New York: Oxford UP, 2007.

Hubbell, Jay B. *The South in American Literature, 1607–1900.* Durham: Duke UP, 1954.

Hutchison, Coleman. *Apples and Ashes: Literature, Nationalism, and the Confederate States of America.* Athens: U of Georgia P, 2012.

Irving, Washington. *Bracebridge Hall.* 1822. Reprint, London: Macmillan, 1882.

———. *Sketchbook of Geoffrey Crayon, Gent.* 1819–1820. Reprint, with intro. by Perry Miller. New York: Signet, 1961.

Isaac, Rhys. *The Transformation of Virginia, 1740–1790*. Chapel Hill: U of North Carolina P, 1982.

Jacobs, Meg, and Julian E. Zelizer. Introduction to Meg Jacobs, William J. Novak, and Julian E. Zelizer, eds., *The Democratic Experiment: New Directions in American Political History*. Princeton: Princeton UP, 2003.

Jacobs, Robert D. "Poe in Richmond: The Double Image." In R. C. Simonini Jr., *Southern Writers: Appraisals in Our Time*. Freemont, NY: Books for Libraries, 1961.

Jefferson, Thomas. *Notes on the State of Virginia*. 1787. Reprint, with an intro. by William Peden. Chapel Hill: U of North Carolina P, 1982.

Johnson, Walter. *River of Dark Dreams: Slavery and Empire in the Cotton Kingdom*. Cambridge, MA: Harvard UP, 2013.

———. *Soul by Soul: Life Inside the Antebellum Slave Market*. Cambridge, MA: Harvard UP, 1999.

Jones, Paul C. *Unwelcome Voices: Subversive Fiction in the Antebellum South*. Knoxville: U of Tennessee P, 2005.

Jordan, Winthrop. *White over Black: American Attitudes toward the Negro, 1550–1812*. Chapel Hill: U of North Carolina P, 1968.

Kaiser, Carl William, Jr. *History of Academic Protectionist–Free Trade Controversy in America*. Philadelphia: self published, 1939.

Kasur, David. *Cost Book of Carey and Lea*. Philadelphia: U of Pennsylvania P, 1963.

Kasson, John F. *Civilizing the Machine: Technology and Republican Values in America, 1776–1900*. New York: Penguin, 1976.

Keehn, David C. *Knights of the Golden Circle: Secret Empire, Southern Secession, Civil War*. Baton Rouge: Louisiana State UP, 2013.

Kennedy, John Pendleton. *At Home and Abroad: A Series of Essays: with a journal in Europe in 1867–8 . . .* New York: Putnam, 1872.

______. *Horse-Shoe Robinson: A Tale of the Tory Ascendency*. Philadelphia: Lea and Blanchard, 1835.

———. *Horse-Shoe Robinson*. 1835. Reprint, with an intro. by Ernest E. Leisy. New York: Hafner, 1962.

———. *Memoirs of the Life of William Wirt*. 2 vols. Philadelphia: Lea and Blanchard, 1849.

———. *Mr. Ambrose's Letters on the Rebellion*. New York: Hurd and Houghton, 1865.

———. "No Piles of Hoarded Wealth." In George E. Probst, ed., *Happy Republic: A Reader in Tocqueville's America*. Gloucester, MA: Peter Smith, 1962.

———. *Occasional Addresses and Letters of Mr. Ambrose on the Rebellion*. New York: Putnam, 1872.

———. *Political and Official Papers*. New York: Putnam, 1872.

———. *Report of Mr. Kennedy, of Maryland, from the Committee on Commerce of the*

House of Representatives of the United States on the African Slave Trade. 27th Congress, 3rd Session. 1843. Reprint, Freeport, New York: Books for Libraries, 1971.

———. *Quodlibet.* 1840. Reprint, Upper Saddle River, NJ: Literature House, 1970.

———. *Rob of The Bowl: A Legend of St. Inigoe's.* Philadelphia: Lea and Blanchard, 1838.

———. *Rob of the Bowl: A Legend of St. Inigoe's.* 1838. Reprint, Whitefish, MT: Kessinger, 2007.

———. *Swallow Barn; or, A Sojourn in the Old Dominion.* Philadelphia: Carey and Lea, 1832.

———. *Swallow Barn; or, A Sojourn in the Old Dominion.* 1851. Reprint, with an intro. by William S. Osborne. New York: Hafner, 1962.

———. *Swallow Barn; or, A Sojourn in the Old Dominion.* 1851. Reprint, with an intro. by Lucinda H. MacKethan. Baton Rouge: Louisiana State UP, 1986.

———. "The Swiss Traveller." In *The Portico: A Repository for Science and Literature,* vol. 1 (Feb.–Aug. 1816). Baltimore: Neale Willis, 1816.

Kennedy, John Pendleton, and Peter Hoffman Cruse. *Red Book.* 2nd ed. 2 vols. Baltimore: J. Robinson, 1820–1821.

Keyssar, Alexander. *The Right to Vote: The Contested History of Democracy in the United States.* New York: Basic, 2009.

Kirwan, Albert D. *John J. Crittenden: The Struggle for the Union.* Lexington: U of Kentucky P, 1962.

Klein, Lawrence. "Addison Afterlives: Joseph Addison in Eighteenth-Century Culture." *Journal of Eighteenth-Century Studies* 35, no. 1 (March 2012): 102-118.

Kohl, Lawrence Frederick. *The Politics of Individualism: Parties and the American Character in the Jacksonian Era.* New York: Oxford, 1989.

Kolchin, Peter. *American Slavery, 1619–1877.* New York: Hill and Wang, 1993.

Larkin, Jack, *The Reshaping of Everyday Life, 1790–1840.* New York: Harper, 1988.

Latrobe, John H. B. *The History of the Mason-Dixon Line.* Philadelphia, 1855.

Lepler, Jessica M. *The Many Panics of 1837: People, Politics, and the Creation of a Transatlantic Financial Crisis.* New York: Cambridge UP, 2013.

Levin, Harry. *The Power of Blackness: Hawthorne, Poe, Melville.* 1958. Reprint, Athens: U of Ohio P, 1980.

Lewis, Jan. *The Pursuit of Happiness: Family and Values in Jefferson's Virginia.* New York: Cambridge UP, 1983.

Lewis, R. W. B. *The American Adam: Innocence, Tragedy, and Tradition in the Nineteenth Century.* Chicago: U of Chicago P, 1955.

Lott, Eric. *Love and Theft: Blackface and the American Working Class.* New York: Oxford UP, 1993.

Maier, Pauline. *American Scripture: Making the Declaration of Independence.* New York: Knopf, 1997.

Mabee, Carleton. *The American Leonardo: A Life of Samuel F. B. Morse.* New York: Knopf, 1943.

MacKethan, Lucinda Hardwick. *The Dream of Arcady: Place and Time in Southern Literature.* Baton Rouge: Louisiana State UP, 1980.

Machor, James L. *Reading Fiction in Antebellum America: Informed Response and Reception Histories, 1820–1865.* Baltimore: Johns Hopkins UP, 2011.

Majewski, John. *Modernizing a Slave Economy: The Economic Vision of the Confederate Nation.* Chapel Hill: U of North Carolina P, 2009.

Manning, Chandra. *What This Cruel War Was Over: Soldiers, Slavery, and Civil War.* New York: Vintage, 2007.

Marine, William M. *The British Invasion of Maryland, 1812–1815.* Baltimore: John H. Saumenig, 1913.

Marszalek, John F. *The Petticoat Affair: Manners, Mutiny, and Sex in Andrew Jackson's White House.* New York: Free Press, 1997.

Martineau, Harriet. *Society in America.* 1837. Reprint, with an intro. by Seymour Martin Lipset. New York: Anchor, 1962.

Masur, Louis P. *1831: Year of Eclipse.* New York: Hill and Wang, 2001.

Matthews, Jean V. *Toward a New Society: American Thought and Culture, 1800–1830.* Boston: Twayne, 1991.

May, Robert E. *Southern Dreams of a Caribbean Empire, 1854–1861.* Baton Rouge: Louisiana State UP, 1973.

McCloskey, John C. "The Campaign of Periodicals after the War of 1812 for National American Literature." *Proceedings of the Modern Language Association* 50, no. 1 (March 1935).

McCormick, Richard P. *The Second American Party System: Party Formation in the Jacksonian Era.* Chapel Hill: U of North Carolina P, 1966.

McCurry, Stephanie. *Confederate Reckoning: Power and Politics in the Civil War South.* Cambridge, MA: Harvard UP, 2010.

———. *Masters of Small Worlds: Yeoman Households, Gender Relations, and the Political Culture of the Antebellum South Carolina Low Country.* New York: Oxford UP, 1995.

McDaniel, W. Caleb. *The Problem of Democracy in the Age of Slavery: Garrisonian Abolitionists and Transatlantic Reform.* Baton Rouge: Louisiana State UP, 2013.

McLaughlin, Jack. *Jefferson and Monticello: Biography of a Builder.* New York: Holt, 1988.

McLoughlin, William. *Revivals, Awakenings, and Reform.* Chicago: U of Chicago P, 1978.

McPherson, James M. *Battle Cry of Freedom: The Civil War Era.* New York: Oxford UP, 1988.

———. *Crossroads of Freedom: Antietam.* New York: Oxford UP, 2002.

———. "The Historian Who Saw Through America." *New York Review of Books* 55, no. 19 (Dec. 4, 2008).

———. *Tried by War: Abraham Lincoln as Commander in Chief.* New York: Penguin, 2005.

———. "What Drove the Terrible War?" *New York Review of Books* 58 no. 12 (July 14, 2011).

Merry, Robert W. *A Country of Vast Designs: James K. Polk, the Mexican War, and the Conquest of the American Continent.* New York: Simon and Schuster, 2009.

Meyers, Marvin. *The Jacksonian Persuasion: Politics and Belief.* Stanford, CA: Stanford UP, 1957.

Miller, Douglas T. *The Birth of Modern America, 1820–1850.* New York: Pegasus, 1970.

Miller, Perry. *The Life of the Mind in America: From the Revolution to the Civil War.* New York: Oxford UP, 1965.

Mintz, Steven. *Huck's Raft: A History of American Childhood.* Cambridge, MA: Belknap Press of Harvard UP, 2004.

Morgan, Philip D. *Slave Counterpoint: Black Culture in the Eighteenth-Century Chesapeake and Low Country.* Chapel Hill: U of North Carolina P, 1998.

Mullins, Jeffrey A. "'The Sweat of Thy Brow': Education, Manual Labor and the Market Revolution." In Scott C. Martin, ed., *Cultural Change and the Market Revolution in America, 1789–1860.* Lanham, MD: Rowman and Littlefield, 2005.

The National Union Catalogue, Pre-1956 Imprints. London: Mansell, 1968.

Neely, Mark E., Jr. *The Boundaries of American Political Culture in the Civil War Era.* Chapel Hill: U of North Carolina P, 2005.

Nevins, Allan. *Ordeal of the Union.* 2 vols. New York: Scribner's, 1947.

North, Douglass C. *Economic Growth of the United States, 1790–1860.* New York: Norton, 1966.

Oakes, James. *The Ruling Race: A History of American Slaveholders.* New York: Norton, 1982.

Oates, Stephen B. *The Fires of Jubilee: Nat Turner's Fierce Rebellion.* New York: Harper, 2004.

O'Brien, Michael. *Conjectures of Order: Intellectual Life and the American South, 1810–1860.* 2 vols. Chapel Hill: U of North Carolina P, 2004.

———. *Rethinking the South: Essays in Intellectual History.* Athens: U of Georgia P, 1993.

Osborne, William S. "'The Swiss Traveller Essays': Earliest Literary Writing of John Pendleton Kennedy." *American Literature* 30 (May 1958): 228–233.

Osterweis, Rollin G. *Romanticism and Nationalism in the Old South.* Baton Rouge: Louisiana State UP, 1968.

Paquette, Robert L., and Douglas R. Egerton. "Of Facts and Fables: New Light on the Denmark Vesey Affair." *South Carolina Historical Magazine* 105, no. 1 (Jan. 2004).

Parfait, Claire. *The Publishing History of* Uncle Tom's Cabin, *1852-2002.* Abingdon, UK: Ashgate, 2008.

Parrington, Vernon L. *The Romantic Revolution in America.* Vol. 2 of *Main Currents of American Thought.* New York: Harper, 1927.

Perry, Lewis. *Boats Against the Current: American Culture between Revolution and Modernity, 1820–1860.* Lanham, MD: Rowman and Littlefield, 1993.

Peterson, Merrill D. *The Great Triumvirate: Webster, Clay, and Calhoun.* New York: Oxford UP, 1987.

———, ed. *The Portable Jefferson.* New York: Viking, 1975.

Pitch, Anthony S. *The Burning of Washington: The British Invasion of 1814.* Annapolis: U.S. Naval Institute Press, 1998.

Poe, Edgar Allan. *The Narrative of Gordon Pym of Nantucket.* 1838. Reprint, New York: Modern Library, 2002.

Pollock, Anthony. "Neutering Addison and Steele: Aesthetic Failure and the Spectatorial Public Sphere." *Early American Literature* 74, no. 3 (Fall 2007): 707–734.

Potter, David M. *The Impending Crisis, 1848–1861.* New York: Harper, 1976.

Quigley, Paul. *Shifting Grounds: Nationalism and the American South, 1848–1865.* New York: Oxford UP, 2012.

Rehnquist, William H. *Centennial Crisis: The Disputed Election of 1876.* New York: Knopf, 2004.

Remini, Robert V. *Andrew Jackson and the Bank War: A Study in the Growth of Presidential Power.* New York: Harper, 1967.

———. *The Battle of New Orleans: Andrew Jackson and America's First Military Victory.* New York: Penguin, 1999.

———. *Henry Clay: Statesman for the Union.* New York: Norton, 1991.

Reynolds, David S. *Beneath the American Renaissance: The Subversive Imagination in the Age of Emerson and Melville.* Cambridge, MA: Harvard UP, 1988.

———. *Mightier than the Sword:* Uncle Tom's Cabin *and the Battle for America.* New York: Norton, 2011.

———. *Waking Giant: America in the Age of Jackson.* New York: Harper, 2008.

Rezneck, Samuel. *Business Depressions and Financial Panics: Essays in American Business and Economic History.* Westport, CT: Greenwood, 1971.

Richards, Leonard L. *Slave Power: The Free North and Southern Domination, 1780–1860.* Baton Rouge: Louisiana State UP, 2000.

Ridgely, J. V. *John Pendleton Kennedy.* New York: Twayne, 1966.

———. *Nineteenth-Century Southern Literature.* Lexington: U of Kentucky P, 1981.

Riesman, David, with Nathan Glazer and Reuel Denney. *The Lonely Crowd: A Study of the Changing American Character.* Garden City, NJ: Doubleday, 1953.

Robert, Joseph Clarke. *The Road from Monticello: A Study of the Virginia Slavery Debate of 1832.* 1941. Reprint, New York: AMS Press, 1970.

Robinson, Ray Edwin. "The History of Peabody Conservatory of Music." PhD diss., Indiana University, 1969.

Rockman, Seth. *Scraping By: Wage Labor, Slavery, and Survival in Early Baltimore.* Baltimore: Johns Hopkins UP, 2009.

Roediger, David R. *The Wages of Whiteness: Race and the Making of the American Working Class.* Rev. ed. London: Verso, 1991.

Romine, Scott. *Narrative Forms of Southern Community.* Baton Rouge: Louisiana State UP, 1999.

Rothman, David J. *The Discovery of the Asylum: Social Order and Disorder in the New Republic.* 1971. Reprint, New York: Aldine de Gruyter, 2002.

Rubin, Louis D., Jr. *The Edge of the Swamp: A Study of the Literature and Society of the Old South.* Baton Rouge: Louisiana State UP, 1989.

Ruland, Richard, and Malcolm Bradbury. *From Puritanism to Postmodernism: A History of American Literature.* New York: Viking, 1992.

Ryan, Alan, ed. *The Reader's Companion to Cuba.* New York: Harper, 1997.

Ryan, Mary P. *Cradle of the Middle Class: The Family in Oneida County, New York, 1790–1865.* New York: Oxford UP, 1986.

Schama, Simon. *Landscape and Memory.* New York: Vintage, 1996.

Scott, Walter. *Ivanhoe.* 1819. Reprint. New York: Signet Classic, 2001.

Seaborn, Adam [pseud.]. *Symzonia: A Voyage of Discovery.* New York: J. Seymour, 1820.

Seidel, Kathryn Lee. *The Southern Belle in the American Novel.* Tampa: UP of Florida, 1985.

Sellers, Charles. *The Market Revolution: Jacksonian America, 1815–1846.* New York: Oxford UP, 1991.

Semmes, John E. *John H. B. Latrobe and His Times, 1803–1891.* Baltimore: Remington, 1917.

Silbey, Joel H. *The American Political Nation, 1838–1893.* Stanford, CA: Stanford UP, 1991.

———. "To One or Another of These Parties Every Man Belongs." In Byron E. Shafer and Anthony J. Badger, eds., *Contesting Democracy: Substance and Structure in American Political History, 1775–2000.* Lawrence: UP of Kansas P, 2001.

Simms, William Gilmore. "Kennedy's Life of Wirt." *Southern Quarterly Review* 17 (April 1850): 192-229.

———. *The Letters of William Gilmore Simms.* Columbia: U of South Carolina P, 1953.

Simpson, Lewis P. *The Dispossessed Garden: Pastoral and History in Southern Literature.* Athens: U of Georgia P, 1975.

Skeen, C. Edward. *1816: America Rising.* Lexington: UP of Kentucky, 2003.

Slotkin, Richard. *The Long Road to Antietam: How the Civil War Became a Revolution.* New York: Liveright, 2012.

Smith, Henry Nash. *Virgin Land: The American West as Symbol and Myth.* Cambridge, MA: Harvard UP, 1950.

Spelman, Georgia Peterman. "The Whig Rhetoric of John Pendleton Kennedy, Spokesman for Industry." PhD diss., Indiana University, 1974.

Stagg, J. C. A. *The War of 1812: Conflict for a Continent.* New York: Cambridge UP, 2012.

Stahr, Walter. *Seward: Lincoln's Indispensible Man.* New York: Simon and Schuster, 2012.

Stansell, Christine. *City of Women: Sex and Class in New York, 1789–1860.* New York: Oxford UP, 1986.

Stanwood, Edward. *American Tariff Controversies in the Nineteenth-Century.* 2 vols. New York: Russell, 1903.

Staudenraus, P. J. *The African Colonization Movement, 1816–1865.* New York: Columbia UP, 1961.

Stevenson, Brenda E. *Life in Black and White: Family and Community in the Slave South.* New York: Oxford UP, 1996.

Stover, John F. "Canals and Turnpikes: America's Early-Nineteenth-Century Transportation Network." In Joseph R. Frese and Jacob Judd, eds., *An Emerging Independent American Economy, 1815–1875.* Tarrytown: Basic, 1980.

Stowe, Harriet Beecher. *Uncle Tom's Cabin.* Boston, 1852. Reprint, with an intro. by Darryl Pinckney. New York: Signet, 1998.

"Swallow Barn." Review. *North American Review* 36 (1833): 519–520.

Swift, Jonathan. *Gulliver's Travels.* 1726. Reprint, with an intro. by Michael Seidel. New York: Bantam, 2003.

Symmes, Clive. *Symmes' Theory of Concentric Spheres.* Cincinnati, OH: Morgan, Lodge and Fisher, 1826.

Taussig, F. W. *Tariff History of the United States.* New York: Putnam, 1892.

Taylor, Alan. "Dual Nationalism: Legacies of the War of 1812." In Pietro S. Nivola and Peter J. Kastor, eds., *What So Proudly We Hailed: Essays on the Contemporary Meaning of the War of 1812.* Washington, DC: National Council, 2012.

Taylor, George Rogers. *The Transportation Revolution, 1815–1860.* New York: Harper, 1951.

Taylor, William R. *Cavalier and Yankee: The Old South and the American National Character.* 1957. Reprint, New York: Oxford UP, 1979.

Termin, Peter. *Jacksonian Economy.* New York: Norton, 1969.

Thackeray, W. M. *The Virginians.* Philadelphia: Lippincott, 1868.

Tise, Larry E. *Proslavery: A History of the Defense of Slavery in America, 1701–1840.* Athens: U of Georgia P, 1987.

de Tocqueville, Alexis. *Democracy in America.* Vol. 2. 1835. Reprint, New York: Oxford UP, 1945.

Toll, Robert C. *Blacking Up: The Minstrel Show in Nineteenth-Century America.* New York: Oxford UP, 1976.

Tomlinson, David. "A Publisher's Advice to Young Authors: John Pendleton Kennedy and Peter Hoffman Cruse Serve a Literary Apprenticeship." *Southern Literary Journal* 14, no. 1 (Fall 1981).

Trachtenberg, Alan. *Lincoln's Smile and Other Enigmas.* New York: Hill and Wang, 2008.

Tracy, Susan J. *In the Master's Eye: Representations of Women, Blacks, and Poor Whites in Antebellum Southern Literature.* Amherst: U of Massachusetts P, 1995.

Trautsch, Jasper M. "'Mr. Madison's War' or the Dynamic of Early American Nationalism?" *Early American Studies* 10, no. 3 (Fall 2012).

Trollope, Anthony. *North America.* Vol. 1. Leipzig: Bernard Tauchnitz, 1862.

Tuckerman, Henry T. *The Life of John Pendleton Kennedy.* New York: Putnam, 1871.

Varon, Elizabeth R. *We Mean to Be Counted: White Women and Politics in Antebellum Virginia.* Chapel Hill: U of North Carolina P, 1998.

Wade, Richard C. *Slavery in the City: The South in 1820–1860.* New York: Oxford UP, 1964.

Walsh, Richard, and William Lloyd Fox, eds. *Maryland: A History, 1632–1974.* Baltimore: Maryland Historical Society, 1974.

Ward, John William. *Andrew Jackson: Symbol of an Age.* New York: Oxford UP, 1962.

Ward, Susan Page. "The Development of the Theme of Chivalry in Nineteenth-Century Southern Literature." PhD diss., Duke University, 1980.

Whalen, Terence. "Average Racism: Poe, Slavery, and the Wages of Literary Nationalism." In J. Gerald Kennedy and Liliane Weissberg, *Romancing the Shadow: Poe and Race.* New York: Oxford UP, 2001.

Whitehorne, Joseph W. A. *The Battle for Baltimore, 1814.* Baltimore: Nautical and Aviation Publishing, 1997.

Wickberg, Daniel. "What is the History of Sensibilities? On Cultural Histories, Old and New." *American Historical Review* 112, no. 3 (June 2007): 661–684.

Widmer, Ted. *Martin Van Buren.* New York: Times Books, 2005.

———. *Young America: The Flowering of Democracy in New York City.* New York: Oxford UP, 1999.

Wilentz, Sean. *Chants Democratic: New York City and the Rise of the American Working Class, 1788–1850.* New York: Oxford UP, 1984.

———. *The Rise of American Democracy: Jefferson to Lincoln.* New York: Norton, 2005.

Wiltse, Charles M. *John C. Calhoun: Nullifier, 1829–1839.* New York: Bobbs Merrill, 1949.

Winik, Jay. *April 1865: The Month That Saved America.* New York: Harper, 2006.

Woodward, C. Vann. *Reunion and Reaction: The Compromise of 1877 and the End of Reconstruction.* New York: Oxford UP, 1951.

Wyatt-Brown, Bertram. *Southern Honor: Ethics and Behavior in the Old South.* New York: Oxford UP, 1982.

Zieger, Susan. *Inventing the Addict: Drugs, Race, and Sexuality in Nineteenth-Century British and American Literature.* Amherst: U of Massachusetts P, 2008.

INDEX